THE EU & BELARUS

Between Moscow & Brussels

edited by
Ann Lewis

THE FEDERAL TRUST
europe's eastern borders

This book is published by the Federal Trust, whose aim is to enlighten public debate on federal issues of national, continental and global government. It does this in the light of its statutes which state that it shall promote 'studies in the principles of international relations, international justice and supranational government.'

The Trust conducts enquiries, promotes seminars and conferences and publishes reports and teaching materials. The Federal Trust is the UK member of the Trans-European Policy Studies Association (TEPSA), a grouping of fifteen think-tanks from Member States of the European Union.

Up-to-date information about the Federal Trust can be found on the internet at www.fedtrust.co.uk

ISBN 1 903403 02 2

NOTE: All contributors to this volume are writing in a personal capacity. Views expressed should not be taken as those of their government or institution.

This book is the fourth title in the Federal Trust series *Europe's Eastern Borders*. The three previous volumes are available from the publisher: *The EU & Kaliningrad: Kaliningrad and the Impact of EU Enlargement* (2001, 0 903573 18 3) edited by James Baxendale, Stephen Dewar and David Gowan; *The EU & Ukraine: Neighbours, Friends, Partners* (2002, 1 903403 18 9) edited by Ann Lewis; and *The EU & Russia: The Promise of Partnership* (2002, 1 903403 14 6) by John Pinder and Yuri Shishkov.

The Federal Trust is a Registered Charity No. 272241

Dean Bradley House, 52 Horseferry Road,

London SW1P 2AF

Company Limited by Guarantee No.1269848

Marketing and Distribution by Kogan Page Ltd

Printed by J W Arrowsmith Ltd

Contents

Part 2
Belarus: The Economy

Part 3
International Relations

Introduction

Belarus is a small country of only 10 million inhabitants on the south-west fringes of Russia. It has few natural resources, does little trade with the West, has virtually no tourism and shows limited interest in the world to its west. But it has one feature which is bringing it to the attention of a wider European public: following EU enlargement it will have more than 1000 kilometres of frontier with the EU.

This book is designed to give the reader a picture of where Belarus stands more than a decade after independence, how it may develop internally, and prospects for relations with its neighbours; and to put forward a variety of ideas about the EU's policy towards Belarus and how, if at all, it might be made more effective.

Left to its own devices, it is doubtful whether Belarus would ever have sought independence. It was a contented and successful component part of the Soviet Union, especially in the last decade of the latter's existence. Its well-educated and skilled population made it a centre for high-tech industries serving the broad Soviet market. With its close ethnic, cultural and linguistic ties to Russia, and lengthy historical links, there was little friction with the dominant neighbour. Belarus (or the Belorussian Soviet Socialist Republic) was prosperous by Soviet standards.

But Belarus could not be immune to the turbulence of the late Soviet years, and a modest movement developed in favour of national independence, democracy and economic reform. Sympathy with Russia remained widespread, however, and following independence and the collapse of the Soviet Union, it was entirely natural that Belarus should be a founder-member, with Russia and Ukraine, of the Commonwealth of Independent States (CIS), seen by some as the continuation by other means of key aspects of the deceased Soviet Union.

The early years of independence were a disaster for Belarus. Well-intentioned but weak leadership, an entrenched and self-serving bureaucracy and a failure to make necessary economic reforms, combined with an economic crisis in Russia, led to plummeting living standards and a disaffected populace. At the first free presidential election in 1994 the electorate rejected all established politicians and voted into office an obscure state farm chairman whose only claim to fame was as the leader of an anti-corruption campaign: Alexander Lukashenko. Since then two strands have dominated Belarusian politics: President Lukashenko's successful drive to secure more and more power for the presidency and thus for himself, and his attempt to forge an ever-closer union between Belarus and Russia.

While Lukashenko came to power quite legally, he has since paid less attention to the niceties of law and constitution. The referendum he initiated in 1996 (widely regarded as manipulated), and the subsequent constitutional changes and parliamentary elections, have not been recognised as valid by the European institutions. But Lukashenko's policies, which strive to recreate as far as possible the Soviet economic model of centralised planning and control, were not unpopular with the people, who felt safe and secure in this familiar environment. His landslide victory in the presidential election of 2001 against a divided and disorganised opposition was not recognised as legitimate by the OSCE and others. But despite a decline in his popularity, his position looks unchallengeable until at least 2005.

Belarus is arguably the least democratic country in Europe. As such it has posed problems for the EU and other European and Western institutions. In its early years of independence, as with other states created from the former Soviet Union, the EU tried to promote reform and develop relations through a Partnership and Co-operation Agreement (PCA). But Lukashenko's increasingly autocratic style and in particular the events of 1996 caused a break-down in relations. Subsequent Western attempts to promote liberalisation in Belarus have met with scant success.

This book addresses some of the most important questions facing Belarus. Is the current system sustainable? Will President Putin be willing to continue the massive economic subsidies which keep the Belarusian economy afloat? If so, will he demand some pay-back for his support? Can any kind of credible opposition develop? Will the younger generation want a different system or way of life?

The book presents a multi-faceted view of Belarus and its relations with the EU and others. The contributors include academics and analysts, politicians and practitioners, from Belarus (official and unofficial), all over Europe and beyond. All the articles are self-standing, and a certain amount of overlap is inevitable as key factors recur when one looks at any aspect of Belarus. But this permits the reader to view the facts from different angles and form a rounded view.

The four sections mostly begin with a broad outline of the subject area, followed by more detailed analyses of particular aspects of the topic. Each section contains both Belarusian and EU viewpoints.

The book opens with a short survey of Belarus's history, which sets the scene for the rest of the book. Part 1 then deals with the internal political scene. It begins with a broad perspective by one of the West's leading specialists on Belarus, Professor Marples from the University of Alberta. More detailed studies follow: on political leadership by a Belarusian academic working in the UK, Elena Korosteleva; on the 2001 presidential election by the Special Coordinator of the OSCE Limited Election Observation Mission, Kimmo Kiljunen; on human rights by the Belarus specialist at Amnesty International, Malcolm Hawkes; on the media by an analyst from the BBC World Service, Steven Eke; and on Belarusian values and attitudes by a team of leading sociologists from Minsk headed by Professor Rotman.

Part 2 deals with the Belarusian economy, with two detailed articles by eminent Belarusian experts, Leonid Zlotnikov and Jaroslav Romanchuk, and a short but pithy examination of the Belarusian economic model by a leading Western specialist, Anders Åslund.

Part 3 looks at Belarus's international relations, opening with a broad overview from the Belarusian Foreign Minister, Mikhail Khvostov. Given the vital nature of Belarus's links with Russia, there follows a trio of articles on political, economic and military relations between the two countries, by Clelia Rontoyanni of Chatham House, Anastasia Nesvetailova of the University of Aberystwyth, and Steven Main from the Royal Military Academy Sandhurst respectively. We then turn to a view of Belarus's relations with its neighbours to the west, written by Grzegorz Gromadzki from Warsaw, and a detailed account of the role of the OSCE and the Council of Europe in Belarus by the former head of the OSCE office in Minsk, Ambassador Hans-Georg Wieck. The section closes with a thoughtful article by Heinz Timmermann which looks at Belarus's relations with Russia in the broader European context and considers how the EU might modify its approach to Belarus in the light of Russia's wish for close relations with the EU. This piece forms a bridge to Part 4.

Part 4 takes a more detailed look at aspects of the EU's relationship with Belarus. It opens with an article by Belarus's Ambassador to the EU, Sergei Martynov, which argues eloquently for a new approach from the EU in the light of Belarus's changing policies and prospects. Catherine Guicherd argues for a new strategy towards Belarus and others involving an 'Eastern Dimension' to EU policy. The European Parliament's views are set out in forceful fashion by Rob van de Water and Jan Marinus Wiersma MEP. Moving to more detailed aspects of policy, a former opposition activist from Minsk, Vitali Silitski, offers an inside view on why the democratic opposition has failed so disastrously up to now, and considers the West's attempts to help and how this might be done better in future. Astrid Sahm examines the justice and home affairs issues (migration, crime, drugs, people-trafficking, terrorism) which are right at the top of the EU's current agenda, and Kenneth Charman, a consultant working with the European Commission, analyses the EU's aid programme and proposes a new strategy. We close with a case study by Margaret Bamford which shows what can be achieved in the most unpromising circumstances with care and commitment.

The book closes with some personal observations by way of conclusions.

All contributors to this book are writing in a personal capacity and the views expressed should not be taken as those of their government or institution.

I have taken the controversial decision to use all Belarusian proper names in a form transliterated from the Russian rather than the Belarusian language. This is entirely a matter of convenience: where Belarusian names are familiar to non-specialists, it is usually in the Russian form, and the Russian versions of names are commonly used in academic writings about Belarus both in that country and in the West.

This book had its origin in a seminar in Brussels in October 2001 organised by the Trans-European Policy Studies Association (TEPSA) and attended by some but by no means all of the contributors to this book. I am grateful to Dorota Pyszna for organising such a stimulating seminar, to Elena Korosteleva, Clelia Rontoyanni and Elizabeth Teague for help and advice at various stages, and to all the authors not only for their contributions but for an enjoyable exchange of views in the course of editing this book.

Ann Lewis
London
July 2002

Map of Belarus:

Belarus and its neighbours

Belarus: A Brief History

Elizabeth Teague

The name Belarus (White Rus or, in its Russian form, Belorussia) has been in use since the mid-fourteenth century. A vast, flat area of mixed forest and marshland, the region that is today Belarus lacks mountains and comparable natural frontiers and has throughout the centuries been both a crossroads for trade and a battleground for invading armies, cultures and religions. Indeed, it has been described as 'the fastest route between Poland and Russia.' To this day, forest covers a third of the country. The Belovezhskaya pushcha in the west of the country, home to elk, lynx, beaver and bison, and scene of the December 1991 meeting at which the USSR was dissolved, remains the largest primeval forest in Europe.

Today's Belarusians are divided into two distinct cultural groups. Having been for many years under Russian influence, those living in the country's eastern and central regions are mainly Russian-speakers and Orthodox by religion. Those in the western parts of the country tend to be Greek Catholic (Uniate) or Roman Catholic by religion. Belarusian is spoken in rural areas but, while Belarusian enjoys official status, Russian remains the most commonly used language.

Early history

The Belarusians are descended from the Eastern Slavs, nomadic cattle-breeders who settled, some time between the sixth and eighth centuries AD, in the territory between the Vistula and the Don. Believed by historians to be the original homeland of all the Slav peoples, the region today constitutes Belarus, Ukraine and western Russia. The principality of Polotsk, fortress-port on the River Dvina, which flows into the Baltic Sea, was the nucleus of today's Belarusian state.

The ninth century saw the arrival of the Scandinavians, variously known as Normans, Norsemen, Vikings or Varangians. These were the same Normans who conquered Ireland in 820, Iceland in 874, Normandy in 911 and England in 1066. Those who turned eastward came, however, as traders rather than as conquerors, and built a chain of ports along the riverways that link the Baltic Sea to Constantinople and the Black Sea. Along this route they traded slaves, furs, honey and beeswax from the north for the silks and spices of the east. One of their largest trading posts was at Kiev on the River Dniestr. A loosely organised cluster of city-states, Kievan Rus was the first centre of Slav civilisation. It was there that, in 988, Grand Prince Vladimir had his people officially baptised into Orthodox Christianity. The religion quickly spread northward and eastward to the territory of the modern Belarusians and Russians.

Kiev remained the dominant power in eastern Europe until, in 1240, it was conquered and destroyed by the Mongol Horde. The Mongol invasion precipitated the separate development of the major Eastern Slav nations – Russians, Ukrainians and Belarusians. While Muscovy to the east submitted to Mongol rule, the western principalities, including Polotsk, Pinsk, Minsk and the rest of today's Belarus, as well as parts of what today forms Ukraine and western Russia, found refuge in an alliance with the warlike Grand Duchy of Lithuania. It has been suggested that the term 'white' in 'White Rus' may refer to territory that was not incorporated into the Mongol Empire and was not, therefore, liable to taxation by them [Fernandez-Armesto, p.329].

The Polish Lithuanian Commonwealth

Lithuania was itself in search of allies against the Teutonic Knights to the north and the Tatars to the south. Meanwhile, to the east, the Muscovite princes had assumed the role of the Mongols' tax-collectors and were growing increasingly powerful. In 1389, Lithuania's Grand Duke Jagiello married eleven-year-old Jadwiga, heiress to the throne of Poland, forging a dynastic alliance that was to endure until the end of the eighteenth century. When Jadwiga died young and childless, the Polish crown passed to Jagiello and his descendants by his second wife.

While formally united, the Kingdom of Poland and the Grand Duchy of Lithuania were separately administered, each retaining its own laws and customs. Ethnically, the two states were remarkably diverse and their subject peoples enjoyed considerable autonomy. Catholic, Jewish and Orthodox Christian communities all flourished. At first, Belarusian language and culture bloomed under the new dispensation. Although Catholicism was declared the official state religion, Belarusian peasants were able for several centuries to continue to practise their Orthodox religion. From the thirteenth to the seventeenth centuries, Belarusian served as the official language of the Grand Duchy and Lithuania's legal codes (the sixteenth-century 'Lithuanian Statutes') were accordingly written in Belarusian. It was during this period that the Belarusians developed the distinctive language and culture that today differentiate them from the Russians to their east and the Ukrainians to their south; at that time, indeed, Belarusian was the most developed of the eastern Slavonic languages. A high point of Belarusian cultural development was marked in 1517, when the scholar and mystic, Francis Skaryna of Polotsk, produced the first translation of the Bible into Belarusian.

Gradually, however, Poland became the senior and the Grand Duchy the junior partner in the dynastic alliance. In 1569, the two entered a political union as the Polish-Lithuanian Commonwealth (Rzeczpospolita). Polish was declared the language of the Commonwealth, displacing Belarusian as the official means of written communication and initiating a gradual decline in Belarusian culture. In 1596, the creation of the Greek Catholic (or Uniate) Church brought the peasants in the Grand Duchy under the authority of the Vatican. They were not, however, required to change their religious practices: the Greek Catholic Church recognised the supremacy of the Pope but retained Orthodox forms of worship and the Old Slavonic language.

At its furthest extent, the Commonwealth stretched from the Baltic to the Black Sea and embraced not only present-day Poland, Lithuania and

Belarus but also Ukraine, parts of today's western Russia, Latvia, Estonia and Romania. It naturally attracted the envious interest of its powerful neighbours. Geography played a crucial role in this process, since the region's lack of natural barriers rendered it particularly vulnerable to armed invasion. Russia made numerous military attacks on Belarusian-inhabited territory in the seventeenth century. Toward the end of the eighteenth century, Russia allied with Prussia and Austria-Hungary and, in the course of three partitions, stripped Poland of its dominions and shared the spoils among themselves. By 1794, the whole of what is today Belarus had been absorbed into the Russian Empire. The third partition, in 1795, wiped Poland from the map of Europe.

Belarus under Tsarist rule

Russian rule was accompanied by a campaign of linguistic and cultural russification. In 1839 the Greek Catholic (Uniate) Church, to which three-quarters of the Belarusian population at that time belonged, was abolished and the population returned to Orthodoxy. In his informative history of Minsk, Guy Picarda argues however that Moscow's efforts to eliminate national consciousness among the Belarusian population had the opposite effect to that intended. Instead of being deterred, Belarusian intellectuals began to think and feel like a distinct nation. Accordingly, the early nineteenth century saw the first shoots of Belarusian nationalist sentiment. Uprisings against Russian rule in 1812, 1831 and 1863 were put down with increasing severity. Moscow retaliated by banning the printing of material in the Belarusian language on any topic other than ethnography. Even the use of the name Belarus was prohibited, and Minsk was designated the administrative capital of the 'North-West Territory' of the Russian Empire.

In 1861, the serfs were liberated throughout the Russian Empire. While the majority of the Belarusian population remained on the land, the spread of the railways and the founding of small industries such as timber-milling, glass-making and boat-building began to lift parts of the population out of rural poverty. In 1870, the first dictionary of the Belarusian language was published, while the literary language was boosted by the publication of writings by poets such as Janka Kupala, Jakub Kolas and Maxim Bahdanovic in the influential journal Our Cornfield.

Ethnic diversity continued to characterise the region. During the nineteenth century, Belarus formed part of the so-called Pale of Settlement, the area of the Russian Empire in which Jews were legally required to reside. In the late Middle Ages, many Jews had migrated to the Polish-Lithuanian state to escape increasing persecution in western Europe. As in other countries, they tended to settle in the towns and to engage in commerce. By the end of the nineteenth century, Jews formed over fifty per cent of the populations of such Belarusian towns as Minsk, Grodno and Mogilev. When the painter Marc Chagall was born in Vitebsk in 1887, for example, Jews constituted the overwhelming majority of the population of the city. The small house in which he and his family lived and from a room of which his father ran a shop, and the ruins of the nearby synagogue at which his father worshipped, have been lovingly maintained and can be visited today; they are a vivid reminder of a lost way of life. As the nineteenth century drew to a close, poverty and anti-semitic pogroms prompted many of the Jews of eastern Europe to emigrate westward, chiefly to the United States, in search of a better life. Of those who stayed behind, many lost their lives in the holocaust. At the time of the 1989 Soviet census, Jews constituted only 1.1 per cent of the population of Belarus. Ten years later, in 1999, emigration had reduced that figure to 0.3 per cent.

Belarus under Soviet rule

World War One saw Russia and Germany locked in combat on Belarusian territory. When Russia, engulfed in the revolutions of 1917, made its separate peace with Germany, Belarus received its first fleeting taste of independence. In March 1918, under German occupation, an independent Belarusian National Republic was proclaimed. It enjoyed only nine months of independence before it was deposed by Soviet forces. In its place, in January 1919, the Belarusian Soviet Socialist Republic was set up, only to be invaded later that same year by Poland, eager to challenge Soviet Russia for control of the territory. In 1921, under the terms of the Treaty of Riga, Poland and Russia agreed to divide the territory between them. The western regions were ceded to Poland. As the Belarusian (Belorussian in its Russian form) Soviet Socialist Republic (BSSR), the remainder of the territory became a founding member of the Union of Soviet Socialist Republics (USSR) when that was established in December 1922.

Initially, the Soviet government encouraged Belarusian language and culture. But the rise of Soviet leader Josef Stalin ushered in a change in policy, as a result of which Belarus and other Soviet republics were subjected to intense sovietisation and russification. As Stalin tightened his grip, the 1930s saw the forced collectivisation of agriculture and rapid industrialisation. Peasant resistance was violently suppressed; thousands lost their lives or were deported to Siberia. Toward the end of the 1930s, when Stalin turned on the intelligentsia, Belarus's entire national elite was destroyed in the purges. Belarus became, in David Marples' words, 'a denationalised nation', the only one of the fifteen Soviet republics to lose its national language.

World War Two

Belarus suffered particularly severely during World War Two. Under a secret protocol to the Molotov-Ribbentrop Pact of August 1939, the USSR and Nazi Germany agreed to divide central and eastern Europe between them. In September 1939, the German army occupied western Poland while the Soviet army invaded eastern Poland. The areas that Soviet Russia had ceded to Poland in 1921 were incorporated into the BSSR.

Belarus was the first constituent part of the USSR to find itself under Nazi occupation when the German army invaded the USSR in the summer of 1941. Soon a strong partisan movement sprang up behind the enemy lines. One in four members of the Belarusian population (more than two million people in all) lost their life before the Soviet army drove the Germans back in 1944. Three-quarters of all the republic's housing and almost all its industrial infrastructure were destroyed. Hundreds of villages were burned to the ground, many of them with their inhabitants locked in their homes. The capital, Minsk, was reduced to rubble. After the war, Stalin had hundreds of thousands of people imprisoned or deported to Siberia for alleged 'collaboration' with the Nazi occupiers. Under the terms of the 1945 peace treaty between the Soviet Union and Poland, much of the territory that had been ceded to Poland in 1921 was incorporated into the USSR; it now constitutes western Belarus.

Economy

Until the Second World War, Belarus's economy was primarily agricultural. The post-war period brought a major change, with substantial centrally-directed investment aimed at developing the country's industrial capacity. The leader of Belarus's communist party, former World War Two partisan Petr Masherov, so skilfully represented Belarusian interests in Moscow that the republic became one of the most prosperous in the USSR. Weapons production dominated Belarus's economy, followed by construction materials, agricultural machinery, electronics, chemicals and textiles. Agricultural produce included grain, sugar beet, flax, fruit and potatoes. Cattle, pigs and poultry were all raised. The country's lack of raw materials and, in particular, of sources of energy, made Belarus heavily dependent on Russia and other Soviet republics. Officially-encouraged migration of labour, mainly Russian and Ukrainian, into Belarus from other parts of the USSR boosted the urban industrial workforce, further weakening the fragile sense of national identity of the Belarusian population.

During the Soviet period, the BSSR was considered the most conservative and loyally communist of the USSR's Slav republics. Only in the late 1980s, under Soviet President Mikhail Gorbachev's reformist leadership, did a nationalist revival begin to manifest itself. Many of its members were students interested in rediscovering their nation's history and culture through archaeological excavations and voluntary restoration work. There was also considerable popular resentment over the way in which the Soviet authorities had handled the Chernobyl nuclear catastrophe of April 1986. Belarus was hardest hit by that disaster. Its territory, lying only a few miles north of the afflicted Ukrainian power plant, received some 70 per cent of the fallout. Rain sent radiation onto unsuspecting people and contaminated tens of thousands of acres of agricultural land. The consequences of the tragedy are felt in Belarus to this day.

The discovery in 1988 of mass graves of Stalin's victims at Kurapaty, just outside Minsk, further shocked the population and encouraged the establishment that year of an opposition party — the Belarusian Popular Front. Led by archaeologist Zenon Pozniak, the Popular Front focussed on the issues raised by the Chernobyl disaster and the decline in the use of the Belarusian language. Parliament responded to the rise in national sentiment by declaring state sovereignty on 27 July 1990; also that year, Belarusian was declared the republic's official language.

Particularly influential at that time was the physicist and academic Stanislav Shushkevich. He became involved in politics in 1986 when he criticised the government's negligence in failing to inform the public about the Chernobyl catastrophe. With the backing of the Popular Front, Shushkevich was elected to the Belarusian Supreme Soviet (parliament) when the country held its first multi-candidate elections in 1990. The following year, Shushkevich was elected its chairman or speaker, nominally, at that time, the highest post in the country. Parliament as a whole, however, remained dominated by the communist old guard, as did the rest of Belarus's political and economic leadership.

Belarus's national revival came late and was low-key compared with those in the Baltic states, Ukraine or Moldova. Steven Eke and Taras Kuzio have pointed out that almost all the major popular demonstrations that occurred in Belarus prior to the collapse of the USSR were economically, not politically, motivated. Though there was widespread popular discontent over food-price rises, there was little if any support for Belarus to secede from the Union. The Belarusian Popular Front was not allowed to register until July 1991, eighteen months after the analogous Rukh (Movement) in Ukraine, and held only 7.5 per cent of the seats in the Supreme Soviet elected in 1990. Prior to the August 1991 coup in Moscow that precipitated the collapse of the Soviet state, Belarus had been one of five republics that had declared their intention of signing the Union Treaty, the aim of which was to reconstitute the USSR on a new basis. Only the failure of the August 1991 coup prompted the Belarusian Supreme Soviet, on 25 August 1991, to issue a declaration of national independence. In September, the country's name was changed to Republic of Belarus, in place of the russified 'Belorussia' used until that time. Unlike Ukraine, however, Belarus did not hold a referendum to endorse its post-Soviet independence. Indeed, it was not immediately clear what Belarus's declaration of independence really meant, or what was going to happen to the USSR of which Belarus was still, officially, a constituent republic.

Independence

At the end of the first week of December 1991, Shushkevich met at an elite rest-home in Belarus's Belovezhskaya pushcha with President Yeltsin of Russia and President Kravchuk of Ukraine. The following day, the three leaders announced to a startled world that they had disbanded the Soviet Union and created a new association, the Commonwealth of Independent States (CIS). Overnight, Belarus and the other former Soviet republics became fully independent countries. Gorbachev resigned as Soviet president and the USSR ceased to exist. Shushkevich, by virtue of his post as chairman of parliament, became the first head of state of independent, post-Soviet Belarus. Minsk was designated capital of the CIS.

The Communist Party had been banned in Belarus, as in other Soviet republics, following the failed coup of August 1991. In other respects, however, members of the old communist political and economic elite remained in power. Shushkevich found himself virtually isolated, increasingly at odds with the old guard who still dominated parliament, which had been elected in 1990. To international acclaim, in 1993 Belarus relinquished its nuclear weapons. In other respects, the country seemed caught in a time warp. Civil society was weak. Political parties failed to command support. The media remained largely under state control, with most publications heavily dependent on state subsidies. Rejection of reform was exemplified by the fact that, in Belarus, the Soviet-era secret police, the KGB, was (and remains) unreconstructed; it did not even change its name.

Belarus's leaders dragged their feet over political or economic liberalisation. The Communist-dominated parliament rejected all attempts by the small reform wing to embark on marketisation. Only a tiny fraction of state-controlled enterprises were privatised, while state and collective farms remained intact. This protected the Belarusian population from the sharp increases in unemployment that afflicted those transition economies that opted for the 'short sharp shock' of rapid marketisation.

Belarus was not however immune to the changes taking place in neighbouring countries, in particular the Russian Federation. The Belarusian economy had been highly integrated into that of the rest of the USSR. When, therefore, the Russian government in 1992 launched its ambitious economic reform programme, the Belarusian economy almost immediately experienced a sharp decline. Export markets were lost and industrial and agricultural output plummeted, even as Belarus found itself facing a sharp rise in the price of imported energy – the result of Russia's decision to stop supplying heavily subsidised energy to the other former Soviet republics. Inflation soared as industrial output slumped and real wages fell.

The impact on the Belarusian population, which had in the post-war years grown used to being financially better off than the population of most of the other Soviet republics, was predictable. They approved of their leaders' refusal to embark on the path of economic reform. Fearful of losing the relatively privileged economic situation they had enjoyed during the Soviet period, many Belarusians looked back with nostalgia to the years before the break-up of the USSR, and hankered for the reinstatement of links with Russia and the other newly-independent, former Soviet republics. Shushkevich grew increasingly out of step with the old guard in the Supreme Soviet. He was dismissed from office in January 1994, when he lost a parliamentary vote of confidence over fabricated allegations of corruption.

In March 1994 Belarus introduced a new constitution that provided, for the first time, for an elected president to lead the country. The first direct presidential elections were held in July 1994. Vyacheslav Kebich, a communist who had served as prime minister since 1990, lost to Alexander Lukashenko, the man who had orchestrated the anti-corruption investigation that unseated Shushkevich. The populist Lukashenko, one-time manager of a chicken farm, promised during his campaign to reverse price rises, put a stop to privatisation, crack down on corruption, and renew Belarus's ties with Russia. The story of Lukashenko's leadership and the subsequent history of Belarus is detailed in the various articles which go to make up this book.

Further reading

Aslund, Anders, *Building Capitalism: The Transformation of the Former Soviet Bloc*, Cambridge: Cambridge University Press, 2002.

Davies, Norman, *Heart of Europe: A Short History of Poland*, Oxford: Oxford University Press, revised edition, 1986.

Eke, Steven M. and Taras Kuzio, 'Sultanism in Eastern Europe: The Socio-Political Roots of Authoritarian Populism in Belarus,' *Europe-Asia Studies, Vol. 52, No. 3*, 2000, pp. 523-47.

Fernandez-Armesto, Felipe (ed), *Guide to the Peoples of Europe*, London: Times Books, revised edition, 1997.

Marples, David, contributions to Britannica Book(s) of the Year, Chicago: *Encyclopedia Britannica*, 1996-2001 inclusive.

Marples David R., *Belarus: A Denationalized Nation*, Amsterdam: Harrowed Academic Publishers, 1999.

Noble, John et al., *Lonely Planet Guide to Russia, Ukraine and Belarus*, London: Lonely Planet Publications, 1996.

Picarda, Guy, Minsk: *A Historical Guide, London and Minsk*, Technology Publishers, 1994.

Pipes, Richard, *The Formation of the Soviet Union: Communism and Nationalism, 1917-1923*, Cambridge, MA: Harvard University Press, revised edition, 1964.

Pipes, Richard, *Russia under the Old Regime*, Harmondsworth: Penguin Books, 1977.

Roberts, Elizabeth, *Belarus, Ukraine and Moldova*, London: Franklin Watts, 1992.

Stone, Daniel Z., *The Polish-Lithuanian State, 1386-1795*, Seattle, University of Washington Press, 2001.

Wixman, Ronald, *The Peoples of the USSR*, London and Basingstoke: Macmillan, 1984.

1

Belarus: Government, Politics and Society

Belarus: The Last European Dictatorship?

David R. Marples

Introduction

On 25 August 1991, following the failed putsch in Moscow, when an Emergency Committee tried to revive centralised power within the USSR, Belarus declared itself independent. In many respects the decision was a surprise. Of all the Soviet republics, the Belorussian Soviet Socialist Republic (BSSR) had appeared the most compliant, with few indications of regeneration of civic and political life in the period of Gorbachev's leadership. In fact, Belarus's Communist leadership had little choice. In Moscow, the Communist Party was banned in late August. The Communist leadership in Minsk was left without direction and with the prospect of an immediate loss of power unless it agreed to radical changes. Belatedly, it followed the trend elsewhere in the USSR and adopted a platform supporting an independent Belarus. The BSSR, creation of Lenin and the Bolsheviks, became the Republic of Belarus in July 1991, still within the USSR. Within the Belarusian parliament (the Supreme Soviet), the chairmanship fell to Stanislav Shushkevich, a respected former Vice-Rector of Belarus State University, political opponent of the hard-line Communist Prime Minister Vyachaslav Kebich, and a man thought able to lead the country at a time of crisis. To the Supreme Soviet, as the arbiter of change, and its chairman would fall the task of carrying Belarus into independence the following month and beginning the difficult task of constructing a new nation-state.

This chapter examines the traumatic period since 1991 to provide an overview of Belarusian politics, with particular focus on the lengthy period in office of President Alexander Lukashenko.

The Soviet legacy: a sovietised republic?

It is impossible to comprehend events in contemporary Belarus without some understanding of the legacy of the Soviet period. Ironically, the Soviet era in a sense enhanced national consciousness in the republic. After the Russian Revolutions of 1917, a small group of nationally-conscious intellectuals tried to form a new state – at first one that would be autonomous within Russia – but they failed for a variety of reasons. The relatively late development of national consciousness was one factor. Only in the early twentieth century did the Belarusian regions of the Russian Empire experience a revival of cultural development. At the time of the revolutions, this was still in its infancy. The declaration of a Belarusian National (People's) Republic (BNR) on 25 March 1918 was ambitious, particularly given the circumstances in which it was declared. The Bolsheviks were in power in Moscow (the new capital), but following the Treaty of Brest-Litovsk on 2 March much of Belarus's territory was under the control of the German High Command. The territory of modern-day Belarus was a virtual battleground. After the collapse of the BNR, Lenin included a rump Belarus as one of the four founding nations of the Soviet Union. The Belorussian Soviet Socialist Republic (BSSR) was not the antithesis of the BNR, but rather an attempt to allow the development of a republic that was 'nationalist in form, socialist in content'. The 1920s would see a further spurt in Belarusian cultural and national development, the founding of new institutions and publications, and the revival of the national language.

By 1928, however, once Stalin had consolidated power in the USSR, the BSSR, like other national republics, was regarded as a potential threat through 'national deviation' and policies that did not accord with those of Moscow. The repression of the Belarusian national and cultural elite in the 1930s was the most thorough in any of the republics, partly because that elite was relatively small. The purges destroyed the native leadership of the BSSR. After 1939, the BSSR almost doubled in size with the incorporation of territories annexed from Poland, though the major city, Wilno (Vilnius), was shortly thereafter transferred to Lithuania. (In the 1920s the BSSR had also been given territories that were formerly part of the Russian Soviet Federal Socialist Republic). Its territory in September 1939, by which time had been added the northern regions of former Poland annexed by the Red Army, was divided into the provinces (oblasts) of Minsk, Grodno, Brest, Vitebsk, Mogilev and Gomel. The territory, almost doubled as a result of the Nazi-Soviet Pact and the ensuing destruction of the inter-war Polish state, would remain the territory of the state through to independence. However, there was to be a significant interlude of foreign occupation.

The German invasion began one of the most difficult periods in Belarusian history. The BSSR was one of the chief battlegrounds of the Second World War. It was conquered rapidly by the German Wehrmacht and then subjected to harsh rule. Approximately one in four residents of the BSSR died between 1941 and 1944. The Partisan movement was also centred here, and, at Stalin's behest, placed under the control of the State Committee for Internal Affairs (NKVD) so that operations could be co-ordinated through Moscow. At the same time, by mid-1943 some nationalist groups were collaborating with the occupiers in the hope of bringing about an independent Belarusian state. In mid-1944, the Soviet armies returned in triumph and the capital Minsk was recaptured on 3 July. The period of the war remained the strongest influence on the population of the BSSR and became the stuff of legends. The 'Partisan tradition' remained very strong, and following the death of Stalin two former Partisan leaders gained the leadership of the Communist Party of Belarus in succession, Kyril T. Mazurov (1956-1965) and Petr M. Masherov (1965-1980). Though their leadership was traditional and firmly Communist, they also oversaw the BSSR's development as an industrial republic relatively free of the growing corruption in Brezhnev's Moscow. Masherov's death in a car crash in October 1980 was mourned as a national tragedy in the BSSR.[1] .

The Gorbachev period brought changes in the BSSR, though they occurred slowly compared with those in other national republics. A key influence was developments in the Baltic states, two of which, Lithuania and Latvia, border on Belarus. Two events of that time had a profound impact on Belarus. One was the disaster at the nuclear power station at Chernobyl in northern Ukraine on 26 April 1986. A substantial proportion of the radioactive fallout from that accident fell on Belarusian territory, contaminating approximately 20 per cent of the land, on which lived 1.9 million people (out of a population of 10 million) including 400,000 children. Official secrecy ensured that information about the extent of the fallout did not reach the population for three years. The second event was the Moscow-inspired campaign to re-investigate the Stalin years and to rehabilitate innocent victims of the 1930s purges. The discovery of a mass burial ground of people executed by the NKVD at the Kurapaty Forest just outside Minsk led to mass demonstrations in Belarus, and was one factor behind the formation of a Popular Front, mirroring the establishment of similar organisations in the Baltic states.

On the other hand, there was equally a desire in the ruling leadership to prevent the BSSR going through the sort of changes taking place to the north. Party authority in the BSSR remained particularly strong. Nationalists suffered from propaganda that equated them with German Nazis and wartime collaborators. The Belarusian Popular Front (BPF) was formed in 1989 but lacked authority, and many citizens found the movement's anti-Russian sentiment repellent. The Partisan tradition remained strong, and the BSSR was perhaps one of the more successful examples of a Soviet republic, one in which the USSR was regarded as a positive experiment that had succeeded in raising the living standards of the population. An essentially peasant community had become urbanised, it was largely Russian-speaking, and its memory was short. It regarded Russia not only as its chief neighbour but also as a country to which Belarus was linked historically (thus ignoring the lengthy periods during which Lithuania and Poland exerted a particularly strong influence). The Stalin purges and the war-time losses had deprived Belarus of a national leadership tradition to carry the republic into independence. Instead, by 1991, the Belarusian Supreme Soviet, elected the previous year, was dominated by Communists, with only 32 independent deputies representing the opposition, most from the Belarusian Popular Front.

From independence to Lukashenko

In December 1991 Shushkevich invited the leaders of Russia and Ukraine (Boris Yeltsin and Leonid Kravchuk) to Belarus, and at the Belovezhskaya nature reserve in Brest region they contrived to form a new Commonwealth of Independent States (CIS) that would deprive the USSR, and Gorbachev, of any meaningful existence. For Belarus, gaining independence from Russia, whatever the circumstances, was a significant achievement, but the early months of the post-Soviet period were an economic disaster for most sectors of the population. In January 1992, when the Russian government, under the guidance of its economic guru Yegor Gaidar, released prices, the effects were devastating, not only in Russia but in neighbouring territories such as Belarus which were heavily dependent on Russian trade and imports. The catastrophic drop in living standards that ensued in Belarus served to alienate the Belarusian people and make them wary of pursuing a market economy.

Belarus was also asked to give up its nuclear weapons as part of the US-backed Non-Proliferation Treaty. Its new currency, quaintly called the *zaichik* (after the rabbit on the banknote), soon collapsed as hyperinflation set in. This experiment with a market economy (it was never more than a hollow emulation of the policies introduced in Moscow) proved to be disastrous for the leadership of Shushkevich. In reality, he was never in full control of the country because his power base was the parliament and he was supported in that body by only a small minority of deputies. Until Belarus had a constitution there was no clear division of power between the parliamentary chairman (and de facto head of state) and the prime minister. Shushkevich's policies were constantly undermined by the Supreme Soviet and by Prime Minister Kebich, who promoted a policy of military and security union with Russia. The main opposition movement remained the BPF led by Zenon Pozniak. It had gained in popularity toward the end of the Soviet period, though it never secured more than a solid 10-12 per cent of the popular vote. Early in 1994 Shushkevich was forced from office on alleged (and fabricated) charges of corruption. On 15 March 1994 Belarus introduced a new Constitution under which the powers of the state would be shared between a new presidency and the unicameral Supreme Soviet (parliament), which was based on the former Soviet model. After its adoption, political factions in the country began preparing for the first presidential election scheduled for the summer of 1994.

Among the candidates were the two leaders Kebich and Shushkevich. Pozniak also joined the contest, as did Vasily Novikov, chairman of the Communist Party of Belarus, Alexander Dubka, a state farm chairman, and

Alexander Lukashenko, a former KGB border guard and also a state farm chairman. Shushkevich and Pozniak split the nationalist vote, garnering between them about 23 per cent. The surprise result, however, was that Lukashenko gained most votes and was in the lead going into a second round with Kebich. What had happened? The answer seems to be a general view in Belarus that Kebich would not be the best choice for president. He was regarded as a corrupt politician of the old school. The much younger Lukashenko offered the old traditions, especially a sincere affection for Russia and nostalgia for the Soviet period, but with none of the baggage; he had even been the chairman of a parliamentary commission to eliminate corruption. He also demonstrated a flair for populism, identifying with an audience and making it appear that he was speaking to each listener personally (a political gift also enjoyed by Yeltsin in his heyday). Lukashenko proved an easy victor in the second run-off vote in July 1994. Belarus had its first president. The BPF decided to allow the new president what it termed a '100-day grace period' before making any critical statements.

In the summer of 1994, one could not term Belarus a democracy. Parliament was not fundamentally different from that of the Soviet years. The Communist Party had been banned, but a new party called the Party of Communists of Belarus (PCB) was now in place. The military had a strong influence because the republic had long been a training ground for the Soviet army (there were also several Russian military bases on Belarusian soil), as did the Committee for State Security (KGB), which retained its name in Belarus, unlike in other new states. The major Soviet newspaper, *Sovetskaya Belorussiya*, remained in place. Parliament had its own newspaper, *Narodnaya gazeta*, which had articles in both the Belarusian and Russian languages. (*Sovetskaya Belorussiya* was entirely in Russian.) There were dozens of smaller newspapers, some of which appeared in Belarusian, including the BPF organ, *Svaboda*. As in other post-Soviet republics, the division of powers between the new presidency and the parliament was unclear. On paper, parliament had the decisive voice. There was also the Constitutional Court, which could in theory turn down decrees issued by the President. Belarus had its own flag (the white-red-white version having replaced the red-green flag of the BSSR) and national symbols. It seemed possible therefore for Belarus to develop as a new national republic with close links to Central Europe and the Baltic states. It was by no means preordained that the orientation toward Russia would be revived.

However, Lukashenko began a quest for power which few had anticipated. In so doing he was able to exploit the general fear of change induced by the country's brief and disastrous experiment with economic reform. First, he began to reassert Belarus's traditional links with Russia. These links served as an alternative to the policy of the BPF, which was oriented toward Europe and the development of a national state based on the Belarusian language and Belarusian cultural development. Lukashenko began with the media, replacing newspaper editors who were not completely behind him with more compliant figures. He also conceived the idea of using referenda to make changes to the Constitution which would increase his own powers vis-à-vis parliament and the Constitutional Court. The first such referendum took place in the spring of 1995, when Lukashenko asked the electorate to express its views on whether the president should have the authority to dissolve parliament; whether Russian should be elevated to a second state language in Belarus; whether the national day should be changed from 27 July (when Belarus had declared sovereignty) to 3 July (when the Red Army recaptured Minsk from the Nazis in 1944); and whether the national flag and symbols should be replaced by a new flag that appeared to many a virtual replica of the Soviet version (only the hammer and sickle were missing). A barrage of propaganda accompanied the referendum campaign, which coincided with parliamentary elections. Several deputies staged a sit-in at the parliament building, and were eventually removed by force. The referendum delivered large majorities in favour of all the President's proposals. The 'new' flag was run up on the President's residence before the results were officially known. Meanwhile, in the newly-elected parliament the BPF had won no seats and the new centrist United Civic Party occupied the middle ground.[2]

The November 1996 referendum: a big step backward?

By 1996 the political pattern in Belarus had become established. The President was considered a dangerous figure not only by the nationalist segment of the population but also by the predominant groups in parliament, including the

Communist and Agrarian Parties. The BPF, now outside the political mainstream, reverted to street demonstrations to protest against official policies. These protests took place on major anniversaries and began to develop into ugly clashes with the militia. Most of the anniversaries occurred during the spring, beginning with the date of the establishment of the BNR (25 March) and ending with the anniversary of the Chernobyl disaster (26 April). On 26 April 1996, a large Chernobyl protest developed into a clash with the police and the authorities arrested a large number of protesters. By the summer of that year Pozniak had fled the country, citing harassment by the authorities. (He was subsequently granted political asylum in the United States but moved to Poland to be nearer the Belarusian political scene.) The main focus of the power struggle was however the parliament of the thirteenth session, led by chairman Semion Sharetsky. In July Lukashenko decided to hold a new referendum later in the year in which the electorate would vote on his ideas to amend the Constitution to form a new, smaller parliament with an upper house and to strengthen considerably the authority of the president vis-à-vis parliament, giving him, for example, the power to dissolve parliament in case of conflict. He also proposed changes to the Constitutional Court. This decision led to the most intense conflict in the political history of independent Belarus. While Lukashenko began to prepare for the new referendum, parliament tried to impeach the president and the PCB recommended the abolition of the post altogether. Ultimately, Russia, with which Belarus had signed a new Treaty of Friendship and Co-operation, entered the conflict as an intermediary.

Prior to the referendum in early November, Viktor Chernomyrdin arrived in Minsk to broker a deal between the two sides. Parliament agreed to withdraw its impeachment bill on condition that the questions in the referendum were for consultative purposes only. The referendum duly took place on 24 November under conditions that most international observers agreed violated democratic procedures in a number of respects. The result was another victory for the President, who then proceeded to act as if the referendum had indeed given him a mandate to make changes to the Constitution. The President now dissolved parliament, which in turn became a smaller assembly (House of Representatives), reduced in size from 260 to

110 seats. The upper house (Council of the Republic) consists of 64 deputies, 56 of which are chosen by local councils (8 from each region and 8 from the city of Minsk). A further 8 deputies are chosen by the president directly. In practice, the government has been able to exercise close control over the selection of deputies at the local level.

The Constitutional Court had proved one of the biggest stumbling blocks for Lukashenko in the early months of his presidency, sometimes blocking presidential decrees. Under the amended Constitution, 6 judges were to be chosen by the president directly, and 6 by the Council of the Republic. The choice of chairman of the Court was the prerogative of the president, in theory requiring the consent of the Council. The constitutional changes served to increase considerably the authority of the presidency. Correspondingly, parliament became a much weaker body, with its authority further diminished by the restrictions placed by the government on election campaigning, and harassment of democratic opposition parties during such campaigns. In this way, Lukashenko effectively removed any potential sources of opposition.[3]

The new parliament consisted of deputies of the thirteenth session of parliament (retaining the seats they gained in the 1995 election) who were for the most part well disposed toward the President. By early 1997 the President had published an amended version of the Constitution which made him one of the most powerful presidents in post-Soviet space. Moreover, he extended his own mandate in office from 20 July 1999 to November 2001, five years from the referendum date. The November 1996 referendum was the most decisive event in the history of independent Belarus. It effectively ended opposition through legal state procedures (parliament and the Constitutional Court). The opposition continued to regard the original Constitution as valid, arguing that Lukashenko would only legally be president until July 1999. Just over 40 deputies in the original parliament refused to accept the decision and began to meet surreptitiously under the leadership of Sharetsky and the Chairman of the Electoral Commission, Viktor Gonchar. The referendum, constitutional amendments and subsequent election were not recognised as valid by the European institutions (EU, Council of Europe, OSCE), and deputies from the old Supreme Soviet continued to occupy the seats allotted to Belarus in the Council of Europe and OSCE Parliamentary Assemblies.

Nevertheless, the OSCE opened an office in Minsk in 1997, forming an Advisory and Monitoring Group (AMG) under the leadership of Ambassador Hans-Georg Wieck, a German diplomat. The AMG's goal was to establish a new dialogue between the government and the opposition with a view to securing a restoration of democracy. It took the view that the Lukashenko administration was not monolithic, and that there was scope for manoeuvre within it. One of the supporters of dialogue who helped lend substance to this view was a former chairman of parliament (in the pre-1995 session), Myacheslav Hryb. Pozniak (from his new base in Warsaw) denounced the idea of dialogue as compromise with a dictator, but several political parties were prepared to take part in an effort to persuade the Lukashenko regime to make concessions, and in particular to put an end to the arrest and persecution of protesters, give the opposition equal access to the official media and create a legislature with genuine authority. Lukashenko in turn paid some attention to the dialogue in an effort to raise his international standing, and to use the AMG as his main form of contact with the West.

Belarus and Russia

More than any of the other former Soviet republics, Belarus has been dominated by its relationship with Russia. Russia is its chief economic partner, and has maintained close security relations with Belarus. The intensive russification of the postwar period has meant that although ethnic Russians constitute only 13 per cent of the population, a majority of the population is fluent in the Russian language, and in Belarusian cities in particular the Russian language is predominant. Lukashenko came to power with a promise to move Belarus closer to Russia. Yet so did Leonid Kuchma in Ukraine (and at the same time, the summer of 1994), and he subsequently appeared to lead his state in the opposite direction. However, Lukashenko, unlike Kuchma, has a direct bond with the populace, and has been anxious to demonstrate that he has lived up to his promises. Lukashenko's political outlook was formed in the Brezhnev period, in a heavily russified area, as a former state farm chairman, used to giving orders but at a regional rather than a national level. His outlook seems parochial. His ideas are not original and his thinking has clearly been conditioned by the Soviet era. He is Russian-speaking (though he is capable of speaking Belarusian) and Russophile, but he does not find the present leadership in Russia particularly congenial. Rather, he has developed contacts with left-leaning circles in Russia: he perceived the former Russian premier, Yevgeny Primakov, as a potential ally and reliable partner. However, Lukashenko's outlook seems conditioned more by pan-Slavism than by socialism. It is the 'imperial' dimension of former Soviet foreign policy which attracts him. Nonetheless, Belarus's foreign policy in the early years of the Lukashenko presidency was single-minded and pervasive: Belarus had to return to its partnership with 'Mother Russia'. This change of policy was advanced in several ways, but it was far from straightforward.

Later in 1995 the senior partner refused to accept closer economic ties. The Russian side rejected a plan for monetary union with Belarus since this would have placed a huge financial burden on Russia. The economic relationship was one-sided. Belarus was heavily reliant on Russia for supplies of oil and gas at subsidised prices. Belarus frequently defaulted on payments and was heavily in arrears to Russia. However, Lukashenko argued that the partnership was one of equality: first, because Belarus remained a base for Russian weapons factories and military personnel, and second, because Belarus did not charge Russia for the transit of oil through its territory to Poland and Western Europe. By the end of 1995, Russian security guards were permitted to police the old Soviet border with Poland at Brest and the two security police forces continued to collaborate closely. Despite his definite pro-Russian orientation, Lukashenko kept his foreign policy options open in 1995 and up to November 1996. Belarus removed all its nuclear weapons in compliance with the Nuclear Non-Proliferation Treaty (though with frequently-voiced official regrets), and held negotiations with organisations such as the IMF and World Bank, implying a commitment to develop a market economy and a more rational economic base. The Soros Foundation also had an office in Minsk, suggesting that Belarus would also begin to develop a more democratic society. Concomitantly, Belarus served as the capital of the CIS and a reliable partner for Russia, and made known its strong opposition to the proposed expansion of Nato to include Poland and the Czech Republic (with possible future entry for the Baltic states). As for international contacts, Lukashenko made several visits abroad, but principally to Ukraine and parts of Russia. However, the relationship with Russia was perceived as a critical part of the success of the 1994 election platform, and clearly the President himself wished to go in this direction.

On 2 April 1996 a 'Russia-Belarus Community' was formed, to some extent a symbolic gesture foreshadowing an eventual Union with a joint parliament dealing with matters encompassing security and foreign policy and, over the long term, close collaboration in other matters too.[4] Its creation had been facilitated by President Yeltsin's desperate need for votes in the June 1996 Russian presidential election. The merger with Belarus demonstrated to Russian voters, particularly nationalists, that Yeltsin was thinking in terms of reuniting former Soviet territories, and particularly the three Slav states, Russia, Ukraine, and Belarus. There was little of real substance to this new Community, however. It seemed more of a propaganda ploy than a move signifying a serious change of policy, let alone structure, by the independent Belarusian state. However, in Belarus it was heralded with great fanfare and demonstrated the direction in which the authorities wished to go. An actual Union Treaty was signed on 2 April 1997, four months after the referendum, and ratified over the summer by the respective parliaments. In Belarus, 2 April became a national holiday. As for the Treaty, a detailed draft running to eighteen pages submitted by the Belarusian side was reduced to three rather vague pages by the Russians, indicating that a Yeltsin firmly in power was not so readily compliant as one seeking votes. The Belarusians appeared not to be rebuffed and signed the Treaty in its abbreviated form. It was ratified by the upper house of parliament on 10 June 1997. Belarus, as the weaker of the two parties, appeared to be relinquishing its independence and its self-proclaimed role as a new small state in Central Europe.

However, the Union gave rise to as many questions as it answered. First, how did it relate to the CIS? If the CIS was functioning adequately, for example, why was the Russia-Belarus Union necessary? On 29 April 1998 Russian entrepreneur Boris Berezovsky was appointed Executive Secretary of the CIS in an obvious attempt to revitalise the organisation. Lukashenko had long been dissatisfied with the progress of the CIS and was at once hostile to the leadership of Berezovsky. In early May, at the eighth session of the parliamentary assembly of the Russia-Belarus Union held in the city of Gomel, Lukashenko lashed out at the CIS, remarking that at its meeting of member states in April in Moscow it had not made one concrete decision or signed a single document. He declared that the CIS had suffered a 'clinical death'. Lukashenko maintained that he was especially concerned because over the next two years there would be presidential elections first in Ukraine (1999) and then in Russia (2000) which could further undermine the stability of the CIS. The CIS, then, was not to detract from Belarus's union with Russia. Over the summer of 1996, an economic union had been formed between Russia, Belarus, Kazakhstan and Kyrgyzstan. Was this union superseded or undermined by the Russia-Belarus Union? Would laws passed by the new joint parliament take precedence over those issued by the office of the Belarusian presidential administration (clearly laws issued by the Belarusian parliament no longer had any authority because it was closely controlled by the presidency)? And last but not least, would there be a joint Belarus-Russia citizenship? Would politicians in one country be permitted to run for office in the other? How much sovereignty would actually be given up? None of these questions had clear answers. It appeared that the rush to merge the independent state with Russia had precluded clearly thought out solutions to the fundamental questions that must surround any union of two states.

Once Lukashenko had reached this point, the pinnacle of two and a half years of policy-making and pro-Russian orientation, there was no way to go but backwards. At some stage (the precise point is uncertain) he appears to have recognised that the ultimate result of the Russia-Belarus Union would be the relegation of Belarus to a secondary player, a mere western province of an expanded Russian Federation, possibly with the same authority as one of the autonomous republics of Russia.[5] Moreover, events in Russia may also have precluded the consummation of the Union, especially the financial crisis in the summer of 1998. One can posit that a finalised Union would not be in the best interests of the Lukashenko administration and indeed that the Belarusian government would be likely to take steps to impede a process that would render the Union more than a symbolic agreement by two like-minded states. The foremost reason for slow progress on the Union has been the personal ambition of the president of Belarus. One would have to construct a psychological profile to provide a satisfactory analysis of his reasons. Official secrecy and the impossibility of ascertaining many details about the President's past make it a difficult task to know precisely what he is thinking at any time. His speeches are long and frequent, full of emotion and anger, hitlerian in gesture; but they do not always make clear what he is thinking. Ultimately, his speeches are intended to convey an image of how the Lukashenko state should be perceived by the citizens of Belarus: as one faithful to 'proud Communist traditions,' maintaining a close relationship with the fraternal peoples of Russia, and hostility (sometimes concealed, sometimes overt) to the West, particularly Nato and the United States.

Several writers have speculated that the Union with Russia was but a stepping-stone for Lukashenko himself to make a bid for the presidency of Russia in 2000.[6] Lukashenko never claimed such an ambition, and Putin's succession to Yeltsin put paid to any such notion, but it is clear even to a superficial observer that his ambitions go beyond the boundaries of Belarus. He has frequently stressed the importance of a Union which puts the eastern border of his country on the Pacific Ocean. He has tried to involve Belarus as a link between the Russian Federation and its 'lost' province of Kaliningrad, offering Belarusian territory instead of Lithuanian as a conduit for the exchange of goods between the two disconnected parts of Russia. He has visited powerful Russian statesmen such as Gennady Zyuganov and the late Alexander Lebed, in addition to numerous provincial governors. In summer 1998 sixteen of Russia's provincial governors were invited to visit Belarus, evidence that the administration was forging close contacts with various players on the Russian political scene. This was an unusual move for the leader of a foreign country, but it made sense from the perspective of one who intended to play a role in the politics of Russia in the immediate future. Since 2001, however, these ambitions have receded into the background. Lukashenko's regime has become an international pariah. Putin's Russia, no matter how flawed the Union, has become Belarus's only legitimate partner, but there are no further prospects for Lukashenko in the Russian political spectrum.

The Lukashenko dictatorship, 1999-2002: a *muzhik* in power?

The President has surmounted three political 'pinnacles' since the summer of 1999: the transition from a legitimate presidency to one based on disputed amendments to the Constitution; parliamentary elections in October 2000; and a presidential election in September 2001. In the background have been Belarus's obvious economic failings, especially when compared to its neighbours: Russia, Ukraine and the Baltic states. Increasingly the United States and the West European states (with the partial exception of Germany) have begun to isolate Belarus, to regard it as an anomaly in Europe, particularly after the fall of Milosevic in Serbia. Disturbingly, many of Lukashenko's major opponents have 'disappeared' and are widely suspected to have been the victims of political murder. They include Yuri Zakharenko, the former Minister of Defence, and Viktor Gonchar, former Deputy Chairman of the parliament of the thirteenth session.[7] Others have fled the country (including Sharetsky, who was in theory the temporary leader of the country once the President's official mandate expired in July 1999) or have been persecuted persistently (such as Mikhail Chygir, former Prime Minister). Lukashenko survived the shaky period of July 1999 (when his mandate in power expired, according to the original version of the Constitution) mainly because he ruled de facto if not de jure.

The opposition held a mock election in the spring of 2000 as a protest against the failure of the regime to allow the formation of a truly representative parliament in the elections of that year. These elections did not receive international recognition and very few opposition deputies entered the new parliament. On several occasions thereafter the opposition came close to achieving a semblance of unity. The main common ground between the Communist Party, the two wings of the Social Democratic Party, the United Civic Party and the two branches of the Belarusian Popular Front was opposition to the emerging dictatorship of Lukashenko. The OSCE AMG assisted in the process of encouraging a united opposition to campaign against Lukashenko and also to work within the official structures of the Belarusian authorities. The key event proved to be the presidential election, which was seen by many as the last hope of removing a dangerous demagogue who had become psychologically unstable. Ultimately the Electoral Commission accepted the candidacies of four men: Lukashenko, Semion Domash, former leader of the Grodno region, Sergei Gaidukevich, leader of the Belarusian Liberal-Democratic Party, and Vladimir Goncharik, chairman of the Federation of Trade Unions. Goncharik was the choice of the united opposition. After he promised the position of prime minister to Domash should his campaign prove successful, the latter also joined the Goncharik camp.

Once again, the electoral methods failed to satisfy international observers. The President announced his own victory before the official vote tally had been completed. According to the authorities, the President received more than 75 per cent of the votes, but polls conducted just prior to the election indicated that although Lukashenko was ahead of his closest challenger, Goncharik, he did not have enough votes to secure a majority. His popularity was particularly low in the capital city of Minsk.[8] However the elections demonstrated the failure of any opposition candidate to capture the attention and allegiance of the electorate. True, they lacked access to newspapers and television (though there was access to Russian Television in Belarus), but in some sectors of the population, especially rural areas and the elderly, the President retains significant allegiance. Though wages and pensions are low, they are paid on time. Belarus has retained a large state sector, and Lukashenko has exploited well fears of the global economy and of political interference by the United States.[9] Perhaps most important, in the latter stages of the campaign Lukashenko received the backing of President Putin, who had earlier seemed undecided and even uninterested in the campaign. Putin may have decided that Lukashenko in power, whatever his idiosyncracies, was more reliable than Goncharik.

The future

The Western powers have not recognized the legitimacy either of the 1996 referendum or of more recent election campaigns in Belarus, particularly the presidential election of September 2001. Western policy has not always been united, however, and Lukashenko is a skilled politician who can suggest improvements of policy (according to Western standards) at opportune times. The OSCE-backed dialogue with the opposition was a case in point. For some time the EU, led by the Germans, appeared to support the notion of a gradual transition to democracy using existing state structures. The American presence in Belarus until recently has been relatively passive. However, although the Americans have been a supportive OSCE member state, they have also begun to express particular concern about Lukashenko's actions through their Minsk embassy. For instance, Michael Kozak, US ambassador to Belarus, described Belarus in an opposition newspaper in 2001 as 'the Cuba of Europe.' Following the events of September 11 2001 and Russian support for the US-led attack on world terrorism, Belarus faces the possibility of becoming more isolated. To date, however, the Russians have not abandoned his regime, and as long as Putin's support is in place (as it was during the latter stages of the September 2001 presidential election), Lukashenko can maintain his authority in Minsk. Russia, rather than the West, is the key element in the stability of the Belarusian government.

The most notable aspect of independent Belarus for many observers has been the lack of change since the Soviet period. Guide-books refer to the country as a 'Soviet theme park'. Those foreign businesses which operate in Belarus are either prepared to tolerate official restrictions and legal impediments in the short term (McDonald's restaurants, for example) or are Russian-owned. The future of the OSCE, one of the few international organisations remaining in Belarus (the EU Tacis office is another), is no longer secure at the time of writing. Attacks on the opposition continue, the media is heavily censored and several independent newspapers have shut down. At times Belarus appears like an armoured camp, defending itself against intrusions from all sides, determined to resist change and opposing globalisation and US influence.

On the other hand, it would be a mistake to dismiss the current regime simply as a hangover from the past. Lukashenko has adhered, however loosely, to the trappings of procedure. He has held elections, no matter how flawed, and he has not completely dismissed negotiations with the opposition. At times he has also expressed his frustration at Russia's unwillingness to make more of the Russia-Belarus Union.[10] His dalliances with various undemocratic regimes (North Korea, Iran and Milosevic's Yugoslavia, for example) have not been very deep or lasting. Ultimately, Belarus's future depends on its contacts with its neighbours, particularly Russia but also Ukraine, Poland and the

Baltic states. The expansion of the EU may prove a greater threat to Belarus's future than the expansion of Nato, particularly in view of its failure to reform areas such as agriculture and to modernise industry. Perhaps also the Lukashenko regime should be seen in the post-Soviet perspective. It can be compared with the regimes of Central Asia more easily than with those of other former Soviet republics in Europe, and it is considerably less corrupt than countries such as Uzbekistan and Kazakhstan. In some respects, an analogy can be made with Ukraine: both have Presidents prepared to violate the Constitution and to destroy political enemies. But Ukraine has received considerably more aid from the West and maintains a foreign policy oriented more toward Europe than toward Russia. Belarus, smaller and without a significant Western diaspora, has, lamentably, received considerably less international aid and attention. Nevertheless, it has survived for a decade as an independent state. That in itself is a significant achievement, no matter how difficult the transition period may have been for the majority of the population.

Notes

[1] There are some interesting examples of the Masherov legacy. His daughter Natalia was briefly one of the candidates for president in the September 2001 election, but eventually withdrew from the race. One of the major streets in Minsk today is Prospekt Masherova. President Lukashenko frequently cites Masherov as a renowned leader and an example to be emulated.

[2] The BPF, which carried the main hopes of many foreign observers for the development of democracy in Belarus, eventually divided into two factions: the Conservative Christian Party of the BPF led by Pozniak and the mainstream BPF led by Vintsuk Viachorka, a diplomat and a very European-style politician. Viachorka was to support several attempts to unite the opposition on various issues in order to strengthen the forces against the president. Pozniak, who spent 5 years in exile, became more distant from the Belarusian political scene and faded as a political figure.

[3] See, for example, Yuri Drakokhrust, 'Referendum: New Era Begins,' *Minsk Economic News*, No. 23 (December 1996), p. 2.

[4] See, for example, David Marples, 'Belarusian-Russian Treaty: An Analysis,' *Belarusian Review*, Vol. 8, No. 1 (Spring 1996): 8-9.

[5] On this question, see Alexander Potupa, 'BelaRossiya: realnost ili blef?' *Narodnaya Volya*, 19 January 1999, p. 1.

[6] Among them was Yuri Khadyka, 'Alexander Lukashenko and Alexander Lebed may meet face to face in the presidential elections in Russia in 2000,' *Belapan*, 20-26 May 1998.

[7] These disappearances occurred on 7 May and 16 September 1999 respectively. See *Naviny*, 11 May 1999 and *Zvyazda*, 24 September 1999.

[8] Even official sources acknowledge that Goncharik received over 30 per cent of votes cast in the city of Minsk. See, for example, http://www.belarusembassy.org/elections2001.

[9] In mid-1999, a survey suggested that 26 per cent of Belarusians were afraid of Nato involvement in their country. Cited in *RFE/RL Daily Report*, 17 June 1999.

[10] He did so on Belarusian Television, 5 June 2001, for example.

Political Leadership and Public Support In Belarus: Forward to the Past?

Elena Korosteleva*

> 'Perhaps, [some politicians think] it would be better to surrender our independence at once? To be a satellite country may be a bit insulting but it is convenient. [Then] we could legitimise a totalitarian economy, accept a militaristic budget, forget about conversion or privatisation, and cease all reforms. Then we would happily move 'forward into the past' on a wrecked imperial chariot. This period is a real trial for the nation: whether it can retain its sovereignty and whether it really deserves independence ...'
>
> Stanislav Shushkevich, *Narodnaya Gazeta*, 13 May 1993.

Introduction. The façade and the reality of contemporary Belarus

The Republic of Belarus progressively introduced itself to the contemporary world as a country of controversy and defiance. Due to its inflexible policy-making, Belarus is currently cold-shouldered by the West, yet this is counter-balanced by partnership with Russia. However, it can be argued that this partnership is more like 'enslavement' than mutual assistance. In addition, since the mid-1990s Belarus has become a polity which some scholars have described as a 'failed democracy',

* The author would like to acknowledge the invaluable support of INTAS (99-00245) and the British Academy (SG-31102), without which the project on which this article is based would not have been possible.

but others would claim as a type of 'third-way socialism' – an attempt to combine features of the old system with the challenges of transition.

During the Soviet era Belarus was a showcase of socialism, espousing equality, social protection and successful management. Indeed, it set the benchmark of Soviet prosperity more than any other USSR republic. Belarus retains this status even today by offering an affordable set of welfare provisions. However, this has been achieved by employing the politics of façade rather than accepting the bleak reality faced by neighbouring CIS countries. Today the World Bank refers to Belarus as the least reformed but most durable economy in the CIS region. Paradoxically, the policy of state control and central planning brought an unexpected 4.1 per cent growth in GDP in 2001 as against 2000. Furthermore, Belarus's industrial output increased by 5.8 per cent, while agricultural production grew by 1.8 per cent, according to official sources. The annual inflation rate fell from 107.5 per cent in 2000 to 46.1 per cent in 2001 and external debt remained low. In addition, the country has continued to enjoy a low level of unemployment (less than 2 per cent), and wages and pensions are paid regularly. In reality, however, there is an urgent need for reform and modernisation. The country is still drawing on its 'prior economic potential' and subsisting on discounted energy supplies from Russia and barter trade with the CIS. In order to survive, bankrupt state enterprises require urgent privatisation, and state fiscal control needs to be adjusted to attract foreign capital investment. Ironically, according to the World Bank if Belarus embarked on the path of economic reform now, its initial conditions would be far more favourable than those of the other CIS countries in the early 1990s.

Politically, according to exiting surveys,[1] the Belarusian electorate shows signs of democratic awareness. They reject the idea of a one-party system, one-man rule, censorship or a return to the soviet-style past. At the same time, Belarusians express wholehearted support for President Alexander Lukashenko despite the President's intolerance of opposition, the alleged disappearance of his political opponents, state-sponsored death-squads and all-powerful police. The presidential election in 2001 demonstrated the depth of this public trust by giving the President a 75.65 per cent majority. However, this victory must be considered in the context of the electoral violations attested to by the international community, and a more alarming factor – the lack of candidate choice for Belarus's citizens. Vladimir Goncharik, the single opposition candidate and an apparent alternative for the dissatisfied, failed to secure a credible vote (15.65 per cent) even from the most informed strata of the population – urban residents, on whom his election campaign was primarily focused.

So, what is modern Belarus, and why are there so many paradoxes associated with its contemporary status quo? Is it indeed a reformist laggard, fallen into some kind of post-communist coma? Or is it a country that reflects a cacophony of interests more concerned with personal ambition than the well-being of society?

These questions will be addressed below and will reveal that Belarus's contemporary landscape is a conglomeration of discrete realms where each player – the government, the opposition or the international community – plays its own part irrespective of the others.

Belarus's disrupted political realm

The dissolution of the Soviet Union presented a challenge to the existing power structures in Belarus. Unlike the Baltic States, Russia or Ukraine, Belarus was not ready for wholesale modernisation and it continued living on the accumulated capital of the soviet past. The population and the leadership were united in interpreting perestroika not as a necessity or the outcome of an internal crisis, but as a selfish initiative by certain political elites seeking personal benefit. In the early stages of transition negative images were often deployed of Moscow 'democrats' and home-grown nationalists such as the Belarusian Popular Front – at that time the most popular movement and later party.

Belarus's power elites naturally sought to preserve their positions, and in many instances were successful. Until July 1994 there was no major change in the governing elite with the notable exception of the emergence of Professor Stanislav Shushkevich, elected from the 'outsiders' to become Speaker of the first Belarusian parliament (Chairman of the Supreme Soviet), and a handful of oppositionists in the 1990 parliament (originally not more than 40 out of 346).

Despite the limited change, the period between 1990 and 1994 was quite troublesome for the Belarusian elite, which was no more than the party nomenklatura of the soviet past. It had to survive the pressure of domestic changes in Russia, including numerous coups d'etat and subsequent economic-cum-political reforms, alongside the growing clamour of nationalist voices within Belarus. Some developments did take place, of which the most salient was the awakening of national consciousness. The ancient national symbols were re-introduced, the teaching of Belarusian was established in schools, and history textbooks were amended. The publication of Belarusian-language books had increased substantially by 1993, and by 1994 the curriculum was taught in Belarusian in 60 per cent of primary schools.

However, only these, limited and secondary, changes took place during those years. No major economic reforms were launched; quite the reverse. Major enterprises continued to be heavily subsidised by the state, and fiscal policies remained centrally controlled. In the words of the then member of parliament Alexander Lukashenko, the Supreme Soviet only discussed

> '...urgent budgetary measures, the introduction of a state of emergency, empowering the Council of Ministers with more authority, the introduction of presidential procedures for recalling MPs to their constituencies, and the redistribution of rights and responsibilities between key power structures...' (A.Lukashenko: 'Dictatorship: a Belarusian Variant?' *Narodnaya Gazeta,* May 1991)

The issues of altering the electoral code, privatising the mass media or allowing minimal freedoms to small businesses were not on the immediate agenda of the legislature, which by 1992 had about 100 democratically-minded MPs. The only amendment to the electoral law was the lowering of the turnout threshold for voters from 50 per cent to 25 per cent, which was passed but not enacted.

The economic crisis of 1993 did not stimulate reform strategies. By then three programmes of market reform had been discussed by parliament.

Instead the nomenklatura sought a way to return to the 'rouble zone' and economic partnership with Russia. This desire to re-unite was partially realised when Belarus signed a collective security treaty with Russia in April 1993, which caused sharp disputes and polarisation within parliament and resulted in the dismissal of Shushkevich from his position.

Politically, the nomenklatura worked hard not to allow any radical measures which could deprive it of power. This resulted in the preservation of most of the electoral code, the dominance of the state-owned media and the introduction of the presidency in 1994. This last idea was of course 'borrowed' from Russia, but designed to fit a local candidate, Viacheslav Kebich, the first Prime Minister of Belarus. The first presidential election took place in July 1994, and the result swept away the former soviet-era elite. The unexpected outcome was the election of a low-ranking member of the nomenklatura to the centre of the political stage. Alexander Lukashenko, formerly director of the Gorodetz collective farm in Shklov district and then MP and head of the anti-corruption committee in the 1990 parliament, became the first President and the new face of the national elite. At the outset of his political career, as a young communist, he demanded the end of official harassment of democrats and the initiation of market reforms, decentralisation of the economy, and privatisation. He was particularly concerned at the prospect of dictatorship by the nomenklatura if no reforms were undertaken:

> 'Can't you see that we wish to implement perestroika by the hands of those who were in power years ago (in Belarus there is no new face among the management, only cadres from the 'golden years') and who now attempt to discredit the democrats. But I wish to reassure you that there are honest deputies in the Supreme Soviet who wish to support changes, and we know that we have the full support of our voters.' (ibid)

Alexander Lukashenko won the 1994 election because the voters opted for new faces and action rather than pledges. But at the same time, while head of an independent European state, the new President unexpectedly found himself in complete economic and political disarray. He had to choose between painful reforms with no guarantee of success or preservation of the status quo and the familiar soviet-style background primarily associated with the re-union with Russia.

Inasmuch as no structural changes were introduced which would lead to fuller representation of popular interests in parliament, the role of parties remained limited. Paradoxically, the electorate strongly endorsed the need for a multi-party system, independent legislature and judiciary (about 80 per cent), but belief in the efficacy of parties themselves was rather low and volatile: in the public perception overall party popularity fell from 13.4 per cent in 1991 to 4.1 per cent in 1994, and continues at a minimal level.[2]

Nevertheless, between 1990 and 1996 Belarus managed to sustain two parliaments and develop relatively structured party political competition with classic divisions and interest groups. Although elected as largely non-partisan, the 1995 parliament subsequently enjoyed factional polarisation, allowing the emergence of five organised groups, two of which were pro-democratic (Civic Action and Union of Labour), another two left-wing conservative (the Communists and the Agrarians) and the largest, *Zgoda* (Consensus), pro-presidential. Even non-partisan deputies acted as if they belonged to a single group having many parameters in common. The principal issues around which the initial polarisation took place were the dissolution of the USSR, the prospect for re-union with Russia, and the change of state symbols from nationalist back to soviet-style. There was no constructive discussion of reform; instead the old elite actively promulgated a strategy of silent withdrawal from the process of democratisation.

Lukashenko's succession to power sharpened the political situation. He immediately came into conflict with parliament, in whose perception he was encroaching on their rights and prerogatives. On a few occasions, acute conflicts resulted in petty fights and stalemate between President and parliament. Lukashenko countered this outspoken 'disobedience' by issuing decrees and holding referenda, which subsequently allowed effective institutionalisation of his political ambitions and radically changed Belarus's chance of further democratisation.

Between 1996 and 2001, in order to safeguard his mission, the President successfully enacted a system of personal control and patronage in recruiting government officials based on the principles of (i) personal loyalty to himself and (ii) favours to old associates, plus, recently, (iii) regionalism – Lukashenko appears to avoid appointing Minsk-based personnel, believing that the Minsk nomenklatura failed to support him in recent elections.[3] As a result, from 1997 the national political elite was replaced by middle-level regional administrative managers (a stratum forsaken since soviet times but eager to regain power and hence loyal to its immediate 'liberator') and representatives of the security forces (many from the Mogilev region – Lukashenko's place of birth). Second, by altering the 1994 constitution in 1996 he reinforced his authority allowing for personal control throughout the system (see discussion below on structural constraints of the system). Subsequently he introduced the 'presidential vertical' (executive control through the appointment of heads of regional executive committees) and established certain rights for the presidential administration. Legislative and judicial changes enabled him to hand-pick the 1997 parliament and to appoint 60 per cent of the Constitutional Court.[4] Since 1997 the President has exerted absolute control over the political elite and its recruitment in Belarus. No significant appointment can be made without presidential endorsement, and no disobedience to the President goes unnoticed. As a result, the hierarchical structure created by Lukashenko permits vertical and horizontal control throughout, with senior officials watching junior, and the latter divided by mistrust.

As a consequence of Lukashenko's efforts to concentrate power in his own hands, the ideologically diverse but weak parties came closer together, introducing a new anti-Lukashenko divide into Belarusian politics. This considerably altered not only the structure of party competition but also the future of interest representation in the republic. As Furman et al state:

> 'The political spectrum in Belarus began to take on a strange shape. It seemed that parties managed to fully cover the political field (from nationalists, social democrats and liberals to communists, pan-slavists and greens), and there were no vacancies for the newcomers. However, a new force, the president, had emerged. As this force grew, it began to exert pressure on the entire party spectrum. Because of this pressure, the parties naturally grew closer together, into one big force – a retreating force.'[5]

This was the end of party politics, in the sense that parties were no longer the channels for mass participation but rather a poorly-managed opposition dogged by infighting. Ironically, they fought the president – the embodiment – rather than the system itself, and failed to concentrate on vote canvassing in an era of diminishing public interest in politics.

Over time, the opposition underwent structural changes and acquired a three-part structure. First, there was a weak but classic right-wing opposition. It included the leading nationalist, liberal and social democratic parties. They were united under the Co-ordinating Committee of Democratic Forces (CCDF), which, after a string of disagreements between the parties on the eve of the 2001 presidential election, was challenged by the alternative coalition 'For Social Changes', set up by the Belarusian Popular Front and the United Civic Party. After the election the CCDF resumed its activity, with the same parties demanding a more structured approach to planning the opposition's activity in the future.

The second group of parties formed a satellite relationship with the right-wing opposition, but represented smaller and largely left-wing organisations. These include the Party of Communists of Belarus, the Agrarian Party, the Party of Labour and Justice, the Greens, the Slavic Union 'White Russia' and the Liberal Democratic Party. They have not openly opposed Lukashenko's regime, but occasionally find themselves in disagreement with some of his policies.

The third cluster is relatively new but salient in the sense that it epitomises a crack in the monolithic nomenklatura crafted by Lukashenko. This group of oppositionists is non-partisan and mainly consists of former members of the establishment, including such ex-officials as Mikhail Chygir (ex-Prime Minister), Vladimir Goncharik (Chairman of the Federation of Trade Unions), Semion Domash (ex-Chairman of Grodno Regional Council), Pavel Kozlovski (ex-Minister of Defence), Vasily Leonov (ex-Minister of Agriculture) and Mikhail Marinich (ex-Ambassador to Latvia). It is also unofficially supported by a group of military functionaries who 'secretly' foresee a more amicable national leader.

The opposition has also undergone generational changes through renewal of the leadership echelons in the major parties. For example, after the split in 2000 Vintsuk Viachorka became leader of the liberal wing of the Belarusian Popular Front. Anatol Lebedzka replaced Stanislav Bogdankevich in the United Civic Party.

Despite these changes, public support for the opposition in Belarus remains very low and is still declining. Alexander Lukashenko continually tops the opinion polls with an average popularity ranking between 54 per cent in 1994 and 53 per cent in 2001. The fact is that Lukashenko had no problem defending his presidency, as he was the only possible winner of the contemporary political game in Belarus, a country with little credible opposition and powerful institutions which he himself created.

The questions are: why is the opposition failing to promote itself even with the help of the international community, and why does the public's opinion of them remain so stubbornly low even when they are informed about the government's malfunctioning?

There are grounds for believing that political parties and interest organisations failed in Belarus not only because of their lack of enthusiasm and initiative, but also due to the still largely intact soviet-era structural framework. The latter includes, among other things, the preservation of the old management elite, an absence of political reforms and economic initiatives, and the maintenance of the old-style electoral code. With time, these 'soviet legacies' became institutionalised, allowing the presidential system to become dictatorial, with a 'flexible' constitution and robust bureaucratic and administrative resources. In response the international community has moved from a policy of isolating Belarus to a more client-based approach involving subsidies to political parties and NGOs. This policy has created more problems than it has solved; but it remains intact and ineffective in forging democracy in Belarus. Let us pursue these arguments.

New presidential regimes in general and Lukashenko's regime in particular are structurally incompatible with a robust party system and naturally favour personality-based politics. But institutional engineering plays a no less influential role than historical legacies and Lukashenko's charismatic personality. Instead of facilitating democracy-building in the country, the 1996 changes to the constitution reinforced the authority of the president, and the unreformed local councils stuffed with Lukashenko's appointees remain there to prevent access to power by outsiders. As amended by presidential decrees, the financial provisions of the current electoral law considerably limit candidates' ability to organise effective election campaigns unless the president supports them. In addition, the system of majority voting in single-member constituencies, in a country dominated by an apolitical rural population (60 per cent according to the 1999 census), creates a natural barrier for an urban-based opposition.

The present parliament pursues an agenda set by the president, who exercises a veto as well as having control over the Council of the Republic (the upper chamber) by appointing 8 members himself and having the rest elected under the vigilant eye of his appointees in the regions. The president also selects six members of the constitutional court as well as its chairman (7 of the 12 available seats), which permits a presidential bias in the judicial system. Furthermore, the mass media operate under strict state control and not even limited anti-Lukashenko commentary is allowed to filter through the news.

A great deal of blame for party failure should be attributed to the opposition itself, which has been unable to act cohesively over the past thirteen years. The 2001 presidential campaign deserves particular criticism. The united opposition, which enjoys the patronage of Western sponsors, in fact never unified or engaged decisively in the campaign. It was torn by petty conflicts over political appointments in a post-Lukashenko government as well as suffering from poor campaign management and weak financial accountability. In the 2001 campaign the opposition seems to have been more interested in redistributing the financial support received from the West than in a serious attempt to fight the incumbent President.

The rural campaign pledged by the opposition never took place, so 60 per cent of voters were left floating, to the President's advantage. The mobilisation campaign was poorly directed, operating with unrealistic slogans, and incongruent actions. Thus 2000 and 2001 demonstrated once again that even with Western support political parties are unable to overthrow the government either institutionally or with electoral consent. In many cases opposition politicians have adopted a strategy of opposing the establishment as a long-term and well-paid vocation, rather than from a real desire for political power. By contrast, Lukashenko's practical policy of increasing wages and paying pensions regularly appealed to the electorate.

The question now is whether the opposition in Belarus is past resuscitation, and whether Western agencies should continue wasting their taxpayers' money on the client-based policies that have proved so ineffective over the past five years. Some scholars believe that the political standpoint of the European Union and the USA, including the policy of isolation and the client-based approach to certain members of the opposition, has been rather short-sighted and counter-productive and has compounded problems in Belarus. By pumping enormous sums of money into the Belarusian opposition, which primarily needs ideological and moral guidance, the West did not alleviate the tension but widen the gulf between the regime and the opposition, making the former stronger in public opinion and obliterating the latter. Naturally, the regime robustly defended its domestic interests and continues to act defiantly.

Russia, on the other hand, made its support for Lukashenko clear before the campaign even began. Not only were the TV channels advised to avoid negative reports on Lukashenko, but they were also politically 'selling' such cultural events as the Slavianski Bazar (July 2001) which involved the three Slav presidents (Vladimir Putin, Alexander Lukashenko and Leonid Kuchma) attending a rock/pop music show and making political statements about the future, and Dozhynki, the post-election celebrations. Vladimir Putin was the first of a limited number of foreign leaders to congratulate Lukashenko on his presidential election victory. He was also among the few politicians who explicitly supported him throughout his campaign.

To recapitulate, Belarus's structural and institutional environment leaves little room in the system for outsiders. These structural impediments, as well as the public ones (including popular trust), remain by and large unnoticed by the external observer, and will only cease with a change in the operating framework. What is more disturbing today is that Belarus is a dislocated realm in which no dialogue takes place between leading policy-makers inside and outside the country. The government acts defensively and defiantly to secure its power and the opposition is corrupt and self-centred. More importantly, there is great and often counter-productive external pressure, which has a limited effect on the regime but impedes the development of a productive relationship between the opposition and the government.

The question is: what do the voters do in this disturbing situation?

Public support: what lies behind public loyalty to the President?

New democracies are known for their tendency to like non-partisan politics, favouring sole candidates and single-issue campaigns. Belarus is no exception to the rule, and presents an example of how representative politics in a democracy can become 'depoliticised' through having 95 per cent non-partisan MPs in the current parliament, which in addition is externally ruled by one man, the president.

Lukashenko's popularity rating has been relatively stable over the years. Conversely, public expectations of parties' effectiveness and their importance in building democracy have declined significantly. In 2000 only about 10 per cent of the population identified with political parties,[6] and less than 0.7 per cent were directly involved in party membership. If in 1991 79.9 per cent of the population believed that parties were essential to democracy-building, in 1999 only 29.6 per cent did so. In 2000 the aggregated index of trust (percentage of trust based on a cumulative estimation of answers to related questions) of various political institutions in the country was 50 per cent;[7] 65 per cent of people trusted the President, 49 per cent the government; 42 per cent the local authorities; 45 per cent the heads of regional administration, and only 15 per cent political parties. In fact the level of trust in Lukashenko's government has grown by about 6 per cent since 1997. This suggests that power is the issue which determines the distribution of 'political investment' by the electorate.

As, Table 1 opposite demonstrates, Lukashenko is the only major figure on Belarus's political scene. Public support for him has never been lower than 42 per cent, and reached as high as 53 per cent in 2001, on the eve of the presidential election. As argued previously, Lukashenko did not even need an election to prove that he would be the only credible candidate for re-election. The system he engineered so masterfully, and pre-existing public support, were already working in his favour.

Table 1: Ratings of political leaders, 1993-2000*

	1993	1994	1995	1996	1997	1998	1999	2000
Bogdankevich		2.0	1.1	3.1	1.5	1.5	0.9	1.7
Gaidukevich	–	0.2	0.1	–	0.1	0.3	0.1	0.4
Grib	–	0.7	0.1	0.9	0.8	0.5	–	–
Ermoshin	–	–	–	–	0.2	0.6	0.2	6.6
Kaliakin	–	–	–	0.5	0.2	0.2	0.2	0.2
Lebedko	–	–	–	–	0.3	0.4	0.1	2.1
Lukashenko	0.3	54.4	49.0	43.6	46.0	50.7	54.2	42.0
Myasnikovich	–	0.3	0.2	0.8	0.3	0.9	0.5	0.7
Pozniak	3.3	7.9	8.6	4.4	0.4	0.2	2.8	3.4
Chygir	–	1.0	0.9	2.4	2.2	0.9	3.8	6.3
Sharetski	–	–	0.2	2.3	0.8	0.7	0.3	0.7
Shushkevich	4.1	7.4	6.4	5.9	5.1	4.2	4.3	6.1

*Defined as the percentage of public support expressed in response to the question: 'Whom would you vote for if elections were held tomorrow?' (Source: Rotman, D. 'President and opposition: specific features of the Belarusian political scene', in Korosteleva et al. (2002) Contemporary Belarus.)

Lukashenko's system of personal rule involves an intimate linkage between the voters and their president, which is reinforced by the institutional and structural frameworks. This has proved to be an effective mechanism to protect the President from occasional discontent among his electorate and to maintain his image of efficacy. In this convoluted system of personal rule, parliament, along with the mass media, presidential administration, multi-level courts of justice, and government officials, is one of the many auxiliary means to unite the voters with their president. However, when the linkage fails or the regime spawns public displeasure, there is always someone else to blame in the President's system of delegated trust. Here are only a few examples of the President's personal handling of government as highlighted by the media:

- 'Belarusian president slams cabinet for failing to meet 2001 target' (RFE/RL, Vol.6, No.29, Part II)
- 'Belarusian president wants better performance from banks: 'You will double the amount of resources you attract next year, and have it as an agreement, or you can have it as an order'' (RFE/RL, Vol.6, No.26, Part II)
- 'Belarusian president approves the annual report of Leonid Maltsev, Minister of Defence, and suggests further military reforms' (BDG, No. 1109, 8 February 2002, http://bdg.press.net.by)
- 'Belarusian president raises pensions' (RFE/RL, Vol.6, No.22, Part II)

- 'Belarusian President Alexander Lukashenko met representatives of Belarusian business circles today. The head of state believes that the floodgates of transparent and fair enterprise should open' (BT, 19 October, reported in Financial Times, http://globalarchive.ft.com)
- 'Egor Rybakov, newly appointed head of the national TV company, expressed his deep gratitude to the president for investing his trust in him. He announced the launching of a new framework for national broadcasting, which should facilitate the implementation of campaign pledges by the president' (*Nasha Svaboda*, 24 October, 2001, www.svaboda.com)
- 'Belarusian president outlines agricultural policies' (RFE/RL, Vol.6, No.12, Part II)
- 'Belarusian president stiffens control over economy, issuing an edict that empowers the State Control Committee, police, Finance Ministry, tax and local authorities to impose fines on economic entities for violating various business regulations' (RFE/RL, Vol.6, No.11, Part II)
- 'Mr Lukashenko believes in an authoritarian style of government because the alternative, he says, is instability' (BBC World News, 10 September, 2001)

Clearly such reports create the impression that the President cares for his people and voters continue to support him no matter what. One must remember that voters in transition countries may not adequately reflect on politics while struggling on low wages, supporting their families and homes and queuing in shops for food and medicine.

Who are Lukashenko's supporters, and what are their beliefs and hopes for the future?[8] Three groups can be initially identified: (i) consistent supporters who voted for him in 1994 and will do so in any circumstances (about 23-28 per cent); (ii) about 40 per cent of 'hesitant voters' who were not convinced by the opposition; and (iii) those who voted for Lukashenko because there was no alternative and they felt it safer to vote for the incumbent (mainly the nomenklatura).

As demonstrated, the electorate behaves in both rational and irrational ways. It sets its priorities in a situation of limited choice, reinforced by a belief in Lukashenko's effectiveness. Most staunch supporters actually believe that Lukashenko is the only 'right person' for the job, endorse him with almost absolute trust and hope that he will be able to define a national destiny.

A certain dynamic can be observed in people's motivation for their support of Lukashenko. In 1994 they perceived him as 'their man', 'one of us', 'a man of the common people', which was the right impression for that time, when he was competing against the nomenklatura. In 2000 they believed him to understand people's needs better than anyone else, to suffer with them, and to know how to 'cure' the country. Lukashenko has been described as a doctor who understands the patient's needs, and who knows how to eradicate the disease. There is a feeling of absolute trust: he is often referred to as 'the people's last big hope' for the future. According to public opinion Lukashenko's principal shortcoming is his lack of a reliable team whom he can hold responsible for economic and political disruptions. This recalls a traditional belief about the tsar, perceived as personally good and fair but given bad advice by his retinue. People also believe that Lukashenko is *chelovek dela* (one who tends to fulfil his promises).

Lukashenko's supporters seem to be very confused about the difference between democratic and non-democratic regimes. They are ready to support both socialist and liberal forms of transition, co-operation with both Russia and the West, and both democratic and authoritarian leadership. Nevertheless, when it comes to a practical choice, they tend to support strong leadership and power by proxy as they believe it can do more for the country than consensual politics alone.

The principal impression is that Lukashenko's supporters feel very secure with their leader and do not fear that such issues as delays in payments or the threat of unemployment will ever concern them. Knowing that Lukashenko holds all the reins of power in Belarus, they nevertheless do not see any impending prospect of dictatorship, either because of their 'traditionalism' (adherence to strong leadership) or absolute trust in their leader.

Lukashenko's supporters seem to be financially stable (though not necessarily well off), dominated by the older population, mainly in the provinces and with only school or vocational education. However, there seems to be a tendency towards an evening-out of his support throughout the country. For example, the majority of people (60.59 per cent) in Minsk (traditionally a stronghold of dissidence) nevertheless voted in support of Lukashenko in the last election. This might suggest that there is either a vacuum of alternatives, resulting in public investment in the incumbent as the lesser of two evils, or that his election campaign was very effective in mobilising voters across the board.

Opposition leadership

There are of course opposition leaders, but together they attract less than 10 per cent of voters' interest and receive less then 1 per cent of active support. Although voters' support is minimal, it is based on an informed choice and has an ideological background. Two opposition leaders, Stanislav Shushkevich and Zenon Pozniak, enjoy relatively stable identification by voters (see Table 1). Until recently they had more popular support than any other opposition candidate in the country. Nevertheless, they did not stand for the presidency in 2001 for the following reasons. First, Pozniak would have failed to qualify for election because he had lived abroad for the previous five years. Shushkevich, like many other opposition leaders, would not have been able to obtain enough support to challenge the principal candidate, Alexander Lukashenko. So the opposition voted to put forward a non-partisan and non-controversial candidate who would be able to unite the non-official parties and their voters, thereby attempting to prevent an effortless victory for Lukashenko in the 2001 election. The locally-grown contestant, Vladimir Goncharik, chairman of the Federation of Trade Unions, was promoted to represent the 'unified' opposition in the election on the basis of rough consensus and increasing Western pressure. If one were to add some speculation about the future, the above-named opposition leaders would be highly unlikely alternatives to the incumbent President in their struggle for power even in five years' time. However, they might (if they so decide) become a viable battering-ram in the parliamentary elections in 2004.

Voters' support for these two opposition leaders will be examined in contrast to that for the President. Opinion research demonstrates that people's attitudes to them are rather contradictory. For example, voters support Pozniak for his well-articulated party manifesto, but somehow do not identify him with his own Christian Conservative Party. They seem to be very concerned with the government's client-based approach and the growing autocracy: about

75 per cent of them deem these issues highly important. At the same time they do not seem to be troubled by such every-day problems as shortage of money, food and medicine, or corruption and incompetence in the elite; less than 30 per cent give these priority. There is another obvious contradiction between the real issues and their view of an ideal presidential candidate. Pozniak's voters tend to demand strict legality and market reforms but are also eager to support governance by decree, delegated leadership and a centrally-controlled economy. They blame the government (75 per cent) and the President (50 per cent) for regime failures and declining living standards. They also believe that Pozniak could be an able leadership contender. But a third of his supporters still think that Alexander Lukashenko is a stronger alternative.

Stanislav Shushkevich's supporters seem to be more rational in prioritising their choices. For example they are concerned more about declining living standards than the incompetence or corruption of the authorities. They blame the government and themselves for their falling standard of living. They also demonstrate a higher degree of appreciation of the values of democracy, and unanimity in rejecting governance by decree or by proxy. In other words, they are less ideological, but more informed in their judgements on issues of social order. Like Pozniak's, Shushkevich's supporters believe in his leadership potential but consider Lukashenko a more viable alternative. These are middle-aged, urban people with professional and higher education, as opposed to Pozniak's group of workers and students.

In summary, the difference between the three politicians is reflected in their audiences: they are ideological and militant in Pozniak's case; rational and pragmatic in Shushkevich's case; and all-embracing in Lukashenko's case.

Conclusion: populist dictatorship or possible democracy?

This chapter has attempted to demonstrate how disruptive and discordant Belarus's political system is today. At present there are three main players: the government, which acts defensively and defiantly to preserve its power; the opposition, which is self-centred and oblivious to its past experience; and finally, the West, whose claimed understanding of the situation in Belarus often results in shallow, manipulative and counter-productive aid. Concerted efforts are required to bring together President Lukashenko, a re-invigorated opposition and Western diplomacy to help to prevent Belarus sinking into authoritarianism. Lukashenko indeed shows signs of willingness to develop a dialogue, which already exists between the other two parties.

One question, nevertheless, remains intact: the sustainability of the regime in Belarus. Formally Belarus satisfies the normal criteria of a democracy. In particular there are regular and contested elections which international observers have described as 'free but not fair'. Belarus's government has been freely elected at constitutionally established intervals, and enjoys political continuity. Political practices are based on the 1994 constitution, subject to minor alterations in 1996, which theoretically commits the new state to ideological pluralism, freedom of association, and multi-party politics. Classic liberal freedoms are formally guaranteed, as is the dominance of the civil over the military power. In addition, there is little likelihood of massive fraud, open use of coercive mechanisms by the authorities, or explicitly manipulative use of the mass media.

Nevertheless, this chapter has shown that behind Belarus's democratic façade there is an undemocratic interior. What is really alarming is that this regime may be rather sustainable, and more importantly may develop into a populist dictatorship. Timing is very important here. If no action is taken to bring the interior into line with the façade, the country might be subjected to unspoken abuse of human rights and absolute tyranny indefinitely.

Notes

[1] C. Haerpfer (2002) 'Electoral politics of Belarus compared', in Korosteleva. E. et al. (eds) *Contemporary Belarus: Between Democracy and Dictatorship*, London: Routledge Curzon; S. White and R. Rose (2000) *Nationality and Public Opinion in Belarus and Ukraine*, CSPP, No. 346.

[2] See Rotman, D. et al. *What kind of Belarus can we see?* (annual sociological reports) Centre for Social and Political Research, Belarusian State University.

[3] For more details on elite change see O. Belova 'Difficulties of elite formation in Belarus after 1991', in Korosteleva, E, R. Marsh, and C. Lawson eds. (2002), *Contemporary Belarus: between Democracy and Dictatorship,* London: Curzon Press Ltd.

[4] See Korosteleva (2001) *Explaining Party System Development in Post-communist Belarus*, PhD Thesis, University of Bath.

[5] Furman, D. (ed.) *Belorussiya i Rossiya: Obschestva i Gosudarstva* [*Belarus and Russia: Societies and States*]. Moskva: Prava Cheloveka. 1998

[6] S. White and R. Rose (2000) *Nationality and Public Opinion in Belarus and Ukraine*, Glasgow: CSPP Publications.

[7] These trends of electoral behaviour have been confirmed by data gathered in recent polls. See 'Charismatic Political leadership in Russia, Belarus and Ukraine', University of Bath, European Research Institute. For example, 40.8 per cent trust Lukashenko, and consider his leadership effective. About 75.1 per cent believe that Lukashenko's presidency is the most powerful institution in the country; and so are his government (23.2 per cent) and the police (30.4 per cent) supported by the president. December 2000.

[8] The findings presented above are corroborated by evidence from other sources, such as Oleg Manaev (www.iiseps.by) and David Rotman (2002) 'President and Opposition: specific features of the Belarusian political scene', in Korosteleva, E, R. Marsh, and C. Lawson eds. (2002), *Contemporary Belarus: between Democracy and Dictatorship,* London: Curzon Press Ltd.

Belarus 2001 Presidential Election: Somewhat Free but not Fair

Kimmo Kiljunen

'This was a brilliant, elegant and persuasive victory', presidential candidate Alexander Lukashenko told the press on 9 September 2001, one hour before the polling stations closed and when no official election results had yet been released.

This premature statement was next day confirmed by the Minister of Foreign Affairs, Mikhail Khostov:

> 'The Republic of Belarus has passed through an important stage in its democratic development. On 9 September 2001 the Belarusian people elected Alexander Lukashenko President of Belarus for the second time.
>
> The high level of voter participation is indisputable evidence of popular support for the incumbent president of Belarus: 83.86 per cent of the enfranchised population of the republic took part in the election; of these 75.76 per cent supported Alexander Lukashenko. This confirms the confidence of the Belarusian people in Alexander Lukashenko and the political system in the country.
>
> The presidential election in Belarus took place in a climate of political, social and informational transparency unprecedented for the states of the former Soviet Union. More than twenty thousand international and domestic observers – MPs, representatives of European and other international institutions, non-governmental organisations, political and public figures as well as citizens – took part in observing the election.'

In my role as Special Co-ordinator for the OSCE Limited Election Observation Mission to Belarus (ILEOM), I concluded on 10 September at a press conference on behalf of the international election observers:

> 'The 2001 presidential election process failed to meet OSCE commitments for democratic elections as formulated in the 1990 Copenhagen Document and Council of Europe standards.'

What went wrong? Why such contradictory conclusions? The Minister of Foreign Affairs added in his statement:

> 'The presidential election also demonstrated that the election process was based on compliance with national electoral legislation. At the same time it indicated that international electoral standards need to be further elaborated and defined.'

Thus, internationally agreed criteria for free and fair elections do not match Belarusian national electoral legislation and standards. It was a brilliant, elegant and persuasive victory for President Lukashenko, but on his own terms. The legislative framework in Belarus failed to meet universally-agreed provisions for democratic elections.

There were several fundamental flaws in the electoral process, some of which are specific to the political situation in the country:

1. The international election observation has to be called 'limited'. Due to the late invitation from the authorities in Belarus, the OSCE – the leading international election observation body – had to limit its observation to the last three weeks of the electoral process only. Furthermore, the authorities arbitrarily denied visas to two key members of the long-term observation team.
2. An independent domestic observer network was created. Out of these 16,000 observers only 12,000 were allowed to be registered. In 4000 cases accreditation was refused. Furthermore, two days before the election the Central Electoral Commission (CEC) cancelled the accreditation of 3000 observers. In the end 9000 independent domestic observers were deployed. The network observed about 70 per cent of all polling stations.
3. This domestic observer network documented altogether on election day and during the early voting more than 5000 violations of the existing laws and regulations pertaining to polling stations and their procedures. They even documented falsifications of the counting processes.

4. The major problem of the electoral process was not, however, what happened on election day itself. The independent observers estimated that Lukashenko received some 70 per cent of the votes cast. The problem was what happened before election day. A proper environment for free and fair elections was lacking. The executive structures, with their extensive and uncontrolled powers, including rule by presidential decree, permitted arbitrary changes in the electoral environment.

5. The registration of presidential candidates was somewhat arbitrary. Initially 22 candidates were registered subject to their gathering the requisite 100,000 signatures. There were several complaints regarding the signature-gathering process. In the end four candidates were registered by the CEC, but one, the former governor of Grodno region, Semion Domash, withdrew his candidacy. Ambassador Mikhail Marinich was not registered, although his supporters had collected some 110,000 signatures; some 13,000 of these were declared invalid by the CEC. President Lukashenko admitted to me at our tête-à-tête discussion that the other candidates, Vladimir Goncharik, the head of the Federation of Trade Unions, and Sergei Gaidukevich, the leader of the Liberal Democratic Party, had also failed to collect the requisite 100,000 signatures. It was only thanks to the flexibility of the authorities, he said, that their candidature was finally accepted! In the end, nevertheless, a genuine choice was available to voters in the Belarusian presidential election.

6. The Electoral Code failed to ensure the representation of various political interests in the electoral commissions. As a result, the election administration system was overly dependent on the executive branch of government, from national to local community level, and was therefore partial. For example, the model ballot paper on display in every polling stations had a cross against the name of Mr. Lukashenko – by pure chance of course.

7. No presidential candidate was able to conduct a proper election campaign. The incumbent President did not want to campaign (he was occupied with his presidential duties – with good publicity, of course) and the challengers did not have the means or opportunity to campaign. The rigid restrictions imposed on candidates by the legal and administrative framework, including presidential decrees, made for a skewed political contest. There was no need to use the presidential decrees to disqualify any candidate, but that option was available.

The most controversial decrees included a) a ban of foreign aid to political parties, b) restrictions on organising public mass meetings and c) a requirement to disclose the sources of income of not only the candidates but also their families. Each candidate was entitled to spend only the equivalent of $12,500 provided for the campaign by the state. They were not allowed to use funds other than those contributed by the common election fund. By way of comparison, the funds available for the presidential election in Belarus were around half of my personal election budget in the last parliamentary elections in Finland!

8. There were repeated incidents of human rights violations during the electoral campaign. The opposition or independent media were subjected to special tax inspections, their equipment and print were confiscated and facilities were closed. There were even reports from some regional campaign centres that the opposition had been surrounded by militia and threatened. That obviously created an atmosphere of uncertainty and fear.
9. State-owned outlets dominated both the broadcast and print media, and they were highly biased during the election campaign. Russian TV channels are widely watched in Belarus, but they were astonishingly quiet about the electoral process except for the very last week of the campaign. The only alternative sources of political information were the independent or opposition print media. However, these were handicapped by higher prices that those of the state, if not censored or confiscated altogether. As a result, opposition views were unattainable for the majority of the public.

Nevertheless, some positive features also emerged in Belarus, in particular with regard to the democratic awareness of the people and the emergence of vibrant political structures of civil society. These manifested themselves in the political coalition of the opposition around a single candidate and in the grass-roots nation-wide organisation of independent election observers, including those favourable to the government. With three candidates competing in the presidential election, the voters of Belarus were offered a genuine political choice. Thus, the elections were somewhat free, but clearly not fair.

Nevertheless, there should not be any illusions: the development of democratic structures in their current form has taken place thanks to the brave commitment of the people in the face of intimidation by the authorities and because of the work of international organisations in Belarus.

On this basis the international observers welcomed and acknowledged 'the emergence of a pluralist civil society, being the foundation for the development of democratic political structures representing all segments of the population.' Furthermore, we concluded that 'the isolation of the country is not in the best interest of the people of Belarus and is not conducive to strengthening democratic development.'

Republic of Belarus: An Elegant Dictatorship?

Malcolm Hawkes

President Alexander Lukashenko described his victory in the September 2001 presidential election as 'an elegant victory'.[1] Notwithstanding pronouncements from international organisations and governments that denounced the elections as fundamentally flawed and undemocratic, this 'victory' marked the culmination of years of hard work by the Lukashenko administration to ensure that there could be only one possible outcome. This state-sponsored campaign has subverted the notion of respect for basic civil and political rights and the rule of law, and fostered a climate of fear in Belarus, through targeted 'disappearances', beatings, imposition of censorship and a wholesale attack against civil society in that country.

In 2001, the London-based freedom of expression NGO Article 19 published a report on the state of freedom of expression in Belarus entitled 'Belarus: The Mechanics of Repression: Obstacles to Free and Fair Elections'.[2] Based on testimony taken from journalists and newspaper editors in the field, the report detailed the methodology of repression, primarily against these front-line exponents of freedom of expression, used by the government to quash dissent in all its forms. In response to this report, the Belarusian government refused to grant Article 19 staff visas to visit the country to release the report in July of that year.

The mechanics of repression extend far beyond the fundamental right to freedom of expression and indeed permeate every aspect of civil society in Belarus. This article will chart out those structural areas of repression, constructed by the President, which the state employs in an attempt to silence the voices of democracy and human rights in Belarus.

It is worth noting that while President Lukashenko devised and implemented his campaign of repression, Belarus's neighbours – notably Poland and the Baltic states – made strong advances towards building civil society institutions with respect for human rights and democracy. Alone among East European states, Belarus remains outside the Council of Europe, membership of which requires respect for human rights and democratic governance.

The first building blocks: the election of Alexander Lukashenko and the November 1996 referendum

While few predicted Alexander Lukashenko's election as president in 1994, fewer still believed that it would lead so swiftly to such authoritarian levels. Early evidence of his authoritarian rule came in December 1994. Although elected on an anti-corruption platform, that month President Lukashenko moved swiftly to block publication of a report on corruption he had commissioned using direct censorship of newspapers; those newspapers that had intended to carry the report were forced to print their editions with blank spaces.

The November 1996 referendum heralded sweeping changes to the Belarusian political and constitutional system and radically changed the Constitution adopted in 1994.[3] Defying multiple constitutional court rulings from 1994-1996, including a ruling in 1996 that the constitution may not be changed by referendum, President Lukashenko pushed through several key amendments to the 1994 Constitution. First, that the current parliament, the Thirteenth Supreme Soviet, be dissolved and replaced by a new bicameral legislature, an upper and lower house, whose members were to be handpicked by the President himself. Second, the President's current term of office was extended from five to seven years. Third, the President granted himself the power to appoint and dismiss members of the country's judiciary, including six of the twelve members of the constitutional court along with that court's chairman; those members of the constitutional court who had opposed the referendum were promptly dismissed and more subservient members appointed. And fourth, the President granted himself the power to rule by decree. The new bicameral parliament is unable to overrule or amend presidential decrees.

A policy of russification

The formation of a Belarus-Russia union has long been a foreign policy goal of the Lukashenko administration, probably due to the inherent economic advantages that such a union would bring to Belarus. No less important a goal was the openly stated desire of President Lukashenko to head such a union, a prospect that seemed likely under the ailing leadership of Russian President Boris Yeltsin. Although Yeltsin encouraged and supported this policy, his successor, Vladimir Putin, has been less than enthusiastic about the idea. However, in pursuit of this goal the Belarusian government has embarked on a policy of russification in which the Belarusian language has been systematically downgraded and sidelined by the authorities.

Although Belarusian and Russian both have the status of official languages in Belarus, speaking in Belarusian has, in itself, become a political statement, linking that individual with the opposition and pro-democracy movement. Whether in court as a defendant or in an oral university entrance exam, those who choose to speak or write in Belarusian are often put at a disadvantage and are perceived more negatively than those who speak in Russian. Similarly, newspapers that publish in Belarusian automatically carry the tag 'opposition' and arguably face greater censure for carrying articles critical of the authorities. Academic researchers together with publishing houses have incurred the ire of the authorities for researching and publishing materials on Belarusian independence, a topic that is considered anti-Russian. Many schools whose language of tuition is Belarusian have either been closed by the state or forced to switch to teaching in Russian instead.[4]

A subservient judiciary

Following the 1996 referendum, the President has the power to appoint all judges in the Belarusian legal system. Many observers suspect that post-1996, judges in Belarus lack impartiality, particularly in political cases, as evidenced by their reluctance to acquit members of opposition political parties. Local observers frequently complain that judges ignore evidence presented by the defence. In other cases, judges reportedly ignore allegations from defendants that their confessions were elicited under torture and ill-treatment.

Lawyers have also gradually been brought to heel. In 1997, a Ministry of Justice decree ordered that qualified legal advice may be given only by lawyers who are members of a state-run bar association. The Ministry of Justice controls these associations, has a deciding influence over who may be given a licence to practice law, and sets qualifying exams. As a result, lawyers have become reluctant to defend members of opposition political parties.

In at least three cases in 1998 and 1999, the Ministry of Justice has, either directly or indirectly, stripped their licences to practice law from lawyers who were involved in the defence of members of the opposition.

For example, Nadezhda Dudareva defended several opposition party members including, in 1998, two teenagers who had been accused of writing anti-presidential graffiti and displaying the banned white-red-white flag in the town of Stolptsy, south of Minsk. Shortly after this case, the Ministry of Justice revoked her licence to practice law, ostensibly for violating lawyers' ethics in an earlier case. International observers and indeed Ms. Dudareva herself believe that it was her role in defending opposition figures that led to the Ministry's action. Other cases include that of former member of parliament Miacheslav Gryb, who lost his licence to practice law, he believes, for his political activity, including participation in a peaceful opposition demonstration. In 1998 the defence lawyer Garry Pogonyailo, who had defended numerous high-profile figures, including the former chair of the National Bank Tamara Vinnikova and a journalist from Russian public television (ORT), Pavel Sheremet, pre-empted exclusion from the bar association by leaving voluntarily. He is still unable to practice law in Belarus.

Other lawyers are the subject of harassment and intimidation from the authorities. Lawyer and human rights activist Vera Stremkovskaya has faced numerous attempts by the authorities to hamper her work as head of the non-governmental organisation the Human Rights Centre and as a defence lawyer. Stremkovskaya has defended some high-profile figures, such as Vasily Starovoitov, a successful farm manager prosecuted on charges that included ebezzlement.[5] In 1999 she faced criminal charges of slander after asking in court what had happened to Starovoitov's property, which had been confiscated by the police; the charges were ultimately dropped, but not before Stremkovskaya had been threatened with losing her licence to practice law.

Restrictions on academic freedom[6]

The repressive methods of the Lukashenko administration have extended to the university campus and the sphere of education in general.

The Lukashenko administration has sought to exert political control over universities at the expense of academic freedom. It has achieved this through the appointment, and dismissal, of university rectors by the President. This goal is assisted by the Belarusian Patriotic Union of Youth, a state-sponsored and heavily pro-presidential youth movement which is present on every university campus despite a ban on political organisations in academia.

Students who are politically active in opposition parties are closely monitored by university authorities, who, in collusion with police, work to identify those of their students attending opposition demonstrations. In addition to administrative or criminal sanctions levied against student participants in peaceful demonstrations, university authorities subject students to academic sanctions that can include suspension or expulsion from their place of study. For example, in March 2002 the pro-democracy movement Charter 97 reported that two activists, Alexander Koliada and Alexander Pavlovich from the youth opposition movement *Zubr*, were expelled from the Mogilev Polytechnic Institute after a local court convicted and fined them for insulting the President. The two activists allegedly performed street theatre in August 2001 which included impersonations of the President.[7] According to reports, in 2001 over thirty students were expelled from university for participating in opposition demonstrations.

Privately-run universities are not beyond the reach of the state authorities. These universities are granted five-year licences to operate and many believe that the renewal of these is dependent on pro-presidential loyalty. Some faculty members of private universities have stated that they were instructed by their rectors not to criticise or permit criticism of the President by students.

Smaller educational initiatives, such as evening or weekend classes and schools aimed at empowering Belarusian citizens to learn about their rights and freedoms under national and international law, have been the focus of attack by the authorities. These projects are commonly denied access to premises in which to hold their classes on spurious grounds; the administrators who run halls, cafes or any space in which classes may be held are reportedly reluctant to rent these spaces to classes out of fear of negative repercussions from the authorities. Local authorities also use overly broad and restrictive provisions on the holding of meetings to prohibit these classes. In 1999 Human Rights Watch reported the case of Galina Drebezova of the Belarusian Association of Women Lawyers who runs evening and weekend classes in human rights for adults and children.[8] She stated that her classes had been banned 'a great many times', most often through local authorities refusing permission to rent premises.

Harassment of NGOs

NGOs are the subject of concerted efforts by the state to hamper and curtail their work. NGOs that work on human rights are more likely to have problems than those which do not. However, organisations that are perceived to be political and in opposition to the President, or which promote the Belarusian language or culture, have continual problems. These problems range from difficulties in obtaining premises from which to work, to members of these organisations being arrested at demonstrations, to onerous and bureaucratic registration and re-registration requirements.

In one example, on 3 December 2001 the Supreme Court ordered the closure of the Belarusian Students Association (BSA). The BSA is apolitical, but chooses to work in Belarusian and, in addition to promoting the rights of students in the country, also promotes the Belarusian language. In September 2000 the BSA received warnings from the Ministry of Justice including for using the 'wrong' colour for its registered logo on its letterhead and for using the spelling 'Belarusan' in English as opposed to 'Belarusian'. The warning about the logo was issued apparently because the organisation had registered a red and white coloured logo, whereas it actually used black and white, since the organisation did not have a colour printer.[9]

Belarusian NGOs have been the target of persistent burglaries in which computer equipment, essential to the operating of these organisations, is stolen. There is no hard evidence that points directly at state involvement in these burglaries, and the theft of expensive equipment in an impoverished economy may be expected. However, the absence of prosecutions for these burglaries, coupled with a reported uninterested attitude by law enforcement officers, raises suspicion. Indeed, in some of these burglaries, the thieves took only computer hard drives and left untouched other valuable equipment. In one of the latest examples, in March 2002, computer, office and other electronic equipment was stolen from the local branch of the *Viasna* human rights centre in Brest. The thieves reportedly entered through the front door.[10]

The climate of fear: attacks on dissent, 'disappearances', arbitrary arrests and politically-motivated trials

A series of unresolved 'disappearances' has contributed greatly to the climate of fear in Belarus, and has proved to be an effective tool to quash dissent.[11]

In May 1999, former minister of interior Yury Zakharenko telephoned his wife to say he would be home shortly. He did not return. Zakharenko had complained of being followed by persons unknown in the weeks leading up to his 'disappearance'. As interior minister, Zakharenko had reportedly enjoyed popular support among the police and law enforcement agencies. In the months prior to his 'disappearance', he had been working actively to form a union of officers from the police service and was involved in opposition politics. This activity appears to be the most likely explanation for his 'disappearance'.

Viktor Gonchar was an outspoken member of the opposition movement and a member of the Thirteenth Supreme Soviet dissolved by the 1996 referendum. In September 1999, he and his companion, businessman Anatoly Krasovsky, went to a sauna in Minsk in a large four-wheel-drive vehicle. An employee of the sauna reportedly stated that the two men visited the sauna and that he saw them leave. Small patches of blood and broken glass from a vehicle's headlight were found in the street outside. There has been no further information as to the fate and whereabouts of the two men.

Dmitri Zavadsky worked as a cameraman for the Russian television station ORT in Belarus and in Russia. Together with Pavel Sheremet, he filmed a piece on the lack of border security in 1997 and the pair were prosecuted in a trial viewed as politically motivated. Following this trial, both men continued to work for ORT but in Russia. In July 2000, Zavadsky drove to Minsk-2 airport to pick up Sheremet from his flight from Moscow. However, upon arrival at the airport, Sheremet could not find Zavadsky. Zavadsky's car was in the car park, reportedly wiped clean of fingerprints.

There has been no clear explanation as to why Zavadsky was targeted. Theories have included the work he and Sheremet had done in Chechnya, in which they had filmed a documentary piece which also allegedly revealed the work of Belarusian security service personnel working as mercenaries.

In a closed trial that Zavadsky's relatives and lawyers denounced, two men were sentenced to life imprisonment for their involvement in the abduction and murder of Zavadsky. However, Zavadsky's relatives complained that the trial ignored evidence from two men who worked in the state security services alleging state involvement in the case; these men subsequently fled the country. Zavadsky's body has never been found.

Attacks on dissent

The tenure of Alexander Lukashenko is littered with examples of unfair and politically motivated practices. The case of Ruslan Zgolich disturbingly echoes the pernicious Soviet practice of imprisoning dissidents in mental asylums.[12] In May 2002, during the trial of Zgolich, who worked as a producer for Belarusian state television, a judge ordered that he be sent a second time for psychiatric examination at a hospital for the mentally ill. Zgolich is being tried for theft for stealing video tapes on which an unfinished film he was producing had been recorded. Upon his arrest in December 2001, police severely beat Zgolich. Prior to his arrest, Zgolich had been an outspoken critic of Belarusian state television, reportedly stating that it was being used by the Lukashenko administration to brainwash its audience. Observers such as the Belarusian PEN Centre believe the arrest and trial is likely to be an act of political reprisal.

Other figures who publicly oppose the President face criminal charges. Former prime minister Mikhail Chygir rose to prominence in opposition to the President in 1999 during the so-called alternative presidential election organised by a coalition of opposition parties. Chygir stood as a candidate in the election, which was symbolic and intended to highlight the expiry of Lukashenko's tenure as president prior to its extension in the 1996 referendum. In 1999 Chygir spent eight months in jail, ostensibly on charges of embezzlement and theft relating to his tenure as prime minister, but the charges appeared clearly linked to his political activities. He received a three-year suspended sentence. However, in December 2000 the Belarusian Supreme Court annulled this verdict but sent the case back to a lower court for Chygir to be tried on charges of negligence and tax evasion.

Meanwhile, in 2001 Mikhail Chygir's son, Alexander Chygir, was arrested on charges of car theft and in March 2002 was sentenced to seven years' imprisonment in a high-security facility, with confiscation of property. The timing of Alexander Chygir's arrest and the severity of the sentence point to a political motive.

Mikhail Chygir was also a candidate in the September 2001 presidential election, although he later withdrew his candidacy, in line with other opposition candidates, to back a single candidate, Vladimir Goncharik.

In May 2002 Mikhail Chygir returned to court to face allegations of tax evasion and negligence connected with his former position as prime minister and his business activities for a German company in Moscow.

Violations of freedom of expression: the independent media

In September 1995 the Lukashenka administration moved to block access to state-owned broadcast media by members of the opposition. State-owned television became a mouthpiece for the president and does not feature criticism of any kind of his activities or policies. Local cable television stations ceased to broadcast news programmes of substance and radio stations followed suit. In August 1996, a popular independent and commercially-run radio station, Radio 101.2, was seized by the government and closed down. The government later handed the frequency to the fervently pro-presidential youth organisation, the Belarusian Patriotic Union of Youth. In November 1995, the state barred opposition politicians from publishing articles in state-owned print media.

That year also saw the state curtail independent newspapers' access to state-owned printing presses and newspaper distribution networks. Some of these newspapers, such as *Belaruskaya Gazeta* and *Narodnaya Volya,* elected to print their copy abroad and import their editions. The government responded by introducing sweeping restrictions on the import of printed matter deemed harmful to the state, or to its political or economic interests. In several cases independent newspaper editions were either confiscated at the border by Belarusian border guards or subject to inspection before being allowed through.

The key moment in repression of freedom of expression in Belarus came with the entry into force of the Law on the Press and Other Mass Media in January 1995. This law handed draconian power to the State Committee on the Press which enabled it to issue warnings to offending publications; the accumulation of two or more warnings in any given year could result in that publication's closure. In February 2001 the Minsk-based news agency Belapan reported that, in 2000, the State Committee on the Press issued warnings to twenty different publications for violating the Law on the Press.

This system has led to the at times farcical situation exemplified by the newspaper *Svaboda,* which has been closed down by the State Committee on the Press several times, each time reopening under a different name but with exactly the same format and staff.[13]

Restrictions on freedom of assembly

The right to freedom of assembly in Belarus is severely restricted. Repressive laws that regulate public assembly strictly control the time, place and number of participants. Demonstrators who do manage to get permission to hold a march and rally must adhere to these rules by the letter or else face fines and/or imprisonment. For instance, some organisers have been jailed or fined when participants have strayed from the pavement to the street. The law also regulates the symbols used in the demonstration; the use of an unregistered symbol, including the former national white-red-white flag, is prohibited.[14]

In May 2001, further restrictions on the right to assembly were introduced by a presidential decree restricting the number of participants at a demonstration to under 1,000 and banning unregistered organisations from holding demonstrations.

Typically, the Belarusian authorities deploy large numbers of riot police at all opposition demonstrations, especially in the capital, Minsk. Violence between the demonstrators and the police is common, with the demonstrators often alleging provocation from the side of the authorities.

At one such demonstration in April 2002 entitled 'We Can't Live Like This!' police detained over one hundred persons amid reported clashes with riot police; over sixty of these persons were variously fined or sentenced to jail terms from two days to two weeks. Much larger clashes, injuries and arrests took place in the first 'Freedom' march in October 1999. Detained demonstrators complained of severe beatings in police custody that amounted to torture and ill-treatment.

The work of the OSCE

In 1998, the OCSE opened an Advisory and Monitoring Group (AMG) in Minsk. The office's designated tasks were to conduct monitoring of the human rights situation and to provide advice to the Belarusian government on legal matters, including the redrafting of legal instruments such as the Criminal Code. The office further attempted to mediate between the opposition political parties and the government to try to resolve questions such as access to the state-owned media in the run-up to parliamentary and presidential elections.

The AMG became the increasing focus of attack from the Lukashenko administration, with its head, Ambassador Hans-Georg Wieck, accused variously of spying and supporting the opposition. The vitriol increased and reached its apogee following the end of Ambassador Wieck's term of office in December 2001. Following Ambassador Wieck's departure, in 2002, the Lukashenko administration demanded that the office substantially scale down the range and scope of its operations, accusing the office of having exceeded its mandate. When the OSCE refused, the Belarusian government effectively expelled the senior members of the mission by not renewing their visas. [See Hans-Georg Wieck chapter in this volume].

Conclusion

As evidenced by the examples listed above, under the authoritarian rule of President Alexander Lukashenko Belarus has become a state where the rule of law and respect for human rights have been subverted to crush dissent and violate fundamental human rights.

The engagement of the international community has yielded little in terms of concrete results, the action against the OSCE's Minsk office being only the latest example of Lukashenko's refusal to comply with external requests to reform. The government of Russia, the country with the greatest power and influence over Belarus, still does little to encourage Belarus to improve its human rights record. The current Russian president, Vladimir Putin, appears more concerned with the impact of the largely unreformed Belarusian economy on Russia in any future much-touted union between the two states, than about Lukashenko's dismissive attitude towards democracy and human rights.

Belarus remains stubbornly isolated from the West, and is not even a member of the Council of Europe. How long Lukashenko may enjoy his latest elegant victory appears a moot point, unless, and until, Russia decides to exert its influence to bring its authoritarian neighbour to heel.

Notes

[1] Sergei Shargorodsky, *Authoritarian Incumbent Claims Victory in Belarus Presidential Vote*, Associated Press, 10 September 2001.

[2] Article 19, *Belarus: The Mechanics of Repression: Obstacles to Free and Fair Elections*, May 2001, available online at: http://www.article19.org

[3] In its fourth periodic report on the implementation of its obligations under the International Covenant on Civil and Political Rights, the Belarusian government stated that the 1994 Constitution demonstrated that 'Belarus had opted definitively for democracy and human rights'; UN ref: CCPR/D/84/Add.4, 3 September 1996

[4] In a June 2000 report, the Belarusian Helsinki Committee stated that in Minsk, out of a total of 242 high schools, 11 used Belarusian as the language of instruction.

[5] Many observers believed the case to be motivated by political reprisal, since Starovoitov's business practices were a direct challenge to the state's agricultural policy. Some reports also allege that Starovoitov was involved in supporting then Prime Minister Kebich, who stood against Lukashenko in the 1994 presidential election.

[6] See, generally, Human Rights Watch, *Belarus: Violations of Academic Freedom*, July 1999.

[7] As reported by the International League for Human Rights, *Belarus Update*, Vol. 5, no. 12, March 2002.

[8] Human Rights Watch, *Violations of Academic Freedom*.

[9] See Radio Free Europe/Radio Liberty Newsline, an electronic news bulletin, on 4 December 2001.

[10] Other suspicious burglaries include: in March 2001, at the Minsk office of the Belarusian Helsinki Committee; in February 2001, computer and office equipment stolen from the independent newspaper, De Facto, in Mogilev; in November 2000, the newspaper *Shag* in Minsk was burgled; in June 2000, thieves broke into the Minsk-based Human Rights Centre and stole computer equipment; and in May 2000, the Legal Assistance Centre was broken into and equipment stolen. None of these burglaries has been solved.

[11] The term 'disappearance' is commonly used as a euphemism for acts of politically-motivated murder. The European Court for Human Rights has ruled that 'disappearance' constitutes torture for the relatives of the victim, who suffer constant anguish, not knowing the fate or whereabouts of their loved ones.

[12] See, International League for Human Rights, *Belarus Update*, Vol. 5, no. 22, May 2002.

[13] *Svaboda* first reopened as *Naviny*, then became *Novaya Svaboda*. The owner, Pavel Zhuk, has reportedly registered several other names in anticipation of further closures of his newspaper.

[14] The white-red-white national flag, introduced in 1991, was replaced by the red-green Soviet-era flag by referendum in 1995.

With the State or Against the State: The Media in Belarus

Steven Eke

Introduction

There is a certain irony that President Lukashenko, who ran his first election campaign in 1994 on a strong anti-corruption theme in which defending the 'need for free media' was a key feature, should have become an implacable enemy of media freedom. Yet the metamorphosis from a (self-declared) ardent supporter of media liberation from political interference to a leader who views the media with almost paranoid suspicion, occurred surprisingly quickly. The overall effect has been to monopolise access to, and the dissemination of information in, Belarus at all levels. Repressive administrative measures and legislation have established the framework for a sophisticated system of state control which finds reflection in active censorship, the closure of some independent media outlets, and the harassment of journalists.

The difficulties imposed on the independent media in Belarus have striking similarities with the rough treatment of many other independent or non-state organisations at the hands of the Belarusian authorities. At all levels, from the president down, there is a genuine reluctance to foster open debate or to encourage pluralism of opinion, and a clear unwillingness to accept that there is a place for the expression of dissent. In its psychological manifestations, much of this has clearly been inherited from the recent Soviet past. But in conditions where ideology is almost totally absent from the ethos and language of the executive, the result is a repressive state in which fear severely curtails the free flow of information.

President Lukashenko himself is unambiguous in his characterisations of the non-state media. He has referred to them as 'fascist', while calling on the state media 'to reveal the real goals' of the political opposition. Occasionally this gives rise to reports that look like nothing more than crude propaganda and are understood to be deliberately false. For example, state-owned Belarusian Television told its viewers after a summit meeting between Lukashenko and the Ukrainian President Leonid Kuchma in 2000 that 'Ukraine will soon be joining the Union of Russia and Belarus'. In reality, there was no such plan. Another report said that President Lukashenko and former US President Bill Clinton held a meeting in Turkey at an OSCE summit, when all that had happened in reality was the briefest of (chance) handshakes between the two men. More often, the attempts by the official media to portray the authorities as benevolent and working against 'enemies of the people' for the good of the 'popular masses' result in outright slander of the opposition, whether in journalism, politics, business, science or the arts.

The application of these restrictive measures is not however consistent and much of the media in Belarus practice self-censorship within what it perceives to be the bounds of acceptability. Theoretically, there is no official state censorship of newspapers and magazines. Equally, there is no official body to regulate cable and satellite broadcasting. This may seem like a green light for a free flow of information. In reality, however, it means that much of the media operates in a legal vacuum and is subject to the authorities' whims. At best, in some urban areas, there is access to a wider range of information outlets than would seem likely. There are more than a dozen daily newspapers. Most of them are nominally non-state-owned. In the capital it is common to find opposition newspapers being sold directly on the streets. It is possible to purchase a satellite dish in order to watch foreign television, or to have cable television installed. Access to the internet is growing although not widespread in what is, by all measures, a poor country.

This chapter looks at how this situation has evolved, and shows that its degree of institutionalisation is such that there is little if any hope for short-term liberalisation. The situation outside Minsk is particularly difficult, with local officials proving themselves more enthusiastic in their campaign of harassment of the independent media than the authorities in the more cosmopolitan capital. The consequence is that only a minority of the population of Belarus has regular access to anything but pro-governmental, pro-Lukashenko propaganda. On state television and radio in particular this propaganda takes on peculiarly crude tones. Commentators and news-readers talk of 'plots', 'foreign spies' and 'hostile security services', accuse opposition political activists of sexual deviancy – a powerful weapon in a morally highly conservative country – and praise Alexander Lukashenko as a man of peace, limitless economic wisdom, and the 'reuniter of Slav peoples'.

International legal obligations and the guarantee of freedom of expression

The Republic of Belarus is a signatory to the Universal Declaration of Human Rights (UDHR), a UN General Assembly resolution. Although not legally binding, it is widely considered that the resolution has acquired the equivalent force of international law since it was adopted after the Second World War in 1948. Belarus is also a signatory to the International Covenant on Civil and Political Rights (ICCPR). This international treaty formally obliges its state-signatories to adhere to certain legal norms, and in many ways enhances the provisions of the Universal Declaration of Human Rights. Furthermore, the UN has repeatedly expressed its view that freedom of expression is an inalienable human right and forms one of the cornerstones of democracy. The first-ever General Assembly of the UN in 1946 passed Resolution 59(1), which established:

> 'Freedom of information is a fundamental human right and... the touchstone of all the freedoms to which the United Nations is consecrated.'

The Constitution of the Republic of Belarus, in Article 8, establishes the supremacy of international law over national legislation:

> 'The Republic of Belarus shall recognize the supremacy of the universally acknowledged principles of international law and ensure that its laws comply with such principles'

Furthermore, Articles 33 and 34 set down unambiguous guarantees of the freedom of expression and exchange of information:

> *Article 33*
>
> (1) Everyone is guaranteed freedom of thought and belief and their free expression.
>
> (2) No-one shall be forced to express his beliefs or to deny them.
>
> (3) No monopolisation of the mass media by the state, public associations or individual citizens and no censorship shall be permitted.
>
> *Article 34*
>
> (1) Citizens of the Republic of Belarus shall be guaranteed the right to receive, store, and disseminate complete, reliable and timely information on the activities of state bodies and public associations, on political, economic, and international life, and on the state of the environment.
>
> (2) State bodies, public associations, and officials shall afford citizens of the Republic of Belarus an opportunity to familiarise themselves with material that affects their rights and legitimate interests.

Despite these obligations and legal provisions, all parts of the media in Belarus have been subjected to extra-constitutional controls by the executive. In some cases, the legality of these controls is highly dubious. The legal system has offered few opportunities to redress the balance, since the Belarusian executive has established full control over the judiciary by the appointment of judges favourable to the President and by trying to exclude 'awkward' lawyers from all levels of the system of justice through an arbitrary and punitive system of registration and supervision.

The impact of media legislation on the non-state media has been made considerably harsher during the two Lukashenko presidencies. The 1995 'Law on the Press and Other Media', part of the Belarusian Administrative Legal Code, was amended in 1998 to create a Public Council on the Implementation of the Press Law. The Council, the first organisation of its type in post-Soviet Belarus, was charged with examining published materials to decide whether they violated current legislation. It is open to question whether this was, in effect, a form of direct censorship, but of the Council's 23 members none were drawn from the independent media. Instead, they were all government-appointed. The Council was designed to act as superviser, but acted to censor where and when it felt necessary. A further heavy blow to the media came in the form of an amendment to the Criminal Code, which established sentences of imprisonment of up to five years for insulting the 'dignity' of the President. Further restrictions on the free flow of information were established with the introduction of the requirement that the non-state media get official licences to receive information on new laws and government decrees from the Ministry of Justice. The conditions attached to the receipt of such licences are draconian, and even include stipulations on the minimum educational levels required of members of staff. It has therefore become difficult to even obtain official information on legislation relating to the media.

Today, the Belarusian State Committee on the Press has the right to suspend publication of newspapers and periodicals without a court order. The Committee can also prohibit any information it deems to inflict damage on the personal or professional reputation of government officials.

Primary target: The printed media

State-owned publications were the first target of President Lukashenko's campaign to monopolise the media. In December 1994 a report by parliamentary deputy Sergei Antonchyk claimed instances of corruption within the Presidential Administration, Lukashenko's power-base. Press coverage of the report was banned by the government, and three newspapers – *Sovetskaya Belarussiya* (Soviet Belarussia), *Zvyazda* (Star) and *Respublika* (The Republic) – revealed the attempt at censorship by publishing editions with empty columns where the parliamentary report had been due to appear. An early sign of Lukashenko's thought patterns emerged when he explained why the newspapers had been censored. He stated that state-owned media, by virtue of receiving financial support from the state, should work exclusively for the benefit of that same state. This self-identification of Lukashenko as the only factor capable of working for the good of his country against implacable enemies has become a persistent feature of his political discourse in the period since the winter of 1994.

That episode was followed shortly afterwards, in the first half of 1995, by a concerted effort to apply the 'only for the good of the state' notion to independent newspapers, whose printing and distribution depended on maintaining good relationships and political favour with the Presidential Administration and the total oversight of the (then) Ministry of Culture and Press. The Belarusian authorities organise thorough control over the technical means of production since they own all the printing houses in Minsk and run the distribution service as a state monopoly through the postal system. This is the main reason for the frequent unavailability of independent newspapers outside Minsk.

Following the creation of Belarus's bi-cameral legislature in the deeply flawed and undemocratic referendum of November 1996, legal measures to curtail the independent press were reinforced. In December 1997, new amendments were added to an already harsh press law. The owners of banned papers faced the ignominious prohibition of not being allowed to open another newspaper within two years of the date of the ban. Other provisions that caused deep concern amongst both Belarusian journalists and foreign human rights campaigners included the right of the authorities under the amendments to suspend the registration of print media, to decide which international publications can be distributed in Belarus (it is almost impossible to find anything other than Russian newspapers), and to extend the reach of these provisions to small-scale publications of even just a few hundred copies. Of equally repressive consequence was the official ruling that all newspapers must be registered from an office address. Newspapers such as the independent *Narodnaya Volya* (The People's Will), which was registered at the editor's home address, faced serious difficulties as a result of this, especially when local authorities in Minsk also tried to prevent private landlords from agreeing rent contracts for accommodation with the editorial staff. And in the clearest example of the cultural values that underpin the Belarusian authorities' approach to the printed media, the State Committee on the Press issued a warning to the one independent, nationalist-oriented newspaper about its use of pre-1933 Belarusian orthography. Stalin had outlawed the traditional Belarusian script and literary style as part of a campaign of russification, but the post-Soviet Belarusian authorities warned that the 'unofficial' orthography was illegal and would lead to the closure of newspapers using it.

The year after the referendum was arguably the most difficult for those newspapers which had led the campaign against what they portrayed as an increasingly dictatorial regime. *Naviny* (News) was the successor to the leading post-Soviet independent newspaper *Svaboda* (Freedom), which was itself shut down after a succession of official warnings. Both newspapers found themselves in trouble with the authorities on multiple occasions. Shortly prior to the formal closure of *Svaboda*, one of the official warnings it received incredibly accused the editorial board of trying to mount a coup d'etat. Its editor came in for particularly harsh treatment. On one occasion a bullet was fired by unidentified assailants through the window of his apartment. *Naviny*'s first official warning was the result of a piece of satire on the corrupt Belarusian militia. The second warning, over claims that the State Security Secretary Viktor Sheyman had built a luxury house for his parents without making the appropriate declarations, led to a libel suit. The newspaper was ordered to pay 15 billion Belarusian roubles, the then-equivalent of $50,000, a huge sum of money in Belarus. *Naviny* closed down as a result. The authorities argued that the newspaper's editorial staff were responsible for their own predicament, after it was revealed that the photograph of the house supposedly built by Viktor Sheyman was not actually the property in question.

The independent printed media were also the first targets for the use of unexpected tax audits and forced evictions. A local newspaper in Grodno, for example, fell foul of both methods of coercion. It was fined thousands of dollars for alleged irregularities after a tax audit, and then evicted with almost no notice and only allowed to re-register in an office with no water or sewerage facilities.

Independent printing facilities

It is not just journalists and editors who have been subjected to harassment as part of the authorities' efforts to curb the printed media. Magic, a private printing company based in Minsk, was by 1998 printing more than twenty major non-governmental newspapers, including *Narodnaya Volya* and the widely-read *Belorusskaya Delovaya Gazeta* (The Belarussian Business Newspaper). The printing shop was visited by the Government Tax Inspectorate with the purpose of doing an inventory of all equipment belonging to the Belarusian Soros Foundation (BSF). (The Soros Foundation closed its office in Minsk after massive tax demands were levelled against it.) Following the visit by the Tax Inspectorate, equipment worth almost $500,000 was impounded. The Open Society Institute sued the Tax Inspectorate for wrongful impounding, arguing that the equipment belonged to them and not to the BSF. On 18 December, at a court hearing observed by the OSCE, the US Embassy and Article 19, the judge ruled that the equipment belonged to the BSF and that, therefore, the Tax Inspectorate had acted legally. This meant that the government had the right to sell the equipment, leaving Magic to print the vast majority of non-governmental newspapers on its one remaining press.

Radio and television

With the ability of the Belarusian population to buy newspapers regularly limited by the country's economic decline, radio and television are their primary sources of information. As such, the authorities' attempts to control and regulate them had been more concerted, and much more effective, than similar attempts to control the print media. There is only one national television company, the Belarusian State Television and Radio Company (BSTRC), which issues licences and distributes frequencies for all the country's radio and television companies. There are a number of cable and local television network operators, but they feature mainly light entertainment and music programmes and avoid coverage of politics. The first independent radio station in Belarus, Radio BA, began broadcasting in 1993. It is a joint venture between the Belarusian Ministry of Communications and the US Family Radio station. It now operates a 24-hour service and is popular. However, it also limits its coverage to music and light entertainment and is not available outside the Minsk region. The only fully independent radio station to have existed in post-Soviet Belarus, Radio 101.2, was closed down on official orders after it was claimed that its frequencies interfered with government communications. Foreign radio is popular: Russian-language programming leads, although there is a small regular listenership for the Belarusian-language service of Radio Liberty. The BBC World Service does not have a Belarusian-language service, but enjoys a small listenership in Belarus for its Russian Service.

Given the poor quality of BSTRC television output, Russian television commands considerably greater popularity in Belarus than the domestic service. Russian television has frequently been at the centre of accusations from the Belarusian authorities of biased reporting of an 'information war' in relation to events in Belarus, or of adopting an 'unfriendly' attitude to the Belarusian authorities. The Belarusian Foreign Minister in March 1998, Ivan Antonovich, called Russian television's coverage of events in Belarus 'innuendo, inventions and fabrications', and warned of a new tool the authorities were prepared to use, the removal of accreditation – a highly effective yet simple way of preventing journalists from working. Shortly after this statement, an official order, termed 'On Stepping Up Counter-propaganda', appeared. It banned official structures from disclosing information of any kind to the independent media, serving to starve them of primary sources of information about official decision-making, and further reduce the possibility of the authorities being held to account by an active and probing media.

It seems more realistic to presume that the Russian broadcast media have been targeted due to their popularity in Belarus and their sometimes open criticism of Belarusian government policy. Journalists from ORT (Russian Public Television) were evicted from their premises following accusations of biased reporting. Three ORT journalists – Anatoly Adamchuk, Valery Ostashkin and Alexander Oganov – whose detention ignited an angry row between Moscow and Minsk, were handed over to the Russian embassy after spending a week in police custody for illegally filming at the Belarus-Lithuania border. The head of the NTV (Russia's Independent Television) office in Minsk, Alexander Stupnikov, an Israeli citizen, was deprived of his accreditation for 'doing harm to the friendly relations between Belarus and Russia' and ordered to leave the country. Foreign television companies have, at times, been prohibited from entering the National Radio and Television Centre (NRTC), and materials due for transmission to Russia seized. Copies of news reports are now demanded by the NRTC for preview and can be filed only after examination.

Television camera crews, along with photo-journalists, have frequently been assaulted at public demonstrations, in some cases being subjected to beatings by riot police or members of the security service in plain clothes.

Equipment is usually seized or smashed on the spot as part of these acts of intimidation. Other television journalists have been subjected to petty harassment, such as having their car or apartment windows smashed, being trailed whilst in the street, or being 'invited' to the KGB for conversations about their activities. The Belarusian authorities have always been keen to avoid losing any part of the propaganda war, and state television and radio regularly portray political demonstrations as the actions of hooligans bent on violence and anarchy.

A second state television channel was established by residential decree in Februaury 2002.

Pavel Sheremet and Dmitry Zavadsky

Perhaps the most revealing (and tragic) stories of harassment of the Belarusian media by the state concern Pavel Sheremet and Dmitry Zavadsky. The case had considerable international resonance during the second half of 1997, and its echo is still heard in Belarus today. Sheremet was head of the Minsk office of Russian Public Television until he was stripped of his accreditation in July 1997. His coverage of demonstrations in Belarus had already led to a series of angry protests at governmental level from Minsk to Moscow. The authorities lost patience after Sheremet, accompanied by his cameraman, Zavadsky (who once worked as Lukashenko's personal cameraman), filmed the Belarus-Lithuania border, which had not been demarcated. They alleged that it was a smuggling route, deliberately overlooked by the Belarusian border guards with the purpose of providing funds for President Lukashenko's various undeclared slush-funds. They were arrested by the Belarusian KGB and charged with illegally crossing the border. Sheremet spent three months in prison after his arrest. Before the court hearing, President Lukashenko declared Sheremet to be a 'foreign spy', provoking an angry exchange with then-President Boris Yeltsin of Russia. Pavel Sheremet and Dmitry Zavadsky received suspended jail sentences of two years and eighteen months respectively for crossing the border with Lithuania illegally. The sentence was seen as a compromise to ease tensions between Russia and Belarus.

Later, Dmitry Zavadsky disappeared without trace after travelling to meet Sheremet, who was flying from Moscow, at Minsk-2 airport outside the city. He has not been heard of since, with very little official information appearing about the investigation into his disappearance. Rumours immediately began to circulate in Minsk that Zavadsky had been murdered by the Belarusian KGB or the Presidential Security Service. Others suggested that Zavadksy had been killed by rogue elements within the military because he had apparently filmed Belarusian mercenaries from elite units fighting alongside Islamic rebels against Russia in Chechnya. More revealing was the information provided by two former employees of the Prosecutor General's Office, Dmitry Petrushkevich and Oleg Sluchek, who received political asylum in the United States. They alleged that President Lukashenko had personally derailed the investigation into Zavadsky's disappearance because of evidence linking a government 'death squad' to his murder. Security officials had arrested Dmitry Pavluchenko, the commander of an elite Interior Ministry rapid reaction unit, who led officials to what he believed was the burial site of Zavadsky's body. As the search was being mounted, an order came from Lukashenko to stop the proceedings and release Pavluchenko. The Prosecutor General and the head of the KGB were both removed from their posts. Sluchek claimed that Viktor Sheyman, the former Secretary of the State Security Council, had ordered Zavadsky's murder, along with those of several other key opponents of the President. Yet Sheyman was promoted by Lukashenko to become Prosecutor General, despite having no higher legal education, and now heads the on-going investigation into Zavadsky's disappearance.

The impossibility of dialogue

Despite the overwhelming atmosphere of intimidation, some efforts have been made by international organisations to bring the authorities and opposition media together in an attempt to start a dialogue. These efforts have been co-ordinated particularly by the Organisation for Security and Cooperation in Europe (OSCE). When it became clear that the authorities would not consider even an internationally mediated 'truce', the OSCE found itself accused of interfering in Belarus's internal affairs and its staff were subjected to campaigns of vilification in the official media. The most common accusations are that the OSCE is, in reality, a front for foreign secret services, and that its various pro-democracy initiatives merely conceal programmes designed to destabilise Belarus with the aim of overthrowing President Lukashenko. These accusations have been made at the highest level, and reached their peak during the presidential election of 2001, when President Lukashenko declared that the OSCE mission in Minsk was preparing a coup, together with a number of Western embassies, under the code-name 'White Stork', and said he would 'throw out' the chairman of the OSCE's Advisory and Monitoring Group, Hans-Georg Wieck, as soon as the election campaign was over. Meetings organised by the OSCE in Minsk, at which opposition media representatives and officials were present, passed in a tense atmosphere of mutual recrimination and were simply a forum where diametrically opposing opinions could be expressed. There was never any possibility of such meetings changing the authorities' approach and attitude towards the independent media.

Technical facilities, telecommunications and the internet

The Belarusian authorities are aware of the power of the internet, even though its growth in Belarus has been slow and its use remains at a pitifully low level. Unknown hackers have attacked websites hosted by opposition groups both within Belarus and abroad in order to render them inaccessible. An Internet Service Provider (ISP) has to apply for a licence by promising to connect through BelPAK, the Internet division of the state-owned monopoly Beltelekom. The licence makes provision for technical inspections by the Ministry of Communications, and orders ISPs to provide lists of their subscribers. Belarusian Internet users could, theoretically, connect via a foreign ISP, but the poor condition of the Belarusian telephony infrastructure and the high cost of the international calls needed make this an unrealistic option.

During the presidential election campaign of 2001, all the major opposition Internet newspapers became unavailable after the Belarusian national Internet domain '.by' suddenly stopped working. Access was blocked to the sites of a number of independent outlets posting real-time reports of alleged violations at polling stations. The independent news agency BelaPan and the Belarusian Service of Radio Free Europe/Radio Liberty also found their services interrupted. More revealingly, the campaign site of the main opposition candidate, Vladimir Goncharik, was also jammed. The authorities suggested that purely coincidental technical faults were the cause of the outage. Curiously, these were resolved as soon as President Lukashenko's overwhelming victory was officially announced.

Conclusion

Given the generally contradictory picture on access to information and official attempts to control the information flow, it is difficult to judge just how well-informed the citizens of Belarus are about events in their own country and abroad. But there is good reason to assume that the thinking of a very significant part of the population is at least shaped by official propaganda and measures against the free dissemination of information. Three-quarters of the population lives outside Minsk. In villages and small towns there is much narrower access to a diversity of media than in the capital. Opposition newspapers are not distributed in these areas. The internet is still unknown. Russian television and radio may go some way to redressing the lack of information, but they too have become largely sympathetic to the Lukashenko regime, as well as uncritical of the Russian government and authorities, which maintain active and warm contacts with their Belarusian counterparts. A growing number of Belorusians travel abroad. Again, this helps to redress the official line on what is happening in the West, a line which is often blatantly propagandistic. But even in the larger cities of Belarus the politically active part of the population is small. There is an enthusiastic third sector of NGOs and human rights organisations, but in any realistic assessment their impact on Belarusian society as a whole is limited. As long as there remains little popular demand for greater political pluralism and faster democratisation in the wider sense, it seems unlikely that there will be a concomitant demand for better, freer and more open sources of news and information. Not unexpectedly, the Belarusian media continue to resemble many other parts of Belarusian society: conservative, narrow and nostalgically attached to the (perceived) omnipotence of authority – as well as the socio-economic benefits – of the recent Soviet past.

Value Systems and Social Transformation in Belarus*

David Rotman, Lidia Novikova,
Nadezhda Golubkova and Larisa Filinskaya

Values and reforms

Values are an important component of both individual and public consciousness and as such act as regulators of social behaviour. Both individuals and groups behave in a particular way on the basis of what they consider to be right, useful etc. In the course of historical development a totality of basic values is formed in every society which determines its mental framework. This value frame is characterised by great historical stability and hardly changes through successive social cataclysms. That is why any radical reform can only take society to a higher level of development when new subcultures mature on the basis of other values, and these are strong enough to take a dominant position in society. If this does not happen, the fragmented social texture will be reconstructed in practically the same form, rejecting any sub-cultures that are not firmly established and rebuilding traditional value systems. It is here that the main danger lies for countries of 'secondary modernisation' (Belarus among them), those countries where reforms are imposed from above by ruling elites who seek

* This article is based on research carried out by the Centre for Sociological and Political Research of the Belarusian State University in the framework of the 'European Values Study' organised by Tilburg University in the Netherlands in 1999. The opinion poll was based on a sample of 1000 respondents from 55 locations throughout Belarus.

to overcome resistance from the traditional mentality. That is why the scale of values in a society in a period of radical transformation is linked with the socio-political cost of the reforms and the very possibility of carrying them out.

The reforms started in 1991 aimed at a gradual transition to democracy and a market economy. This process was and is taking place, amid some hardship, in all the countries of the former USSR. Factors causing this hardship include a break-down in the economic links which existed between the regions of that vast country, ethnic conflicts, and a struggle for power among the new political elites. The population was not prepared for serious changes. In this context Belarus's specific characteristic was its special position in the structure of the USSR: not only its high level of economic development by Soviet standards, but also its ability, as a consequence, to supply the population with sufficient food and primary goods. In such conditions people are usually very sceptical about change, especially if they are not sure of the result. This leads to conservative attitudes and internal resistance to innovation. It is no accident that in Belarus people leaned towards leftist politicians, successors to the totalitarian tradition of government, whereas the Russians, Ukrainians, Moldovans and Georgians supported their democrats with enthusiasm. The conservative mood in Belarus was also determined by the fact that a 'dictatorship of development' was formed too slowly after the break-up of the USSR. By 'dictatorship of development' we mean a coalition of governing elites objectively interested in the modernisation of the country and ready to carry it through by any means (alas, not always classically democratic means). The present state of the country is also a result of the long-standing weakness of the opposition. The opposition were unable to strengthen their position in society, and indeed were themselves responsible for the processes which led to their self-destruction (constant internal conflicts, careerism in the leadership, attempts by every opposition leader to play the sole and leading role and exclude all the others, complete unwillingness to compromise, and at the same time helplessness and lack of decisiveness at important historical moments). Belarus is going through a painful and long-drawn-out process of seeking 'its own way' in the hope of building a new democratic society while preserving the old social reality. This would suit both the authorities and the people.

Of course Belarus, situated as it is in the geographical centre of Europe, cannot stand aside completely from the broader historical process. A definite, albeit slow and inconsistent, movement towards world civilisation is taking place in Belarus; the period of storm and turmoil of the late eighties and early nineties of the twentieth century was not without effect.

That is why the Belarusians' system of values today is significantly different from that which dominated in the Soviet period. This applies above all to political and democratic values. However we must concede that these particular values were and are far from the top of people's scale of priorities. They are significantly less highly-rated than factors such as family, friends, career, work, leisure, health or religion. For instance, only a quarter of the citizens of Belarus who have the right to participate in elections state that political questions are important in their lives. Nevertheless, these questions are directly linked with the processes taking place in the country, with its present and the future of generations to come, as society becomes ever more self-aware.

The inhabitants of Belarus are more interested in establishing modern, civilised relations between the state, society and the individual, and in the intensity of the processes of democratic change, than in political clashes, power struggles, or the successes or defeats of a particular politician or group. To all appearances, the attitude of citizens (especially the young and middle-aged) towards totalitarian government and communist slogans has become more and more negative. For instance, while recognising that both freedom and equality are unquestionably very important, the majority would opt for freedom if they had to choose between the two. About two-thirds of citizens are sure that 'though democracy has its problems and drawbacks, it is better than any other form of government'. About the same number would like to see 'a democratic political system' in their country. It is possible to draw the conclusion on the basis of data from sociological questionnaires that the majority of the population are oriented towards democratic values. At the same time, many people do make a realistic assessment of the real state of affairs in the country, for good or ill, and the actual results of the democratic reforms up to now. Only one in four is satisfied with the way reforms have been carried out. The picture is much the same as regards respect for human rights. Only every third Belarusian considers that human rights are respected.

The overwhelming majority of the citizens of Belarus (75 per cent) think that society must change and achieve democracy through gradual reform while avoiding revolutionary or radical innovations. So democratic values have, to all appearances, already become close to the heart of our citizens. Moreover, these are real values and not a tribute to political fashion. This thesis can be demonstrated. While people support the need for democratic reforms, they are critical of the speed with which they are being carried out. This testifies to the fact that people's attitude to democracy is conscious and rational, and not formed under external influence or at an emotional level. On the other hand one cannot say that most people's understanding of democracy is correct and unequivocal. Sociological surveys reveal an interesting aspect of Belarusians' attitudes. Slightly over half the population are sure that the main task of society is to maintain law and order and not, for example, to combat inflation or provide greater scope for participation in the making of important political decisions. It is clear that all the signs of situational thinking are present here. People express what they consider to be the basic reason for their personal problems. In this case they assume that poor living standards, price increases and crime can be overcome by administrative methods. This is probably a sign of renewed commitment to the former socio-political system.

As mentioned above, real political values are less intensively developed than democratic values. More than half the population are not interested in politics, and three out of four citizens consciously do not want to take part in any political activity except voting in elections. (The majority of the Belarusian electorate took part in the presidential election and a significant majority voted for the president in power.) The electorate shows little interest in politics. Many citizens do not support any political party or movement and do not subscribe to any ideological or political trend. It is also noteworthy that, knowing little about the political spectrum (leftist parties are, as a rule, confused with right-wing parties and vice versa) people most often refer to themselves as 'centrist'. On the one hand this shows a relatively low level of political culture, while on the other hand it underlines once again the desire to avoid even virtual extremes, preferring 'reform' to 'revolution'. Finally, democratic values, as noted above, enjoy higher priority.

Thus some difficulties emerge when we try to define the key value orientations in Belarusian society connected with the political processes and democratic transformation taking place in the country. Nevertheless, we can state that these values are forming, and starting to act as social norms. Their bearers are, first of all, the young and middle-aged, the inhabitants of large and medium-sized cities, and people with professional and higher education. However, this general level of value-consciousness is not applicable to individual behavioural strategies, regulated as they are by certain archetypes grounded in the traditional value system.

It is clear that radical reform is possible only if the ruling elite shows a high degree of political will and professionalism. If it does not, and is not interested in reform, society will slowly drift this way or that depending on political and economic conditions. Undoubtedly, the nation's capacity for modernisation is essentially linked with its ethnic, family, work, religious and moral traditions and values.

Nationality and ethnicity

Any nationality, as an integrated association of people, possesses qualities and traits peculiar to itself. It is constantly nourished by the deep and strong roots of national culture, and by traditions passed on from generation to generation. That leads to the formation and development of definite 'subjective values', attitudes formed over centuries and expressed in patterns of behaviour. Such traditional values allow the nation to preserve its unique originality, specific peculiarities and mentality.

The origins of the Belarusians go back to the historical roots of the Slav tribes, their interaction and conflicts. Relations between the Belarusians and Russians were especially close. This link emerged not only because of the common origin of the two peoples but the closeness of their cultures, languages, customs and way of life.

The ancestors of the modern Belarusians lived together on this territory not only with Russians but also with Poles, Baltic peoples (ancestors of modern Lithuanians and Latvians) and Tatars. Cross-cultural contacts had a definite influence on the formation of the Belarusian nation. For example, the culture and way of life of the Belarusians living in the western part of the country came under Polish influence. Catholicism and West European culture came mostly from Poland. Polish influence can also be traced in the Belarusian language, which has many similar words to Polish.

Living alongside Lithuanians in the framework of a single state (the Grand Duchy of Lithuania of the fourteenth and fifteenth centuries) brought new elements into Belarusian culture.

Thus, a multi-ethnic state emerged historically on the territory of Belarus, a state enjoying a considerable degree of tolerance and freedom of opinion and doctrines. There were no mass religious or ethnic persecutions. Such a multi-ethnic, multi-confessional and multi-cultural environment instilled in the Belarusians a spirit of tolerance and humanism, and an ability to understand one another. These features became the pivot of the Belarusian tradition, determining the particular way of life and national character of the Belarusians.

Even today, many nationalities or ethnic groups are represented in Belarus, though most with small communities. According to the 1999 national census, the population of Belarus includes the following groups: 81 per cent Belarusians, 11 per cent Russians, 4 per cent Poles, 2 per cent Ukrainians, 0.3 per cent Jews.

In the former USSR ethnic affiliation was not a matter of personal choice but was determined by the state according to the individual's origins (parent's, most often father's nationality) and recorded in official documents. Today, Belarusians' national self-identification is, above all, a matter of a person's individual feelings as someone living in Belarus (for example, 'I think I am a Belarusian ').

However, such inner self-determination is based on an awareness of being Belarusian by origin. Thus 95 per cent of people who consider themselves to be Belarusian are Belarusian by origin as well.

Some of the people (especially those from multi-ethnic families) identify themselves with a particular nationality not on the basis of their ethnic origin but on the basis of their cultural, ethnic and territorial identification. For instance, the most powerful factors underpinning the ethnic identity of Russians living in Belarus are 'common language' and 'national culture and traditions'. The importance of these particular factors stems from the processes involved in the formation of Belarusian national statehood. The Russians in Belarus, an ethnic minority, have to some extent lost their historical and cultural links with Russia. Only the Russian language unites them with other Russians. The new realities of life in Belarusian society stimulated many nationalities' understanding of their ethnic status in the new state. Each of these ethnic groups forms its own ethnic image ('we are Belarusians', 'we are Russians', etc.).

Relations between the Russian and Belarusian communities are one of the most important issues in the national-cultural development of Belarus. Data from various sociological studies show that ethnic Russians show a high degree of identification with the Belarusian nation and the state of Belarus. Internal identification with the Belarusians ('the Belarusians consider me to be one of them') is important for the Russians. At the same time, the Russians identify emotionally more with the country than with the Belarusian ethnic group. They are proud of Belarus, just as the ethnic Belarusians are, and with the fact that they have managed to become part of Belarusian society. Only 4 per cent of the Russians living in Belarus do not feel attached to the country.

All these factors form the basis for the integration of ethnic Russians into Belarusian society: the national consciousness of the Russians goes beyond the limits of their ethnic consciousness; they consider themselves part of the Belarusian people. General national identification of the Russians with Belarus is stronger than ethnic identification. At the present moment 98 per cent of Russians living in Belarus are citizens of the republic; 66 per cent of those are proud of belonging to the state of Belarus.

The Belarusians, in their turn, are actively involved in Russian culture in Belarus. This is explained by the long tradition of living together, and the closeness of cultures and life-styles. This closeness does not lead to any loss of ethnic feeling on the part of Belarusians, nor does their self-identification with their own ethnic culture prevent their inclusion in the Russian culture.

In other words, it is possible to remain a Belarusian and be included in two cultures simultaneously.

One of the key traditional features of any people is its language. The language is the basis of its culture, and the preservation, reproduction and development of the language reinforces its cultural identity. It is no coincidence that the movement for national revival in all the former Soviet republics started with language issues. Official policy in the sphere of inter-community relations is reflected in the law on languages. In Belarus both Belarusian and Russian have the status of official languages. However, the majority of the population of Belarus speak Russian. Russian is actively used in all spheres of life (at home, at work, in public places). Only half the ethnic Belarusians can speak Belarusian fluently, and even they rarely use it to communicate verbally. There are far fewer ethnic Russians who speak Belarusian fluently: only 16 per cent. In practice there are no particular problems between Belarusian and Russian speakers. The closeness of the languages means they can understand each other easily. The ethnic Poles and Lithuanians who live in Belarus speak their native language as well as Russian and Belarusian. This is possible because they live close to the respective borders. They can pick up TV and radio programmes from Poland and Lithuania and can communicate easily with their fellow language-speakers living there.

The majority of the population do not perceive the high status of the Russian language in Belarus as a sign of russification; only 18 per cent of Belarusians believe this to be so. In the opinion of this group, russification is manifest in the estalishment of equal status for the Russian and Belarusian languages; in the inadequate number of educational institutions teaching in Belarusian; and in the dominance of Russian TV programmes.

The special characteristics of Belarusians' national self-identification show that traditional values are changing and gaining new features. Preference for this or that language is not so much determined by the individual's level of competence in the language and its use as by the communicative value of the language in carrying out particular activities or meeting personal goals in life.

Young people show greater language tolerance. The majority of young people (67 per cent) consider knowledge of their native language to be a personal matter. They are rather pragmatic in their attitude to their native language. They do not believe that by not using their national language they risk weakening their national identity or switching to another nationality, provided individuals preserve their own ethnic-cultural self-identification.

At the same time, a significant number (60 per cent) of ethnic Belarusians expect their children to study and know their native language and the history and culture of their people. Their desire to preserve their ethnic-cultural values shows that there have been changes in the ethnic behaviour of Belarusians during the last decade. State independence brought into being a definite striving for ethnic identification for all the country's national groups. This has deepened the psychological boundaries of identification between Russians, Poles, Lithuanians and others living in Belarus on the one hand, and Belarusians belonging to the dominant titular nation on the other. But these tendencies towards separation have not taken on any concrete form. A huge majority (90-95 per cent) of people from all the nationalities have never faced any negative attitude to themselves from either the authorities or the police. This indicates that inter-ethnic relations have stabilised, thanks to balanced state policies, the Belarusians' national tolerance, and the use of Russian as an inter-ethnic language.

As we can see, life experience affects traditional values. Each generation chooses one tradition or another, accepts some features and rejects or expands others. The changes in the traditional value system taking place today are linked with those taking place in the main social institutions: the family, the media and the education system. In a multi-ethnic environment such institutions act not only as an important factor in socialisation but also as a support to ethnicity.

A transformation in the institution of the family is taking place today in many ethnic groups, including a fall in the number of multi-generational families and an increase in the number of nuclear families, leading to a decline in the immediate influence of the older generation on succeeding generations.

All this is leading to a change in traditional ways of life, the loss of traditional values such as deference to parents, relatives and ancestors, and the upholding of traditions and specifically ethnic features of family life. The situation is becoming more complicated with the dissemination of Western mass culture through all possible channels. This is leading to a cultural reorientation, especially among young people.

Modernisation of the education system is leading to increasingly varied teaching programmes, including in the sphere of language. Mastering other languages lets students escape the bonds of their own ethnicity and make contact with other cultures. The national language is a kind of cultural boundary between one ethnic group and the others. A multi-lingual environment opens up new opportunities.

Traditional national values are reflected in the national character. This becomes apparent in ethnic paradigms, which create a nation's ethnic image. Sociological research shows that ethnic Belarusians believe they are distinguished by love of their motherland, kindness and showing kindness to other people, tolerance towards other ethnic groups, restraint, patience, openness and diligence (but not initiative or entrepreneurship). These values, demonstrating satisfaction with their national affiliation, show that Belarusians have a stable positive image of their own people and country.

Thus, the specific characteristic of the Belarusians' national self-identification is that in adjusting to other people they treat them as one of their own, extending to them an inclusive 'we' which applies not to the ethnic group but to the whole nation. Tolerance of the 'alien', and socio-cultural adaptation to widen the bounds of the Belarusian national identity, are adding a new dimension to traditional values.

Family values

In Belarus the family traditionally comes top in people's order of priorities. The family acts as the main guardian of cultural values, the main agent of child socialisation, and a necessary condition for happiness.

When asked what is necessary for happy family life, people rate highest: children, mutual respect, patience, mutual understanding and conjugal fidelity. These factors are considered to be the most important by 70-76 per cent of the adult population of Belarus. Next in the hierarchy of importance (45-52 per cent) are readiness to discuss emerging problems, good housing, living apart from parents (a rather painful problem for young families on modest income), harmonious sexual relations and sharing a joint household. A third group of factors is rated most important by a third of respondents: high income, common interests and being able to spend a lot of time together. Common ethnic or social origin and shared political views and religion are not considered to be significant for family life. In other words, according to the majority of Belarusians family stability depends on specific psychological qualities in the partners (and to some extent on their material circumstances), but people do not link the presence of such qualities with ethnic or religious factors.

Three quarters of the population have a positive attitude to the institution of marriage and think that a woman must have children to fulfil her destiny. At the same time, less than half the population approve of single women wishing to have children out of wedlock. Attitudes to marriage are differentiated by a range of socio-demographic factors: the institution is considered old-fashioned by people who have had negative experiences of marriage (who are divorced or separated), by single people and by people over 60.

Although children are highly valued in the family, adults differ about how far parents should make sacrifices for the sake of their children. About half consider that parents must do their best for their children even at the expense of their own happiness. A smaller but still quite significant number are more pragmatic and are sure that parents must lead their own lives and should not sacrifice everything for their children.

The first model is traditional and goes back to the time when human populations depended for their survival on their ability to reproduce. In poor communities people who became parents had to 'die' (devote their lives to their children) in order to ensure the reproduction of the species.

Such views are still popular in Belarus, particularly with the 18-40 age-group, the widowed and the poorly-educated. The opposite view, characteristic of modern developed societies, also has many adherents, especially among the middle-aged and elderly (people who have already brought up their children and want to live for themselves), the divorced and people with a middle or high level of education.

What qualities do parents want to develop in their children? First of all, industry, a sense of responsibility and respect for other people. About half want to see their children well-behaved above all, and also thrifty and decisive; a third wants to see their children independent or, alternatively, dutiful. The least popular qualities to adults are imagination, unselfishness and interest in religion. This scale of values and qualities testifies, to our mind, to an increase in the element of rationality in the consciousness of a society in transition. Industry, sense of responsibility, tolerance and decisiveness – this set of qualities serves to describe a person with what Weber called the 'spirit of capitalism'. And diligence, so important in the Soviet system of upbringing, and independence, the distinguishing mark of a free person, are relegated to a secondary role. Unfortunately, such non-rational qualities as self-sacrifice and imagination are not appreciated; they are easier to cultivate in wealthy societies, whereas for poor ones they are superfluous.

The role of religion

The situation is different with interest in religion (or 'religiosity' in the neutral sense used by sociologists). The low rating of this factor within the family can, in our view, be explained by two circumstances. Firstly, interest in religion is not a stand-alone phenomenon in post-Soviet society; it is seen as significant more for its ability to affect morality. That is why it is not religion itself that is valuable, but what it can contribute to the formation of a child's personality.

The second circumstance merits detailed consideration. We refer to the role of religion in contemporary society and the processes taking place in this sphere in societies in transition.

The artificial isolation of the majority of the Soviet people from religion and church was an important aspect of life in the Soviet Union. Though the church continued to exist as a social institution, the official (and obligatory) communist ideology was based on the ideas of atheism and treated religion as a relic of previous epoques, destined to die out in the future.

Religion was forced out of all spheres of public life, and religious traditions could only be preserved in the private sphere of the family as a set of moral precepts and rules of conduct. Nevertheless their historical durability was so high that the destruction of the communist system throughout the former Soviet Union caused a phenomenon which sociologists have called a 'religious renaissance'. The essence of this was a mass rejection of atheism as one of the main elements of the official ideology, the growth of religious and pro-religious attitudes, and a radical change in the social role of the church, which was transformed in a short time from an insignificant and rudimentary social institution into quite an important public force. Between 1994 and 1998 the number of believers in Belarus increased from 33 to 47-49 per cent of the total population, while in 2000 the figure was 52 per cent of the adult population. We should also note that growth in the number of believers slowed at the end of the nineties and may have come to a halt. (The 3-4 per cent difference falls within the margin of error.) Thus a definite 'saturation point' has been achieved, since when an extensive has given way to an intensive process: a kind of 'crystallisation' of religious consciousness.

In talking about the increasing level of religious sentiment, we must remember that the mass rejection of atheism in the post-Soviet period was accompanied by the spread not so much of traditional religion but of a vacillating, amorphous and eclectic consciousness and an undefined attitude to religious belief. Alongside those who believe in God (or more correctly, believe they believe), the adult population of Belarus contains a significant number of people (31 per cent) vacillating between belief and atheism, and 8 per cent who say that they do not believe in God but in supernatural forces. Atheists make up 13-14 per cent, a figure which has been constant since 1994.

However, it would be incorrect to judge the level of religious sentiment in Belarus only on the basis of self-evaluation by its inhabitants. Moreover, in

2000 only 26 per cent of the population described themselves as really religious people; twice as many agreed that they believed in God. That is why, in addition to self-identification as a believer, affiliation to a particular religious and the practice of stable forms of religious behaviour are all traditionally included among the essential features of 'religiosity' in sociology.

As regards confessional self-identification, the proportion of adherents to the main Christian confessions and atheists has remained stable over the last decade: 77 per cent Orthodox, 15 per cent Catholics, 0.6 per cent Protestants, 2.5 per cent undifferentiated Christians (in practice mainly from the evangelical communities).

However, not only believers but the overwhelming majority of the population (about 80 per cent), irrespective of their personal interest in religion, identify themselves with a particular confession. Of course, in this case we are dealing with cultural rather than religious identification, when a person referring to a particular religion is in fact identifying himself with a specific cultural environment historically formed by that religion. In this sense the population of Belarus is mostly oriented to the Orthodox faith (63 per cent), much less to Catholicism (10 per cent) or Christianity in general (6 per cent).

The third and last feature indicating individual religious sentiment is religious practice. The main and most visible forms of practice are attending religious services and taking part in religious rites.

Only when the believer strives for a dialogue with the object of his belief through the performance of ritual actions can we speak of the institutionalisation of religious belief.

In Belarus 23.4 per cent of believers attend religious services regularly, 61 per cent sometimes, and 15 per cent never. The proportion taking part in religious rites is even smaller: 21 per cent regularly do so, 54 per cent sometimes and 25 per cent never. If we single out believers showing all the signs of religious behaviour simultaneously (attending religious services regularly, taking part in religious rites and knowing the texts of prayers and the Bible), they amount to just 14 per cent of all believers.

Nevertheless, religion is important in Belarusian society. 72 per cent of adults think that people need religion, while 66 per cent think that today's children should be given a religious education in order to inform them about the history of religion, the religious world-outlook and the main religious texts. In other words, they want religion to be a significant factor in the general cultural and moral education of the younger generation.

The majority of Belarusians see the social role and value of religion as follows: religion promotes people's moral improvement (56 per cent of the population) and helps preserve culture and traditions (44 per cent). Its spiritual functions, together with the inculcation of a religious outlook, are much less appreciated by both believers and atheists: only 27 per cent assess highly the capacity of religion to promote reconciliation and humility (32 per cent of believers); 21 per cent to find meaning in life through religion (27 per cent of believers); 12 per cent to provide an explanation and understanding of the world (13 per cent of believers). Thus, for the majority of the population the value of religion is determined not so much by its specific spiritual-intellectual potential, but rather by the fact that it acts as some kind of vehicle for accumulating, preserving and transferring the cultural heritage (as a basis for national integration) and moral experience of the society. In scientific language, we are talking about two social functions not specific to religion: its ability to integrate people on the basis of common beliefs and to regulate their moral behaviour.

In the Soviet period these functions were exercised by the Communist ideology. This was followed by 'internal de-ideologisation' – a loosening of guide-lines as a result of the rapid, historically momentous destruction of the political-economic system the ideology had served – when the understanding and vision of the world produced by the Communist ideology lost its meaning. The effect was aggravated by the absence of any developed alternative ideological systems suitable for assimilation by the general population. The search for a new ideological framework inevitably had to reach out to some ready-made value standards formed by the culture of the past, appropriate to the majority and historically stable. Religious ideology meets these requirements quite well. At the same time, the abolition of all restrictions on religion during perestroika revived suppressed memories of religious culture and even gave birth to a fashion for religion. This led to a swing of the ideological pendulum: having broken free from the prison cage of atheism, people inevitably swung to the opposite side, to religion. Moreover, Christian and Communist ideologies are very close typologically: they are both built on the unconditional acceptance of certain dogmas (Christian theology in the first case, dogmas about the historic mission of the proletariat, the withering away of the state and the inevitability of Communism in the second); personal trust in the object of belief (God or state/party) as governor and saviour of the believer; and, lastly, personal devotion to the object the believer serves. That is why for many people the replacement of one myth by the other took place almost automatically in that period of radical change. If we are right, this would explain not only the weakness of the churches in the religious life of believers, but also the wide-spread adherence to non-orthodox forms of belief: quasi-scientific (belief in astrology, extra-sensory perception, UFOs) and quasi-religious (fortune-telling, the evil eye, sorcery). Thus, 57 per cent of those who believe in God simultaneously believe in sorcery and the evil eye; 42 per cent in fortune-telling; more than half in reincarnation, perhaps unaware that this is a fragment of non-Christian religions.

These data testify that an active process of erosion in the clear boundaries of the churches' dogmas is taking place in the general religious consciousness.

The 'religious boom' of the nineties in Belarus (mirrored in all the former Soviet territories) was rather superficial. The number of believers actually increased, but their belief is weakly institutionalised and is not connected with a religious way of life. Moreover the growth of religious sentiment has been accompanied by a significant growth in quasi-religious beliefs, an eclectic mixture of the relics of pagan cults and fragments of eastern religions and quasi-scientific mythology.

The level of expectations of religion is quite high in society today, above all as a force for social integration and support for public morality. However less than half the population (43 per cent) think that religion can solve concrete personal moral problems. At the same time, believers are no different in their moral precepts and values from those with other outlooks. Consequently, at the individual level religious belief does not create some special, higher morality.

A particular feature of Belarus, arising from its geopolitical position, is its multi-confessional society, a product of its history. Research has shown that different confessional trends satisfy the religious needs of different socio-demographic groups. Those with the most traditionalist views (mostly social outsiders) are more often attracted to the Orthodox religion; those with the most modern outlook to Protestantism. However, the proportion of believers who are Protestants is small, and moreover their value systems and patterns of behaviour show that Protestantism in Belarus is rather sect-like and that its work ethic cannot serve as a spiritual basis for modernisation as it did in the West.

It is clear that the 'religious boom' is coming to an end in Belarus. The phenomenon was probably caused by a swing of the ideological pendulum, which has already gone through its highest point. We will clearly be faced with the supremacy of the ill-defined and amorphous outlook which is a natural feature of the global collapse of rigid systems of ideas. However, religion and church have already become firmly established in our life, and the extent of their influence on society, the direction and effectiveness of their interaction with society, will be determined by the capacity of society and church to modernise in line with the main vector of development in world civilisation.

We have already talked about the closeness of the Belarusian and Russian character and behaviour. Both cultures are based on a less pragmatic outlook than that of Western Europe. Krichevsky, Ilin and Berdyaev wrote at length about this: 'West European humanity is moved by will and reason. The Russian lives, above all, by the heart and imagination, and only after that by the will and mind'.

However, this tendency cannot dominate people's behaviour for all time. Belarus's first steps towards the market have led to some changes in the country's general attitudes and people's values. These changes are evident first of all in the young and educated. In general, one can talk about significant contradictions and ambivalence in the value systems of the Belarusian people.

Attitudes to work

Of particular interest is the work motivation of the inhabitants of Belarus. In this analysis we will study only one component of work motivation: the requirement to work, which depends both on personal value systems and how far the working environment allows (or does not allow) people to act in accordance with these values.

During our research, respondents rated the importance of 17 aspects of work. We compared the motivation of young, middle-aged and elderly people.

Ranking the priority factors singled out by respondents shows that a high salary comes first in all age groups. Advancement of material interests to the first plane means that the individual has to spend most of his strength and energy on sustaining life at a socially acceptable level. It is also important to note that numerous studies carried out in Belarus and Russia show that such attitudes are not clearly linked with work efficiency (productivity, quality, cost-effectiveness).

Good relations with work-mates, or collective spirit, follows in the evaluation of factors relating to work. This characteristic has strong support from people of different ages (70-75 per cent of respondents). Collective spirit and justice are among the highest values as regards the Belarusian way of life. These are the most vividly expressed features of the national character, highly appreciated both in others and in oneself. The presence of collectivist principles in young people shows how socio-cultural experience is passed on from generation to generation. It is worth mentioning that collectivist concepts presuppose egalitarian justice. Unwritten rules of personal behaviour in the collective are well known to the community: 'do not make yourself conspicuous', 'be like the others', 'initiative is to be punished'.

'A comfortable work-schedule' and 'good working conditions' are equally important for people of different generations. Patriotism is a less important motivating factor, but one which is constant over generations. About one in four respondents noted the importance of 'work useful to society'.

Economic hardship and major upheavals have not managed to weaken Belarusians' desire to have 'an interesting job'. However, as the analysis shows, this means different things to the young and middle-aged. If young people associate an interesting job with creative work, career prospects and the possibility of going abroad, the middle-aged and elderly do not aspire to challenging work, nor are they ready to re-qualify, or widen or renew their knowledge and skills. They consider work that only they can do to be interesting work. The socio-economic changes in society cannot but stimulate people to form positive attitudes to work and to seek to achieve a new quality of life. Today, the distinctive feature of young people's attitude to work in Belarus is that they say that scope for initiative, career growth, self-fulfilment and job prestige are the most important factors in relation to work. Consequently, intellectual motivation and achievement dominate. Orientation towards success is less characteristic of older Belarusians. The opportunity to show initiative is not so important either.

Research into young people's life strategies shows that they are less ready to sacrifice their health, take jobs not commensurate with their abilities and skills or do monotonous work. They will seek to overcome difficulties to get into a good university, take on work with a high degree of responsibility, re-qualify and study for new professions, and put off having a family until they have achieved a certain level of education and material and social position. Attention to quality of life has also increased.

The way of life espoused by young people rejects the conditions of many workers in an industrial society (low qualifications, monotonous work), and the principles of social stratification embodied in the Soviet social system. Typically, young people's attitudes, as we have seen, are different from those of the general population brought up in the Soviet system; the values of active self-denial, hard work, striving for status and sense of responsibility play an active role for the latter.

Undoubtedly, young people favour liberal values. Traditionalist values are rather wide-spread among the middle-aged and elderly, who resist market values.

Our research shows that there is a contradiction between two values in society: personal responsibility for one's own material well-being on the one hand, and economic paternalism and state guardianship on the other. 13-18 per cent of Belarusians over 30 categorically state that 'first of all, the state must care for its citizens', and almost a third of Belarusians are sure that 'the state must provide for its citizens in old age' and 'provide housing'.

The adaptation of labour relations to market conditions is taking place in a painful and complicated manner. Guaranteed employment, job security and income stability are all declining, while the number of people in casual or part-time employment, and employment in the non-formal, grey sector, is increasing. One of the peculiarities of the labour market in Belarus is the existence of the 'working unemployed' or 'retained unemployed', which demonstrates the presence of excess labour. This is accompanied by enforced idleness and breaks in the work-process, late payment of salaries and low earnings. Today the problems of under-employment, and of well-educated people having to do work for which they are over- qualified, are especially topical.

In 2000 the official level of unemployment in Belarus was 2 per cent. 8.2 per cent of those employed in the economy were either on compulsory unpaid leave or working part-time on the initiative of the enterprise. Depending how radical the change to a market system is, 8-33 per cent of those currently employed could find themselves thrown onto the open labour market, with a consequent rise in the level of unemployment. Young people aged 16-29 accounted for half the unemployed in 1999-2000.

The labour market situation is forcing our citizens to demonstrate active forms of economic behaviour in order to seek and find additional income. Young and educated Belarusians are more successful in this. In general about 45 per cent of the adult population need more money.

We have covered only a few of the problems of modern Belarusian society and its citizens. The list could be extended. However, neither material hardship nor psychological discomfort, neither scepticism nor pessimism about the reforms being carried out in the country (for instance, more than half the young citizens of Belarus do not see any real results from the reforms aimed at improving the life of the population), nor the peculiarities of the national character can change the main direction in which society is heading.

In this article we have not covered all the values traditionally studied by sociologists. Nevertheless, the analysis presented allows us to show both the positive and negative tendencies in the development of Belarusian society. Life goes on, and if democracy and the market are really our future, compromise is inevitable. Belarus has to change. This change must start from the people, not be imposed from above. 'Self-improvement' and 'self-development' will help to bring the new society closer.

2

Belarus: The Economy

In the Noose of Populism: Eleven Years of the Belarusian Economic Model (1991-2001)

Leonid Zlotnikov

In the late eighties Belarus was considered an economically developed country within the USSR structure. Before the dissolution of the Union it had the highest growth rates of industrial output and labour productivity, and with the Baltic republics had one of the highest levels of GDP at $6,500 – 7,000 per capita (in parity prices). In 1991, the last year of the USSR's existence, the annual volume of goods exports to the other republics exceeded imports from them by $2.5 billion. Belarusian politicians drew from this the conclusion that Belarus was subsidising other republics.

By the beginning of the twenty-first century Belarus appeared to be one of the countries with the least reformed and most backward economies of all the former Soviet republics. The situation would have been even worse but for Russia's subsidies to the Belarusian economy. Why did this happen? What objective processes in the economy and what miscalculations in economic policy caused the present situation? The author tries to give answers to these questions in the present article.

Belarus is the only post-socialist country where early, albeit hesitant, market reforms were brought to a halt – after Alexander Lukashenko was elected president in 1994. That was the beginning of a new stage in the country's development. The various periods of development are reflected in the structure of this article. The first section considers the first phase of economic development and attempts to explain the causes of the 'conservative revolution' of 1994. The second and third sections analyse the formation of economic mechanisms and economic processes after the election of the country's first president.

1991-1994: Slow movement towards oligarchic capitalism

The village gains the upper hand over the town

The roots of the deep conservatism of Belarusian society must be sought, above all, in the particular characteristics of the country's economic development. One should note the low level of its industrial development before the 1917 revolution and the higher economic growth rates in the following years, especially after 1945.

Although Belarus was situated close to some industrial centres it was part of the backward borderlands of the Russian empire. The main industries were small-scale peat and logging enterprises, and paper and cement production. Capitalist relations here were much less developed than in Russia or Ukraine. In 1940 only 21.3 per cent of the population lived in towns (in Russia 34.4 per cent).

But in 1960-1985 industrial output increased 900 per cent, whereas the USSR average was 490 per cent. This led to more rapid growth of the urban population: by 262 per cent in Belarus in 1959-1987 as against 173 per cent in Russia. In particular, in the same period Minsk's population tripled, with a growth rate second only to that of Mexico City.

Thus, recent history has given rise to two economic factors which have, in our opinion, had a negative influence on the population's readiness to accept market reforms.

First, a greater proportion of the urban population and the elite than in other republics are only first or second generation city-dwellers. These classes largely retained their feudal-patriarchal values, in particular a negative attitude to incomes received from financial dealing or trade, a weak understanding of the principles of human rights and the rule of law, and a predisposition to an authoritarian system of government.

Second, in the Soviet period Belarusians' welfare grew faster than in other republics (the highest national income growth rate, starting from a low base), which led to a greater degree of satisfaction with the existing regime and the absence of a reformist wing in the Communist Party leadership.

Opinion polls conducted during the last years of the USSR showed that the population of Belarus was less ready to embrace market economy values than it was in other regions.

For example, in 1989-1990 the population of Belarus appeared to be the least well disposed to the privatisation of enterprises by making them joint-stock companies: only 19 per cent of those polled were ready to buy shares (in Georgia 44 per cent, in Estonia 40 per cent). The highest proportion of people who wished to own land was registered in Moldova and Central Asia (57 per cent) and the lowest in Belarus (23 per cent).

The end of the myth of the effective economy

Belarus is poor in natural resources. The exceptions are mainly potassium salts and raw materials for the production of building materials. Domestic oil production meets only 10-12 per cent of Belarus's needs. The rest of its energy supplies are imported from Russia. In 2001, for example, 80 per cent of the country's energy requirements was covered by Russian gas deliveries.

Manufacturing industry was developed during the Soviet period. Belarus specialised in the production of tractors, trucks, machinery, agricultural machines, electronic and radio products and petrochemicals. More than 65-70 per cent of these products were exported within the Soviet block. A substantial proportion (20-30 per cent) of the output of the light and food industries was also exported to other Soviet republics.

Let us note that Belarus developed the production of goods at the end of the technological chain involved in turning raw materials into finished products. This means that the quality of goods obtained from quality raw materials deteriorated at each stage in the operation while the cost per unit of output grew rapidly.

This fact, which is important for our analysis, can be explained through an example. In Belarus the yield from cereals is approximately a third of that in the EU. So in order to produce 1 tonne of cereals in Belarus it is necessary to cultivate an area three times the size. Furthermore, a locally-produced tractor consumes 20-30 per cent more fuel. The result is that it takes 350-400 per cent more fuel to produce a tonne of cereals in Belarus than in EU countries. In animal husbandry, where productivity is rather low (for example the average milk yield per cow was 3,058 litres in 1999 and 2,400 litres in 2001, daily weight gain in pigs in 2001 was 399g), the quantity of cereals consumed per unit of production is almost double that in developed countries. Losses in storage of cereals (up to 15 per cent) and potatoes (30-40 per cent), greater energy consumption in food processing (up to 30 per cent) etc. should be also taken into account.

As a result, we get an astonishing fact: the input of raw materials per unit of finished product was 8-10 times higher in the former USSR than in developed countries. That is why 150 per cent more raw materials per capita were consumed and three times as much land cultivated, but GDP per capita was only a sixth to an eighth. Ten years later little has changed in Belarus or in Russia, with which Belarus has close production ties.

The pricing methods used in the socialist period hid the great inefficiency of the Belarusian economy because energy, metals and other raw materials were imported from Russia at not much more than a third of the world price, while light industry goods and food products were sold to Russia at three times the world price.

In 1991-1995 foreign trade prices were brought closer to world market prices, which did not favour Belarus. This led to a considerable worsening of the economic situation in Belarus. We estimate that Russian subsidies fell in that period by one billion dollars.

The second negative consequence of the predominant development of manufacturing was the non-competitiveness of Belarusian products following the liberalisation of foreign trade. This was because the technical level, quality and price of communications equipment, TV sets, computers and many other goods produced in Belarus were only superficially equivalent to analogous foreign products.

Thus, Belarus's economic situation before the dissolution of the USSR was not as good as it appeared from the statistics. In this situation a country poor in natural resources needs reform more than others. But it was precisely in Belarus that reform was promoted least.

Liberalisation whether you like it or not

The constant discussions in the eighties about possible ways out of the crisis served to instil in the mass consciousness the notion that state property generated thoughtless management, the embezzlement of public funds, a slowing down of scientific and technical progress and poor efficiency. Wide strata of society gained access to information on the barbaric exhaustion of natural resources, on the country's militarisation, on its immensely generous aid to other countries, on trashy and expensive projects, and on the abominable crimes of the communists.

At the same time, the mass media showed the outward face of life in capitalist countries. All that created the psychological basis for the implementation of market reforms. At the end of 1990 62.6 per cent of those polled in one survey spoke up in favour of transition to a market economy and only 17.2 per cent against.

However, this positive view of market reform on the part of the population was partly a spontaneous reaction, without their having any clear idea of what market relations entailed. Popular attitudes were contradictory. When asked whether prices should be freed, only 21-25 per cent of those polled agreed. At the same time most people favoured a 'market economy'. This contradiction in popular attitudes in transition countries was noted by many specialists.[1] The values of liberalism were not fully understood. The notion of 'the market' took on the nature of a myth linked with dreams of a horn of plenty.

The 'velvet' revolution in the countries of Central Europe left the Belarusian ruling elite or nomenklatura in a state of shock. It was unable to speak out openly against the myth of the market economy and democracy that overcame the majority of the population. In October 1990 parliament adopted a programme of transition to a market economy which envisaged the formation of market structures by the end of 1991. It was expected that in the first year of reform 30 per cent of industrial enterprises and 60 per cent of building firms would be privatised. Laws were adopted permitting the private ownership of means of production, the creation of joint-stock companies and private enterprises of other kinds. Farmers were given land for their permanent use, though without the right to sell, lease or mortgage it.

However, the nomenklatura, who remained in power, were in no hurry to give up either property or power. The programme of transition to the market was soon forgotten. 'When the economy cracks, relationships collapse, the rouble does not work... then government must take everything into its own hands... regulate everything, govern everywhere', said Vice-Premier Miasnikovich in August 1991, justifying the absence of reforms. The economic recession which followed the disintegration of socialism was used by the nomenklatura to discredit the market system as a whole and to ensure the country developed in accordance with their own interests.

The privatisation plan was abandoned. By the middle of 1996 less than 10 per cent of state enterprises, employing 10.3 per cent of the economically active population, had been privatised. All the large enterprises remained in state hands. Employees bought out the majority of privatised enterprises, so that they turned into collective entities.

To begin with Belarus's leaders tried to reconstruct the simulacrum of a command economy; firstly by creating a system of centralised supply to replace the dissolved USSR State Supply Committee. On the initiative of the Belarusian leadership delivery contracts were signed with almost all the republics of the former USSR. For example, in October 1990 a contract was signed with Kazakhstan under which Belarus was to deliver a specified number of tractors, automobiles and other machines to Kazakhstan at set prices and was to receive in return cereals, metals, chemical products, etc. At the end of

1991 enterprises received 70 per cent of their resources through the centralised supply system. State orgnisations distributed the same volume of goods produced.

The regulation of the flow of goods was accompanied by rigid control of prices for all products and services. The government was proud of the fact that it held prices down. This pricing policy led to the mass export of goods from Belarus. Shop shelves became empty. Within a few years the government and parliament had to take measures 'to protect the domestic market'. In October 1990 an article on speculation was added to the Criminal Code. Purchase of goods for re-sale at higher prices could be punished by imprisonment for up to three years. (This article is still in force in Belarus: it is forbidden to purchase products from state enterprises for re-sale).

The command system began to malfunction. Inter-governmental agreements were not fulfilled. In order to fill their empty shelves, shops had to be given permission to buy at higher prices (at first for imported goods). At the beginning of 1992, when Russia liberalised prices, the Belarusian government had to do likewise. Prices for some foodstuffs and communal and transport services remained fixed. (In addition, the prices charged by almost all enterprises continued to be restricted to a fixed level of profitability in accordance with anti-monopoly legislation introduced in 1992). By 1994, when they were having difficulty in selling because of a reduction in demand, enterprises had to be given the freedom to dispose of their own products. 1994 saw the highest rate of privatisation of state property.

Thus, circumstances forced the Belarusian nomenklatura to carry out a partial liberalisation of the economy. But this forced retreat was on a modest scale[2]. Belarus came 25th out of 28 transition countries in terms of economic liberalisation, ahead only of Azerbaijan, Tajikistan and Turkmenistan.

The dead drown the living

The Belarusian leaders did not admit that it was the inefficiency of the command economy that had caused the crisis of socialism and the dissolution of the USSR. They continued to consider the Belarusian economy to be highly efficient. They attributed the crisis in the economy to the misguided policies of central government. For example, explaining the failures of 1991, Vice-Premier Miasnikovich said: 'We did not manage to give our economy maximum protection from the nationwide disorganisation'.[3] That is why the leaders of Belarus saw no grounds for rejecting the socialist model.

The basis of the command system was large state enterprises in industry and collective farms in agriculture. Ever since the first years of independence the Belarusian nomenklatura have tried to keep these sectors in their own hands.

In the Baltic states unprofitable enterprises were closed down. In Latvia and Estonia, for example, the average annual fall in industrial production in 1991-1993 was 35.4 per cent and 19.4 per cent respectively. Estonia refused to give any state support at all to agriculture. In contrast to its neighbours, Belarus did everything possible to preserve its large enterprises, the majority of which were operating at a loss. That is why the rate of industrial recession was much lower (5.3 per cent per year).

Investment policy was focussed on the development of those branches which, in the opinion of the government, could respond quickly: agriculture and light industry. A substantial proportion of financial support in 1992-1994 was allocated to agriculture. The share of credits going to agriculture, for example, increased in the course of 1992-1994 from 7 to 28 per cent of the total. 25-28 per cent of the budget within this period was also directed to agricultural subsidies.

The liberalisation of foreign trade and a reduction in Russian military orders led to a fall in demand for Belarusian products in the CIS countries. Under these conditions the government should have cut living standards, liberalised the economy and started to restructure production. This was done in the neighbouring Baltic States: in Lithuania, for example, the citizens of Vilnius lived without heating one winter. But nothing of the kind was attempted in Belarus.

Due to a series of objective and subjective factors, the economic consequences of the crisis of socialism were more dramatic in Belarus than in other parts of the former Soviet Union. During the period 1991-1994 prices grew nearly 18,000-fold, inflation slashed the value of savings accumulated over decades, the level of investment halved, and external debt grew from zero (at the dissolution of the USSR Russia took over all external debts) to $1.27 billion. All resources were directed to the maintenance of current levels of production and consumption, rather than being used to solve the problems the country faced.

Unlike in the Baltic States or Poland, Belarus's leaders continued to support the operation of unprofitable enterprises and direct investment in the processing of standard raw materials into expensive and poor-quality goods, which was another factor tending to reduce popular consumption. That is why by 1995, although output had fallen less, the level of incomes and social protection was lower than in the above countries. The Belarusian leadership's policy had had the opposite result to that which they had expected.

Turning power into property

In 1991 the Communist Party was dissolved, but there was still no separation of powers nor any civil society. That is why the economic-administrative nomenklatura remained uncontrolled and at the same time had wide-ranging authority in the sphere of economic decision-making. This created favourable conditions for corruption: for pumping state financial resources into the newly-fledged private sector and into the personal incomes of enterprise managers and officials. And so the process began.

The early nineties was a period of 'gold fever' for domestic business. The hard currency exchange rate was so high that the purchasing power of the dollar was ten times what it is today. Exporting oil, for example, and then importing computers or perfumery with the proceeds, was hugely profitable. Even greater opportunities for the primary accumulation of capital were created by the policy of freezing prices (which aggravated the shortages in Belarus) while they were increasing rapidly in the other countries of the former USSR.

For example, the price of the Minsk truck MAZ set by the state in 1991 ($30-35,000) was approximately half its sale price in the other countries.

Bribes for the right to buy a truck at the official price reached $15-20,000. The plant was surrounded by middle-men. By our estimate, middle-men extracted about $1.5 billion from the state through the Minsk automobile plant alone in the period 1990-1993. A similar situation applied to other plants as well.

The 'privatisation' of finance by various means through which the resources of state enterprises were converted into private resources created the conditions for the privatisation of state property. However, the conservative Supreme Soviet failed to adopt the necessary legislation, so privatisation began under temporary regulations approved by the government. The valuation of property purchased was carried out not at market prices but, in line with the socialist mentality, according to its balance sheet value. This meant that some property was in fact sold dirt-cheap. For example, research carried out by IMF experts at two privatised enterprises in Minsk has established that their purchase price was only 10 per cent of their real value.

Privatisation and the accumulation of capital in the hands of the state and economic bureaucracy went more slowly in Belarus than in Russia. But the trend was the same as in the richer neighbour: the country was moving in the direction of oligarchic capitalism.

Rebellion of the masses

Up to the time the first president of Belarus was elected in July 1994 the economic situation in the country continued to worsen. Real incomes halved between 1990 and 1994. Social stratification increased considerably. The difference in income between the richest and poorest 10 per cent increased up to 13-fold. These two processes created favourable conditions for the establishment of a populist totalitarian regime.

Communist and populist propaganda of various kinds skilfully channelled people's dissatisfaction with their own situation and resentment at the (in their eyes) unjust enrichment of entrepreneurs into rejection of the idea of market reform and democracy. The left achieved an about-turn in the attitude of the masses. If a referendum had been held in December 1994, then, according to the results of a national opinion poll, 30.3 per cent of those polled would have voted for the market instead of the 62.6 per cent at the end of 1990.

Thus, the readiness of the population at the end of 1990 to accept unfamiliar market reforms had been lost by the time of the presidential election. The 'window of opportunity' for the creation of a private sector in Belarus appeared to be closed.

In July 1994 Alexander Lukashenko, a noted fighter against corruption, was elected president. He promised that the country's development would serve the interests of 'ordinary' people; the word 'market' did not appear in his pre-election programme. He promised to 'restore the controllability of the economy and state control over prices with the aim of excluding growth in profits through growth in prices'. He promised that all profits obtained at the expense of unjustified price increases would be confiscated and put into the budget, and that the directors responsible would be called to account, including through criminal liability.

Generalising, it could be said that in 1994 Belarus experienced a 'conservative revolution' or 'rebellion of the masses'. By conservatism we mean the kind which emerged in reaction to the French revolution and the enlightenment, and which is organically incompatible with a developed system of market relations. People who did not belong to the political, economic or cultural elite in Belarus, and had neither the necessary education nor any experience of state government, occupied the top of the power pyramid. They are trying even now to govern the Belarusian economy proceeding from the ideas of 'ordinary' people regarding simple and rapid solutions to complicated social problems.

The German model of socialism

Lukashenko's views, as can be surmised from numerous interviews, are deeply conservative. Here is a short summary of his views on private sector development. All the processes in society must be under the control of a single leader. The separation of powers in Western democracies is, in his opinion, more illusion than reality: even in the United States, one man controls everything. The Belarusian president must have the right to take any decision concerning the governing of society: for example, to dismiss not only the Chairman of the Constitutional Court or the Chairman of the National Bank, but also the director of even the remotest enterprise or school.

The main motive for an entrepreneur, according to the President, should not be the desire for profit but the desire to benefit society; the 'spirit of gain' is incompatible with the spiritual values of the Slav-Orthodox peoples. Lukashenko has an especially negative view of financial and commercial enterprise.

The President prizes the values of justice and equal distribution. He has declared repeatedly that Belarus is seeking its own model of economic development different from both capitalism and socialism. The main characteristic of this new society must be a justice that results, first of all, in distribution according to one's labour. That is why the market principle of price formation based on supply and demand is being replaced in Belarus mainly by strict government control of prices.

In order to retain power, the President must act in accordance with the expectations of his electorate ('ordinary people') by suppressing private trade, middle-men, financiers and bankers, by establishing 'just prices' etc. And that is what he does. A durable system has taken shape: the president scans the people's moods and reflects them in his words and actions, which reinforces the lack of realism among 'ordinary people'. Now it would be difficult for the President to change his negative attitude to the private sector, not only because it would go against his convictions but also because it could lead to the loss of his electoral base.

Lukashenko came to power in defiance of the will of the economic and political elite of the time. Neither he himself (his highest previous position was as director of a state farm) nor his closest colleagues had any experience of government. Because of this he could not immediately change the direction of economic processes in accordance with the demands of the 'masses'. At first he had to rely on the former state bureaucracy and take its interests into account.

The anti-crisis programme worked out on the instructions of the President in October 1994 reflected the interests of different lobby groups in the nomenklatura (industrialists, agriculturalists, civil servants). At the same time it contained a number of reformist measures. In 1995-1996 the National Bank managed to reduce considerably the rate of inflation and even accumulate currency reserves, which helped to attract foreign investment.

However, the situation gradually changed. In 1995-1996 a considerable proportion of the heads of state institutions, including the army, KGB and Ministry for Internal Affairs were replaced. Having strengthened his position, Lukashenko began more decisively to restore the command system of government.

Creeping nationalisation

In Belarus, official statistics divide the economy into two sectors, state and non-state. However 'non-state' does not mean 'private', as a Western reader might assume, because every joint-stock company is considered to be 'non-state' even when the state holds 100 per cent of its shares. The proportion of GDP produced by the 'non-state' sector is known: about 40 per cent. But experts can only estimate the contribution of the genuinely private sector, ie enterprises where the state holds none or less than 50 per cent of the shares. It has increased by 2-3 per cent since 1994 and now accounts for 10-12 per cent of GDP.

Two waves of privatisation can be distinguished. The first ('romantic') wave occurred in 1990 and early 1991, on the basis not of law but of temporary government regulations. At that time the process of privatisation could be initiated by a decision of the labour collective. In this process, 30 per cent of the shares usually went to the state, 40 per cent to the work force, and 40 per cent on open sale. But at that time there were no stock exchanges or investment funds, so 'open sale' was only a symbolic concept. Buyers and sellers negotiated a price and did their deal privately. (This share-trading mechanism is still functioning today.)

At that time a number of profitable enterprises in the light, woodworking and building industries were privatised and turned into collective enterprises.

A wave of indignation arose in society against unfair privatisations. For example, Alexander Lukashenko, a deputy in parliament at the time, asserted that a private sector must emerge using its own capital and credit and not through the privatisation of state property. (He repeated this line several times over the following years). In February 1991 parliament halted the privatisation process until legislation could be adopted on the 'just' distribution of property.

By the beginning of 1994 the entire administrative basis for privatisation was in place and a privatisation programme was put together. Under this, two-thirds of state property was to be privatised, half of that using the vouchers which were given to all adult citizens prior to 1 July 1994. The number of vouchers issued to individuals depended on their age and work experience. Their total nominal value was to be equivalent to 50 per cent of the total balance sheet value of all enterprises subject to privatisation. About 70 per cent of the population received vouchers. Under the 1993 law half the shares of every enterprise had to be exchanged for vouchers. Later on this procedure was changed and the president or another state institution determined the quota of shares to be exchanged for vouchers in the case of each individual enterprise to be privatised.

In the initial stages there was great interest in privatisation. However when Lukashenko came to power (July 1994) he quickly put the brake on. First, some of the privatised enterprises were returned to the state by presidential decree. Everybody knew that the presidential administration was preparing a decree cancelling privatisation and allowing for the punishment of all those guilty of handing over state property. In addition, many in the state nomenklatura were dissatisfied with voucher privatisation, since the demand for property could not be satisfied with the vouchers issued.

The decree stopping privatisation was not issued, but other measures followed which were intended to halt privatisation temporarily. For example, in 1995 the media announced that the President had signed a privatisation programme for 1995. But nobody saw the decree after that, and the law banned privatisations not covered by a programme. People were forbidden to take out credit to purchase shares (which had been allowed in 1990-1991) or to sell their vouchers. The investment funds created before 1995 either changed their sphere of activity or were liquidated once they had returned the vouchers to the people who had bought them.

Only shares in unprofitable enterprises were put on sale. Lukashenko threatened their directors: first sack the management team that had failed to run the enterprise effectively, and only then could the enterprise be privatised.

Finally, civil servants made no attempt to conceal the fact that enterprises were either 'their own' or 'alien'. The state enterprises were 'their own' and were given many privileges. Non-state enterprises were deprived of such support. As a result, directors did not strive for independence. By autumn 1994 a number of enterprises were already opting to become state enterprises again (the shoe factory in Grodno, for example).

Instead of the 20 per cent of property that was to be privatised according to the 1994 programme, only 5 per cent was actually privatised because of implicit official resistance (though it was still the highest percentage in all the years of independence). Then privatisation became sluggish. Although voucher privatisation ends on 1 July 2002 and the savings banks have shares in weak enterprises which could be exchanged for vouchers, nobody in the media reminds the public of this fact and the population has lost interest. Half the vouchers remain in the hands of individual citizens.

The banks have been nationalised. The President issued a decree in August 1995, unbeknown to the shareholders and in defiance of legislation then in force, amalgamating one of the joint-stock banks with the state bank, thereby reducing the share of private capital in the new bank to less than 1 per cent. By another revolutionary decree, in June 1996, he slashed the share of private stockholders in the collective investment fund of all the commercial banks, ensuring the dominant role of the state in these banks.

The President's economic policy caused many industrial enterprises to get into difficulties. The state sometimes took away their shares for non-payment of taxes or energy bills. In addition, from 1994 onwards there were court cases looking into past privatisations. This involved checking whether the process had been in line with subsequent laws and regulations. For example, in 2000, after many trials, the court found that the value of fixed capital had been understated when the Amkodor machine-building works was privatised in 1990-1991. On this basis 15 per cent of the shares were returned to the state.

In January 1998 a 'golden share' was introduced which gave extensive powers to state representatives. For example, they have the right to veto the dismissal or appointment of the enterprise director. This means that in reality the state has total control over the enterprise even when it may hold, say, only 0.1 per cent of the shares.

The strategy adopted for the development of Belarus involves the state keeping hold of the commanding heights. The 'participation' of the state is understood as follows: 'The key role of the state as the director of economic activity will be preserved'[4].

'To control with all our might'

This is how Lukashenko described the essence of his economic policy in one of his speeches.

Price formation

Belarus has several protective lines against freedom of prices. First, prices are fixed for socially significant products (medicines, bread, meat and milk products, transport and communal services). The second price control barrier comes from anti-monopoly legislation. There is a register of enterprises, about 2000 in all, which are deemed monopolistic, which means that prices for the majority of goods and services are regulated on the basis of the anti-monopoly legislation. In practice this legislation serves as a masked tool of price control, because after the creation of the common customs area with Russia all Belarusian enterprises except the 'natural monopolists' (sewerage, water supply, etc.) ceased to be monopolistic. Even milk and cream, for example, can be delivered to a small town from Russia.

Third, in May 1999 an all-embracing limit on prices for all goods 'produced on the territory of the republic of Belarus' was introduced. Under this decree, price indices are established each quarter for the various products. The presidential decree permits the government to remove goods and services from under its umbrella, but such exceptions are only valid for three months.

There are many other forms of price control. For example, purchase prices for agricultural products, social utilities and power supplies are regulated, and wholesale price mark-ups are limited to a fixed rate of profitability.

Controlling material flows

First, at the beginning of each year since 1997 the President issues decrees approving the 'forecast indices' for the development of the national economy for that year. These set growth output rates for each branch. In practice the 'forecasts' become the planned output targets, and then directives to the directors of state enterprises. Contracts made on this basis include a bonus for the director for achieving a level of output growth above that of the previous year: 5 per cent growth means a bonus of 10 per cent of salary. Directors of private enterprises are also summoned by the authorities and asked to increase output.

Second, a decree of April 2000 reintroduced a planning procedure formerly used by the USSR's State Planning Committees, to cover a wide range of consumer goods. This even covers individual entrepreneurs. Six months before the beginning of the year the regional executive committees must present to the Ministry of Trade 'an estimate of the demand for specified goods' for the next (planned) year. The Ministry of Trade 'generalises' the output requirements for the products in question and sends these to the Ministry of the Economy. The latter divides the overall requirements among the executive bodies and sends them to the Council of Ministers for approval.

The result of this system can be shown in an example quoted in *Sovetskaya Byelorussia* ('A net for carp', 31 October 2001). Belarusian fish hatcheries received quotas for the delivery of carp to the retail network. However, for a variety of reasons the demand for carp fell sharply. Carp caught in the autumn were left in storage nets losing weight and marketability. The fishermen could have sold their fish to fish factories for processing instead of to the retail network. But until the planned delivery quotas had been fulfilled, enterprises had no right to use the goods produced at their own discretion.

Third, the system of deliveries to meet state needs has been preserved. The 'Act on the formation and placing of orders for the delivery of goods to meet national state needs' stipulates that deliveries are to be made on a competitive basis. It also says that monopolistic enterprises cannot avoid making delivery agreements 'groundlessly'. As the register of such enterprises includes almost all medium and large enterprises, this is a system of obligatory deliveries at prices dictated by the state. Enterprises that have accepted state orders are given various privileges, including 'priority supply of centrally-controlled materials'.

For agricultural products there are not even formal provisions giving enterprises freedom to make delivery contracts: they are simply informed of the type and volume of produce they must deliver, and told the purchase price at the same time. There are also limits on the movement of agricultural products. For instance, once the plan for state deliveries has been fulfilled, the enterprise can send the rest of its products for processing or sale only to those enterprises that have a licence for that particular type of activity. Licences, in turn, have become instruments of control over the flow of goods and services. When, for example, the government decided to eliminate small commercial enterprises engaged in meat processing, it introduced licences to cover that activity. When locally-produced flour became more expensive than Russian flour, an import licence was introduced in order to force bakeries and pasta factories to purchase the more expensive flour.

Fourth, there are various regulations governing the flow of particular goods. Mainly this applies to material and technical supplies to the agro-industrial complex. Manufacturers are obliged to supply mineral fertilisers to agricultural enterprises at below cost price. Collective and state farms have to be 'supplied' with oil products and electric power at prices below cost price. State bodies decide where and how much should be produced, who must purchase harvesters, etc.

Taxes

The current overall level of taxation is 33-37 per cent of GDP. In most countries at a similar level of development the level of taxation is lower than in Belarus: for example, in Lithuania it is 26.4, in Peru 16, and in Colombia

12.3 per cent. However the payments imposed on enterprises are not limited to taxes. They have to pay a further 10 per cent of GDP into the social protection fund. The government compels enterprises to give approximately 3-4 per cent of GDP to the population and agro-industrial complex through subsidies to electricity consumers. For example, 1 kilowatt-hour currently costs about 2 cents to produce. Households and agricultural consumers pay a fixed tariff of 1 cent per kilowatt-hour, while others pay 4 cents. 4 per cent of GDP is kept by the state due to the difference in prices for gas. (The state buys from Russia at $30 per 1000m^3 and sells to enterprises at $60.) In 1999-2000 obligatory sales of hard currency to the National Bank at one-half to one-third of the market price were equivalent to a 15 per cent tax on hard currency earnings. There are also numerous levies to pay for state events.

Allowing for these and other factors it can be asserted that the real level of central government control of GDP in Belarus is not less than 50 per cent. That is why enterprises have no funds for investment. The rate of renewal of fixed assets is as low as 2.1 per cent per year in industry, 1.7 per cent in agriculture. One cannot speak of the long-term prospects for developing the country under these conditions.

The system of taxation (about 30 taxes) is complicated. Taxes are laid one upon another, and are included in production costs. Fines for violations are huge. Many people, and the best qualified, are engaged in 'correct registration', record-keeping and audit. Violations of the legislation take place on a massive scale. For example, at a meeting in the Ministry for Entrepreneurship and Investment in January 2001, Deputy Minister Shwets announced that only 0.5 per cent of enterprises monitored in 2000 had committed no violations.

Other features of the economy are also entangled in bureaucracy. It is difficult to find any activity that does not require a licence and various certificates. You need a licence to engage in 'help with self-education', hairdressing, the production of tombstones etc. A freight service firm, for example, must have three licences: for city, intercity and international haulage. When unlicensed activity is detected, the firm's income for the whole period of this activity is confiscated. In Belarus four times as many activities require a license as in Ukraine, which is notorious for its bureaucracy.

As a result of the activities of the presidential administration, a huge command economy has been created: according to the American Heritage Foundation Belarus comes near the bottom of the league in terms of economic freedom (141st out of 161 countries in 2000, 146th in 2001). The country's investment rating is rather low. In 2001 the overall share of direct foreign investment was less than 1 per cent of total investment.

At the same time Belarus has some of the attributes of capitalism: private shops, cafes, limited liability manufacturing companies, joint-stock companies. There are 2.7 such enterprises per 1000 inhabitants (for comparison Great Britain has 46, Italy 68, Russia 5.6). The private sector employs about 10 per cent of the workforce.

In Belarus's harsh conditions entrepreneurs survive mainly thanks to bribes (according to one recent poll only 20 per cent of entrepreneurs manage without bribes) and working in the shadow economy. In the September 2001 presidential election 75 per cent of owners of private businesses voted for Lukashenko. This indicates that they do not want to damage the contacts they have established with the bureaucracy, and that the existing situation satisfies the majority of entrepreneurs.

The Belarusian economic model is similar to that created in Germany in the thirties and forties of the last century. The well-known economist Ludwig von Mizes described it as the 'German model of socialism'.

Miracles only happen in fairy tales

The most surprising period in the development of the Belarusian economy were the years 1997-1998, when GDP growth rates were suddenly the highest in Europe: about 10 per cent annually. Newspapers heralded the 'Belarusian miracle'. In reality, this growth was fuelled neither by the development of the private sector, through which growth began in the rest of the post-communist area, nor by investment and modernisation, nor by increased efficiency.

So where did this growth come from?

We can single out factors external to the economy, ie the use of resources not generated by the national economy, and internal factors resulting from the economic policy of the period.

External factors

Cancellation of energy debt. A halt to the fall in output and some stabilisation of the economy was noted in June 1996, three months after Russia cancelled Belarusian energy debt to the value of $1.3 billion (equivalent to about 40 per cent of the country's budget in those years). Belarus's liberation from payment for half a year's consumption of energy served as the initial stimulus to economic growth. But even after the debt cancellation Belarus was in no hurry to pay for current deliveries. Energy debts had grown again to $300 million by the end of 1996.

Creation of the Customs Union with Russia. Belarus's entry into the Customs Union undoubtedly stimulated output growth. Belarus increased its import duties to the Russian level, leading to a reduction in imports of foreign goods, a sharp increase in production of certain goods in Belarus itself, and an increase in exports to Russia. For example, imports of tyres for cars and trucks fell in 1995-1997 from 114,600 to 22,000 units. Exports of Belarusian tyres to Russia in a 9-month period in 1997 increased 260 per cent compared with the same period the previous year (from 635,000 to 1,650,000 units). The introduction of import taxes on TV sets reduced imports in one year from 104,100 to 6,000. Production of Belarusian colour TV sets increased in nine months of 1997 by 60 per cent and exports of TV sets to Russia grew by 27.3 per cent. Overall, exports to Russia increased by 38 per cent in 1998.

The Belarusian leadership was using the Customs Union the whole time to generate additional income at the expense of Russia. One of the first scandals to emerge related to the illegal export to Russia of a large shipment of alcohol which the Belarusian President permitted to be exported duty-free. The last loophole was closed at the beginning of 2002, when Russia abolished the export tax on gold. Before that Russian industrialists had sold their gold mainly to the

National Bank of Belarus, because the import and export of gold to and from Belarus were duty-free. Thanks to its profitable activities as middle-man, the Belarusian bank was able to accumulate a certain amount of gold in 2001.

Differential foreign trade prices. Another contribution by Russia to the support of the Belarusian economy through foreign trade is less obvious. Half the country's imports from Russia consist of energy supplies. In 1996-98 gas (which now accounts for 80 per cent of the country's energy balance) was sold to Belarus at half the price Russia charged other countries; since 1999 at a third of the price. And prices for goods exported by Belarus to Russia are higher than those at which they could be exported to other countries. For example, in 9 months in 1997 Russia imported sugar from Belarus at $513 per tonne and from other countries at $304-324; synthetic fibre and thread at $3182 and $2324 per tonne respectively. Experts estimate that Belarus gained $200-300 million over the 1996-1999 period because Russia refrained from purchasing cheaper goods from other countries.

One should also note Belarus's sizeable income in recent years from the sale of arms accumulated before the dissolution of the USSR (amounting, according to available data, to $400 million in 1996).

Altogether, according to estimates by Moscow's Institute for Economic Analysis, Russian subsidies to Belarus amounted to $1.5-2 billion, not including debt cancellation. We estimate the figure to be $1.3-1.7 billion.

So external factors have a significant influence on Belarus.

Internal factors

To non-professionals, the situation of the Belarusian economy in 1995-1996 seemed paradoxical: on the one hand, storehouses filled with goods and enterprises at a standstill because they couldn't sell their products; on the other, a great need for these products at other enterprises and among the population. But the latter are short of money.

The shortage of money in circulation, it is asserted by proponents of a soft money policy, is caused artificially by too rigid a monetary policy. In other countries the amount of cash and money in circulation is much higher in relation to GDP than in Russia or Belarus. In the USA, for example, this ratio (monetary co-efficient) is much higher than the global average (80 per cent) at 120 per cent. In Russia it was 10-12 per cent as of 1 October 1996; in Belarus 13-14 per cent as of August 1997.

The most active proponent of soft monetary policy was Pyotr Prokopovich, a builder by education and work experience, who was appointed head of the National Bank of Belarus in 1996. (Under authoritarian regimes loyalty rather than professionalism count when appointments are made to leading posts. Belarus is no exception). He promised to increase income levels quickly by raising the monetarisation indicator through credit emission. The President gave his approval.

From autumn 1996 to 1999 the money in circulation doubled or tripled annually. Prices grew similarly. Hyperinflation plus the external factors pushed the economy to the point of artificial balance at a higher level of production and consumption. In 1996-1998 the purchasing power of salaries increased by 25 per cent, and a substantial growth in house-building led to an increase in the share of investment in GDP. (It was expected that house-building would be the locomotive that would pull the economy out of crisis).

In the period of growth 1997-1998 and up to the present, production at unprofitable enterprises has been supported with various subsidies and privileges. Inflation, taxes and subsidies have taken resources away from efficient enterprises and shifted them to unprofitable ones. All enterprises saw inflation lead to exhaustion of their current assets at the rate of 8-10 per cent per year. Enterprises practically stopped renewing fixed assets: in 1997-2000 the wear and tear ratio of machinery and equipment in industry increased from 74.6 to 80.3 per cent, in agriculture from 58.2 to 80.6 per cent.

Thus, the highly-publicised 'Belarusian miracle' was a consequence of Russian subsidies and the eating up of national resources accumulated earlier. The first signs of stagnation became apparent as early as the second quarter of 1998, when industrial output fell and there was a steep fall in the Belarusian rouble exchange rate.

It is curious to note that the huge (by developed country standards) level of credit emission did not lead to an increase but to a reduction in the monetary coefficient of the economy. Enterprises were even shorter of money than before. There was an increase in non-payments by enterprises to each other, and barter arrangements developed. Belarus once again confirmed to the world the truth of monetary theory and showed the world the wrong way to control the economy.

Everything comes to an end... sooner or later

The government tried to overcome the slowing down in growth rates by accelerating the operation of the printing machine. Accordingly, prices grew by 280 per cent in 1998 and 350 per cent in 1999 alone. Russia helped once again by reducing the price of gas in 1999 from \$50 to \$30 per $1000m^3$ (reducing the annual cost by \$320 million). But the growth in GDP that year was insignificant. And if we take the peculiarities of Belarusian statistics into account, we can assert that in 1999 economic growth in Belarus came to a halt.

In 1999-2000 the government continued to live from day to day and raid all possible reserves to maintain current output and support people's incomes. Since 1999 there has been a steady decline in investment (from 23.4 per cent of GDP in 1998 to 15.4 per cent in 2001). Belarusian enterprises have more often withheld payments to their suppliers. For example, their net debt to foreign enterprises increased by \$350-400 million in 2000 and by a further \$150 million in 2001. The debt of Belarusian enterprises to each other almost doubled in 1999-2001 and amounted to \$4 billion. The circulating assets of enterprises fell: in 2000 they were 41 per cent lower than in 1998 in the economy as a whole, and 51 per cent lower in industry.

State support for house-building has fallen considerably. If in 1999 state subsidies of one kind or another covered 70 per cent of the cost of house-building, in 2000 they covered only 30 per cent. As a result, house-building fell by 14.5 per cent in 2001.

The culminating moment in the eliminating of the rest of the country's reserves was the presidential election in September 2001. Real wages from January to August that year grew by no less than 34.1 per cent. Real monthly wages reached $100 as promised by the President.

Some growth in output and in the money incomes of the population in 2001 was accompanied by a considerable worsening in the financial position of enterprises and banks. Artificial support for the Belarusian rouble and a high level of hard currency sales (with the aim of sterilising the money supply) led to a halving in the currency resources available to enterprises and banks. The real profit of all enterprises declined by 23 per cent. Profitability fell from 13.4 per cent (2000) to 8.6 per cent. Budget income was 10 per cent below the planned level. Whereas 21.8 per cent of enterprises were unprofitable in 2000, the figure for 2001 was 35.5 per cent.

It seems that the increase in output and incomes in 2001 was the last heroic deed of the Belarusian economy. Between September 2001 and January 2002 wages and pensions fell by 12.7 and 17.5 per cent respectively. Inflation, which in summer 2001 was at its lowest since independence (all economic entities were forbidden to raise prices), was over 6 per cent in December 2001 and January 2002 because the government again resorted to the printing press. More than a quarter of the emission took place in the last month of the year, so the problem of price growth was transferred to the beginning of 2002.

In 2001 individuals' money deposits in the banks increased, attracted by the positive interest rate. At the beginning of 2002 the population's share in the total money in circulation was 63 per cent. This is hot money, and if the real interest rate on deposits turns negative, people will begin to convert their roubles into dollars. This will lead to a financial crisis. If the real interest rate remains positive, enterprise credit will be too expensive. At least half the enterprises will have to close.

A third possible scenario is an unwinding of the spiral of inflation. But as enterprises' resources have already been exhausted, inflation will not prevent recession but will result in stagflation.

No matter which of these scenarios is realised, there will probably be a considerable fall in the standard of living, and the country will have to bring the social burden and individual incomes into line with its fading production potential.

The people are offered spiritual instead of material sustenance

Lukashenko's regime, even in its current difficulties, refuses to carry out market reforms. The Deputy Minister for the Economy, Zaichenko, declared in February 2002 that the government's main resource would remain 'the administrative resource'. Talk of economic liberalisation, sparked off by some of Lukashenko's pre-election declarations, has ceased.

Instead of initiating reforms, the authorities are again seeking external resources. Belarus is demanding that Moscow reduce gas prices again to $22 (as in the neighbouring Smolensk region of Russia). The largest enterprises in the chemical and petrochemical industries are being turned into joint-stock companies so shares in them can be sold from March 2002. However, the government intends to keep a controlling stock of shares itself. Ministries are planning to attract $500 million in foreign investment.

But even if external resources can be attracted, this will only serve to balance the economy at a lower level. This transition is already taking place.

At the beginning of 2002 average wages, pushed for a short time to the $100 mark, began to come down again. (It should be taken into account that people spend 60 per cent of their money incomes on food products, the prices of which are higher than in neighbouring countries). There is an acute need for funds to cover central budgetary commitments. For example, in Minsk the library of the Academy of Sciences stopped opening in the evenings in order to save electricity, and the heating was off in a number of the Academy's institutes in February. Hospitals put off planned operations because of a lack of medicines. Nor is the situation in the business sphere any better. For example, workers at the Minsk tractor works, the largest factory in the country, received half of their December pay only at the end of February. Many collective and state farms are falling apart. And so on.

The leaders who led their country into bankruptcy are trying to switch people's attention to other problems. They understand that when people are imbued by myths (communist, religious, messianic, nationalist, racial, etc.) they can endure any poverty, as we see in Iraq or North Korea.

Now the media are actively propagating spiritual values and contrasting them with the material values of Western civilisation. We cannot all enjoy the golden life, they say, because global resources are finite and we cannot all consume as many goods as the most highly-developed countries. Specialists in information warfare are thinking hard how to counteract the dangerous virus of consumerism. This virus is dangerous because people's aspirations to material welfare threaten the very existence of the regime. A line is being developed about the messianic role of Belarus as an outpost of opposition to the aggressive civilisation of the West.

Belarus's leaders are convinced that Putin's misguided pro-market and pro-Western policies will be buried in the end, and that in future Russia will borrow from the Belarusian experience of economic renaissance. So the tactic of waiting for the moment when Russia ends its 'march into nowhere' will probably be continued. And until the left returns to power in Russia, Lukashenko will strive to fight for the sovereignty of Belarus and its economic model.

Ludwig von Mizes, the famous liberal economist, while watching the archaisation of social life in Germany in the thirties, came to the conclusion that the only weapon against populist regimes of any kind was economic enlightenment. 'Only the man who has a good understanding of questions of economic theory', said Mizes, 'can elaborate an independent opinion on the problems under consideration. All the rest simply repeat what they have chanced to hear. They are an easy prey to demagogic infiltrators and foolish charlatans. Their credulity is the most serious threat to the preservation of democracy and Western civilisation'.

Today in Belarus only a small part of the population (22-30 per cent according to various sources) understand that their poverty is the consequence of the development strategy Lukashenko has forced upon the country. If the number rises by another 10 per cent, a return to reform by democratic means is quite possible.

Table 1.

Some indicators of development in Belarus, 1990-2001

Indices	1990	1991	1992	1993	1994	1995	1996	1997	1998	1999	2000	2001
Total population Million	10.21	10.21	10.23	10.30	10.32	10.30	10.26	10.24	10.23	10.05	10.02	
GDP, per cent over previous year	-	98.8	90.4	92.4	87.4	89.6	102.8	111.4	108.4	103.4	105.8	104.1
Capital investment per cent over previous year	109	104	71	85	89	69	95	120	125	92	102.1	93.9
New dwellings, per cent over previous year	93	102	82	86	89	57	135	128	108	81	121	85.7
Depreciation of machines and equipment. End of year, per cent:												
In industry						70.4	74.6	77.9	70.8	79.1	80/3	
In agriculture						58.2	66.8	73.5	73.8	80.6	80.6	
Yield, centners per hectare:												
grains and legumes	26.6	24.2	26.8	27.7	22.4	20.4	21.7	23.6	18.3	14.5	19.3	19.9
Potatoes	135	137	115	155	118	131	151	99	109	113	133	123
Consumer price index, December to December of previous year, per cent	-	246	1660	2097	2060	344	139	163	281	351	208	146
Consumer expenditure on foodstuffs and alcoholic beverages (per cent of total)	34.2	35.3	44	52.7	61.4	65.4	61.9			62.6		

Notes

[1] See eg G.M.Tamas, 'Capitalism, Socialism and Modernity', *Journal of Democracy*, July 1992, or S.M.Lipset, 'Thoughts on Capitalism, Socialism and Democracy' in *Predely vlasti v Wek XX i Mir*, Moscow, 1994.

[2] From plan to market. Report on world development-1996. World Bank, Washington. 1996

[3] *Sovetskaya Byelorussia*, 23 May 1991.

[4] Programme of social and economic development of the Republic of Belarus for 2001-2005, *Sovetskaya Byelorussia*, 16 May 2001.

Chasing the Old Ghost: Neo-socialist Policies in an Emerging Market

Jaroslav Romanchuk

After the break-up of the Euro-Asian system of centralised planning and decision-making, 27 new independent states were formed. The Republic of Belarus inherited from the Soviet Union a relatively developed infrastructure of production, transportation, telecommunications and education. Many industrial enterprises (tractors, trucks, meat processing, TV and refrigerators etc.) were built for the Soviet market or the socialist world as a whole. By Soviet quality standards many Belarusian goods were quite competitive provided there was no real market price. Goods and capital were allocated by Communist Party decision rather than consumer and producer preferences. Information distortions were so great that the only rationality in production and investment decisions was the rationality of arbitrary decision by a few authorised institutions. At the same time rational expectations were quite easy to form since the framework for the centralised decision- making process operated under quite rigid rules. The system came close to embodying the hypothetical maxim of economics: 'all other factors being equal'.

Economic foundations and reality ignored

Belarus had no experience of working as an independent country. It had no institutions to carry out independent monetary, fiscal and administrative policies. More important, its economy had never functioned as a closed market.

The declaration of the end of socialism did not per se bring about any meaningful change in the economic system. In order to understand the peculiarity of the Belarusian model the following factors should be taken into account:

1. Belarus did not have a natural production structure, i.e. a structure of production resulting from independent choices by consumers, entrepreneurs and capital owners. That is why all attempts to fine-tune the economy in transition, to nominate 'national champions', to stimulate exports administratively and pursue an active industrial policy were inconsistent with economics and should be considered as tools to squeeze rent from the system rather than exercising a 'scientific pattern of optimal resource distribution'.

2. Belarus did not have a natural price structure, i.e. one based on the preferences of economic entities and their propensity to save and consume. Thus attempts to establish 'fair' prices for certain goods led to blockage in the market information system and to many more investment mistakes. In fact the Belarusian system retained the major drawback of the Soviet system: an inability to make economic calculations and to ensure personal responsibility for investment mistakes.

3. Belarus did not have a natural employment structure. Many jobs were created by administrative and political order from policy-makers in Moscow or Minsk rather than by the private sector. Consequently many 'company towns' (where one plant provides 25 per cent or more of jobs) faced serious problems as the market they sold to no longer existed.

4. There was a clear crisis of trust in the institutions of the state. They were associated with repression and persecution rather than viewed as partners for citizens. This was an important factor in the drafting of economic legislation. Too complicated a law, with many loopholes, benefits and vague propositions based on notions of fairness and equality and protection of the poorest consumers, created further distortions in the economic system. That is one of the reasons why, when a post-socialist copied any Western piece of legislation, it had unintended consequences that had to be tackled with more tax-payers' money.

5. There was no tradition of paying taxes. Belarusian citizens could hardly be called law-abiding. The clash between informal institutions and very complicated legislation led to huge distortions in the official economy and the creation of a dynamic grey sector.

6. Another peculiarity of the systemic transition in Belarus was that the legislative framework was very weak. At the first stage it was shaped by the last communist government and parliament, and at the second stage by the authoritarian President, Alexander Lukashenko. The poor legal base failed to create a reliable system of property protection or to ensure a smooth change of property owners. In fact, the concept of property rights was alien to Belarusian law-makers.

7. Belarus did not have reliable tax-payers producing competitive goods for world and domestic markets. Thus the government worked under severe budget constraints and failed to reform a social security system that was regularly abused by high and middle-income groups. Copying a Western welfare model and its basic patterns of income redistribution in conditions of legislative havoc generates serious distortions. These in turn reduce popular support for democracy, the market economy and private property, as state-controlled media contrast 'the orderly, socially-secure socialist system' with 'the disorganised, chaotic and rich-oriented market'.

8. Belarus did not have authoritative, responsible trade unions. These workers' organisations were turned into pseudo-state structures. On the one hand they resisted systemic reforms. On the other they were used to support government economic policy. Belarusian trade unions could not play the role of Poland's 'Solidarity'.

9. Belarus did not have an independent and well-qualified judiciary. Judges were not ready to solve disputes between legal and physical entities. Old corporate structures involving lawyers and providers of legal services were used to reinstate an oligopoly in this sector. The courts and state prosecution system were used to legalise various discriminatory practices and even to discriminate against competitors with special arrangements with local or national authorities.

10. Belarus did not have internationally recognised accounting practices and norms of financial and corporate transparency. Instead of accepting EU, BIS, IMF and World Bank norms Belarus experimented with national accounting practices, which along with other factors effectively blocked foreign investment.

11. Belarus did not have a market for information or independent mass media. Thus powerful tools of control over government activities were blocked. The state monopoly over the electronic media and newspaper distribution system, and numerous discriminatory practices against the private media, hobbled institutions that are widely used in the West to control the activities of both state structures and corporations.

12. Belarus did not have enough highly-qualified personnel to staff state institutions. Low pay caused highly-skilled people to opt for the private sector or emigration. Civil service jobs were filled with people with a solid socialist management background. Ten years after independence, Belarus is still run by people from the old communist, trade union or administrative system. Attempts to ensure 'soft landing' policies of gradual step-by-step systemic reform led to personnel reshuffles, changing labels and retaining the substance of economic regulation.

Consequences of planning in an information vacuum: main parameters of the system

Belarusian policy-makers made major methodological mistakes in accepting mainstream Western tools of economic analysis. Relying on aggregates calculated by collecting distorted data, and applying demand-stimulating and full employment schemes (using both monetary and fiscal means) in the emerging economy, led to highly inefficient resource allocation. Policy-makers acted as if in a market environment that provided all the economic players with adequate information. In reality the government made it impossible to create an environment in which most economic entities could form rational expectations and reduce investment risks. Neither economists nor policy-makers grasped the meaning of 'complete ignorance' (when at the moment of action an economic entity is not aware of certain factors that may deem his action irrational in the future). Attempts to reach equilibrium, to ensure optimal allocation of resources and full employment (from the point of view of key decision-makers), led to the use of monetary and fiscal levers and a whole array of administrative measures. As a result Belarus is one of the worst performers in Central and Eastern Europe. It is lagging in terms of stabilisation, liberalisation and institutional reform. It has one of the worst records on property rights violation, confiscation, foreign investment and market access regulation. Soviet-style politicians have used bad theories to justify a dangerous combination of Marxist and Keynesian policies. After a decade of serious mistakes in strategy and tactics in pursuing economic reform, Belarus is now an unstable monopolised economic system with a high level of investment and property risk. It has the worst inflation index for 1994-2000 in the world, about 550 per cent per year. Through the system of authorised banks the National Bank continues to finance unprofitable projects by state enterprises and collective farms. The resources of the whole banking system amount to only $2.3 billion. Commercial banks are still obliged (under administrative pressure) to finance various off-budget projects: sowing, harvesting, construction, etc. The real debts of enterprises doubled in each of the last two years. Despite annual subsidies of about $500 million, agriculture generates losses.

The tax system is extremely complex, with 39 national, regional and district taxes. It has numerous privileges, preferences and special conditions, which result in corruption and fraud. After paying all taxes, an enterprise gets to keep only 4 per cent of its net income. There are about 280 regulations fixing prices for various goods and services. The existing state purchasing system forces industrial and agricultural enterprises to sell some of their goods and services at 20-70 per cent below cost price. Discrimination against the private sector and foreign investors is enshrined in law.

A 'golden share' mechanism can be used to gain control over any enterprise irrespective of its form of ownership or country of origin by citing a need to protect state security, economic state interests, morals, health, or the observance of Belarusian citizens' constitutional rights. A 'golden share' can be imposed for any term determined by the authorities. State representatives in companies that have a golden share have the power of veto over a wide range of strategic, financial and personnel issues. Altogether this form of control over enterprise activities has been used in more than 25 cases. This is one of the major breaches of private property rights in Belarus. In addition, systematic re-registration campaigns and the practice of getting registration offices to liquidate enterprises scare off foreign and domestics investors. There are so many cases of theft and confiscation of goods in Belarus that Russian insurance companies sometimes refuse to insure goods on its territory.

Another type of government intervention is licensing. About 180 categories of activity are subject to licensing. (This list grows every year by an average of 13 activities. The current total is about 1500.) The 1995 regulations on activities subject to licensing have been changed no less than 65 times, increasing the number of such activities each time. Licensing and certification costs amount to almost 20 per cent of an enterprise's production costs.

The major beneficiaries of Belarusian economic policy in 1995-2001 are the same persons and entities: agriculture, construction and export-oriented industries. In 2000 it was still more advantageous for a state enterprise to have 'strategic' or 'socially important' status and thus get cheap resources and protection from competitors, than to attempt to achieve market competitiveness. The status of a private enterprise automatically means higher transaction and resource costs. The situation is paradoxical: private and foreign enterprises show much better results, pay more tax, are much more efficient and do not seek subsidies – but all the budgetary support goes to the state production sector.

Article 13 of the Constitution states that 'the state gives everyone equal rights to all economic and other activities except those that are illegal, and guarantees equal defence of and equal conditions for the development of all forms of ownership'. This is violated in practically all spheres of economic activity. The most widely used tools of market monopolisation are subsidies and grants given on a discriminatory basis; credit for state enterprises at extremely low interest rates thanks to National Bank emissions, budgetary resources and off-budget funds; allocation of the most profitable export and import resources; and interference with the price regulation process, with some companies having the exclusive right to fix prices freely and to enjoy a special production, sales and payments regime. A poll of economic entities at the beginning of 2001 showed that 87 per cent of respondents face violations of their rights of equal opportunities and free competition.

Who makes economic decisions in Belarus?

There is a greater concentration of economic decision-making power in Belarus than in the Soviet Union. About 200 people make key decisions on 80 per cent of all capital flows while the other 10 million have control of just 20 per cent. Even these 200 state decision-makers are not a homogeneous class. About 40 of them handle about 80 per cent of the 'state pie'. The official national budget is but one of four sources of financing for projects launched by the President and key decision-makers. The second is the President's Fund. It is not shown in any open document where this foundation gets its money from or how it is spent. In 1999 President Lukashenko said that he did not spend a penny of budget money to build his ice-hockey stadiums but earned the hard currency himself. He was evidently referring to the revenues of this Fund. In 2001 the CIA and Western newspapers reported that Belarus's arms sales had reached $1 billion. Neither revenues nor taxes from such massive sales have been reported in the national budget open for public and legislative scrutiny. The third source of funding is off-budget specialised foundations, including the support funds for agriculture, housing, pensions, science and many others. These funds do not act independently or pursue their own policies. They fulfil direct orders from the government and Presidential Administration, and finance programmes not connected with their direct activities. The fourth source is revenues from specially-designated companies that have the exclusive right to control the most profitable cash and export-import goods flows. The government has expanded this source of finance by including 'voluntary' contributions from state and private companies to agricultural and housing programmes. The local and national authorities force economic entities to pay for energy supplies to, and to cover the debts of, collective and state farms. As a stick to ensure obedience, they cancel licences, close credit lines and create administrative stumbling blocks that may drive a company out of business.

The public has nominal control only over the state budget. The other three sources of finance are closed to public scrutiny. The President appoints the managers of all state property. Belarus has not created a class of owners with nominal rights to handle their capital. One group of managers (the old Soviet economic elite) has been replaced by another (called the Shklov group after Lukashenko's home town). At the same time Lukashenko has kept in position those who pledged loyalty and agreed to accept the new rules of the game. He regularly rotates people from one post to another. There is almost no inflow of new kinds of managers and politicians into the system.

The structure of economic decision-making in Belarus has the following hierarchy:

1. President.
2. Presidential Administration. These first two layers are backed up by the Security Council, KGB and Committee for State Control. These form a powerful analytical and control structure, a kind of information processing unit which is frequently used as a tool to stifle competition and redirect capital flows according to presidential specifications.
3. Council of Ministers, its ministries and their corporations. It would be logical to include the parliament here, but in Belarus this is totally controlled by the president and simply rubber-stamps the president's economic decisions. It has no power to draft laws. Even the state budget is reviewed by the president alone. The National Bank is *de facto* a department of the presidential administration. Its Chairman signs many documents (together with the Minister of Finance)

formally sanctioning financial aid and subsidies to collective farms, various industrial plants and social groups. In fact the resources of the National Bank are just another source of funds (mostly inflationary) for the executive power.

4. State sectoral conglomerates and their factories, big state industrial plants (with 6000 – 10000 employees) which in many cases are the only employers in the city or the region.
5. State companies set up exclusively to control various export-import flows of cash, goods and services. The Belarusian (or rather Russian) Orthodox Church can also be included here as it is one of the major bodies handling large flows of export-import goods. It is granted economic privileges for ideological reasons. It has licences to trade in alcohol, cigarettes, cars and other goods on which high import tariffs and VAT are payable.
6. Local authority officials who handle local budgets and tax revenues and have control over the state border (especially those with free economic zones on their territories).
7. State and collective farms, small and medium sized state industrial, construction and transport companies which enjoy various perks from the government that enable them to make profits at the expense of taxpayers.
8. Small private companies, across-the-border 'shuttles' – semi-legal traders importing various consumer goods and exporting heavily-subsidised and high-tariff goods to Russia, Ukraine, Poland, Lithuania (food products, gasoline, hard drinks, cigarettes).

It is difficult to place another very important element in the economic decision-making structure – the 'grey' world. This permeates through all layers of power as the volume of the grey (broadly defined as unregistered and criminal) economy amounts to about 85 per cent of GDP.

Globalisation clearly transfers economic power from the government to private transnational companies, financial institutions, hi-tech centres and powerful media centres. Privatisation of assets in advanced economies (France, Italy, Germany), numerous international mergers and a reduction of the share of the government in GDP are evidence of this process. By contrast the Belarusian government is pushing the country in the opposite direction to the globalising economic world. Hence it has lost and is continuing to lose much of its competitive potential and many traditional markets.

Industrial development

Despite its supposed priority, industry remains an inefficient sector of the Belarusian economy, with an extremely inefficient distribution of resources, as shown by its cost structure. Over the last 10 years the share of materials in overall costs grew to almost 80 per cent, while wages and salaries dropped from 11.2 per cent to 9 per cent and depreciation charges fell in 10 years from 9.4 per cent to 1.4 per cent. This means that industry is wasting fixed assets, not making even the minimum necessary investment in science, and is firmly plunging into systemic crisis. The paradox of the Belarusian model is that the government announced 4.1 per cent GDP growth in 2001, and a drop in investment of 6.1 per cent at the same time. The magic of accounting and administrative redistribution practices makes the Belarusian bubble look stable, but if you scratch the surface you see that enterprise debt grew almost 300 per cent in 2001, as did stocks of goods.

Such behaviour can be explained by:

- lack of motivation for directors to engage in long-term strategic planning given the complete uncertainty over ownership rights,
- high rates of inflation that 'eat up' current assets,
- poor financial discipline: no incentive to economise and minimise costs if industry, as a national priority, gets various financial and administrative benefits,
- lack of economic freedom and responsibility in corporate decision-making on production, financing and sale of goods,
- inflexible structure of industrial management, hostile towards rational economic policy-making by companies.

For an ordinary investor or a Western analyst it is difficult to understand the condition of the average Belarusian industrial enterprise. In Belarus enterprise balance sheets are classified so that one cannot analyse the risks and benefits of a project. On the other hand, the government itself reacts late to the emergence of an enterprise crisis. (In a civilised economy balance-sheet openness is a necessary condition for the stable development of enterprises and to secure the trust of shareholders, creditors and investors.) As a result of the wide-ranging state assistance to enterprises, taxpayers pay extra for every TV set, tractor, refrigerator or microchip produced. More than half the industrial enterprises would not be able to function in the conditions set for small and medium size businesses: no tax holidays, no writing off of debts and fines, no state credit guarantees, premises costs ten times higher than for state enterprises, with limits on cost efficiency, sales margins and prices for the factors of production, independent supply of raw materials and independent market research.

The Belarusian market is a paradox. Because of discrimination against private business, joint stock corporations with or without a state share and private enterprises initiate their own nationalisation. There is a clear explanation for this. Enterprises within the state system get a number of company benefits: access to cheap materials, privileged credit, monopoly access to a certain market segment; privileges relating to rent, taxes and financial resources; reduced administrative costs (e.g. for fire and health inspections, since local organs are more tolerant to state enterprises); possibility of regular participation in exhibitions, greater opportunities for managerial staff, etc. So the major obstacle to economic development in Belarus is its trade and industry sector, based on the presence of state monopolists which are in reality vertically integrated companies. The state anti-monopoly body does not consider the market share of the whole concern but the smaller shares of its constituent parts.

Discriminatory practices in agriculture

Belarus is the only post-Soviet country to preserve the collective and state farm system and to have restored the socialist planning and regulation system for agricultural production. Agricultural enterprises receive about $500 million from different sources each year, about a quarter of national budget expenditure. Administrative price formation has led to the actual bankruptcy of agriculture. After prices rose more than 600 per cent in 2000, the cost-efficiency of dairy products was about 3 per cent. Investment in new technologies, equipment and social projects is out of question. The state finances and consumers would have been better off if there had been no such help to agriculture. The 2001-2005 programme of social and economic development for Belarus preserves the crisis in this sector and blocks change mechanisms. One typical regulation offers farms a 5-year moratorium on debts and other payment. It should be noted that such policies benefit not profit-generating enterprises but those chosen by a civil servant for some poorly-defined reason. The 'manual' management of resource and financial capital flows continues, and small taxpayers and state employees pay for the special status of some collective and state farms. The regime is not even trying to get out of the crisis through the development of private farming, bringing land into economic use, or the legal introduction of private property rights by way of developing the sale of land to the people who live in rural areas.

Discriminatory practices in foreign trade

Belarus has one of the most complex systems of tariff and non-tariff trade regulation in Europe. As a small open economy, Belarus has limited competitiveness. The average level of customs duty on imports is about 14 per cent, almost four times that in OECD countries, and a mass of regulations deprive enterprises of independence in choosing their production, trade and payment regime. But every discriminatory law and regulation contains exceptions which give civil servants the right to decide the procedure for foreign trade operations.

Currency and foreign trade legislation is the most frequently changing and cumbersome. In December 2001 the head of the Belarusian Customs Office said that in order to abide by the law in international trade a company, or rather the accountant and the director, needed to be familiar with about 10,000 documents. Restricting access by 'non-critical' importers to the currency market was intended to stabilise the exchange rate on a long-term basis, leading to stable prices. But it simply resulted in multiple exchange rates, higher inflation, and other negative consequences on a macro and micro level. It led to numerous restrictions on business access to the market and made the legitimate purchase and sale of foreign exchange impossible. Gradually the Belarusian rouble disappeared from foreign trade, and the official over-the-counter market was replaced by the black market. Officials used further regulations to respond to each 'scheme' contrived to bypass tight legislation, making it illegal. All this significantly damaged the appeal of legitimate exporting. 1999 saw a start to the liberalisation of foreign trade. In autumn 2000 practically all restrictions on the use of the rouble in foreign trade accounts were lifted and the currency market was considerably deregulated. This allowed Belarus to adhere to IMF Article 8. However, these positive National Bank policies are not co-ordinated with the fiscal and institutional policies of the government, leading to considerable discrepancies among the economic sub-sectors.

Trade relations with Russia

Belarus's trade turnover constitutes about 120 per cent of GDP, but its trade policy is not multi-vector, which puts the production sector of the economy in a very difficult position. The fixing of maximum prices, especially for food products at the end of the 90s, led to a huge price disparity between domestic and foreign markets. The President and the government adopted a number of regulatory acts limiting the export of goods. One decree in 1998 banned the export of consumer goods from Belarus, which led to the practice of unconstitutional, administratively-imposed confiscation of property, including the confiscation of state enterprises' vehicles as well as cars belonging to Russian and other European citizens.

The widely-trumpeted Customs Union between Belarus and Russia never corresponded to the documents on which it was formally based. Moreover, Belarus never even had a classical free trade area with its eastern neighbour. Like the CIS, it turned into a discussion club used by lobbyists to defend their profitable interests. By the beginning of 2001, after five years of the Union, Belarus and Russia had still not agreed on import/export duties for 2840 items. These differences illustrate the lack of consensus on strategy and tactics in building Russian-Belarusian relations. Then Prime Minister Yermoshin noted in April 2001 that Belarusian industrial enterprises paid 3.5-4.3 times more for their natural gas than neighbouring Russian regions, and 5.5-6 times more for electricity. This reflects another problem in Belarusian-Russian relations: the lack of equal economic conditions for Belarusian and Russian enterprises. There is no co-ordination of non-tariff regulation, the VAT regime or trade with third countries. The volume of barter deals grew to 30-35 per cent of trade turnover with Russia, then went down to 15 per cent in 2001 due to Russia's policy of getting rid of barter. In 1996-2000 the compulsory sale of 30 per cent of the hard currency revenues of enterprises at the National Bank rate (the market rate was up to three times higher) turned into another foreign trade tax. Operating in this kind of environment led to depreciation of assets, the emergence of a parallel system of payments between enterprises, and corruption in the system of resource allocation. In addition, clearing schemes for the import of Russian electric power, natural gas and oil products led to the emergence of a multi-price system in Belarus when one and the same good had many prices depending on the form of payment and kind of buyer (private/state, foreign/domestic). Such price distortions led to a situation where factory prices were higher than prices to intermediaries involved in barter or clearing schemes.

Major features of the business climate

The successful development of entrepreneurship requires a clear-cut and transparent normative and legal base. The 'rules of the game' in Belarus do not meet the basic requirements for a favourable economic environment. The Civil and Investment Codes which were passed in the first half of 2002 are characterised by:

- non-conformity with the norms of international law;
- contradictions between various regulations;
- instability and a chaotic legislative base, allowing for retrospective legislation;
- ambiguity of some provisions.

The Constitution and the Civil Code are constantly corrected and 'improved' through a variety of decrees and other regulatory measures. The number and incoherence of these induce a vicious circle of never-ending alterations and amendments. There has been an inexorable rise for instance in the number of regulations issues by the Council of Ministers, from 507 in 1991 to 1787 in 1997 and over 3000 in 2000 and 2001. Since 1997 there has been a significant upsurge in the President's participation in the regulation of businesses, with a constant flow of decrees and subsequent frequent amendments.

Climate of investment disincentives

Belarus comes 135th out of 156 countries around the world in terms of an attractive investment climate. In 2002 Belarus came 148th in the world in the index of economic freedom designed by the Heritage Foundation. (Russia came 131st while the most dynamic reformer, Estonia, was fourth.) Belarus's position has steadily got worse on all the major indices of institutional change, liberalisation and stabilisation. These indices point up Belarus's very reactionary and aggressive administrative and legal environment for the development of private companies and private initiative. In one of his speeches Lukashenko compared privatisation with the elimination of state property. This emotional approach has dominated institutional changes over the last seven years. According to the Ministry of State Property, its 2706 enterprises are worth the equivalent of about $5.5 billion. If all these state enterprises had been sold for just $550 million, or a tenth of their balance sheet value, and the money put into the lowest-risk USA state bonds at 5 per cent annual interest, the budget would have received $25 million annually, or 5 times as much. It is very easy to calculate the opportunity cost of this type of property management. According to the former minister of privatization, Novak, 1.9 million square metres of premises are vacant or are used inefficiently. At the lowest rent rate the state loses almost $23 million per year. If we take into consideration other factors, the social and economic cost of blocked privatisation and the profits foregone amount to hundreds of millions of dollars.

Conditional right for entrepreneurship

The state deprives its citizens of the right to make mistakes in business: paragraph 7 of the Regulations on Registration states that 'if after the end of the second and every following fiscal year the value of net assets of a commercial enterprise drops below the statutory capital, then it has to register the reduction of its statutory capital. If the value of the above assets is less than the minimum size of the statutory capital then such a commercial enterprise is subject to liquidation.' There is no businesses without risk. As the future is always uncertain, the risk as interpreted by a bureaucrat will always reflect his own point of view. Belarusian citizens, unlike citizens of countries with market economies, are deprived of the right to use the limited liability principle when registering companies.

Freedom to enter the market is as important as freedom to leave it. Decree No. 22 of November 2000 on the registration and liquidation of legal entities in Belarus did not change the procedure for enterprise liquidation, which may last for years. There are cases where people have not been able to shut down their companies since 1996. Shareholders cannot engage in business activities because the enterprise in which they were involved is in process of liquidation. The decree did not change the rule whereby an enterprise can be liquidated by one of the registration authorities. There were plans to modify presidential decrees on incorporation but no draft paper had been published by July 2002. Practical implementation of this decree violates the constitutional rights of the citizen. If someone has not liquidated the enterprise or has budget debts he cannot get a passport to travel abroad.

Destruction of the social security system

The social security system, based on universal social transfers, subsidies for goods and services, maximum-price indices for consumer goods, obligatory norms for the retail trade relating to the range of goods, and various categories of benefits, is not able to solve the issue of redistribution of goods in favour of the most indigent. The system of interventionism using monetary and fiscal mechanisms leads to social stratification, increasing disparities between rich and poor, diminishing social guarantees for pensioners, teachers, doctors, large families, children and young people. Even the principle of free education and health services is not carried out. Numerous benefits are purely nominal.

Mechanisms to target help on the most indigent have not been developed, nor are there any official criteria for poverty. According to trade union information, 40-60 per cent of the country's citizens are below the poverty line. State social protection is envisaged for 34 broad categories of people, and support is provided in 29 different forms. Half the population (about 5 million people) enjoy them, though many have only nominal benefits. 93 per cent of families with children are on low incomes. Adult incomes are too low to provide adequate provision for children, and the birth-rate has dropped sharply. Today about 600,000 families are on the list of those in need of housing. 60 per cent of average household expenditure goes on food.

Pensioners make up about a quarter of the total population. During the last 10 years the labour force has dropped 18 per cent while the number of pensioners has grown by 13 per cent. The pensions of 35 per cent of pensioners are insufficient to meet basic nutritional needs.

The natural increase in population became negative in 1993. Life expectancy has fallen by 3 years over the last three years and the suicide rate has doubled since 1990. This is one of the worst indices in Europe. Sickness rates have risen sharply, especially among the young. People living in areas damaged by the Chernobyl disaster have suffered particularly, while the government continues to subsidise farms producing contaminated food. Funds earmarked for overcoming the effects of Chernobyl are falling year by year.

Hopelessness, legal chaos, the lack of labour market prospects and the lack of self-employment opportunities stimulate violence. Betweem 1990 and 2000 registered crime grew 170 per cent, drug-related crime 700 per cent. In 1990 35 per cent of marriages broke down, in 2000 almost 70 per cent.

A better way forward

Purely administrative measures of managing economic and social processes in the post-socialist state have led to a sharp decline in living standards, an increased risk of internal destabilisation, and a decline in the country's economic potential. It has been proved once again that good intentions based only on political will cannot lead to growth in a country's welfare if the authorities are economically illiterate. World experience, including experience in the post-soviet regions, proves that systemic reforms both in economic development and social justice are most effective if they accord with the classical triad: privatisation – liberalisation – macro-stabilisation. The actions of the Belarusian regime reject this approach and are directed at the suppression of private property and the strangling of economic freedom.

To get out of this economic, political and constitutional crisis Belarus must follow a social and economic model which will:

- provide the fastest possible restructuring of industry and create an information environment allowing the market to determine the share of consumption, savings and investment as well as the spheres, mechanisms and instruments of economic activity;
- legally provide for equal economic conditions for domestic and foreign entities;
- shift to a market system of national currency regulation and the monetary policy which will enable it to stabilise most quickly (inflation targeting or introduction of euro or dollar parallel currencies);
- use world standards of presentation and analysis of statistic information and of accounting;
- create an economic environment that will help the development of small and medium-size businesses;
- initiate reform of the state management system, clearly differentiating the rights and powers of the centre and regions;
- simplify and make transparent the taxation system. A group of Belarusian economists has worked out a new tax system based on just 6 taxes instead of 39 (retail sales and service tax, personal income tax, social security tax, real estate tax, excise tax and import tariff) and a new budget policy concept based on a balanced budget and the centralisation of all sources of government finance (off-budget funds, presidential funds, branch concern funds, etc.);
- be guided by an independent court system dealing with economic, criminal and administrative issues;
- liberalise prices for all forms of capital, remove limits on interest rates, receipts, rents and allowances;
- minimise the social impact of transition on the poor and least protected, targeting state assistance on the least protected members of society;
- gradually shift to a system of individual pension and medical accounts;
- create conditions for the development of the third sector (NGOs) to act as contractors to the state as well as fulfilling many social functions;
- allow for a volunteer mobile army of a size and character corresponding to the nature of existing domestic and foreign threats.

Such an approach would give Belarus a chance to become competitive in the regional and global division of labour. After 12 years of systemic transformation in Central and Eastern Europe, Belarus has a unique opportunity to take into account the mistakes made and positive solutions found. Bearing in mind the many success stories of post-socialist states, Belarus should choose an economic policy like that of Estonia rather Poland or Hungary in the early nineties. The country cannot afford to copy the classical welfare model of a Western country. It does not have the necessary institutions or, most importantly, the necessary information from the market. Instead of concentrating its efforts on patterns of redistribution, the government should pursue the policies that led to the US economic miracle in the nineteenth and early twentieth century, and the Japanese and German post-war models which were targeted on wealth creation, protection of property rights and contract enforcement. This does not mean that welfare programmes should be slashed. Faced with a choice between corporate welfare and addressing assistance to the most needy, it is economically rational and politically feasible to choose the latter if we want to ensure long-term economic growth and wealth creation.

Is the Belarusian Economic Model Viable?

Anders Åslund

Belarus has chosen a peculiar road of political and economic development, establishing a Soviet-type model without a Communist Party. It may actually be characterised as a Soviet theme park, offering an interesting test case for post-communist transition. The first question is why Belarus has taken this shape. If technical skills and order were decisive, Belarus would be a leader within the former Soviet Union in the establishment of democracy and a market economy, whereas if political and intellectual insights were key, Belarus would be a laggard.

The other question is whether this system will hold. The argument of this paper is that it can hardly be sustained. Economically, this model cannot be very efficient, but its only claim to legitimacy is economic stability and security. Several factors seem likely to undermine the Belarusian system in the longer run. The economy is far too open for a model designed for a closed economy. A marginal but still substantial private sector offers safety to a rising civil society, which is challenging the orthodoxy. While the system is certainly repressive, violence is limited, rendering Belarus a velvet totalitarianism. The current Belarusian regime survives because of subsidies from Russia, but the Russian government shows no enthusiasm for it. Ultimately, the system seems too absurd to last for long. All these key features are actually reminiscent of Poland in the late 1980s. Both the economy and society are too open to allow such a substandard economic and political system to endure. Yet that says little about when a regime change is likely.

Economically developed but politically immature

During the last years of the Soviet Union, Belarus shone. It had one of the highest levels of GDP per capita in the union and a high level of education. Industry accounted for about half of its GDP, predominantly manufacturing, much of it machine-building connected with the military-industrial sector. Two peculiarities stood out. One was that Belarus was the best-functioning and most orderly part of the Soviet economy, with steady high growth rates long after other republics had started declining. The other characteristic was a tiny unofficial economy, and striking honesty. One shortcoming, however, was that the non-technical intelligentsia appeared all but absent. Belarus seemed like the Soviet Union's Prussia – well-functioning but militarised and non-intellectual.

It came as a surprise therefore that Belarus developed a very radical national front in the late Soviet years, inspired by the Lithuanian Popular Front. Yet this radical nationalism alienated most Belarusians, and its very radicalism appeared to reflect a limited national consciousness and the weakness of civil society. The Communist Party won easy victories in the first partially free parliamentary elections in 1989 and 1990. After Belarus became independent in December 1991, more by accident than desire or design, the communist leaders remained in power, although they had supported the abortive hardline coup in Moscow in August 1991.

The communists were conservative and wanted to minimise change, even if Russia compelled Belarus to undertake some price liberalisation at the beginning of 1992 because of the common rouble zone. The Belarusian Popular Front formed the main opposition, but it focused on national issues, paying little attention to economic policy. There was no prominent market-oriented economist to be found. As could be expected, Belarus insisted on the rouble zone till its bitter end in late 1993, causing it to stumble into hyperinflation of 2,000 per cent a year in both 1993 and 1994. Output plummeted, but less so than in almost all other former Soviet republics because the Belarusian governments tried to protect the old Soviet industry with regulations and subsidies. Hyperinflation and inconsistent regulations aggravated corruption even in this most honest post-Soviet state.

In July 1994, Belarus held presidential elections. The general expectation was that the communist candidate would win easily, but the demagogic collective farm chairman Alexander Lukashenko won an overwhelming surprise victory after running on a platform against corruption. While populist candidates achieved over 20 per cent of the vote in both Poland and Russia, Lukashenko's victory with 80 per cent of the vote is a strong indication of the political immaturity and atomisation of Belarus at the time.

Restoration of state control

Belarus had never undertaken much market economic reform, and when its reforms peaked in 1995 only Turkmenistan, Tajikistan and Azerbaijan were less liberalised and privatised among the former Soviet republics. No significant privatisation has ever taken place, and the private sector remains marginal at a maximum of 20 per cent of GDP.

As President, Lukashenko regulated more prices and re-imposed in full an old Soviet system of state orders that had never been abolished. Foreign trade has been controlled through multiple exchange rates, which means that a few people at the political centre can control foreign trade, squeezing out most independent traders.

The economy is most easily understood if we think of it as dominated by about 40 big industrial enterprises and scores of old collective farms. Enterprise taxes are formally high, but in practice industrial managers negotiate both taxes and subsidies freely with the presidential administration. Lukashenko has admonished and subsidised these big factories to restore their Soviet-era output, which means that little structural change has taken place. He claims high growth rates and the steady payment of salaries and pensions as a basis for his legitimacy, but the statistics are probably more doctored than they were in Soviet times.

A late Soviet-type economic system

Most of all, the Belarusian economic model is an old Soviet system, but one in which planning is not very important. Enterprises are asked to make their own production plans, though they must not produce less than before or than planned. The predominant state ownership seems real, and state managers have not managed to seize the enterprises. Profit orientation appears limited, impeding efficiency and innovation. Prices are controlled by indirect means such as limited mark-ups.

About half the shops are still state-owned, as is plain to see. They have generic names such as 'produkty' (food). The products are sparse and frugal, about half of them unsaleable old Soviet goods, which shows how regulated the market is, though by Soviet standards supplies are ample. Whereas problems of shortages are discussed even in state-owned newspapers, blatant shortages are not apparent. The private sector manages to keep them at bay.

Before 2000, Belarus had up to 200 per cent annual inflation because of excessive subsidised credits and other hidden enterprise subsidies. In 2001 inflation abated, but Lukashenko's impulses could easily prompt a new wave of inflation and devaluation. No financial markets have evolved.

Belarus has a not-very-original post-Soviet tax system, but taxes are probably the highest in the region and close to confiscatory. Naturally, tax exemptions are given right and left by various protectors. Book-keeping is enormously complicated, although in the end taxation is arbitrary.

The characteristic post-Soviet inspection hell is well-developed also at Belarusian enterprises, though powerful protectors shield many of them. Private entrepreneurs are enticed to accept state protection and then easily get into difficulties. So private enterprise is hardly developing, and many private entrepreneurs end up in trouble, often in jail, as lawful business is virtually impossible without tax exemptions.

Lukashenko maintains a large presidential fund to provide for his own whims. Much of its financing comes from arms sales, and it is widely alleged that Lukashenko sells arms to anybody, from Iraq to Chechnya. He reportedly sells tanks and rockets from the large Soviet stockpiles that have been left in Belarus. The presidential fund was also used to finance his presidential campaign in September 2001.

A true dictatorship

The power structure appears simple, and is reflected in the economic system. President Alexander Lukashenko is a true dictator, even if he was re-elected with a three-quarters majority in an election in September 2001 which was neither free nor fair. He rules through the presidential administration, the KGB and the state administration. A populist dictator, he has no need for a party but underlines his direct contacts with the people. Nor does he have any ideology, but adheres to unmitigated populism. His power base is the rural, poor, poorly educated, old, religious and Orthodox, making the rural babushki his key supporters. The President does make sure to offer social transfers to many, and while these are small, they are actually paid out. Belarus has one of the worst health records in the former Soviet bloc, and male life expectancy has declined by 4.4 years from 1989 to 1998 with no sign of any improvement. But this is ignored by the authorities.

Lukashenko maintains a minor personality cult, with extraordinary media coverage of himself; the book-shops abound with Lukashenko pictures. Some newspapers are reminiscent of turgid third-rate Soviet newspapers in the mid-1970s at the height of Brezhnevism, while others are little but propaganda sheets. They are full of absurd reports of production successes at state enterprises and collective farms. Lukashenko is presented as enormously humble and popular. The opposition is caricatured, but quite a lot of information is given, and the degree of aggression and information varies greatly between different state newspapers.

The President rules arbitrarily and is as contemptuous of the rule of law as ever the Soviet communists were. Famously, in 2000 he issued a decree entitling himself to nationalise anything at will and without compensation. He bankrupts or arrests any businessman and sacks any official as he pleases. During a visit to a new public office complex he thought it looked too good, so he suddenly ordered that the already high rents should be raised by 40 per cent. Although the private businessmen who had just moved in had concluded standard rental contracts, they found these over-ruled.

As a consequence of this power structure, several groups that are usually powerful in post-Soviet states are remarkably weak. First, the Council of

Ministers functions as a collection of subordinate civil servants rather than as a government. Second, there are no Belarusian oligarchs and the most prominent businessmen seem to be temporary favourites of Lukashenko's. Third, organised crime is minimal. In a luxury shop, I learned that in the early 1990s one-fifth of their customers had been professional criminals, but these had virtually disappeared. Now the rising clientele consists of corrupt bureaucrats, while the number of wealthy private businessmen has also dwindled. Private racketeering only persists for kiosks. Fourth, the regional governors form no powerful group.

This means that Belarus has a highly dictatorial power structure. In many ways, Lukashenko is correct when he says that he stands alone with the people, suggesting an unusual degree of atomisation. The number 2 in the country is logically the head of the presidential administration, followed by the minister of the interior and the chairman of the KGB, while the prime minister is dispensable. As there is no law in Belarus, political protection of business is vital. A bank that won a case against the state in court found itself cut off from the bank account system by the National Bank. The best protection is obviously the Ministry of the Interior. Yet neither the protected nor the protectors experience much stability, since Lukashenko disdains stability. This means that businesses do not invest much or adapt, nor do they support Lukashenko more than necessary for survival.

Both politically and economically, this system appears similar to the 'goulash communism' of Hungary and Poland in the 1980s, when the communists had given up any claims of ideological superiority and implausibly argued that they could deliver more economic welfare. But Lukashenko is far more voluntaristic.

An emerging civil society

Yet this picture is incomplete in so far as it presents Belarus as a continuation of the old regime. In fact, the old system seems not so much intact as withering away. Several new elements have emerged that appear to be causing cracks in the current Belarusian model. The most striking of these dissonant elements is a surprisingly vibrant civil society.

When I visited Minsk the first time in 1986, I was struck by how well the Soviet system functioned there, the honesty and the absence of a real intelligentsia. In the mid-1990s, I repeatedly met wild Belarusian nationalists who believed any conspiracy theory about Russian domination over Belarus, implausibly arguing that Lukashenko only obeyed orders from Moscow. Now, all that is gone, while a high-grade civil society and intelligentsia have emerged with a good and nuanced understanding of reality. The liberal opposition studies and details the shortfalls of the Lukashenko regime, but appears more interested in understanding than condemning, as the moral flaws are so obvious.

The evidence that two opposition leaders were murdered by top Lukashenko aides in 1999 appears beyond doubt. People have started speaking their minds frankly, without looking over their shoulders for informers, while opposition activists take it for granted that their words and actions are being observed. The chairman of the liberal opposition party, the United Civic Party, Anatoly Lebedko, argues on the one hand that Belarus is 'the last enclave of totalitarianism in Europe.' On the other hand he calls it a 'velvet dictatorship.' Many Belarusian intellectuals speak English well, and they are modern, open, tolerant and cosmopolitan. The opposition economists are radical free-marketeers, but they are thoughtful and well-read. Unlike reformers in other post-Soviet countries, they have been given a lot of time to study. This Belarusian environment is much more accessible than corresponding Ukrainian circles.

While 80 per cent of the population are dependent on the state, at least one-tenth operate in a very independent small-scale private sector. The oppositionists work in private institutes, enterprises, media and NGOs. Trusting in the value of their human capital, they move from one institution to another, as little financial capital is involved. Lukashenko frequently closes down such institutions, but there are always others they can go to. The President does not try to co-opt them but ostracises them. As a consequence, he cannot corrupt them.

In this regard too, the situation is reminiscent of Poland in the late 1980s. The system is economically and politically too absurd to last, while both the economy and society are too open to allow its survival. It is enough to enter a shop in the capital to see that this substandard system is condemned. A strong civil society has developed in a substantial private sector, which is an enclave in the larger state-controlled economy. The private sector is big enough to provide considerable security for the opposition, while unable to dominate the state on its own. Yet it is impossible to say how soon the regime will crumble. I encountered a similar situation in May 2000 in Belgrade, where the demise of the dictatorship occurred much faster than anybody imagined at the time.

Lukashenko undertakes all kinds of actions against the independent media, but they do exist. It is enough to go to an ordinary newspaper kiosk and you will find not only the official state newspapers but also two or three opposition newspapers with substantial independent information and criticism of the regime. Belarus has quite open borders and is relatively western in location, so it cannot block all the kinds of information that enter the country.

Lukashenko's repression has actually helped the opposition to unite. Unlike in most other transition countries, the democratic right has been united in two substantial parties, the liberal United Civic Party and the nationalist Belarusian Popular Front. In addition, there are two social democratic parties and two communist parties.

The nomenklatura and state enterprise managers are not satisfied with Lukashenko either. While Lukashenko allows them to steal, he does not offer them stability and security. They can make money, but not invest it. Time and again, ministers and top enterprise managers are thrown out of their jobs and into prison, accused of anything from murder to major theft. Although the nomenklatura and the liberal and national right have different values, they all want to get rid of Lukashenko, and this desire is sufficiently strong to make them co-operate with one another.

Too open an economy to permit isolation

Another peculiarity of the Belarusian system is that, in spite of its retrograde Soviet system, the country has a very open economy with total foreign trade exceeding GDP. Enterprises live in a dual world and have to export to survive, primarily to Russia. The most surprising change in recent years is Lukashenko's unification of the exchange rate in September 2000. Although both the IMF and the World Bank had long advocated this, the decisive reason was that Russia insisted on unification of the exchange rate as part of their planned union. Another explanation was that the head of the presidential administration, who had made a fortune out of the multiple exchange rates, had been sacked the previous year, so there was no longer any strong economic interest opposed to exchange rate unification.

However, unification of the exchange rate is arguably the critical borderline to currency convertibility and a market economy. The economic system has become too contradictory to be tenable for long. The situation has been aggravated by many factors. Belarus was hard hit by the Russian financial crash in 1998. In its aftermath, as World Bank materials show, Russia has sharply reduced its subsidisation of Belarus. Clearly output has fallen or stagnated as a consequence, although official statistics show a splendid rise, as the old industrial production is inflated and statistics presumably falsified. Russia has also insisted on a transition to monetised trade, replacing the previously dominant barter trade. An interesting measure of well-being is the dollar wage, which has fallen since 1998. Undoubtedly, old-fashioned Belarusian products will lose out on the vibrant Russian market, while superior Russian goods are making inroads in Belarus.

If Lukashenko goes, the economic reform programme that should be pursued looks pretty obvious. A thorough liberalisation of domestic trade and prices is needed. A major tax reform is vital, reducing income tax (the liberals propose a flat tax of 10 percent) and profits tax (the liberals want 24 percent, as in Russia) while abolishing a lot of cascading turnover taxes. The budget will need to be balanced at long last, and the presidential fund should be brought under treasury control, while huge non-transparent enterprise subsidies should be eliminated. Small enterprises must be liberalised.

The most complex problem is privatisation. On the one hand it must be done. On the other hand, however it is done Russian enterprises will no doubt buy up large parts of the Belarusian economy in no time, which might become the main political issue in Belarus in future. The natural solution would be to give the enterprises away to those who work in them, while making sure that the employees receive genuinely individual and tradable shares. Liberal Belarusians are anxious to pursue a very radical reform to avoid the creation of an oligarchic system. Their other special aspiration is to undertake a case-by-case privatisation that would make it more difficult for Russian oligarchs to buy up Belarusian enterprises cheaply and tacitly.

Russia's multiple roles

One of the most complex and important aspects of Belarus's economy is the role played by Russia. Lukashenko would hardly be in power and his system would not survive were it not for Russia's tolerance. Russian communists and nationalists, led by Zyuganov and Zhirinovsky, as well as a large part of the old Russian establishment, including many regional governors, actively support Lukashenko and his regime. This is his only international support of significance. As a result, Russia has provided Belarus with huge subsidies. They come mainly in three forms. First, Belarus buys energy, especially natural gas, at very low prices, the difference apparently being borne by the partly state-owned Gazprom company rather than the Russian government. Second, Belarus pays for many of its purchases from Russia with goods, which means that it can sell a lot of merchandise to Russia that would otherwise be hard to sell, and at better prices. Third, Russia has repeatedly written off Belarusian debts. These subsidies have been very substantial, amounting to up to 20 per cent of GDP. Recently, however, Russia has been much more reluctant to bankroll Belarus and is insisting on cash payments, resisting barter.

The official Russian position on Lukashenko may be described as guarded neutrality, but as long as he has such a strong domestic position Russia has to deal with him. President Putin clearly wants to keep a distance from Lukashenko, while not criticising him outright. In opinion polls Belarusians favour the Union with Russia, but predominantly between two sovereign states, which makes no sense. Nobody seems to take the Union seriously, and the liberal Belarusian oppositionists reckon that Lukashenko's single achievement is that he has made Belarus's sovereignty irreversible. The most popular politician in Belarusian polls is Putin, who leads over Lukashenko by a huge margin.

Big Russian business is eyeing concrete assets in Belarus. Some Russian enterprises have entered the fray, but Lukashenko refuses to sell them the mismanaged assets they aspire to. Even after accepting their purchases and receiving substantial payments to the Belarusian treasury he has repeatedly cheated Russian companies of their targets. Thus, the Moscow mobile phone company MTS and the St Petersburg brewery Baltika have each paid $10 million but received nothing. Lukoil has some petrol stations but it wants to buy a big refinery, and it has one of the grandest new office buildings in Minsk. Its competitor Tiumen Oil has already acquired 20 per cent of the Russian-Belarusian joint venture Slavneft through subsidiaries, and wants the rest of that oil company. Most of the modern food in the shops, like dairy products and juices, is produced by the biggest Russian company in that industry, Wimm-Bill-Dann. Belarus used to export a lot of beer to Russia, but now St. Peterburg's (Nordic-owned) Baltika had become the dominant beer brand in Belarus. Moscow's leading restaurateur, Rostislav Bianco, has opened three prominent restaurants in the city centre. It will be difficult to keep these aggressive capitalists at bay, and they will inevitably be the first large enterprises to enter the Belarusian economy on a big scale.

Another prominent Russian presence is the four major Russian TV channels, which are all watched widely in Belarus and which report extensively on Belarus. The opposition sees these channels as their best media support because they report Belarusian events relatively objectively and they are quite independent of Lukashenko.

Where is Belarus going?

At a conference in Minsk in August 2001, the United Civic Party Chairman, Anatoly Lebedko, suggested that Belarus had the choice of three alternative models:

- Africanisation with continued Lukashenko rule;
- Ukrainisation with rule by strong oligarchic clans;
- Europeanisation, which requires radical and early reforms.

While these choices appear stark, their very formulation clarifies how far the Belarusian discussion has developed. The Lukashenko dictatorship appears both too inefficient and too open to last, while civil society is so strong and self-confident that it is bound to take over sooner or later, more or less like Poland in the 1980s.

The regime is openly repressive, but not sufficiently so to incite true fear. The opposition is calmly cataloguing all the transgressions of the regime, and this evidence will haunt Lukashenko in years to come. Information flows seem too large and open to permit the survival of any dictatorship.

Most of all, the Lukashenko regime appears terribly old-fashioned, and is legitimised by neither ideology nor party. Concocted statistics and a certain level of social support to the poor from a probably stagnant pie do not inspire confidence in the future of the Belarusian system. Lukashenko's electorate is not likely to grow but to dwindle, since he is such an unreliable patron. His new presidential mandate will only last four years, and the only question is whether he can keep the country under economic and political control that long. In fact, there are good reasons to be optimistic about Belarus's future, even if the breaking-point is not apparent. A peaceful liberal revolution is likely within the next few years, and is likely to lead to democracy and a market economy as in all Belarus's neighbours.

3
International Relations

The Foreign Policy of the Republic of Belarus: Meeting the Needs of the Time

Mikhail Khvostov

The world has changed a great deal in the last decade. Globalisation is developing apace. There has been a significant increase in the number of actors on the international stage, non-governmental as well as governmental. The list of those with a direct influence on foreign policy decision-making is constantly growing. Also growing is the range of domestic issues that have an external dimension: these now include questions relating to finance, the environment and migration. It is now nigh on impossible to separate domestic from foreign policy.

Big changes are also taking place in what constitutes state power. Moving ever more insistently to the fore are such issues as financial power and the level of development of banking systems, communications and information infrastructure.

Regional integration has become particularly important in recent years. Integrated units are playing an increasingly influential role both in foreign policy and in the world economy.

Foreign policy on both the geopolitical and the economic plane has become tougher and more pragmatic and has assumed radically new forms. Ideological confrontation is a thing of the past and attention has shifted from the application of military might to the employment of political and economic means in the pursuit of national interests. The conflicts that inevitably arise between states no longer fall into neat categories: sometimes, states find themselves co-operating on the basis of shared interests; at other times, they find themselves on opposing sides of the barricade. And, as the experience of the past decade shows, it can be just as hard to resolve small, localised conflicts as to settle large, multinational ones.

The defining characteristic of the current international situation is the transition to a system based on relative consensus on such concepts as political democracy, human rights and the market economy. International co-operation is playing an increasing role in the economic, financial and ecological sphere and in the battle against organised crime, drug trafficking and other important issues.

All this means that states can no longer afford to base their foreign policy on such simple considerations as 'yes-no ally-opponent'. Nowadays, states must be on the lookout for new ways of combining their key interests with new forms of international co-operation in partnership with a widening range of allies.

Unfortunately, the 'iron curtain' that for almost half a century divided Europe into two military blocs (Nato and the Warsaw Treaty Organisation) and two economic organisations (the European Economic Community and the Council for Mutual Economic Assistance) lives on in the minds of certain politicians. Old misunderstandings constitute a formidable barrier to progress. In my opinion, one of the main impediments today to the establishment in a whole range of states of democratic, open societies is the lack of tolerance on the part of rich and powerful countries. These rich countries are afraid to shed their old ideological dogmas, to remove their blinkers, and to see that it is in their own economic interests not to try to drag other states into economic transition or to export democracy.

The fate of the Belarusian people has always depended on the state of relations between East and West. It made little difference whether Belarus was part of the Grand Duchy of Lithuania, the Polish-Lithuanian Commonwealth or the Russian Empire: every conflict brought death and destruction on the territory of Belarus. Napoleon's invasion of 1812 resulted in the deaths of over one hundred thousand Belarusians; during the First World War, one in six Belarusians died; during the Second World War, Belarus lost over a quarter of its population.

For us, therefore, it is axiomatic that any conflict between East and West represents a potential threat for Belarus. We are unable – and have never tried – to play on the contradictions between Russia and Western Europe or to exploit an imaginary 'threat from the East' or 'threat from the West'. Quite the contrary: Belarus is perhaps even more vitally interested than other states in the establishment of a favourable political climate on the European continent.

The long history of the Belarusian people, who have always sought friends and partners, the current international situation and pragmatic economic considerations lead us to one simple and logical conclusion: Belarus's foreign policy cannot be anything other than multivectored. It must be actively engaged in constructive work in all directions, predictable for the rest of the international community, while at the same time oriented toward meeting our national interests.

Belarus's foreign policy priorities are plainly and precisely formulated: realisation of the Union of Belarus and Russia; devotion to integration within the ranks of the CIS and the Eurasian Economic Community; active participation in common European political and economic processes; joint action to strengthen regional and global security; all-round co-operation, both bilateral and multilateral, with the states of Asia, Africa and Latin America; and co-operation in international organisations, first and foremost the UN.

Belarus sees its foreign policy and its international economic activity as a whole, and does not try to rank one above the other. For us, there are no 'more important' or 'less important' partners. This is the essence of our multivectored approach. It follows that our international strategy is founded on promoting Belarus's organic inclusion in the universal system of political, economic, cultural and humanitarian ties. We can attain the aims we have set ourselves only through the civilised, step-by-step inclusion of our country in the integrative processes unfolding on the European continent.

We take a realistic approach to the situation that is taking shape. Europe is witnessing the development, in the form of the European Union, of a powerful centre of gravity that is political as well as economic. Virtually all the states of Europe are to a greater or lesser extent being pulled into its orbit. Such processes as EU enlargement, the formation of an economic and monetary union, the introduction of a single European currency and the establishment of new integrated institutions in the political, military and other spheres, are having a significant impact on the course of events in Europe as a whole; they will undoubtedly have a decisive impact on the shape of Europe in the twenty-first century.

The establishment on the western borders of our country of a single economic and monetary space is bound to have a significant impact on how Belarus operates in the world economy. The EU is already, after the Russian Federation, Belarus's second largest trading partner. Following EU enlargement, the role of the EU in the Belarusian economy will practically double. We are accordingly keen to develop mutually beneficial and long-lasting co-operation with the EU.

Key Belarusian documents such as the Constitution, the National Security Concept and the Programme of Social and Economic Development for the years 2001-2005 all state that Belarus has no alternative other than to build a law-based state, create effective guarantees for the observance of human rights, develop civil society and liberalise the economy. Alongside these priorities, we place the highest importance on the maintenance of social stability and economic growth, since these guarantee that the democratic transformation will be irreversible. We empathise with the social aspects of the EU's market economy and are keen to ensure that Belarus is a reliable and worthy partner for Europe's democratic states.

Progress in attaining these goals has not gone unnoticed at international level. Specifically, the statement issued by the Belgian presidency of the EU on the outcome of Belarus's presidential election recognised the existence of civil society in Belarus. A bilateral political dialogue is developing, as witness the series of consultations, meetings and visits that have taken place during the past year. We co-operate with the EU within the framework of the Tacis programme. On the whole, economic relations between the EU and Belarus are developing quite dynamically, and the volume of trade is increasing.

Unfortunately, the potential for partnership is not being fully exploited. We count on the EU to come forward with further, really substantive approaches. The present freezing of the status quo in EU-Belarus political relations is counter-productive in the light both of the serious positive changes that have taken place inside Belarus, and of the transformation of international politics on the global scale.

Belarus is making a tangible contribution to the development of common European processes. It contributes to military, political and inter-ethnic stability; acts as a check on negative migration dynamics in the region; and guarantees the efficient functioning of the international transport and energy infrastructure. We have consistently met our obligations within the framework of the OSCE. Our efforts to co-operate with this organisation are aimed both at strengthening all aspects of security and at furthering the progressive reform of OSCE institutions. In the first place, the OSCE should take fuller and more balanced account of the interests of each of its participating states. Our consistent adherence to this position was confirmed by the active way in which the Belarusian delegation participated in the meeting of OSCE foreign ministers in Bucharest in 2001.

In this connection I cannot fail to mention another task of our foreign policy, namely, the construction around Belarus of a belt of good-neighbourliness. In addition to Russia and Ukraine, we invite our northern and western neighbours, Latvia, Lithuania and Poland, to join this belt. What these three countries have in common is that they all firmly link their future with the European Union and the North Atlantic alliance. This in itself gives them an objective interest in maintaining stable relations with Belarus, since absence of conflicts with neighbours is an essential precondition for EU membership.

Europe is coming to understand that the domestic and foreign policy strategy of the Republic of Belarus represents the will of the Belarusian people as expressed in parliamentary and presidential elections, the democratic conduct of which the international community has not questioned. To ignore this fact would be to contradict the basic principle of democracy: that state power belongs first and foremost to the people.

It is in the application of democratic principles that I see the key to the development of an all-round Belarusian-American partnership. Belarusian-American relations today are not straightforward. We for our part are doing everything we can to put recriminations behind us and to build relations with the United States on a foundation of understanding and constructive, mutually beneficial co-operation. The key to the attainment of this goal lies in a series of consistent steps aimed at the gradual development of contacts in the sphere of bilateral relations and *having significant potential.*

Following the events of September 11, 2001 in the USA, the problem of international terrorism has moved to the top of the international agenda. The terrorist attacks gave new meaning to the concept of security since they revealed how fragile and interconnected today's world is. It became clear that countering the current threats will require unity of political will and a pooling of resources by states world-wide, a careful calculation not only of military and political but also of social and economic factors. Reacting to the rebalancing of the European and world security system that has taken place since September 11, Belarus approaches the issue of international security, and its relations with the organisations that provide it, even more attentively than before.

Belarus declared itself a member of the coalition against terrorism, welcomed the adoption of UN Security Council Resolution No 1373, and demonstrated, by concrete actions, its dedication to international co-operation against the terrorist threat. At the present moment, Belarus is one of only a handful of states that have adhered to all twelve UN conventions on the struggle against international terrorism. We are determined to fulfil our obligations and to participate in the elaboration and realisation of further measures agreed by the international community in the struggle against terrorism.

Our country has shown itself a reliable and active participant in international agreements on disarmament and arms control. Belarus was the first state to ratify the adapted Treaty on Conventional Forces in Europe (CFE) and, at the end of last year, the Open Skies Treaty. It is punctiliously meeting its obligations under the Chemical Weapons Convention, and plays an active role in the Executive Council of the Organisation for the Prohibition of Chemical Weapons. Belarus strictly adheres to UN General Assembly Resolution No 46/36L of 9 December 1991, which guarantees complete transparency in the export of weapons and military technology, and submits an annual declaration of relevant information to the UN register of conventional weapons.

A clear example of our readiness to take decisive measures to guarantee international security and arms control is provided by our voluntary renunciation of the status of nuclear power and the removal from Belarusian soil of all nuclear weapons and delivery systems. Belarus's approach to the nuclear issue was underlined by its proposal, reinforced by UN General Assembly Resolution 53/77H, to create a nuclear-free zone in Central and Eastern Europe. Belarus's proposal was aimed at strengthening regional security and stability, reducing the danger of renewed nuclear confrontation in Europe, assisting the disarmament process and, in particular, eliminating weapons of mass destruction.

Our policy toward Nato takes account of the fact that it remains an influential inter-state institution, capable of effectively defending its members' common interests in the security sphere. We take our relations with Nato with the utmost seriousness, doing everything we can to strengthen the mechanisms of mutual co-operation in those areas we judge necessary, useful and feasible both for us and for our partners. Co-operation is growing within the framework of the Council for Euro-Atlantic Partnership and the Partnership for Peace programme. Belarus's own partnership programme with Nato for the years 2000-2001 has been successfully fulfilled. Following September 11, the Ministry for Emergency Situations provided information on Belarusian rescue services to the Euro-Atlantic Centre for co-ordinating action in liquidating catastrophes. Belarusian units are ready, if and when required, to come to the assistance of the USA. Contacts are improving with members of parliament of Nato member-countries. Belarusian scientists are playing an active role in the Nato programme 'Science in the Interests of Peace'. A draft partnership programme between Belarus and Nato for the years 2002-2003 has been submitted to the Nato Secretariat for consideration and approval; five additional areas of co-operation have been announced.

Concentrating only on the military aspects of international security will not, however, resolve the problem. The task confronting the international community is, it seems to me, larger than that. It is essential to combat a range of new negative political, social and economic threats, of which terrorism is, without a doubt, one of the most serious.

A pre-eminent role in the resolution of this first task is destined to be played by the United Nations. This remains for us the most important priority of multilateral diplomacy. At the UN General Assembly and Millennium Summit in 2000, Belarus spoke in favour of preserving the United Nations as the unique, universal institution uniting states both large and small and directing the further development of international relations. It is by co-ordinating the activity of the world community in the political and economic sphere that it will be possible to iron out differences in the level of development of different states, and by that means to eliminate the political, social and economic grounds for the development of deformed phenomena such as terrorism. For this reason, Belarus supports the process of reform and renewal of the United Nations Organisation and its Security Council. The creation of the necessary conditions for the effective work of the United Nations is an imperative for us all. On this hinges the future not only of the UN but of the entire world community.

Belarus's policy toward Russia is organically linked with our policy toward the CIS and the Eurasian Economic Community. Belarus's support for integration in the post-Soviet space is not an attempt to spawn a new 'empire', but flows from our pragmatic evaluation of existing political and economic realities. The collapse of the USSR, the rupture of economic, scientific and human contacts between the former Soviet republics, and the forced and sometimes hasty transition to the free market led to substantial loss of economic potential. In a decade of sovereign existence, the new states have experienced an economic decline. The proportion of their economies occupied by manufacturing and high technology has shrunk, while the share occupied by raw materials production and less highly processed manufactures has increased.

The similarity between economic processes taking place in the CIS member-states determines their mutual complementarity. Slowly but surely, the significance of factors encouraging economic integration on CIS territory is increasing. Particularly striking is the emergence of preconditions for economic stabilisation and growth in several CIS countries. For this reason, Belarus speaks in favour not of abstract integration of the post-Soviet states, but of the mutual structural adaptation of the economies of the CIS member-states on a market basis, the creation of a fully-fledged free trade zone between them.

Attaining this objective will lay the basis for the transition to a higher state of economic co-operation and the creation of a common economic space conducive to adaptation to globalising processes, norms and demands. In other words, the preconditions for the smooth entry, on an equal footing, of the CIS countries into the world economic system.

I see the Republic of Belarus not only in a Euro-Atlantic context, but also in a complex global system of different but mutually interacting states and peoples.

Significant positive movement has been achieved in our relations with the Asian states. A range of priorities has been identified offering significant potential for co-operation. Political dialogue with the Asian states – first and foremost with China and India – is characterised by mutual understanding and coincidence of positions on a majority of issues in world politics and international relations, effective co-operation in international organisations and constructive contacts at parliamentary level.

The efforts of Belarus and the Asian countries toward active bilateral partnership springs to a large extent from the complementarities of our economies. Many Asian states are interested in importing Belarusian machinery, agricultural technology, electronic and consumer goods, scientific and technical products, and so on. I have an optimistic view of future relations with the countries of Asia and have no doubt that, as they become deeper and richer, these relations will serve the interests of both Belarus and our foreign partners.

History has determined that the Belarusian economy has always been oriented toward foreign markets. Therefore, Belarus's strategic goal is to become a producer of highly competitive goods and services. All our efforts are directed toward that aim. Our country's stable economic development is all the more vital in view of the need to overcome the consequences of the Chernobyl catastrophe. Chernobyl continues to cast a heavy and destructive cloud over Belarus's transition to robust development.

We understand that full integration into international markets will require the resolution of a whole complex of issues relating to the protection of ownership rights, improving corporate governance and increasing financial transparency. But we have made a good start: Belarus is already a leader among the CIS member-countries when it comes to openness in the economy. It ranks among the top ten European states as regards the share of foreign trade in gross domestic product. We are proud that the trademark 'Made in Belarus' can today be found in practically every corner of the globe.

Belarus aspires to full membership of the World Trade Organisation and is synchronising the negotiation process with internal reforms. At the same time we understand that membership offers not only advantages but also responsibilities. We are drafting a package of draft laws to remove 'white spots' as regards international standards and WTO regulations. I hope that EU member-countries will support us, for Belarus's entry into the existing European economic network is in the interest of all the states on the continent.

We consider that among the most important aims of our foreign economic activity are to increase our export potential and attract foreign investment into the Belarusian economy. Our priorities accordingly include the establishment of a favourable investment climate. We aim to create conditions of maximum openness for business, while providing it with protection against bureaucracy and crime. The Investment Code that came into force in Belarus in October 2001 strengthened the juridical position of foreign investors. The government has created a Consultative Council on Foreign Investment with the participation of representatives of a number of leading foreign firms and international organisations. Business circles work in our country independently, but we consider it appropriate to offer them assistance and government support. A national regime is provided for foreign investors, as is, in a number of instances, a privileged tax regime. For us, it is just as important to co-operate with a small firm, regardless of what it is producing, as it is with a world-famous enterprise. There is no contradiction here: I speak of the principle and of our approach.

Our priorities are clearly defined: development and support for enterprise, small and medium business, is the most important direction of state policy.

Belarus's investment policy guarantees a stable legislative framework for commercial organisations with foreign investment. Such bodies are guaranteed a five-year moratorium, from the moment of their registration, on the application of any legislation that would be unfavourable to their business activity. Long-term conditions for the leasing of land are in operation, as are tax incentives. All joint and foreign enterprises have the right to set their own prices on their products. They can use accelerated amortisation at rates of their own choosing. Other privileges are also offered. As a result, foreign investors are finding Belarus increasingly attractive.

Belarus's relations with international financial and economic organisations are not always such as would correspond to the condition of our country's economy. Nevertheless, we have sought, are seeking and will find ways of resolving the problems that arise, and of harmonising the recommendations made by such organisations with the priorities of our national economic development. The recent past has accordingly seen an intensified debate over key issues relating to our country's economic transformation and the provision of credit. Dialogue has increased between Belarus and the World Bank. The Bank's leadership evaluates positively the steps we have taken in the field of market reforms, as witness the resumption, after quite a long interval, of lending by the Bank to Belarus.

Positive results have also been achieved in relations with the IMF. The economic policy that has been made and carried out in Belarus in the past year has taken account of the Fund's recommendations. An IMF monitoring programme is being carried out successfully in Belarus. A single exchange rate has been established for the Belarusian rouble, and monetary-credit and budget-taxation policy has been tightened up. Serious strides have been made on the road to liberalisation of exchange regulation and price formation. Restrictions on foreign trade have been reduced and significant progress has been made in privatisation.

Also developing well is our co-operation with the EBRD, as is the Programme for Co-operation between Belarus and the World Intellectual Property Organisation. Belarus continues to support the work of the UN Economic Commission for Europe and takes an active part in its activity.

Of course, we still have a lot to do both to liberalise the domestic economy and to expand international trade. But, taking account of the restricted nature of our natural resources, the remorseless impact on our country of crisis phenomena in the world economy, and the rise in world energy prices, we have achieved remarkably good results.

In our foreign policy, we have succeeded in finding and maintaining a dialectical balance between our national interests and the expectations of our foreign partners, between defending our rights and taking account of the needs of other members of the international community. All states must aim to ensure that their foreign policy corresponds to the demands of the time. At the same time, the world community should understand that the greater your contribution to international stability, the greater the dividends you will receive. I am profoundly convinced that politicians must not be afraid to invest in stability, in establishing links even when these do not appear to have an immediate practical purpose, and in building a democratic civil society.

Not to export democracy, but to invest in it.

This is perhaps the essence of a pragmatic foreign policy.

Belarus and Russia: Ever Closer Allies?

Clelia Rontoyanni

Unlike its Baltic neighbours, Poland and Ukraine, Belarus has shown little inclination to associate its future with European integration. Instead, the Belarusian leadership has embarked upon a course of bilateral integration with Russia, which has been at the centre of Belarusian diplomatic efforts since the early 1990s. Economic dependence and a sense of cultural-historical affinity with Russia were crucial in prompting a Russia-centred external orientation in the first place. Belarus has subsequently been deprived of other foreign partners with the potential to assist its economic prospects and support its participation in European affairs, primarily as a result of the Lukashenko administration's unresponsiveness to American and European criticism of its heavy-handed treatment of the opposition and the non-state media. Belarus has been effectively locked into an almost exclusive reliance on Russia in economic and political terms alike.

As allies, Belarus and Russia are already very close. Indeed, Russian policy-makers value Belarus as Russia's most loyal ally. In addition, the process of bilateral integration has extensive implications for Belarusian domestic policy and occupies a central position in the country's internal politics. Economic integration requires convergence of economic conditions and legislative harmonisation, thereby limiting the Belarusian leadership's scope for social and economic policy formulation, at least in principle. At times, the conclusion of bilateral treaties with Russia has been accompanied by international speculation about the continued survival of Belarus as a separate state. This chapter addresses this question by looking at the content of integration agreements, their impact on Belarusian domestic policy and also the sources of support for different forms of integration. Finally, it considers the extent to which Belarus functions as an independent international actor, taking into account the military dimension of integration.

From Community to Union; from Union to Union state; from Union state to what?

The current institutional set-up of Belarusian-Russian relations is described as a 'Union state' following the relevant treaty signed in December 1999, the third stage after the establishment of a Belarus-Russia Community in April 1996 and of a Union a year later. There can be little doubt that such a rapid 'forward and upward' movement has had little to do with actual progress in implementing the provisions of earlier treaties. It can be viewed as a series of solemn declarations of political will spelling out the objectives that a process of integration is to strive towards. Of course, these declarations of intent have the status of international treaties and are, therefore, legally binding. It has often been argued, in the Belarusian as well as the Russian national press, that the modest (and sometimes almost non-existent) results in terms of treaty implementation testify to insufficient political will. Such criticisms take little account of the magnitude of the targets set by the spectacular progression in upgrading the legal basis of bilateral relations.

Belarusian and Russian officials acknowledge that the integration treaties have largely been inspired from those of the European Community/Union. This is most visible in the institutional structure of the Belarus-Russia Community, Union and Union state. The two countries aspire to establish a common economic space marked by the 'four freedoms' of the European single market (freedom of movement of goods, services, capital and labour), an objective contained in the treaty setting up the Belarus-Russia Community. To this end, the two countries are to form a customs union, harmonise national legislation regulating economic activity and co-ordinate policies in a multitude of policy areas, including monetary policy. According to the treaty, these objectives were to be achieved within less than two years (by the end of 1997), a highly unrealistic time-scale. The Union and Union state treaties provide for longer periods of implementation, while extending the scope of joint policy-making to new areas such as environmental protection and employment legislation. The Union State Treaty specifies the stages that are to lead to a monetary union by 2005.

The integration process, however, aims to create more than a single economic space. Foreign policy and defence have featured among the areas of policy co-ordination from the very inception of the process. Indeed, they have been perhaps the only policy areas where actual progress in meeting integration targets has preceded the formulation of further objectives. The scope of policy co-ordination has been widened to include common policies to combat terrorism, while the Union State Treaty brings border control and military procurement policies under the exclusive jurisdiction of common institutions.

The political aspect of the process is most clearly reflected in the concept of a Union (now Union state) citizenship, which was introduced in the Union treaty. It was subsequently given substance by the Treaty on the Equal Rights of Citizens which was concluded in December 1998. The treaty covered social and economic rights, namely rights of residence, equal conditions in employment and equal access to healthcare, education and other social services throughout the territory of the Union. The introduction of a Union citizenship, which was actively advanced by the Belarusian authorities and the Union Parliamentary Assembly, raised some concern in Russian political circles as well as in the ranks of the Belarusian opposition. According to the Union treaty, Union citizenship entitles one to stand for election to Union institutions. During Yeltsin's second term in office, there was widespread speculation – particularly in the Russian press – that President Lukashenko had his sights on the office of Union president.

Such fears have so far proved ungrounded, as even the Treaty on the Formation of a Union State does not provide for a directly-elected president. Instead, the so-called Union state preserves the rotating presidency of the Supreme Council, held by the presidents of the member-states for alternate terms. The Supreme Council is the highest joint decision-making body. According to the Community treaty, which initially created it, the Supreme Council 'considers and decides the most important questions regarding the development of the Community, and controls and directs the activities of its institutions regarding the implementation of (its) decisions'. It consists of the heads of state, the heads of government and the four chairs of national legislatures (both Russia and Belarus have bicameral parliaments). It operates on the principle of 'one state, one vote' and meets at least twice a year.

The Community treaty also set up two supranational bodies whose members are responsible for acting on behalf of the Community rather than their member-states: the Executive Committee and the Parliamentary Assembly. The Executive Committee was established as the permanent administration of the Community. It is a much weaker analogue of the European Commission, particularly after the conclusion of the Union State Treaty, which renamed it 'Permanent Committee' and deprived it of its most significant powers.

The authority to issue decrees and directives and propose legislation to the Union state parliament, the preparation of the Union state budget and the role of advising the Supreme Council were transferred to a new institution, the Union state's Council of Ministers. The treaty designates it as the 'executive body of the Union state'. It meets regularly, usually on a bimonthly basis. Unlike its EU counterpart, the Union state Council of Ministers is not a purely inter-governmental body. It is made up of the two countries' Prime Ministers, Foreign Ministers and Ministers of Economy and Finance, the Secretary of the Union state (a new supranational office) and also the heads of various Union state agencies. A former member of Yeltsin's Presidential administration, Pavel Borodin, was appointed as the first Secretary of the Union state.

The Parliament of the Union state, which is to replace the Union Parliamentary Assembly, is to be bicameral. The lower chamber (Chamber of Representatives) is to be formed on the model of the European Parliament, i.e. by directly elected deputies, 75 to be returned by the Russian electorate and 28 from Belarus, to take account of the different size of the two countries' populations. The Chamber of the Union, as the upper house is to be called, will consist of an equal number of deputies appointed by the national parliament of each of the two member-states. It therefore retains the formula used for the Parliamentary Assembly, as set by the Community and Union treaties.

The Union-state parliament will be stronger than the Parliamentary Assembly, whose legislative role is limited to proposing legislation to the Supreme Council and national governments. The Union-state parliament will have the power to pass legislation which, in the areas of exclusive Union state competence, will have direct applicability throughout the Union state. The decrees and directives of the Supreme State Council and of the Council of Ministers are also immediately valid without the need for enabling national legislation. The Union State Treaty delineates the areas where legislative competence is shared between Union state institutions and national governments and lists a number of policy areas of exclusive Union state jurisdiction. These include measures aimed at the creation of a unified legal and economic space, joint military procurement and issues related to regional troops (discussed later in this chapter). In the remaining areas, shared jurisdiction means that national laws will still be required to enact Union state legislative acts. The Union State Treaty, however, states that national legislation contradicting a decision of the Supreme State Council will have to be amended.

At present, treaty provisions remain impossible to enforce, as a Union state Constitutional Court (envisaged in the Union State Treaty) has not been formed yet. This delay is due to the fact that the first elections to the Union-state parliament, which is to appoint the members of the Court, have not taken place. The parliament is also to confirm the members of another new institution, the Union state Accounts Chamber, whose establishment has been postponed as well. The Russian and Belarusian parliaments have taken more than two years to adopt the relevant electoral legislation.

The ongoing debate on a Union state Constitutional Act, which is to be submitted to national referenda, may push the elections further back. The eventual ratification of a Constitutional Act will require amendments to the two member-states' constitutions. According to the Union State Treaty, it was to be the successor of the Parliamentary Assembly (the Union state Parliament) that was to draft the Constitutional Act. The Assembly has been consistently active in pressing the national administrations to step up the process of integration, widen its scope and increase the resources allocated to it. Not surprisingly, it has given precedence to the adoption of the Constitutional Act over the conduct of elections to the new Parliament, thereby contravening the provisions of the 'Programme of Action' attached to the Union State Treaty. Indeed, it has put forward its own draft Constitutional Act, one of several currently being considered by a special working group created by the two countries' administrations.

Although it is not possible to speculate as to the final content of the Constitutional Act, it is clear that, from an institutional point of view, the Union state could be compared to the European Union, but hardly to a state. The Union State Treaty states that Belarus and Russia are fully sovereign states with separate government institutions, state constitutions and international representation. Common institutions of an inter-governmental character (Supreme State Council, Council of Ministers) have a dominant role. In terms of policy formulation, Belarus and Russia have acted in a less co-ordinated manner than the treaties would suggest, particularly on economic issues. Fears that Belarus might cease to exist as a state appear exaggerated, not least because neither the Belarusian political elite nor the country's population would accept such an outcome.

Who supports integration and of what kind?

President Lukashenko has built his political reputation as an ardent promoter of integration with Russia, making it his personal task to complete a project which the previous administration had unsuccessfully tried to get off the ground. At home, the electorate seems to consider the integration process to be the policy area in which the President has been most successful in keeping the promises that brought him into office.[1] In April 2001, President Putin honoured his Belarusian counterpart with a state medal for his contribution to the unification of the 'two brotherly' nations. Especially prior to Putin's rise as the dominant figure on the Russian political scene,

Lukashenko figured among the most highly-esteemed politicians in the eyes of the Russian public.

Alexander Lukashenko has been particularly vocal, not only in his advocacy of integration with Russia and with the CIS, but also in his support for Slav-Orthodox solidarity. He condemned the Nato campaign against Yugoslavia in very harsh terms reminiscent of those used by Russian nationalist politicians. He has repeatedly urged Ukraine to join the Russia-Belarus Union and his speeches have been full of positive references to the achievements of the Soviet Union. Such public discourse has tapped into the politically powerful combination of the Belarusian electorate's notion of historical and cultural closeness to Russia (and Ukraine) and its nostalgia for the Soviet era. The referendum of May 1995 testified to the popular appeal of the President's rhetoric, as over three-quarters of the votes were cast in favour of restoring the Soviet state symbols, giving official status to the Russian language and continuing economic integration with Russia.

The conclusion of integration treaties with Russia has elicited public protests, primarily in Minsk, organised by the Belarusian Popular Front and other national-minded political forces concerned about what they see as a threat to Belarusian sovereignty. It is rather difficult to estimate the actual participation in such demonstrations, as figures given by state-controlled and opposition-leaning media tend to diverge significantly. However, extensive public opinion research conducted by reputable institutes independent of the state indicates that integration with Russia remains a popular cause in Belarus without marked differences among regions, unlike in Ukraine. Support for integration tends to be strongest among those sections of the populations that form President Lukashenko's core electorate, namely the older generation, the less educated and the residents of rural areas.[2]

Most of the Belarusian public have a positive view of the integration process, which is perceived to have a beneficial effect on the Belarusian economy. Exports to Russia and, more importantly, imports of Russian energy at subsidised prices have been instrumental to the sustainability of the Belarusian government's social and economic policies. The so-called 'Belarusian model' has been the main pillar of the Belarusian president's approval rating, as most people credit him with the regular payment of salaries and pensions, the maintenance of almost full employment and relatively satisfactory provision for the state education and health services. However, the Belarusian authorities' wish to preserve certain elements of the Soviet system (subsidies to enterprises; price and currency controls) has led them to postpone or water down the implementation of several treaty obligations relating to convergence with Russian reforms and economic conditions. Intergovernmental negotiations have often been strained as a result. During the governmental instability and uncertain policy agenda of the second Yeltsin administration, it had been the hope of the Belarusian president that Russia would come to espouse the principles of the Belarusian model. Mixed signals on economic policy given by the Primakov government (particularly Deputy Premier Maslyukov) encouraged such hopes. Under Putin, however, such a possibility has been effectively ruled out and Belarus has been faced with the choice between economic reform and the stalling of the integration process.

Most of the Belarusian public perceive Russia's influence on Belarus positively. Russia was not blamed even for the economic downturn that hit Belarus after the Russian financial crisis of August 1998.[3] However, if economic reform is introduced and is seen to be driven by Russian pressure, popular support for integration may decline. When large-scale privatisation begins, the take-over of major Belarusian enterprises by Russian big business appears highly likely. This would aggravate concerns expressed by large sections of the Belarusian public regarding the possible 'export' of what are perceived as negative aspects of the Russian system such as organised crime and asset-stripping privatisation.

For the time being, repeated surveys suggest a 'yes' vote as the most likely outcome of a referendum on the Union state, while surveys of the Russian public suggest comparably high levels of support. The Belarusian electorate's readiness to support the Union state in a referendum reflects more a general inclination towards alignment with Russia (as opposed to the West) than a preparedness to do away with Belarusian state independence. Only a small minority of around 5 per cent appears willing to accept the option of Belarus becoming part of the Russian Federation.[4] The notions of a federation or a confederation, in which Russia and Belarus would have equal standing, appeal to the majority of the Belarusian public. A large section (around 40 per cent) of the population would, however, prefer Belarus and Russia to remain separate states. The overlap between those in favour of this form of relationship and those intending to vote in favour of the Union state in a referendum suggests some confusion as to the implications of integration.

Preferred type of relations

	Nov 97	Sep 98	Mar 99	Nov 99	Nov 00
Good-neighbourly relations	34.5%	50.8%	43.2%	42.4%	40.6%
Union of two states	26.2%	28.1%	30.5%	33.4%	29.2%
Union in a single state	27.5%	20.1%	24.1%	21.8%	15.9%

Sources: Oleg Manaev, 'Na vostok ili na zapad?', *Analytical Bulletin of the Independent Institute for Socio-Economic and Political Studies (IISEPS)*, no.7, 1999, p.5; *IISEPS News*, December 2000, p.82

The Belarusian President has increasingly insisted that Belarusian sovereignty will not be negotiated, a position largely aimed at maximising the weight of Belarus in Union state institutions – particularly the common currency emission centre, which is to be set up in 2003. The Belarusian elite is intent not only on preserving all the attributes of Belarusian sovereignty, but also on reducing the influence of Union state policy-making over their control of the national economy. The privatisation of major enterprises, many of which are targeted by Russian business groups, is proving particularly unpalatable for the Lukashenko administration, partly because state ownership of large enterprises constitutes one of the pillars of the Belarusian model.

Reform-oriented opposition politicians such as Semion Domash and Anatoly Lebedko are critical of the Belarusian model and of the current course of integration with Russia, questioning the desirability of common political institutions and military integration. The economic rationale dictated by the country's reliance on its heavily export-oriented, energy-intensive industry continues to call for a Russia-first foreign policy. As in the early post-independence period, the appeal of Belarusian nationalism remains rather narrow, even among the political elite. An aspiration to distance Belarus from Russia and join the Baltic states and Poland on the path to European integration has not provided a vision for the country's future that could unite the opposition, let alone inspire the mass electorate.

In the run-up to the presidential election of September 2001, the united opposition's candidate Vladimir Goncharik campaigned on a pledge to keep Belarus on the track of integration with Russia. At the same time, reversal of the Lukashenko administration's record of stagnating relations with the West was the foremost external priority in the united opposition's programme, not least due to pragmatic considerations. Russia is not in a position to provide investment and new technologies on the scale required for the modernisation of the Belarusian economy. A foreign policy acceptable to most opposition forces would have to be more balanced than that pursued by the Lukashenko administration. It would aim at co-operative relations with the West, while preserving integration with Russia as the primary focus.

Is Belarus an independent international actor?

To the extent that Belarus has an international role, it has been primarily as Russia's closest and most reliable ally. The positions of Belarusian diplomacy on every major international issue from the Chechen conflict to Nato's eastward enlargement have been essentially identical to those of Russia. The two Foreign Ministries engage in annual joint planning and closely co-ordinate their positions on a regular basis, as laid down in the integration treaties. In international organisations in which both Russia and Belarus participate (United Nations, OSCE, CIS), their representatives take the same line.

The Russian foreign policy establishment appreciates the political loyalty of Belarus, particularly against the background of the other CIS countries' wavering responsiveness to Russian concerns. In the economic and military fields alike, Belarus has proved its reliability by providing secure and low-cost transportation routes for Russian trade with Europe (most crucial to Russian oil and gas exporters) and free access to key military installations located on its territory. The Belarusian President has contended that these contributions are invaluable to the Russian economy and security to counter arguments referring to Belarus as a net burden on Russian resources. It appears that his point has been taken, as Russian economic liberals have ceased their objections to continued support for the Belarusian economy, even as such support has increased in preparation for monetary union.

The tensions in Russia's relations with Nato that surrounded the Alliance's first round of eastward enlargement and its intervention in the Kosovo conflict added impetus to military integration between Belarus and Russia. Bilateral defence-related agreements have been proliferating since the early 1990s. Initially, they covered temporary arrangements for the withdrawal and demobilisation of troops formerly stationed in Central Europe and inter-enterprise deliveries in the military industrial sector.

In early 1995, Russia obtained the right to use two important military installations in Belarus for 25 years free of charge, essentially in exchange for a separate agreement cancelling $1.5 billion of Belarus's debt to Russia. These installations are the radio location facility in Vileyka, which serves as a major communications and control centre for the Russian navy, and the Baranovichi air-defence station, which hosts the CIS air-defence administration and, since 2000, the Volga early-warning missile station. The removal of controls on the common border later in 1995 saw the start of joint guarding of Belarusian borders with Poland, Lithuania and Latvia. A supranational Border Control Committee was set up in 1997 to organise related activities and contribute to the formulation of a Union border policy. The relevant common doctrine was adopted in 1999.

Much of the military co-operation between Belarus and Russia takes place within the framework of the CIS Collective Security Treaty, to which Belarus has been a party since 1993. Joint monitoring of CIS air space, in operation since 1996, is one example. The two countries have subsequently moved further on a bilateral basis by taking steps to form a common air-defence system. Belarus regularly participates in CIS military exercises (always in the annual air-defence exercise). Bilateral exercises have also been held at least annually since 1996 on the territories of both countries.

Since 1998, Belarusian military officers have been included in the same training programmes attended by Russian officers, which goes beyond the preferential access that Russian military academies grant to officers from member-states of the Collective Security Treaty. The two Ministries of Defence have held joint collegial sessions on a regular basis since 1998. They engage in joint planning, work on common doctrine and, since the conclusion of the Union State Treaty, decide on the structure of the combined armed forces and their procurement needs.

The Union State Treaty provides for a regional force. The creation of such a force, combining the entire Belarusian armed forces with the Moscow military district and numbering up to 300,000 troops, was announced in spring 2000 during Putin's first visit to Belarus after his election to the presidency. It was specified that the regional force would be deployed in Belarus only in the event of an immediate threat to the country's security and would not lead to the permanent stationing of Russian troops on Belarusian territory. Nevertheless, the news raised concern in Poland and the Baltic states, particularly as many Belarusian and Russian observers presented it as a direct response to Nato expansion. In practice, the regional force has essentially been confined to strategic planning and exercise policy, with troops remaining under national command structures. Arrangements for the joint use and modernisation of military facilities located in the two countries' border regions have been in place since 1998.

Russia's rapprochement with Nato appears to have made little difference to the military alliance with Belarus. In March 2002, the Russian Chief of Staff Anatoly Kvashnin argued that Nato's 'Strong Resolve 2000' exercise in Norway and Poland was evidence that the Alliance 'is preparing its forces for two simultaneous military conflicts near Russian and Belarusian borders'.[5] Russia's military leadership remains sceptical of Nato intentions and counts on Belarus as a key strategic ally.

For the Belarusian administration, the deterioration in relations with the European Union and the United States in the latter half of the 1990s prompted an increasing reliance on Russian diplomatic support and military protection. The Belarusian authorities have been very suspicious of the motives underlying Western criticism of Belarus on the grounds of non-compliance with international democratic norms. They have shown very little inclination to address Western concerns, which they have dismissed as the result of a biased approach and as a cover for unwarranted external interference in Belarusian internal affairs. Nato's air strikes on Yugoslavia during the Kosovo crisis and the subsequent downfall of Slobodan Milosevic exacerbated President Lukashenko's preoccupation with alleged CIA plots to remove him from office. Prior to his re-election in September 2001, he had been acutely concerned that the West (and the US in particular) might attempt to organise mass protests in the wake of the elections, seeking to replicate the sequence of events that toppled Milosevic.

Lukashenko's suspicion of Western intentions – he even suggested there was a serious threat of a military intervention aimed at his overthrow – reinforced the value of the military element of integration. Russia's nuclear capability came to be regarded as the most effective guarantee of Belarusian security, a view also reiterated by Lukashenko's main rival for the presidency and favourite of Belarusian officialdom, Vladimir Goncharik.[6]

At the same time, Russian political support has been instrumental to Belarusian efforts to regain international legitimacy and participation in European affairs. Russia has recognised both the parliamentary elections of autumn 2000 and the presidential election of 2001 as 'free and fair', an assessment shared by all major political forces in Russia, including the liberal Union of Rightist Forces and Yabloko. Russian diplomacy has also criticised Western governments and international organisations for applying double standards in refusing to recognise the legitimacy of Belarusian elections. Russian officials have been very reluctant to discuss Belarusian domestic issues in their contacts with the European Union and its member-states, urging them to engage directly with Belarus.

To Europe via Moscow?

The process of integration with Russia has not in itself been the cause of the international isolation of Belarus, although it has contributed to the country's low visibility on the European stage. Neither have European institutions (the European Union and the Council of Europe in particular) ostracised Belarus for its pro-Russian orientation, nor Russia pushed Belarus to limit its ties with the West. Russia itself is keen to develop its economic interaction and political dialogue with Western states and organisations (including Nato and the European Union), which are already so extensive as not to allow for any comparison with Belarus. As a result, Belarus, which Russia sees as the gateway of choice for its trade with Europe, has, somewhat paradoxically, come to consider its eastern neighbour as its political bridge to Europe. Russia's continued willingness and actual ability successfully to advocate Belarus's return to international legitimacy cannot be taken for granted if the Belarusian leadership remains intransigent in resisting political liberalisation in the face of international criticism.

Belarusian policy-makers by and large appreciate the need for an improvement in the country's relations with the West and for the development of economic co-operation in particular. However they do not see the path of European integration as a credible alternative to the current Russia-oriented course, at least in the medium term. The queue to join the EU appears too long, the reforms required too daunting, and the immediate economic rewards unlikely to substitute for Russian support. A long-term strategy of integration with Europe together with Russia, as suggested by Belarusian Foreign Ministry planners and moderate opposition politicians, may be a more promising option, and would also be in line with the preferences of the Belarusian public.

The Putin administration's efforts to come closer to European norms (particularly in the economic sphere) and develop a solid political partnership with the West give the Russia-Belarus Union a new perspective. It is up to the Belarusian leadership to find the resolve to reform the country's economy and over-centralised political system so that integration with Russia can move forward and Belarus can follow Russia's path in drawing closer to Europe.

Notes

Research for this paper was conducted with the support of the UK Economic and Social Research Council, award Nos R 00429834663, T 026271003.

[1] US State Department Office of Research, *Opinion Analysis*, M-162-00, 13 September 2000, p.4

[2] Oleg Manaev, 'Na Vostok ili na Zapad? Sotsiologichesky Portret Protivnikov i Storonnikov Nezavisimosti Belarusi', *Novosti NISEPI*, December 1999, pp.3-9

[3] Most Belarusians blame the government for their country's economic situation. 'Novak' Sociological Institute, *Belarus and the World*, Minsk, March 2000

[4] Ibid.; *Zerkalo Sociological Bulletin* (Belapan News Agency), no.40, December 2001

[5] AVN Military News Agency via *BBC Monitoring*, 4 March 2002

[6] Interview in *The Viewer* (Belapan News Agency), no.32, 8-14 August 2001, p.6

A Friend in Need... or a Friend in Need? Russia and the Belarusian Economy

Anastasia Nesvetailova

The way they were: why Belarus was happy in the USSR

Of the fifteen members of the former Soviet Union, Belarus is probably the only republic that had no revolutionary ambitions for independence from Russia. The need to re-discover Belarusian national identity and sovereignty did not come from within civil society (as, for example, in the Baltic states), but was largely imposed on the country at the meeting in the Belovezhskaya woods in 1991. More than a decade on, the Belarusian national idea is still weak: national self-identification is far from being a primary concern for most people; even at the state level, governmental self-determination is indecisive and shaky.

As visitors to Belarus unanimously observe, today the country resembles a living museum of Communism: Lenin's statues are still standing, three central streets in Minsk bear the names of Marx, Engels and Lenin, and newly-weds lay flowers at World War II monuments. In Minsk you won't see the negative symptoms of savage capitalism that have spread through Moscow or St Petersburg. The city is tidy, orderly and elegant in its dignity. But communism proved to be long-lived not only on the streets and in the life-style; crucially, it penetrated deep into people's psychology and sentiments. The mentality of Belarusians remains fundamentally soviet. Ideologically and emotionally, the majority of Belarusians continue to live in the USSR. It is this sovietism of the public mood that is the main reason for identifying Belarus with Russia.

For more than one reason, it is more appealing to Belarusians to look back at Soviet times rather than inquire into the future of their young independent country. Its favourable demographic mix, lack of natural resources and geopolitical position pre-determined Belarus's role as a scientific outpost for the rest of the USSR. The republic was renowned for its high-quality research institutions and specialists. Also, particularly in the late Soviet years, most of the enterprises underwent significant modernisation, were re-equipped and oriented towards the production of competitive consumer goods. The stable socio-political and economic climate and prospects of secure retirement attracted labour from other Soviet republics. On the whole, Belarus was a very happy member of the Soviet Union.

Maybe this is why, more than a decade after the USSR collapsed, Belarusians still tend to view their big eastern neighbour as the USSR, not a new Russia. In Belarus, the Russian Federation is still widely perceived as a giant power rich in natural resources, military potential and international weight; her problems of economic crisis, ethnic and social conflict did not seem to affect Belarusians' longing for closer re-integration with Russia.

Due to Belarus's position within the USSR and its close yet subordinate ties with the top echelons of its ruling Communist Party, there has always been a patriarchal aspect to the centre-periphery relationship between Minsk and Moscow. From the communist system, the nomenklatura and technocrats inherited not only their connections and power, but also their methods of rule. As it turned out, these methods appeared perfectly compatible with market economy principles. But rather than destroying the old politico-economic structures, Communist elites have played a decisive role in transforming them into a new economy.

After the collapse of the USSR in 1991, the Belarusian government elite, heavily influenced by Russia's politico-economic groups, actively used the momentum to construct an *apparatus market*, combining the traditional soviet-style command system of governance and state ownership with new market opportunities for the upper layer of the bureaucracy. In doing this, the authorities in post-Soviet Belarus, rather than promoting the development of national industrial, financial or banking systems, were by and large reflecting the interests of Russian capital.

As a result, today Belarus has what the World Bank has called a 'non-competitive political regime'. Typically in such systems, leaders from the Soviet era tend to pursue economic stability while securing their dominance of the post-Soviet political system. They feared the opening to global market forces and the rise of oligarchs in partially reformed economies. Instead, they preferred to maintain continuity with key elements of the previous command system to maintain the state's predominant role and to avoid many painful adjustment costs associated with reform. By maintaining the dominant role of the state in the economy and considerable discretionary capacity to intervene in economic affairs, leaders like Lukashenko ensure their positions remain powerful. Trade unions, business associations and other civil society groups that might represent broader social interests are either circumscribed or tied to the state. The extent of economic reform is thus highly dependent on the political leader's preferences.

It is interesting to note that in other regions, many authoritarian leaders did adopt comprehensive economic reforms; this has not yet happened in any of the post-socialist economies. Why? According to World Bank experts, authoritarian leaders in the region have tended to inherit power and support from the surviving structures of the former communist system. This has created a strong link between authoritarian political power and command administrative methods in the economic sphere.[1]

Real Existing Socialism revisited? The new Belarusian 'miracle'

Could such a system work for Belarus? At first sight, it seems that it could. In 1996, after a five-year decline, Belarus registered a 2.8 per cent growth in GDP. That year was the start of the Belarusian 'economic miracle' of 1996-2000. During those four years, GDP grew by 35 per cent, industrial production by 65 per cent. Yet, with annual GDP growth around 6.3 per cent, prices were increasing by 116 per cent per year. No other transition country has registered such high growth rates with high inflation.[2] Belarus's relatively favourable growth stands in stark contrast to its extremely poor record on macro-economic stabilisation, structural reform and living standards. The EBRD ranks Belarus 25th out of the 26 transition economies in overall progress in economic reform.

The secret of Belarus's miraculous performance has been her close links with Russia; specifically, supplies of Russian oil, gas and energy. Using these crucial components to keep the economy subsidised and the infrastructure running, Belarus not infrequently 'forgot' to pay for them. The accumulated payment arrears were later settled through barter transactions that artificially maintained demand for Belarusian exports – another important form of indirect subsidy from Russia.

Country	Real GDP in 2000 (1990 = 100) per cent	Average inflation (CPI), 1991-2000 per cent	EBRD transition rating, 1999	Government revenue to GDP, 1999 per cent
CSBaverage	*106*	*41*	*3.1*	*39*
Czech Rep	99	13	3.5	41
Hungary	109	20	3.7	42
Lithuania	68	88	3.2	32
Poland	147	26	3.5	43
Romania	83	102	2.8	32
CIS average	*62*	*185*	*2.3*	*24*
Belarus	89	344	1.6	42
Georgia	30	257	2.9	16
Kazakhstan	65	163	2.7	19
Russia	66	163	2.5	34
Ukraine	43	244	2.5	35
Uzbekistan	97	182	2.0	32

Source: World Bank 2002.

The availability of cheap and often free energy inputs produced a paradoxical result. Despite its poor reform record, Belarus is still considered to be one of the most successful examples of post-Soviet development. The new Belarusian wealth may not be as bold as it is in, for instance, the Baltic States or Russia. But analysing its progress to a new capitalist way of living, it is necessary to remember that capitalism does not only include the availability of an extensive range of consumer products and services. Living standards also cover access to education and health care, guaranteed employment and retirement, security and crime prevention. Apparently, authoritarian Belarus has been coping a lot better with guaranteeing these values than corrupt, crisis-stricken and war-torn Russia.

Indeed, when compared with the partial and poorly implemented reforms in many CIS countries, Belarus's inaction did enable it to avoid some key mistakes in the early stages of transition. While continued state ownership did little to promote competitiveness or strategic decision-making at the enterprise level, it did deter the large-scale asset stripping and tax evasion that has damaged growth in the early stages of transition in some other CIS countries.

Moreover, the capacity of the Belarusian state to maintain high levels of tax collection (see table opposite) highlights the importance of these taxes in smoothing the initial output decline. The strength of fiscal revenues has boosted the scope for supporting declining sectors and socially-oriented expenditures. Though it may be tempting to explain this fiscal performance as a product of the authoritarian state, a similar political regime has not guaranteed similar outcomes in Turkmenistan or Uzbekistan.

Together Forever? The Russia-Belarusian Union

In December 1999, nine years to the day after the Soviet Union was dismembered in the Belovezhskaya woods, the then Russian President Yeltsin and the Belarus leader Lukashenko signed a treaty that established a 'Union state' between Russia and Belarus. To this day, most of the clauses of the treaty, as well as its actual constitutional status, remain evasive, unclear and amorphous. The joint economic projects and programmes that are financed out of the Union's budget rarely touch upon people's everyday life, making the viability and, indeed, political legitimacy of the Union a contentious issue. Furthermore, its credibility and progress in integration have clearly been affected by changes in the Russian political arena.

While 70 per cent of Russians support the idea of a Russo-Belarusian Union, it is easy to understand why, in the era of an impaired Yeltsin, Lukashenko, the man of 'stability and order', appealed to many Russians and Belarusians as a potential leader for the new inter-state formation. However, Yeltsin's retreat from the political scene and the March 2000 presidential election in Russia changed these beliefs drastically.

Even before his elevation to the Kremlin, Vladimir Putin emphasised that the integration process, if any, should proceed in a way that would benefit Russia. Unlike Yeltsin, Putin does not bear any guilt for breaking up the

Soviet empire and exacerbating its repercussions. He easily gained great popularity with the Russian electorate without playing with the slogans of 're-uniting fraternal nations' and 're-establishing historical bonds'. Putin's first actions after taking office were to reform Russia's federal governance and strengthen the country's territorial and political integrity and national idea. The early years of his presidency turned out to be a fortunate time for Russia's economic recovery: oil exports shot up and the country replenished its hard currency reserves. With a strong leader in charge of a strong (at least compared to Belarus) economy, it is clear that Russo-Belarusian integration, if any, will proceed according to Russia's preferences.

Despite the much-emphasised historical bonds, Russia's sudden rebirth seems to have irritated Belarus's leadership. Disagreements about the constitutional status of the Union remain painful. Lukashenko is convinced that the governing bodies of the Union should be supranational in status, and not inter-governmental. For Belarus, supranational governing bodies would be a guarantee of its sovereign status; the two countries would at least formally have equal weight in decision-making. Putin, however, would never grant Belarus special independent status under such a confederation, since inevitably other Russian regions such as Bashkiria or Tatarstan would demand equal treatment. Lukashenko in turn, having lost the opportunity to take a leading role on the Russian political stage, would not wish to give up Belarus's sovereignty and the presidency by accepting for Belarus the status of a region within the Russian Federation.

With disagreements about the constitutional rights of the Union so painful, it is easy to see why in November 2000, after his meeting with Lukashenko, Putin firmly stated that Russo-Belarusian integration could only proceed as an economic union; any form of political unification was not even an issue. In the economic sphere, integration is supposed to reach its peak in 2005, when the Russian rouble becomes the common currency for the two countries.

In order to facilitate monetary integration, Moscow provided Belarus with a $200 million loan. This is a very big sum for Belarus; if used properly, it could really help solve the problems of inflation, the budget deficit, dollarisation and the shadow economy. It seems that Russia is anxious to help Belarus achieve a sustainable macro-economic stability and economic growth. But things are not as simple as they seem at first. The money came with strings attached. Belarus must reform its financial system and monetary policy, reduce its budget deficit and inflation rate, and, importantly, stabilise the economy. By January 2005 Belarus is expected to improve the credibility of its domestic currency; adjust its foreign exchange reserves to their Russian equivalents; and revise its foreign currency market mechanisms. Under pressure from Putin, Belarus is also obliged to tailor its tax and customs laws to Russian standards, and, crucially, open the way to the sell-off and privatisation of Belarus's plants and factories.

It is ironic that for Belarus, which has been isolated from international credit resources, Russia is performing the role of a harsh IMF watchdog. There are at least two reasons why Russia found itself involved in settling Belarus's problems. The first is the danger of a non-payment crisis in a country that provides a transit route for Russian gas, electricity and oil to the West. Today non-payments and arrears are rapidly becoming the main problem in Belarus. The year 2001 confirmed a dangerous tendency: a growth in payment arrears and indebtedness corresponding to the slowdown in GDP growth. In November 2001 domestic arrears of enterprises amounted to 2.7 billion Belarusian roubles, which is higher than the aggregate money supply. Belarus may be repeating Russia's financial history pre-1998, and Russia knows all too well the damaging repercussions of a default.

Secondly, and much more worrying for the critics of the Union, there is a strong likelihood that through the integration process Russia may actually demand repayment of Belarus's debt. In principle, this is normal: if you borrow or purchase something, you have to pay for it at some point. But Belarus is not used to playing by these rules; and besides, the country is insolvent. It does not have enough hard currency reserves, and its exports are already employed in settling prior debts to Russia. Therefore, as in a normal case of bankruptcy or acquisition, Russia may simply demand that debts be settled through a transfer of ownership of Belarusian businesses.

Not that Belarus has a lot of offer: 4000 enterprises are loss-making. Effectively, every third economic agent is working for a negative return. But the country has a 'hard artillery' weapon: manufacturing. Unlike the agricultural and construction sectors, Belarusian industry has been able to survive not due to cheap credits and concessions from the state, but due to its ability to realise its potential. So in the immediate future economic growth will depend not on the recovery of the 4000 bankrupt factories but on whether the directors of the few profitable firms are able to sustain the competitiveness of their products.

Around the time of the 2001 presidential election, Lukashenko several times promised that he would finally embark on economic reform. Yet there are no signs of the abolition of concessions to industry and agriculture; even external trade barriers are not likely to be eliminated. After the 2001 election, real wages went down by 11.5 per cent. Wage arrears, previously close to nil, went up by 13 per cent. Overall, workers' real incomes fell by 25 per cent. Even the President was forced to admit that the 'evolutionary' model of development had exhausted itself. There are strong reasons to believe that the fall in income levels will continue in 2002. The situation is aggravated by Russia's demands that Belarus pay for gas and electricity in cash.

It is a striking fact that during the 2001 election, 75 per cent of Belarusian entrepreneurs voted for Lukashenko. This means that those in business and the bureaucracy close to the nomeklatura are keen to preserve the status quo in Belarus and will resist any radical market-oriented measures. This kind of vertical, state-centred organisation of capitalism is typical of most post-Soviet countries. In line with the patriarchal practices of communist times, big Russian capital favours a monopolised, state-controlled economic model in formally independent Belarus. Formal political sovereignty has not prevented large Russian financial-industrial groups from dictating their preferences to Belarus. One of the most vivid examples of this is the experience of the Ford car factory erected near Minsk in 1995-96. Despite the tangible benefits to the economy of the direct foreign investment and new employment opportunities, Minsk was forced to shut the venture down in 1997. The pressure came from Russia, which was concerned that Ford-Belarus products would undermine the competitiveness of Russian-made cars.

With Belarus's economic troubles deepening, the possibility of a wholesale purchase of the Belarusian economy by Russian tycoons is becoming more and more plausible. In Russia, Putin's re-distribution of property is almost completed. The oligarchs are keen to spread their interests to other countries, and Belarus is an easy target on their shopping lists. Large-scale privatisation of Belarusian enterprises has hardly begun, the local private sector is weak, and the chances of grabbing large chunks are very high. Moreover, the price of Belarusian assets can only go down in the future. 80 per cent of Belarus's capital funds are exhausted, according to some Russian experts. In 2-3 years Russian capital will be able to acquire the whole of the Belarusian industry and infrastructure virtually free.

Rumour has it that most of the successful Belarusian enterprises, predominantly in the food and textile sectors, are already half or totally owned by Russians. In the oil business, too, there are signs of all-too-keen Russian investment. According to the journal 'Russia's oil', *Lukoil,* the Russia oil giant, intends to process oil in Belarus in order to supply oil products to its retail chains in Central and Eastern Europe. *Lukoil's* participation in the sell-off of Belarusian oil refineries such as *Polimir, Khimvolokno, Naftan* and *Azot* seems to be an attractive option for Belarus. Russian money would help the enterprises modernise their factories, restore their competitiveness, and claim around half of the profits, while the Belarusian state would retain the right to re-nationalise the venture if anything went wrong. At it turns out however, *Naftan* has almost completed its modernisation using its own resources, and *Polimir* is considered an appealing target for Western companies who have an eye on it. Half of its products are exported to CIS countries or further afield.

Everything seems to confirm the fears of the Belarusian opposition. They insist that Belarus can only be independent if there is some counterweight to Russia's involvement in the form of Western investment, first of all from the EU.

O Brother, where art thou?

Does Belarus have a choice? Theoretically, maybe. To begin with, Belarusian sceptics doubt the whole assumption that the economic union with Russia will help Belarus increase her international competitiveness. In Belarus today more than 70 per cent of consumer goods are produced using domestic inputs, which gives tangible support to domestic industries. In contrast, the Russian economy (apart from the raw materials sector) is essentially import-oriented. Moreover, Russia has begun reforming its energy and communal services sectors and by 2003-2004 will have ceased subsidising communal and transport payments. Putin's government has been remarkably successful in making people pay. Under the reform programme, Russian households now cough up 60 per cent of their running costs. By 2003, local authorities must collect the whole amount, some $40 a month for a typical household. In 2002, Russian tariffs will go up. Energy tariffs will increase by 28 per cent, and gas tariffs by 20 per cent. Naturally, for Belarusian consumers these prices cannot fail to go up. But in Belarus, communal services are still subsidised by the state, and $40 is an average household *monthly income.* While Belarus's major reason for seeking integration with Russia was to get gas and oil at (lower) Russian domestic prices, with tariffs now approaching the world level, the whole idea of lower prices for Belarus may come to nothing.

There are further doubts about the prospects of merging with the Russian economy, so evidently obsolete in R&D terms. Russia's technological potential is decades behind the world level, and she does not have the billions of dollars necessary for an autonomous IT breakthrough.[3] Despite the recent economic recovery, in the medium run things still look pretty bleak for Russia. Around 40 per cent of Russian businesses are loss-making, even after the two best years in the country's economic history. Imports are shooting up, exports (raw materials aside) are still pitifully low. Most factories are direly managed. Their machinery is on average 16 years old, roughly three times the figure in the West. In these circumstances, critics argue, the only strategically sensible option for Belarus would be to join the rest of the Eastern European camp in 'screwdriver production', working for and under the rule of the big multinationals.

Realistically though, Belarus is not in a position to be too fussy, or even to bargain. First, the ambitions of Russian capital in Belarus are well justified. Partly because of its inability and unwillingness to undergo fundamental structural reforms, partly due to the inadequacies of its authoritarian political regime and its resulting isolation from international credit facilities, Belarus is hooked on the Russian economy. Russia supplies Belarus with 100 per cent of its oil and gas, 80 per cent of its energy resources, 80 per cent of its coal and 86 per cent of its crude metals. Russia is also the main market for Belarusian exports, most of the profits from which are skimmed off by the countries' elites under the shield of the customs union.

The Belarusian economy is impoverished; as its condition deteriorates, even top officials and directors are beginning to confront the President and his policy line. Alexander Vaitovitch, chairman of the upper house of parliament, has bluntly criticised Lukashenko for rule by decree. A senior member of parliament, Vasil Khrol, has blamed Lukashenko for breaking his election promise to reform the economy: 'We have wasted ...months already...' On 29 January 2002 the chairman of the government's securities outfit, Valentin Shukhno, complained about the backwardness of the country's state-controlled currency and securities exchange. Two directors of Belarus's most successful factories refused to support Lukashenko in the election campaign, but at a price: both are now in gaol.

Second, probably even the most romantic Belarusian nationalists are not so naïve as to believe that Belarus has any chance of joining the EU. With the 15 EU states still fighting about the accession of such successful countries as Hungary, Estonia and the Czech Republic, there is no way a country like Belarus can get into the EU market. As the Belarusian Ministry of Foreign Affairs has admitted, although in the short term Belarusian exports might benefit from the side-effects of industrial reform in the new Central European member-states, in the long term 'it is difficult to imagine a [Belarusian] presence on the EU market without a reconstruction of production and an improvement in the quality of [Belarusian] products.[4] At the same time, MFA officials like to believe that due to its geopolitical position at the Eurasian crossroads, Belarus is destined for prosperity: 'By 2020, 50-67 per cent of West European gas consumption will come from Russia through Belarus.'

It is true that Belarus's geopolitical position has always been its key asset: the *Yamal-Europe* pipeline transports Russian gas into Europe through

Belarus. With Nato enlargement, Belarus is also Russia's buffer from the West. But the transit of Russian oil and gas is not an exclusive prerogative of Belarus. As the world economy becomes more global in scope, both Russia and the EU countries are aiming to diversify their trade linkages. The *Yamal-Europe* pipeline is not the only route for Russian gas. For example, on 24 April 2001 *Gazprom* signed a co-operation agreement with the German *Ruhrgas* and *Winterstall* and the Finnish *Fortum.* The document is a techno-economic scheme for a new gas pipeline that would link Russia and Germany and go on the Baltic seabed. The pipeline has the potential to become a trans-European network, which would give Russia access to European financial resources.

So there is not much choice for Belarus. Russia is clearly in a much stronger position to negotiate the terms of economic union; and there is reason to believe that Putin has the ability to reinforce economic growth in Russia. A strong Russia may either give up on Belarus and stop subsidising its neighbour, or adopt an even harsher stance in demanding the repayment of debts and reform of the economy. Given Putin's political skills, he will most probably opt for the latter, eventually subjecting Belarus to Russia's political and economic interests.

What about Belarus? Can it revoke the Union agreements? Given the unpredictability of the Belarusian leader, it may well be that when Russian demands get really tough, Lukashenko might decide that it would be better for Belarus not to adopt the Russian rouble and instead change the vector of its foreign policy towards the West. The West, however, may not be particularly happy, ready or indeed credulous enough to extend a helping hand to the suspicious leader. Belarus is poor, it does not have many friends, and if it wants to keep things going, it will have to listen and do what Russia says. At the end of the day, if their lives finally change for the better, the majority of Belarusians will not care much whether the improvement was directed from Moscow or from Minsk. And it is the lives of real people that ultimately matter.

Literature and Sources

'Cracks in the concrete', *The Economist,* 2 February 2002.

'Pay up, please', *The Economist* 26 January 2002.

'Russia's Reforms', *The Economist* December 1 2001.

'Vozmozhnye posledstvija dlja Belarusi rasshirenija Evropeiskogo Soyza', 1999, *Vestnik MID,* no. 3, pp. 54-62.

Chybrik, A., 2001, 'Ekonomika Belarusi: statistichenskii obzor', *Ekovest/Ecowest,* 1:2.

Kobrikov, B., 1999 'Pomozhet li nam Rossija vyiti na dorogy civilizovannogo razvitija?' *Narodnaja Volja,* 27 October.

Kyrochkin, D., 2001, 'Evropeiskaja intergracija: vozmozhnosti dlja Belarusi', *Ekovest/Ecowest,* 1:2.

Makalovitch, I., 2001, 'Naftan i Polimir, na vyhod', *Narodnaja Volja* 16 December.

Manenok, T., 2002, ' Horosh na bymage', *Belorusskii Rynok,* 1/2002.

Nesvetailova, A., 2001, 'Russia and Belarus: the Quest for the Union, or Who Will Pay for Belarus's Way to Recovery?' in E. Korosteleva et al, *Belarus: the Forgotten Heart of Europe,* London: Curzon Press.

Tomashevskaja. O., and Mahovskii, A. 2002, Soyznyi Extrim, *Belorusskaja Delovja Gazeta,* 9 January.

Transition – The First Ten Years: Analysis and Lessons for Eastern Europe and the Former Soviet Union, 2002, Washington: The World Bank.

V Obmen na prjanik, 2002, *Belorusskaja Gazeta,* 14 January.

Zlotnikov, L., 2002, Aleet Vostok, *Belorusskii Rynok,* 1/2002, 8 January.

Notes

[1] *Transition – The First Ten Years: Analysis and Lessons for Eastern Europe and the Former Soviet Union,* 2002, Washington: The World Bank, pp. 46-48.

[2] Chybrik, A., 2001, 'Ekonomika Belarusi: statistichenskii obzor', *Ekovest/Ecowest,* 1:2.

[3] B. Kobrikov (1999) 'Pomozhet li nam Rossija vyiti na dorogy civilizovannogo razvitija?' *Narodnaja Volja,* 27 October.

[4] Vozmozhnye posledstvija dlja Belarusi rasshirenija Evropeiskogo Soyza, 1999, *Vestnik MID,* no. 3, pp. 54-62.

Geopolitics and Security: Belarusian-Russian Military Co-operation 1991-2002

Steven Main

Introduction

As shown in other chapters in this book, there have been a number of stages in cementing and intensifying the political and economic relationship between Belarus and Russia since the collapse of the USSR in August 1991. Within a wider European foreign and security context, however, one of the most important aspects of the relationship between Russia and Belarus has been and continues to be the military aspect; it is in this area that the success of the move towards union has been most striking. In many respects, the relationship between the two states is strongest when one examines the level of military co-operation nurtured and strengthened over the past decade.[1] In contrast to the political and economic 'unifying' process, neither the Russian nor the Belarusian military seem to have had many problems in agreeing on a common set of objectives or in mapping out the way ahead for the development of the military relationship between the two states. However, despite past success, there is a possibility that things may change as Russia re-adjusts its attitude towards the US following the terrorist attacks of September 11, 2001.

Given the events of September 11, the drive behind the growing unification process between the two military establishments may alter, especially if Russia continues to speak in harmony with the USA in the fight against 'international terrorism'. After all, if Nato continues to expand eastward (and following the November 2002 summit in Prague this seems extremely likely), with no obvious negative reaction from Moscow, the military tie-in with Belarus will still be important to Russia (at least on a regional basis) within a wider European context, though its importance to Russia could be reduced, especially if Russia is seen to acquiesce in Nato's further drive east. September 11 did not rob nation-states of their right to determine their own national, state interests, but it did encourage them to think on a different level: after all, the world's most powerful state had been attacked at its very heart by a determined, well-organised group of men, not a nation-state. Thus, the further deepening of the Russian-Belarusian military relationship may begin to bottom out as Moscow re-examines its security picture at the local, regional and global level. September 11 may force Russia into a position where, in the light of the 'international terrorist threat', it will not complain too bitterly if Nato expands into the Baltic Sea region, for instance, in a further attempt to keep the Americans 'on-side'. Russia may concede the argument that, given the evolving security picture around its borders, Nato's expansion eastwards is, in the overall scheme of things, one of Moscow's least important security problems. If November 2002 does see invitations being sent to one, two or all three of the Baltic states to join Nato, for example, with Nato's increasing presence close to Russia's borders, where would the benefit of greater military co-operation between Russia and Belarus then lie? The military tie-in between the two countries would not have achieved one of its aims: preventing the further expansion of Nato in Eastern Europe. It did not prevent the first wave of Nato expansion in mid-1999 and there is no possibility of it preventing a second wave of Nato expansion should one take place in 2002. But this would be only a surface interpretation of events: after all, the whole process, as will be detailed below, began long before Nato expanded into Central and Eastern Europe countries and, as Nato would appear set to expand still further, the military relationship between the two countries has still not been blown off course. In short, while the security picture for the two countries has changed since 1991 – Russia has been involved in two long and bloody wars in the south – and while there is a possibility that the military alliance between the two countries will still fall short of full military union, it is still a relationship from which both countries benefit. Although co-operation between the two armies (especially in relation to anti-aircraft defence) will be very important, the two parts will remain distinct entities. For the time being at least, for instance, there will be no single, unified Russian-Belarusian Army.

Belarusian-Russian military co-operation 1991-1998

According to the official web-page of the Belarusian Ministry of Defence:

> 'At present [2000], 30 agreements have been signed between the Republic of Belarus and the Russian Federation on various areas of military- and military-technical co-operation. The co-operation between the military departments of the Republic of Belarus and Russia covers the whole spectrum of military matters, is active in nature and is based on the principles of equality and mutual advantage. Greatest success has been achieved within the framework of creating a unified system of regional security.'[2]

It is in the military sphere, first and foremost, that both Belarus and Russia have proved themselves to be keenest in forging ever closer links between their respective states. Both economically and politically, Russia has reservations, to put it mildly, in forging the sort of links wanted by President Lukashenko; but, as evidenced by the number of agreements signed and actively fulfilled by both countries, in the military area the picture is very different. This is due to a number of a factors, some of which are related to the geographical position of Belarus in Europe and others to its continuing military significance, not only in the defence of Russia's western regions (particularly Kaliningrad oblast), but also in maintaining two very important Russian military strategic sites, one at Gantsevichi (home to the 'Volga' early warning missile detection site, able to detect the launch of any missile in Europe) and the nuclear submarine command and control centre at Vileyka. The Russians themselves do not underplay the geostrategic and military significance of Belarus to Russia: in a set of theses published by the influential Council on Foreign and Defence Policy back in October 1999 it was stated:

> 'As a result of full integration with Belarus, Russia will acquire a number of incontestable geopolitical privileges: direct access to the borders of the Central European region [in addition to Russia, Belarus borders Poland, Ukraine, Latvia and Lithuania]; removal of the potential threat of the so-called Baltic-Black Sea belt isolating Russia; strengthening of Russia's position with states,

> blocs, and allies, first of all in Europe; increasing the military resources of the state in conventional forces due to integration with the Belarusian Army; development of new perspectives for manoeuvre in the framework of the CFE Treaty; elimination of the military strategic isolation of the Kaliningrad special defence region.'[3]

Following the collapse of the USSR in August 1991, the two countries established formal diplomatic relations on 26 June 1992. Less than a month later (two months after the formal re-creation of the Russian Armed Forces and four months after the formal re-creation of the Armed Forces of the Republic of Belarus), Belarus and Russia signed a package of 24 agreements, consisting of 19 economic accords and 5 military agreements, on 20 July 1992. The five military agreements were concerned with the countries' strategic forces, as well as the technical and material maintenance of both sets of forces, officer training, etc.[4] It should not be forgotten that Belarus had inherited a lot of equipment and personnel from the Soviet Union. The republic had been one of the USSR's old Military Districts (MD), the Belorusian MD, part of the USSR's first echelon in the event of a military invasion of the USSR. Thus, it was staffed by some of the best units and best kit available to the Soviet Armed Forces. On the collapse of the USSR, Belarus inherited, along with 250,000 military personnel, 72 intercontinental ballistic missiles, a weapons system which the country was more than keen to get rid off.[5] By international agreement, all the country's nuclear weapons were removed to Russia by November 1996. On occasion, Lukashenko has expressed a degree of doubt about the sense of Belarus getting rid of its nuclear weapons so readily and one can still hear the occasional dark mutterings emanating from Minsk or Moscow about the potential re-deployment of nuclear weapons to the territory of Belarus in the light of continued Nato expansion eastwards. But such speculation is quickly denounced and quietly forgotten – until the next time Lukashenko wishes to indulge in unnecessary scare-mongering.[6]

Six months of intense debate followed in the Belarusian parliament, the initial package of agreements between the two states being ratified on 4 February 1993. For its part, the Russian duma ratified all 5 military agreements on 27 April 1993. Commenting on the basic provisions of the Russian-Belarusian agreements, the then Russian Deputy Defence Minister, General Gromov, noted that the package created a new basis for bilateral military relations 'in the interests of both states [...] for military security, specific features of the structure of their armed forces during the period of transition and their ties in the military sphere.'

There can be little doubt that, though the military burden of the FSU was great, and though there was talk about the need to create a 'common defence space' incorporating the whole of the CIS, little of practical importance was actually done to achieve this in the initial few years. By the beginning of 1994, the division of the Armed Forces of the USSR had been finally completed and the military might of a super-power had been unevenly divided into 12 parts, with not one of the inheriting states able, rationally or economically, to manage its inheritance adequately. As it was for Russia, so it was for Belarus: military reform quickly followed in an attempt to bring the economic burden down to a manageable level whilst, at the same time, reaching levels of equipment and men that the state could maintain to meet the realistic threat, both internal and external, to the nation's security. In general, for all the FSU states, this has been one of the hardest problems to tackle during the transition period and in many respects is still being dealt with. Thus, Russian-Belarusian military co-operation also grew partly out of a need to assist each another to cope with the defence legacy of the FSU. As nations which had shared much in the past, both good and bad, they had a commonality of interest born through history, language and culture which meant that the two sides were pre-disposed towards each other. The collapse of the USSR had been a wrench to many on both sides of the border, as well as being a potential security headache for both countries unless steps were taken quickly to plug the hole in the nation's defences. The loss of many important Soviet military bases in the Baltic republics, and especially the radar missile tracking station at Skrunde in Latvia, meant that Russia needed to plug the holes in its security fence. Both the political and the military leadership in Moscow realised this very quickly, and the natural choice for a potential military ally was Belarus. Genuinely concerned by the unfolding security situation amongst its neighbours – Poland, Latvia and Lithuania were/are all striving to join the 'aggressive' Nato military alliance – Minsk was more than happy to respond positively to Moscow's overtures.

Following the break-up of the USSR, perceptions of the nature of the military threat facing each country were very different: while Minsk still saw the main danger as emanating from the west, Kazakhstan saw the main threat as emanating from China, and Armenia as emanating from the south. Even now, as pointed out recently by one Russian scholar, only Russia and Belarus are, publicly at least, still alarmed at the prospect of future Nato expansion in Europe: 'The majority of the members of the CIS…are quite indifferent'.[7] The threat of Nato expansion was a reason for the growing military rapprochement between the two states, although it should be emphasised that the Community of the two states created in April 1996 was not designed to be an exclusive 'club' simply for Belarus and Russia. Their growing 'togetherness' in the military sphere was predicated on sharing a joint perception of the military threat to stability and security in the region as a whole. The military inheritance of the USSR was not simply in the number of military personnel, or the number of ICBMs, planes, tanks, etc. left in the MDs, but also included a question of mind, an overall strategic outlook, a view of the world that was either suspicious of the West and/or distinctly hostile to Nato. Of course, in some respects that attitude has changed as both Russia and Belarus themselves have changed in the course of events over the past decade. But initially their main inclination on security matters was to distrust any overtures being made by the West, especially in the military sphere. Sharing a commonality of views meant that it was comparatively easy for them to translate that way of thinking into practical action on the ground. The other members of the CIS had different perceptions of the security threat – even Ukraine did not share Moscow's or Minsk's perception of the threat emanating from Nato – which helped further to underline the intensification of the military relationship between the two countries.

A significant boost was given to the overall drive for closer relations with the election of President Lukashenko in spring 1994. He has been one of the main stalwarts in the overall drive for the closest possible economic, political and military integration between the two states. Thus it was no great surprise that Lukashenko's first foreign trip abroad as President was to Russia in August 1994. Yeltsin returned the compliment in early 1995. Early 1995 marked a significant step forward in relations between the two states, particularly in the military sphere, with the signing of two important agreements. On 6 January 1995, two-year talks on the fate of Russia's strategic bases in Belarus, at Gantsevichi and Vileyka, were successfully concluded. Russia was allowed to begin construction of an early-warning radar site at Gantsevichi, just outside Baranovichi, to compensate for the one it would have to de-commission at Skrunde, Latvia, in the not too distant future, and was also granted the use of both sites for a minimum period of 25 years.[8] On 21 February 1995, on the wider political front, Belarus and Russia signed a Treaty on Friendship, Good Neighbourliness and Co-operation, thus firming up the basis for further military-political co-operation between the two states. In the official Russian delegation in February 1995 was the then Russian Minister of Defence, Pavel Grachev. He was to make a return visit to Minsk in early December 1995 and hold two days of talks with his Belarusian counterpart, General Maltsev. The overall purpose of the talks was 'to discuss the current state of affairs and the prospects for military and military-technological co-operation between the two states, and ways of solving outstanding problems.'[9] Both sides stressed the importance of strengthening relations between them, and at the close of the visit Grachev and Maltsev signed a further 20 documents intended to improve military co-operation between the two countries, including the preparation of joint air defence missions.[10] Provisions covering joint air defence missions demonstrated in particular the practical nature of the military relationship between the two states. On the eve of the signing of the Treaty on the Creation of the Community of Belarus and Russia (2 April 1996), the Anti-Aircraft Defence Forces (PVO) of the two sides had already undertaken a number of joint military patrols of Russia's western border provinces.[11] According to one analyst, this particular aspect of the military co-operation between the two countries should not be under-estimated:

> 'As of 1 April 1996, the national PVO forces of Belarus and Russia began carrying out joint military patrols. The significance of this step from the point of view of increasing the security of both countries is hard to over-estimate.'[12]

The April 1996 Treaty also envisaged both sides adopting a common foreign policy, the creation of a ruling Supreme Council including both heads of state and government, and the establishment of an executive committee and a joint parliamentary assembly in order to ensure that decisions taken were actually put into effect – in short, a further mechanism was being put in place to allow for greater co-ordination of the foreign and security policies of the two countries.[13]

Further evidence of increased military co-operation between the two states was revealed in May 1996, when a joint session of the Defence Ministry collegiums of Russia and Belarus was held in Moscow (14 May). According to the official bulletin of the meeting, the agenda contained 'a dozen issues' and the package of documents signed included measures 'to ensure the fulfilment of the 2 April 1997 Treaty on the Foundation of the Union; to determine the deadline and procedure for the elaboration of guidelines for the development of the armed forces of Russia and Belarus; to plan joint functions in operational training and the use of [each other's] military infrastructure in the interests of ensuring regional security...to train personnel in the military higher schools of the Russian Federation and the Republic of Belarus,' etc.

Unlike many of the agreements signed and adopted by the CIS as a whole, many of the agreements signed and adopted by Russia and Belarus in relation to each other's security in particular were actually put into effect, so that, within a year of this particular meeting, many of the above steps had been translated from paper into concrete action. In a wider context, things began to gather pace politically, especially in January 1997, when Yeltsin wrote to Lukashenko stressing the need for fuller implementation of the integration programme between the two countries, accepting Lukashenko's original proposal that referenda be held in both countries on the idea of formal unification of the two states and a common government duly formed.[14] Referenda were not held, but on 2 April 1997 a new Union Treaty was signed and the Community became a Union, with a Charter. But this was still far from enough for Lukashenko. On 22 May Lukashenko openly stated that, in his opinion, Belarus and Russia should sign up to a formal military alliance: 'It would be logical to assume that we need a military alliance to guarantee our joint policies.'

Although the Charter fell well short of being a formal military alliance between the two countries, it did, nevertheless, contain a number of important provisions concerning the security of the member-states. Thus, according to

Article 11 of the Charter, signed on 23 May 1997, in the area of mutual security the following tasks were agreed upon:

> '(a) to take, if necessary, joint measures to avert a threat to the sovereignty and independence of each of the member-states of the Union;
>
> (b) to co-ordinate the activity of the member-states of the Union in the field of military development and the development of their armed forces, to use jointly the military infrastructure and to take other measures, taking due account of the interests of the member-states of the Union, to maintain their defence capability and the Union's defence capability;
>
> (c) to work out and place a joint order for military equipment and to create a joint system of technical support for the armed forces of the member-states of the Union;
>
> (d) to carry out a co-ordinated frontier policy;
>
> (e) to combat corruption, terrorism and other crimes.'

As one commentator has noted, 'The creation of the Community (2 April 1996) and then the Union of Russia and Belarus (2 April 1997) opened the widest possible opportunities for integrating the countries in the military sphere'.[15] This was further emphasised towards the end of 1997, when the Russian Defence Minister, Marshal Sergeyev, visited his opposite number in Minsk, Colonel-General Chumakov, on an official visit. The meeting was more than a simple courtesy call, ending in the formal signing of a Treaty of Military Co-operation between the two states. Under this new Treaty and the Agreement on the Joint Maintenance of Regional Security in the Military Sphere, the military establishments were to become ever more closely welded together:

> 'On 19 December 1997, in Minsk, the Ministers of Defence of the two countries signed an Agreement on Joint Maintenance of Regional Security...and a Treaty of Military Co-operation. The latter defined joint steps to be taken in repulsing threats to the sovereignty and independence of Russian and Belarus. The use of [each other's] military infrastructure and the adoption of other steps to maintain the defence capability of each other's state, as well as of the Union as a whole, were outlined. A method of defining and placing the joint defence order was worked out; on this basis would be worked out orders for the purchase of weapons and military equipment; and the creation of a unified system for the technical maintenance of the armed forces.'[16]

It should be noted that in the broader context of the security of CIS member-states, the single most important and obvious practical manifestation of the military co-operation between the CIS member-states over the past 10 years, apart from peace-keeping missions, is the creation and maintenance of a single unified PVO system covering the air defence space of much of the FSU. With specific reference to Russia and Belarus, joint patrol missions presuppose 'that if the situation so demands, and in agreement with the commander of the national PVO system...joint measures can be taken to stabilise the [security] situation, including the use of Russian units on patrol'.[17] Thus, if Russia requires the assistance of Belarusian Air Force units on patrol, or vice versa, they can be called upon in an instant and can take the steps necessary to 'stabilise' the situation on hand. In an interview with the former Commander of the Belarusian PVO, Lieutenant-General Kastenka, the latter stated that 'on 1 April last year [1996] we started combat duty with the forces and means of Russian Air Defence Troops. Taking part in this, from the Russian side, are detachments and units of the Moscow Air Defence area and the Air Defence Army deployed in the north-west of Russia. The combined system protects the borders of Belarus and the border of Russia in the western region'.[18]

According to Sergeyev, the agreements signed 'allow us to plan and carry out a whole range of measures, including operational and military training'.[19] For his part, Chumakov made the realistic assessment that he saw 'an improvement in the military capability of our army only in mutual co-operation with the army of Russia'.[20] The two men also discussed the passing, by the Union's executive committee, of the Joint Defence Policy Concept, as well as the need to create a joint Collegium of both Ministries of Defence to work out programmes for the training of Belarusian officers in Russia's military education system.[21]

Thus, by the end of 1998 Russia and Belarus had created a regional military security sub-system within the overall framework of the CIS's collective security system. As mentioned above, given both the common perception of the military threat to the sovereignty and territorial integrity of the two countries, let alone their shared history, language and culture, it was considerably easier for Russia to tie in its security interests with those of Belarus than, say, with Armenia or even Ukraine. President Lukashenko's actions and policies have also been a great asset in the development and intensification of the relationship between the two countries. Ever since coming to power in 1994, Lukashenko has done everything in his power to bring the two nations closer together. Lukashenko has striven to ensure that Belarus is firmly welded to Russia, and in many respects his overall policy of political, economic and military integration with Russia does seem to enjoy the tacit support of the Belarusian people. Such a major policy could not simply be forced upon a nation against its will, and there does seem to be genuine support for closer relations with their big eastern neighbour. On a wider scale, the creation of this regional sub-system of collective security may provide the basis for the reinvigoration of the military security aspects of the Collective Security Treaty. In Russia's future security relationship with, for instance, the republics of Central Asia, it may draw on the 'Belarusian experience' to create a further sub-regional security system there (especially in view of the new American military presence in the region). There are signs that, with the creation of the Anti-Terrorist Centre and the Central Asian Rapid Reaction Force, Russia may begin to create a series of sub-regional security systems, moving away from attempting to create one huge CIS security system. Except in the area of PVO defence, Russia's previous attempts at creating a CIS security system have not to date been crowned with much success.

Belarusian-Russian military co-operation 1999-2002

As stated above, one of the main drivers behind the whole integrationist process between the two countries has been Lukashenko himself. He has been more than keen for his country's defence and foreign policies to be co-ordinated with those of Russia; indeed, Belarus was the only member of the CIS which actively supported Russia in the latter's stand against the Nato bombing campaign against the Yugoslavia in 1999. In many respects, particularly in the military sphere, Lukashenko's attitude towards Russia can be summed up in the title of an interview published in the main newspaper of the Russian Ministry of Defence, *Krasnaya Zvezda*, on 5 May 2000: 'We will defend Mother Russia with our [bare] chests'. On other occasions, he has been quick to emphasise the combined sacrifice of the Belarusian, Russian and Ukrainian peoples in their fight against Nazism in World War II. As a former political officer, he is still struck by the symbols and images of the country's Soviet past and, indeed, if one looks at the current emblem of the Republic of Belarus, it does bear a striking resemblance to that of the old Belorusian SSR. Without diverging too much from the topic of this particular chapter, suffice it to say that Lukashenko is not simply a man stuck in the past, but gives the impression of believing that in many ways things were better then than now. He has a tendency to venerate both the USSR that was and the Russia that is. Occasionally, he tends towards emotive use of language when discussing Russia in the context of military security. Given his perception of the threats facing both Russia and Belarus, as well as his own understanding of history, he sees the defence of Belarus and Russia as one and the same thing:

> 'Russia has a strong interest in military co-operation, with regard to the defence of our state and the Russian state, and of our Union. The reason probably is that the Belarusian Army is the only thing the Russian Federation has in the west...Only the Belarusian Army, which is willing to guarantee the security of its own territory and that of the Russian Federation.'[22]

This view of the common defence of both Union states has received much support from the senior Russian military leadership. The growing military co-operation between Russia and Belarus has allowed Russia to fill a very important gap in its strategic defence system in the western region since the collapse of the USSR and the active expansion of Nato in Central and Eastern Europe since 1999. As mentioned above, Russia's bases in Belarus are important in providing communication with its strategic submarine fleet, as well as ensuring radar cover for the loss of the radar station in Latvia. Geographically, Belarus is also important in easing access to the important strategic exclave of the Russian Federation, Kaliningrad oblast, home to the Baltic Fleet. Then, of course, there are the Belarusian Armed Forces themselves, well-trained and reasonably well-equipped, plus the country's native defence industry, all important factors in determining the importance of Russia's military co-operation with Belarus. To further enhance the security of both nations, the decision was taken in April 1999 to create a unified regional group of troops of Belarus and Russia.[23] Sergeyev alluded to this in an interview published in *Krasnaya Zvezda* on 27 April 1999 a few days after a formal visit to Belarus. An *Interfax* statement dated 6 October 1999 once more alluded to the earlier decision, saying that the two Ministers of Defence, Sergeyev and Chumakov, had signed a resolution 'establishing a regional military coalition [group] in the western region.' According to the statement, Sergeyev pointed out that the creation of the regional group 'is not aimed at a particular enemy' but that the group would be 'ready for action if [the enemy] does appear'. His Belarusian counterpart added that 'if separate, our countries might fail to protect the frontiers. Units of the regional army group will provide defence in the East European region should it become necessary.' The statement also alluded to the fact that 'command and supply headquarters' were being set up so that 'the group could be formed'.[24] The group will be drawn from units already existing in each nation's armed forces, brought into action when the situation so demands.

More detail about the group was released a year after the actual decision was taken to establish it. In his annual address to the Belarusian parliament, Lukashenko spoke about the need to create 'a new concept for the defence system in the western region'.[25] A couple of days later, Belarusian TV interviewed the Belarusian Assistant Minister of Defence for military policy, Major-General Portnov, who spoke about the size and functions of the military group: 'The make-up of the regional group will be the armed forces of the Republic of Belarus and the military formations of the Russian Federation that are assigned to its composition. The group's strength, manning and staffing will be determined by the tasks to be assigned to it by decision of the Supreme State Council'. In response to speculation about its size, he admitted that the figure of '300,000 is a purely theoretical figure' and that its size would reflect the tasks allotted to it. Given that the size of the Belarusian Armed Forces is no more than 80,000, this would imply that Russia was prepared to commit nearly 250,000 men in order to ensure that the group could meet the threat.[26] In effect, Russia would deploy those units to the group already serving in the country's western oblasts, as well as those military units based in Kaliningrad oblast. Fearing an over-reaction on the part of the Russian media, the MOD of the Russian Federation was quick to point out that the figure of 300,000 would include not only army units, but also border guard troops and interior troops. Moscow MD would be the main supplier of men for the regional group (including Air Force and PVO units), supplying approximately

100,000 men; including border guards and interior troops, the overall figure would increase to 150-170,000 men.[27] But it should be stressed that Belarus is not going to be suddenly swarming with 240,000 Russian soldiers marching over the border: the group will only come into being when a threat to Russian/ Belarusian security emerges. There is no large combined Russian/Belarusian military group quartered in Belarus waiting to pounce on any unsuspecting neighbours. When a relevant threat arises, then the machine will be cranked up and the group brought into practical existence. Until then, the only units serving on Belarusian soil, with the exception of the two Russian bases at Gantsevichi and Vileyka, are Belarusian. Referring to speculation over the drafting of a common defence doctrine for the two Union states, one commentator has noted the following:

> 'According to statements in the press, the draft document [common defence doctrine] does not propose the creation of a common army for the Union state; however it does foresee the creation of a powerful Russian-Belarusian military group under a single command. According to the then Commander of Moscow MD, Colonel-General Puzanov, 'The composition and numbers of the regional group have been predetermined and the troops are ready to operate within the group'.'[28]

Thus, the composition and complexion of the group are already fixed. In addition to the Belarusian Armed Forces in their entirety, it will also include those military and security forces of the Russian Federation deployed in Russia's western oblasts (including Kaliningrad oblast).[29] Although command and control facilities would already appear to be in place, it seems certain that the actual main force of the group would not assemble except in the face of a severe and serious military threat to either Russia or Belarus.[30] This was the view recently expressed by Major-General Portnov: 'Every time I am asked where and how we shall see this regional group, I reply: you will see it when there is a real military threat to the Union of Belarus and Russia.'[31] According to one Russian analyst, Nato's semi-official reaction to the news was along the lines that if such a group were created, it wouldn't happen quickly.[32] Despite this cynicism, however, Belarus's neighbours, including Poland and Lithuania, have shown more concern about the potential functions of such a group in the region, worried that the group may re-deploy operational-tactical missiles in the area.[33] In an interview published last year, the Belarusian Minister of

Defence, Maltsev, made a partial allusion to the deployment of the group within Russia's western regions: 'In as much as we are located in the East European region of the Collective Security Treaty (territory of Belarus, Kaliningrad oblast and the neighbouring regions of Russia plus the Baltic Sea region) the regional group of forces...will naturally operate here...thus, questions of its type and who needs it are simply not applicable here. It is our common group. This is the region for which we are both answerable. And the higher the combat readiness of the group, the better it will be for both sides.'[34]

In other words, this is where the group is and this is where it is going to operate, if deployed at all, in the face of a common threat to either Belarus or Russia. This regional group of forces, operating within the Collective Security Treaty of the CIS, is set to operate in the western region: as stated earlier, it can be seen as a regional sub-security system operating within the overall framework of the CIS security system. As one Russian analyst pointed out, 'Within the framework of the Collective Security Treaty, they are only [now] forming the Collective Rapid Reaction Forces, but Moscow and Minsk already have a regional group of troops and are improving ways of controlling it'.[35]

A further indication of how seriously plans were being made in relation to the creation and functioning of such a group was the decision to hold a large-scale command staff exercise in June 1999, involving both Russian and Belarusian military units, under the code-name 'West-99'. This was not quite on the scale of the huge Warsaw Pact exercise of the same name held in 1981, but it was 'the largest strategic command-staff exercise in post-Soviet history'.[36] As well as units of the Belarusian Armed Forces, units from the Moscow and Leningrad MDs and the Northern and Baltic Fleets also took part. The exercise was conducted in three stages. The first stage involved putting the troops on full military alert. The second involved preparing and using the troops deployed 'to repel aggression in the West', including planning joint operations with the Belarusian military command, using the regional group of forces. The third and final stage involved 'inflicting defeat on the aggressor and restoring the territorial integrity of the Russian Federation and allied states'. The Russian MOD was quick to point out that the exercise had nothing to do with contemporary events in the Balkans, but at least part of the exercise did involve repelling aircraft and missile attacks after a long air operation: Nato's air campaign against the Yugoslavia readily comes to mind. Belarus's mobile forces, as well as its regional PVO system, were used in the exercise. The exercise was important not only in its scale and timing, but as the first time the regional group of forces was actually deployed in simulated combat conditions.[37]

On 20 October 2000 a report appeared in *Krasnaya Zvezda* on the conduct of a command staff military game held at the Academy of the Russian General Staff. In charge of the exercise was the Commandant of the Academy, former Commander of the Far East MD, Chechevatov. In terms of the immediate impact of the exercise, the assessment was that the command staff military game was 'a practical step on the path towards the creation of the regional group of forces of Belarus and Russia'. On a not unrelated theme, Chechevatov also alluded to the fact that the 'flower of the Belarusian Armed Forces were studying at the Academy'.[38] In 2000 alone, 19 officers and generals studied there. Overall an increasing number of Belarusian officers train in Russia: in 1999 the figure was 158, in 2000 it was 217. All are financed by the Union budget. Studying together at the Academy should ensure that, in the longer term at least, co-operation between the two sides will be easier.[39]

At a session of the joint collegium held in Moscow in October 2000 Sergeyev and Chumakov stated that the actual process of military integration had assumed particular significance 'under existing conditions'. Within both the bilateral and CIS framework, the two states had taken a number of 'concrete steps' in the area of 'military integration'. Joint defence of the air space and the functioning of the unified PVO system were particularly singled out. According to Chumakov, 'The integration of Belarus and Russia in the military sphere has developed more quickly than in other areas'. Chumakov also alluded to the signing of an agreement on creating a unified regional PVO system for the two countries which would call on the conduct of joint military patrols by both the air forces and PVO forces of Belarus and Russia. Chumakov did not rule out the possibility that under these conditions Russian air force planes could well be deployed to Belarusian air force bases.[40]

Conclusions

In short, ever since the collapse of the USSR in August 1991, a whole series of steps have been taken by two of the three original Slav members of the FSU, namely the Republic of Belarus and the Russian Federation, to re-form an effective military relationship both to answer their own regional security concerns and to try to help counter-balance the impact of the military expansion of others in the region. Given their shared history, language and culture, this was not a difficult relationship to re-forge, and over the past decade the respective military and political leaderships have been keen to promote the process at every possible turn. While the politicians may have been pursuing the policy for their own non-altruistic reasons, the military establishments in both countries would appear to have been keen to plug the gap in the western region of the countries' defence system through the re-creation of a unified PVO system, the creation of a regional group of forces and increased joint training and exercises. The steps taken still fall well short of formal unification, a project which, certainly in the political and economic arena, seems to be far off in the future. But for the time being the military co-operation between the two countries seems to be at a level adequate to meet the security needs of both countries. Given the economic and constitutional constraints, Belarus will not deploy its military forces outside a very confined geographical area, and only when its interests are directly threatened. Obviously Russia, given its size, its resources and its nuclear arsenal, is in a very different geo-political position and will, as has been demonstrated on a number of occasions in the past 10 years, react militarily when required. But the military aspect of the relationship between the two countries is on a different level, both compared with the economic and political relationship and in relation to Russia's military relationship with the other CIS member-states. Practical steps would appear to be more important than simply words on paper: they share a common analysis of the threat to stability in the region and have responded accordingly. The events of September 11 may encourage Russia to take a harder look at its relationship with the USA and to continue to revise its attitude towards the USA in the light of their 'common fight against international terrorism'. If so, then this could have an impact on Russia's relationship not only with Belarus but also with the other members of the CIS. How Russia reacts to the possible incorporation into the Nato alliance of any or all of the Baltic States come November 2002, for example, will provide the West with a strong indication of how it intends to develop its relationship not only with Belarus but also with the CIS. Grudging acceptance of the fact of Baltic accession to Nato may cause Russia to downgrade its military relationship with Belarus as it will have failed to counteract Nato expansion in Central and Eastern Europe. However, if Russia continues to oppose Nato expansion in the region, then the opposite will occur and Russia will continue to develop and intensify its relationship with Belarus. Either way, the only thing that can be said with any certainty is that, in this part of the world, the security picture is going to be very different after the Nato summit in Prague in November 2002.

Notes

[1] In order to define more adequately the word 'co-operation' in this particular context, I will use the geostrategic definition provided by Colonel-General P N Andreyev in a recent essay analysing military-political co-operation in the CIS: 'Co-operation includes co-ordination and rendering mutual assistance in questions of constructing, reforming and developing the national armed forces of member-states; conducting joint measures in operational and combat training of their armed forces and other troops; working out an agreed programme for training different types of troops of the national armed forces in deciding [how best to deal with] joint tasks in various conditions; agreeing matters of operationally equipping territories, the creation and improvement of the military infrastructure in the regions in the interests of collective defence; working out a unified approach to the standards for creating and maintaining material supplies.' (Colonel-General P N Andreyev, 'Geopolitika i bezopasnost'. Voenno-politicheskoye sotrudnichestvo gosudarstv SNG: etapy i osnovnye naparavleniya razvitiya', *Voennaya Mysl'*, No.4, 2000, 25-35; 31).

[2] 'Deyatel'nost' Ministerstva oborony Respubliki Belarus', (http://www.mod.mil/by/megd_sotr.html). According to a later interview of the then Belarusian Minister of Defence, Colonel-General A Chumakov, by February 2001 the total number of agreements in the military sphere had reached 38, (http:news.monitor.bbc.co.uk/pubs/cgi/pubs.pl?temp=view &path=/intake/p.../12+Mar+200 3/12/01)

[3] 'O Rossiysko-Belorusskoi integratsii. Tezisy Soveta po vneshney i oboronnoi politike', *Nezavisimaya gazeta*, 1 October 1999.

[4] R A Woff *The Armed Forces of the former Soviet Union*, London: Brassey's, 1996.

[5] 'Opora na sobstvennye sily', (*Krasnaya Zvezda*, 27 February 1999).

[6] V Grigor'ev, 'V XXI vek – kak soiuznoye gosudarstvo', *Krasnaya Zvezda,* 2 April 1999; E Rostikov, 'Protivoves', *Zavtra,* No.17, April-May 1999; Yu Golotiuk, 'Obratnoi dorogi net', *Izvestiya,* 8 October 1999.

[7] N G Fedulova, 'Problemy bezopasnosti i voennogo sotrudnichestva b ramkakh SNG', *Otechestvennaya istoriya,* no.7, 2000, 77-89; 88.

[8] Fedulova, *ibid.*, no.5, 2000, 69-84; 71.

[9] Woff, *ibid.*, E2-34.

[10] *Ibid.*

[11] Fedulova, *ibid.*, p.71.

[12] *Ibid.*, pp.71-72.

[13] *Ibid.*, SU/2577 B/1, 3 April 1996.

[14] *Rossiyskaya gazeta,* 15 January 1997.

[15] Fedulova, *ibid,* p.72.

[16] *Ibid.*

[17] *Ibid.*

[18] BBC Summary of World Broadcasts, SU/2900 S1, 23 April1997.

[19] 'Osobiy soiuz Rossii i Belorossii ne protivorechit Dogovoru o kollektivnoi bezopasnosti SNG', *Krasnaya Zvezda,* 23 December 1997.

[20] *Ibid.*

[21] *Ibid.*

[22] A G Lukashenko, "*Ostriy razgovor ob integratsii*", *Nezavisimaya gazeta, 25 April /2000.*

[23] O Falichev, 'Ukreplyaya slavyanskiy soiuz', *Krasnaya Zvezda,* 27 April 1999.

[24] 'Russia, Belarus set up military group', Moscow, 6 October (Interfax).

[25] K Shimanskaya, A Neverovsky, 'Lukashenko zashchitit Rossiu ot NATO', *Kommersant-DAILY,* 12 April 2000.

[26] 'Belarusian general interviewed on joint Belarusian-Russian formation', BBC Monitoring Web Database, excerpts from a report by Belarusian TV on 15 April.

[27] V Georgiev, 'Sovmestnaya gruppirovka uzhe sushchestvuet', *Nezavisimaya gazeta,* 19 April 2000.

[28] Fedulova, *ibid.*, p.72.

[29] O Falichev, 'Voennaya integratsiya Rossii I Belorussii…', *Krasnaya Zvezda,* 19 April 2001.

[30] V Marzaliuk, 'Union state: no alternative to military integration', trans., (original appeared in *Vo slavu rodiny!,* 12//6/2001). For a rare English analysis of the group, see V Rich, 'Russia-Belarus force plans flounder', *Jane's Intelligence Review,* October 2000, 19-20.

[31] Major-General Yu Portnov, 'Po edinym zakonam', *Krasnaya Zvezda,* 2/2/2001.

[32] Shimanskaya, *ibid.*, 12 April 2000.

[33] Y Golotiuk, 'Belorussian Army to become Russified', trans., (original appeared in *Vremya Novostei,*29 August 2001, p.2).

[34] Lieutenant-General L Mal'tsev, 'Nashe voennoe sotrudnichestvo razvivaetsya intensivno', *Krasnaya Zvezda*, 15 August 2001.

[35] V Georgiev, 'I obshchaya bezopasnost', i sovmestniy eksport oruzhiya', *Nezavisimaya gazeta*, 1 December 2001.

[36] V Georgiev, 'S sovetskim razmakhom', *Nezavisimaya Gazeta*, 19 June 1999.

[37] *Ibid.*; Yu Golotiuk, 'Dan prikaz emu na 'Zapad-99'', *Izvestiya*, 22 June 1999.

[38] Gavrilov, *ibid.*

[39] *Ibid.*

[40] 'Zasedanie sovmestnoi kollegii ministerstv oborony Respubliki Belarus i Rossiyskoi Federatsii', *Vestnik MID Respubliki Belarus*, No.4, 2000, (http://mfa.gov.by/rus/vestnik/no4_2000/3.htm)

Not All Roads Lead to Moscow: Belarusian Relations with Poland, Ukraine and Lithuania

Grzegorz Gromadzki

That relations with Russia are of great importance to Belarus is obvious enough. Yet the country's relations with other neighbours are also of major significance, especially when looked at not only in terms of official contacts but from a wider perspective. In addition to Russia, Belarus shares borders with Ukraine, Poland, Lithuania and Latvia. The last three are at present carrying on accession negotiations with the European Union and stand a chance of becoming fully-fledged member states over the next few years. Such a turn of events would bring the outer perimeter of the newly-enlarged European Union to Belarus's doorstep, leaving the country with 1248 km of border with the EU. Of the three countries looking forward to EU membership, Lithuania and Poland are of particular importance to Belarus, if for no other reason than their shared history. To a sizeable portion of Belarusian society, the Grand Duchy of Lithuania – which, together with Poland, comprised a single state, the Polish Commonwealth, through to the late 18th century – continues to be very much of a living tradition. But contacts between the individual citizens of the countries concerned are at least as important as diplomatic dealings between their governments. Interaction between Belarus and Latvia is of somewhat less significance here, although there is the issue of the pipeline used to pump Russian oil through Belarusian territory and on to the Latvian terminal at

Ventspils; revenue accruing from the transit of Russian oil is one of the staples of the Latvian economy.

Unlike Latvia, Lithuania and Poland, Ukraine – also a neighbour of Belarus – has no chance of gaining admission to the EU in the foreseeable future. The other major difference between Latvia, Lithuania and Poland on the one hand and Ukraine on the other is that Ukraine is a member of the Commonwealth of Independent States (CIS). As a result, Ukraine's official contacts with Belarus, also a CIS member, are by their very nature bound to be of a somewhat different character. While it may be true that the CIS is much more of a united entity on paper than in practice, the fact remains that, on account of their membership of this structure, contacts between Belarus and Ukraine continue to be infinitely livelier than those between Belarus and those of her neighbours who have oriented themselves towards the EU.

Relations with official Minsk

Poland and Lithuania have been quite straightforward in their criticism of the policies pursued by the Belarusian President, Alexander Lukashenko. Complaints first began to issue from Vilnius and Warsaw in the autumn of 1996, when Lukashenko carried out a referendum which not only flew in the face of all democratic norms but amounted to a de facto putsch, with the entire opposition forced beyond the boundaries of official political discourse. Poland and Lithuania refused to recognise the results of this referendum, and continued to regard the Supreme Soviet (which Lukashenko disbanded) as the legal parliamentary assembly of Belarus. Both Poland and Lithuania joined the European Union and the United States in condemnation of the Lukashenko administration in 1998, when its officials ejected the ambassadors of several countries from their residences. (The ambassadors of Lithuania and Poland were among those evicted.) The Lithuanian and Polish appraisals of the presidential election held in Belarus in September 2001 were in similar vein. The Lithuanian Ministry of Foreign Affairs made known in an official communiqué that 'On 14 September 2001 Lithuania associated itself with the European Union's statement on the course of the presidential election in Belarus. The statement is based on the conclusions of international observers and notes that the presidential election in Belarus was not conducted according to the OSCE rules on democratic elections...' The Polish authorities expressed themselves in like spirit. In December 2001, the Polish Minister of Foreign Affairs, Wlodzimierz Cimoszewicz, announced during a press conference following a meeting with his Belarusian counterpart, Mikhail Khvostov, during the OSCE's Bucharest summit that, 'Belarus's fulfilment of certain conditions, such as respect for democratic standards, trustworthy treatment of the opposition and opposition media, and clarification of the fate of missing persons and punishment of those responsible by due legal process in the event that such persons are found to have been murdered – these are the minimum conditions which must be met before Belarus, as represented by her political leaders, can gain access to the drawing room of European politics'. The official policy statement published by Poland's Ministry of Foreign Affairs in January 2002, meanwhile, emphasised the point that high-level contacts between Warsaw and Minsk would become possible only when Belarus effects 'positive changes in the areas of human rights and freedom of the media, and the fate of opposition politicians who disappeared without trace has been clarified'. Mr. Cimoszewicz took this opportunity to affirm that Poland was willing to pursue economic and local-government co-operation with Belarus on a much larger scale than hitherto, but that any upgrading of official relations must be preceded by Belarusian compliance with the conditions set out. And it is not only the executive branch in Poland which has taken a critical stance vis-à-vis the Lukashenko regime. In January 1999, the Sejm (the lower chamber of Poland's parliament) addressed Belarusian society with a special message in which it elaborated on the need to respect democratic norms and human rights. The reaction of the Belarusian authorities was indignant; the country's diplomatic service attacked this document as interference in the internal affairs of a sovereign state.

This unmitigated hostility to the policies of Alexander Lukashenko notwithstanding, Poland and Lithuania are seeking to avoid the complete isolation of Belarus. When Lithuania took the chair of the Council of Europe in the first half of 2002 it promised to concentrate on relations with Belarus. The speaker of Lithuania's Parliament, Arturas Paulauskas, declared that Lithuania, as a member of the Council of Europe as well as a neighbour of Belarus, could not allow the latter to be isolated on the international stage. A similar position was taken by Antanas Valionis, the Lithuanian Minister of Foreign Affairs.

The stance taken by these Lithuanian officials was consistent with the Belarus policy of all previous Lithuanian administrations irrespective of their political provenance. In September 1997, for instance, President Algirdas Brazauskas invited President Lukashenko to a conference of twelve Central and East European leaders even after the Belarusian opposition had been definitively eliminated from official political life in the country. The Lithuanian government is endeavoring to maintain at least some vestige of working contacts with Belarus at a reasonably high level. A programme of unofficial contacts is being pursued. Among these was a visit to Vilnius by the Belarusian Minister of Foreign Affairs, Ural Latypov, in April 2000, during which he met President Adamkus, Prime Minister Kubilius and Foreign Affairs Minister Saudargas. Earlier, in 1998, President Adamkus had met Lukashenko himself.

The reason Lithuanians are working to keep up some sort of dialogue with Belarus has much to do with their country's geographical location. In addition to Latvia and Poland, both prospective EU entrants, Lithuania abuts on Kalinigrad district (a Russian exclave) and on Belarus. Good relations with Russia and Belarus will be of crucial importance to Lithuania's own future, and the country's politicians are well aware of this. The fear that, even after its admittance to the European Union and Nato, Lithuania may find itself in a hostile environment due to the simple facts of geography runs quite strong in Vilnius. The border between Lithuania and Belarus continues to pose a very real problem. While the Soviet Union existed, this border was of an administrative character only. While the 1990s saw the legal delineation of the border, as is appropriate between distinct entities under international law, there remain the ramifications involved in Lithuania's eventual accession to the EU. Once this has occurred, Lithuania will have to strengthen that border in order to ensure compliance with Schengen standards.

Like Lithuania, Poland has also been seeking to prevent the international isolation of Belarus. In March 2002, the Polish Minister of Foreign Affairs, Wlodzimierz Cimoszewicz, met his Belarusian counterpart, Mikhail Khvostov, for unofficial talks. It is the goal of Poland's government to include Belarus in international co-operation on matters of general concern such as the fight against terrorism. It is for this reason that Belarus was among the countries invited to attend the conference on combating terrorism held in Warsaw in November 2001. The Belarusian representative at this event, which brought together sixteen countries from the region, was Ural Latypov, head of the Security Council. Contacts are also cultivated in the economic sphere. In December 2001, for instance, a seminar entitled 'Good Neighbours' was held in Minsk, with both countries represented by deputy ministers of economics.

By the same token, Poland shares the Lithuanian goal of maintaining good-neighbourly relations along her borders, which provides ample reason for seeking dialogue with the Belarusian government, such as it may be. Another important issue is the Polish minority in Belarus, accounting for some 4 per cent of the country's 10 million inhabitants; the Polish side fears for its fate under the Lukashenko regime.

In January 2002, officials representing Poland's Ministry of Foreign Affairs held consultations with their Belarusian counterparts. Among the issues raised was the tax the Belarusian government had just imposed on charitable donations, in cash as well as in kind, arriving from Poland. Since Lukashenko's assumption of power, activists of the Polish Union in Belarus have been complaining of discrimination; in the view of the Belarusian president, an organisation representing the Polish minority poses as much of a threat as any other non-governmental institution operating in his country and, as such, must be subject to complete control by the state.

The official business links with Belarus maintained by Poland and Lithuania are of limited importance to the economy of either country. At the same time one must bear in mind that, for both, Belarus is important as a transit route for Russian raw materials, primarily natural gas and oil. Poland has the Yamal pipeline, Lithuania the oil pipeline to Mazeikiai and Butinge. Lithuania is also faced with a major problem in the form of electricity exports to Belarus from the generating plant at Ignalina. Lithuania pursues these exports because the output of the Ignalina plant exceeds domestic needs, but the Belarusian side appears to have made a habit of not paying for deliveries, racking up arrears of approximately $90 million by 1999. This state of affairs precipitated an outcry in Lithuania to the effect that the country's government was supporting the authoritarian regime of Alexander Lukashenko by providing electricity on preferential terms. The power exports were stopped; but they resumed in May 2000 on completion of a new contract involving a third party, Russia. Under this new arrangement, Lithuanian electricity is delivered to Belarus by the Russian company Energiya; the Lithuanian provider Lietuvos Energija receives payment in the form of nuclear fuel for Ignalina; and Belarus pays Russia with deliveries of assorted goods.

Ukraine's policy towards Belarus, when set against this rather hard line taken by Lithuania and Poland, seems more accommodating and multi-faceted. While official Ukrainian declarations certainly express some disquiet at the goings-on in Belarus, unequivocal criticism of the Lukashenko regime is absent. This is probably a by-product of Ukraine's own complicated domestic situation. The Ukrainian authorities, President Kuchma and his staff included, have been accused of violating basic democratic freedoms; as a result, they are loath to discuss human rights violations by their neighbour to the north. Unlike Poland and Lithuania, Ukraine has kept up a programme of regular meetings with Belarusian officials at the highest level. It is beyond dispute that this lively interaction owes something to the fact that both Belarus and Ukraine belong to the CIS. Despite this, President Kuchma has resisted Lukashenko's overtures geared at including Ukraine in the Union of Belarus and Russia. In June 2001, the Ukrainian President publicly dismissed this scheme in the following words: 'We did not win our independence in order to go and lose it again'. That said, however, Kuchma does not seem to entertain qualms about meeting Lukashenko and Putin at three-way summits such as that held in Vitebsk during the Slav Fair festival in July 2001. The appearance of Kuchma and Putin in Vitebsk was widely perceived as endorsement of Lukashenko prior to the presidential election held in September of that year. When Ukraine celebrated the tenth anniversary of her independence in 2001, however, Lukashenko was not invited. Some elements in Ukraine would certainly welcome integration with Russia and Belarus, prominent among them the Communist Party of Ukraine and its leader, Petro Simonenko. Ukraine's communists would regard a union of Slav countries as a step towards rebuilding the glory of Soviet times. However, the poor results scored by the communists in Ukraine's parliamentary elections of March 2002 indicate that sentiments of this sort are not shared by the majority of Ukrainians.

Much as in the case of Lithuania and Poland, Ukrainian trade with Belarus is rather modest, with just under 2 per cent of Ukrainian exports going to that country. Belarus's share in Ukrainian imports is only 3 per cent.

In analysing the minutiae of various aspects of official policies adopted towards Belarus by her respective neighbours, however, it soon becomes obvious that this clear-cut division – EU candidates on the one hand, Ukraine on the other – does not always apply in practice. One area where the divisions run along different lines is that of freedom of movement between Belarus and the various countries with which it shares borders. From the very beginning of their independence in the early 1990s, Lithuania and Latvia laid down a visa requirement for citizens of Belarus. This course was informed by their desire to distance themselves from the post-Soviet sphere, to demonstrate that their orientation was, on the contrary, pro-Western, with integration with the EU and Nato figuring prominently among their priorities. Poland and Ukraine, for their part, have allowed Belarusians to travel without restriction. In the Ukrainian case, visa-free movement was, in its essence, a carry-over from Soviet times, when there was little by way of a border between Ukraine and Belarus, two republics incorporated within a single state. Poland, for her part, wanted her contacts with countries lying to the east, Ukraine and Belarus in particular, to be as decent as possible following the downfall of Poland's communist order in 1989; visa-free travel was an important element in this open eastern policy. These days, however, Poland's progress towards membership of the EU is imposing the need for certain changes, with the Schengen rules binding on all prospective member states; in specific terms, this will mean that, as of July 2003, Poland will institute visa requirements for the citizens of several countries, Belarus included.

Given the impossibility of any serious dialogue with the Lukashenko regime, the official policies pursued by each neighbouring country vis-à-vis Belarus have had rather limited effects, especially since 1996. But relations between the various countries, especially Lithuania and Poland, and Belarus are not limited to contacts with the current President and his government.

Contacts with the opposition

For two of Belarus's neighbours, Poland and Lithuania, contacts with the anti-Lukashenko opposition are of considerable importance. The support afforded to the Belarusian opposition by the Polish and Lithuanian governments has assumed a more or less official character. As mentioned above, Poland and Lithuania refused to recognise the results of the 1996 referendum, and their preferred candidate in the 2001 presidential election was Vladimir Goncharik, the main challenger to Lukashenko.

The Belarusian opposition attach particular importance to Vilnius, the capital of Lithuania. It was this city which, in June 1989, hosted the first congress of the Belarusian Popular Front, an organisation already established during the days of perestroika, when Belarus and Lithuania alike were part of the Soviet Union. The BPF chose to hold its event in Vilnius because Minsk was firmly in the grip of hard-line communists, ill-disposed towards initiatives of this sort. Vilnius, furthermore, carried important connotations for the historically-minded; it was there that, in the late nineteenth and early twentieth centuries, the first Belarusian societies and publishing houses were established. When Semion Sharetski, speaker of the Belarusian Parliament (freshly disbanded by Lukashenko), was fleeing Belarus in July 1999 for fear of further repression, he made his way to Vilnius.

Poland has also provided a haven for people faced with political problems in Belarus; if anything, more less-than-willing Belarusian émigrés have made their way to Poland than to Lithuania, numbering a good several dozen. In December 2001 some of them established the Union of Belarusian Political Refugees in Poland, a body duly registered with the Polish courts and pursuing its activities in an open manner. Every now and again, the Belarusian authorities apply for the extradition of specific Belarusians living in Poland, typically citing alleged white-collar crimes. The Polish courts consistently reject such approaches, acting in the belief that, if they did return to their homeland, these people would suffer prosecution on political grounds.

But Belarusian opposition activists travel to Poland not only when they find themselves forced to emigrate, but also for short visits, typically associated with various seminars and training events run by Polish NGOs. Bialystok, a city on Poland's eastern border which is home to a sizeable Belarusian community, has a Belarusian-language radio station, Radio Racja ('Radio Rightful Cause'). Although its primary audience consists of Belarusians living in Poland, its broadcasts can also be picked up in the western part of Belarus, and it has become a source of independent news and commentary free from any tampering by Lukashenko stalwarts. In addition, many Polish institutions, especially NGOs, rank support for the independent Belarusian media among their chief objectives, providing training for journalists and publishers from the independent press of Belarus. In April 2002, the Polish media threw their weight behind support for two Belarusian journalists charged with defaming President Lukashenko, an offence which may carry a penalty of several years in prison under Belarusian law.

The free Belarusian press also benefits from Lithuanian assistance. The Lithuanian Journalism Centre organises meetings for journalists and publishers from Belarus, and a number of independent Belarusian newspapers used to be printed in Lithuania. In some cases this began during Soviet times, with the titles in question shipped to Belarus every day!

Contacts with Belarusian citizens

Lithuania and Poland have been playing an important role in other ways than through their support for Lukashenko's die-hard opponents. Contacts with these countries provide a positive element in the life of ordinary Belarusians. The opening of the Polish border in the early 1990s gave Belarusians an opportunity to escape the isolation which had been their lot until that time. It should be recalled in this context that during the Soviet era there was not just the Berlin Wall separating the Communist bloc from Western Europe, but also another wall, notional but equally effective, isolating the Soviet Union from its satellite states. An ordinary Belarusian simply could not travel across the border, full stop. Now, Belarusians visiting Poland or Lithuania can see with their own eyes that transition from a communist system to democracy and a free market is absolutely possible, and in less than a lifetime at that. Such travels are particularly important for the younger generation.

Normal day-to-day contacts with Poland also have an important economic dimension for Belarusians. While much of this commercial interchange evades official statistics, it is beyond dispute that the figures in question are substantial; it is estimated that, in 2001 alone, its eastern neighbours bought goods worth 800 million euros in Poland, with at least one third of this figure accounted for by Belarusians. This benefits the Polish economy by increasing the exports and turnover of Polish enterprises. This 'suitcase commerce' also has its darker sides however. Every year, considerable amounts of alcohol and cigarettes are smuggled from Belarus into Poland, where such tax-free bargains meet with a ready response from buyers. Another issue is the 'grey' job market. While this is largely seasonal in nature, and any estimates are laden with a high degree of uncertainty, it is safe to say that the number of Belarusians working unofficially in Poland runs into the tens of thousands. Many of these take up employment on the lower rungs of the labour market, taking menial jobs frowned upon by most Poles and at significantly lower wages. Belarusians also trade and work in Lithuania, albeit on a lesser scale (primarily because of the population difference, with some 4 million people living in Lithuania and ten times that number in Poland). To the 10 million Belarusians, particularly those inhabiting the border regions, revenue derived from contacts with Poland is not something to be taken lightly. This is borne out by statistics which indicate that one third of the population of Berastse, a region just east of the Polish border, would much rather see their country allied with Poland than with Russia.

A variety of Polish and Lithuanian institutions are busily organising training events in Belarus geared at supporting the growth of civil society, focusing on areas such as local government, the rule of law, or regional economic development. There are also courses for youth activists organised by bodies such as the Council of Lithuanian Youth Organizations, and scholarship programmes which enable young Belarusians to go to Lithuania and Poland for courses of study. (Each year several hundred people at least receive such study grants.) There is hope that initiatives of this sort pursued by countries which stand a chance of eventual EU membership will help to foster a pro-European elite in Belarus.

Conclusions

It would be hard to speak of any concerted action undertaken to the benefit of Belarus by all her neighbours. There have, of course, been joint statements about the need for democratisation in that country, to mention only the declaration of 20 November 1996 issued by Presidents Brazauskas, Kuchma, and Kwasniewski (of, respectively, Lithuania, Ukraine and Poland) following an initiative by Kwasniewski, calling on the government of Belarus to respect human rights and civic liberties in keeping with the principles of democracy. Joint Polish-Lithuanian initiatives, meanwhile, have been quite common; at the OSCE summit held in Istanbul in 1999, for instance, the Presidents of Lithuania and Poland spoke with one voice against human rights violations in Belarus. There was also a joint move by Brazauskas and Longin Pastusiak, the speaker of the Polish Senate, who suggested in February 2002 that the Council of Europe make an effort to establish a dialogue with Belarus. It is reasonable to expect that, once Poland and Lithuania have joined the EU, they will take advantage of their new status to promote the Belarusian issue in other fora, e.g. the European Council, especially as diplomats from both countries are well aware that they may encounter some difficulty in recruiting other partners truly committed to this cause and, accordingly, may end up relying principally on each other. There are distinct groups within Belarus's political elite and among Belarusian society at large for which contacts with Lithuania and Poland constitute an appealing alternative to a strongly pro-Russian tilt. The younger generation of Belarusians, particularly those with a university education, are increasingly willing to see their country included in the process of European integration, a process which they can witness first-hand by travelling to those of the neighbouring countries which have already set out on that path.

The OSCE and the Council of Europe in Conflict with the Lukashenko Regime

Hans-Georg Wieck

The Council of Europe in support of democracy-building and civil society

After World War II the Belorussian Soviet Socialist Republic was rebuilt on the ruins of this war-stricken part of the Soviet Union as a Soviet model society, in particular in Minsk and other industrial centres.

Nevertheless, the reform process initiated by Gorbachev in the Soviet Union in 1985 set free Belarusian nationalist forces as early as 1986. Belarusian intellectuals demanded the revival of their traditional language. In 1988 the archaeologist Zenon Pozniak, who had discovered a mass graveyard for about 30,000 victims of Stalin's terror near Kurapaty/Minsk, established a Belarusian nationalist party, the Belarusian Popular Front. By the early nineties, more then 150,000 Belarusians had joined the party.

However, the collapse and dissolution of the Soviet Union was resented by the broad spectrum of the population that had enjoyed a comparatively high living standard as specialists in academic institutions, research establishments and high-tech industrial complexes in Belarus. The Communist Party survived the dissolution of the Soviet Union fairly well and maintained its unity in spite of internal disputes about the degree of economic and political independence from Russia the country needed.

On the occasion of the recognition of its independence by the European institutions and their member states in early 1992, the country committed itself among other things to promoting the transformation of the country in the direction of pluralistic democratic structures and a market economy in accordance with the OSCE Copenhagen and Paris Summit Declarations on the Human Dimension adopted in June and November 1990. The members of the twelfth Supreme Soviet, elected in 1990, were admitted in due course to the Parliamentary Assembly of the OSCE, and governmental representatives took their seats on the OSCE Permanent Council. In 1994 the Supreme Soviet adopted a constitution which by and large met OSCE standards.

During the first years of Belarus's existence as an independent state it was the Council of Europe in particular that helped in many ways the development of democratic institutions, the rule of law and civil society in Belarus, as it did in other countries in transition.

The Parliamentary Assembly of the Council of Europe granted Special Guest status to Belarus on 16 September 1992. Its Ad Hoc Committee on Elections in Belarus observed the four rounds of parliamentary elections held in 1995. In 1995 the Assembly appointed two eminent lawyers to report on how far the Belarusian legal system conformed to the standards of the Council of Europe. In December 1996 the lawyers submitted a rather positive report on the basis of a visit to Belarus in May 1996.

Between April 1992 and May 1995 a number of high-level political visits took place. Stanislav Shushkevich, Chairman of the Supreme Soviet and in this capacity President of Belarus, and Foreign Minister Kravchenko held a meeting with the Council of Europe Committee of Ministers in Istanbul in 1992. The Secretary General, Catherine Lalumiere, paid a visit to Minsk in May 1993.

Belarus signed the European Cultural Convention in October 1993, and in March 1997 the European Convention on Foreign Law of 1968 and its Additional Protocol of 1976. In September 1996, Belarus was also invited to accede to the Framework Convention for the Protection of National Minorities.

Following the Parliamentary Assembly's report on the first two rounds of the Belarusian parliamentary elections in 1995 and an exchange of views with Foreign Minister Syanko in May 1995, the Secretariat was instructed by Ministers' Deputies to continue co-operation with Belarus but to place increased emphasis on media freedom.

After the convening of the thirteenth Supreme Soviet in early 1996 the Inter-Ministerial Council for Co-operation between Belarus and the Council of Europe became fully operational, with the task of bringing Belarusian legislation into conformity with the European Convention on Human Rights. Several initiatives were undertaken in the field of law and support for NGOs.

Concerns were expressed by the opposition in parliament about the President's growing disregard for the rule of law and in particular rulings of the Constitutional Court, and for the independence of the media and radio stations. This reached a climax with the constitutional *coup d'etat* of November 1996.

Alexander Lukashenko, directly elected in 1994 as first real President of the Republic with an imposing majority of 80 per cent of the vote cast in the second round, pursued a policy of re-orientation of the country towards the closest possible links with the Russian Federation and the restoration of an authoritarian state structure in line with the Soviet past. The state symbols – national flag and national anthem – were reoriented towards the country's Soviet past and the economy towards that of the Russian Federation. On the basis of a referendum launched by Lukashenko the Russian language was made a second official language, on an equal footing with the Belarusian language. The recent re-emergence of Belarusian traditions was abandoned if not suppressed. Lukashenko sought to strengthen the power of the president's office to the detriment of the Supreme Soviet, and in November 1996 he finally imposed an authoritarian constitution on the country, endorsed by a highly manipulated referendum. Contrary to the provisions of the 1994 Constitution he declared the results of the referendum to be binding, dissolved the thirteenth Supreme Soviet and nominated from among his supporters in that body 110 members for a 'Chamber of Representatives'. A second Chamber was established, the 'Council of the Republic', whose members were to be partly nominated and partly selected by regional parliamentary bodies. The Constitutional Court rejected Lukashenko's rulings. However, the new situation was recognised by the Russian leadership and the other CIS countries, and gradually also by some countries in Asia, Africa and South America. This found its expression in the exchange of parliamentary delegations.

The National Assembly, comprising the two chambers above, was admitted as a member of the Inter-Parliamentary Union (IPU).

European institutions reject Lukashenko *coup d'etat*

A few days after the coup, the Parliamentary Assembly of the Council of Europe adopted a resolution calling for a round table meeting of representatives of interested parties and institutions, to provide an opportunity for a productive dialogue and a more consensual approach to reform of the constitution. The text of the new and illegally imposed constitution was judged by the European Commission for Democracy through Law (the Venice Commission) to reinforce the president's powers excessively, to the detriment of all other bodies, and to be an unacceptable alternative to the 1994 constitution.

In parallel steps, all the European institutions condemned the way in which President Lukashenko had imposed his new undemocratic constitution:

- The Council of Europe's Ad Hoc Committee on Belarus stated that the way in which Lukashenko had carried out the constitutional reform and organised the referendum was contrary to democratic standards and jeopardised the future of democratic development in Belarus.
- In November 1996 the Ministers of the OSCE Troika issued a statement warning that in the prevailing circumstances the referendum was not legitimate.
- In December 1996 the European Parliament confirmed its decision not to take further steps towards the ratification of the Partnership and Co-operation Agreement with Belarus.
- In December 1996 the European Council of the European Union called on the leadership of Belarus to re-establish full respect for internationally accepted democratic and constitutional principles and practices and warned that failure to do so would have a negative impact on relations between the European Union and Belarus and on the Union's support for Belarus's accession to the Council of Europe.

On 13 January 1997 the Bureau of the Parliamentary Assembly of the Council of Europe decided to suspend the Special Guest status of Belarus's National Assembly, which had been granted to Belarus on 16 September 1992 and which constitutes an important step towards full membership. It established beyond doubt that the new Belarus constitution violated minimum democratic standards, and in particular that the way in which the new Belarusian legislature had been formed deprived it of democratic legitimacy. From January 1997 onwards the Council of Europe's relations with Belarus were directed towards supporting civil society and the functioning of independent media.

Accordingly, inter-governmental activities to assist the approximation of Belarusian legislation to Council of Europe standards were discontinued, while the Working Group kept the political situation under review, waiting for the Belarusian authorities to restore the minimal prerequisites for the resumption of such activities (separation of powers, respect for the rule of law and human rights).

Belarus remained an applicant for membership. As a party to the European Cultural Convention Belarus participated in all activities under this Convention and continues to do so. Belarus can also participate with observers in multilateral expert meetings. In can also be invited, subject to general consent, to specialised ministerial conferences, which has happened in a number of cases. But Belarus was not invited to the Second Summit of the Council of Europe in Strasbourg in October 1997.

In January 1997 an EU fact-finding mission, with Council of Europe Secretariat participation, led to the establishment of a tripartite consultative working group to prepare proposals for improvements in the Constitution of Belarus. The group was composed of members of the legitimate representative bodies: the elected president and elected parliamentarians of the thirteenth Supreme Soviet. The EU presidency appointed four experts to provide mediation and assistance, including a member of the Venice Commission and a member of the secretariat of the Council of Europe. The group held three meetings in the period up to July 1997. Since then its work has not been resumed because of a lack of political will on the part of the President.

The new role of the OSCE and the Council of Europe after Lukashenko's coup

The European institutions (the European Union, the Council of Europe and the Parliamentary Assembly of the OSCE) did not recognise the results of the manipulated November 1996 referendum. The members of the thirteenth Supreme Soviet continued to occupy the seats for the Belarusian parliament in the Plenary and Standing Committee of the OSCE Parliamentary Assembly. The European Union and the Council of Europe undertook a mediation attempt in 1997 with the aim of bringing about agreement between the President and the opposition on the restoration of the 1994 constitution. The attempt failed. Belarus had already lost its Special Guest status at the Council of Europe; the European Union suspended the ratification by national parliaments of the Partnership and Co-operation Agreement. High-level political contacts were suspended.

The European institutions continued to work closely together in the handling of the political crisis created by the Lukashenko coup, leading up to the establishment of the OSCE Advisory and Monitoring Group (AMG) in Belarus in autumn 1997 with a mandate to support democratisation and with no time limit.

AMG seeks resumption of democratic transformation

In April 1997, the Secretariat of the Council of Europe participated in the OSCE fact-finding mission to Minsk that resulted in the establishment of the OSCE Advisory and Monitoring Group in Belarus, agreed by the Permanent Council of the OSCE on 18 September 1997, and the Memorandum of Understanding signed by OSCE Secretary General Aragona and Belarusian Foreign Minister Antonovich on 18 December 1997. The Group started work in early February 1998 with Ambassador Hans-Georg Wieck as Head of Mission. The Group was charged

> 'to assist – in co-operation with the Belarusian authorities and other international institutions – the Belarusian authorities in promoting democratic institutions and in complying with OSCE commitments and to monitor and report on this process.'

The mission, which was given diplomatic status, was to consist of five international officers including the Head of the Group and to have access to everyone in the country; everyone in the country was to have access to the mission.

The OSCE Chairman-in-Office, Polish Foreign Minister Geremek, visited Belarus on 27 February 1998 to emphasise the political importance which the OSCE in general and the Chairman-in-Office in particular attached to the unfolding activities of the AMG in Belarus. He qualified Belarus as an integral part of democratic Europe and expressed the hope that, with the assistance of the AMG, the country would accept, in the course of its transition to democracy, common European standards regarding the rule of law, human rights and adherence to the principles of pluralist democracy. The Chairman-in-Office expressed concern about politically-motivated trials of young people and members of the thirteenth Supreme Soviet. On that occasion the Foreign Minister accepted the proposed working method of the AMG: to conduct parallel consultations on issues of democracy with governmental structures, political parties and NGOs. Round table consultations were to take place at a later stage.

At the OSCE's summit in November 1999 the Presidents and Heads of Government of OSCE participating states adopted, in paragraph 22 of the Istanbul Summit Declaration, an extensive interpretation of the mandate of the AMG, stating

> 'We strongly support the work of the Advisory and Monitoring Group in Belarus, which has worked closely with the Belarusian authorities as well as with opposition parties and leaders and NGOs in promoting democratic institutions and compliance with OSCE commitments, thus facilitating a resolution of the constitutional controversy in Belarus. We emphasise that only a real political dialogue in Belarus can pave the way for free and democratic elections through which the foundations for real democracy can be developed. We would welcome early progress in this political dialogue with OSCE participation, in close co-operation with the OSCE Parliamentary Assembly. We stress the necessity of removing all remaining obstacles to this dialogue by respecting the principles of the rule of law and the freedom of the media.'

This interpretation endorsed in particular the mission's practice of having direct dealings with the opposition and with the NGO sector. Over time this turned into the main bone of contention between Belarus's authoritarian leadership and the European institutions, which supported the functions of the group as defined by the OSCE's Istanbul Summit. This ensured continued support for the democratic opposition, a support that, for fundamental political and humanitarian reasons, could not be sacrificed.

The AMG proceeded in three ways in its efforts to bring about the development of democratic institutions and the country's compliance with its OSCE commitments:

1. Assistance to the government and legislature in the development of legislation relevant to the development of democratic institutions, such as

- an appropriate law for democratic and fair elections;
- laws on the media and opposition access to the media, ending the monopoly of state institutions over the mass media, which is also contrary to the constitution of 1994 and its revised version of 1996 – the constitution currently in operation;
- the establishment of the office of an independent Ombudsman as mediator between citizens and the administration in case of complaints;
- revision of the criminal code and criminal court proceedings in order to establish the independence of the judiciary and the rule of law.

However, the legal and administrative framework adopted for the local elections in April 1999 provided ample evidence that the government was not willing to establish a fair and democratic framework for the elections. In preparation for the annual session of the OSCE Parliamentary Assembly in midsummer 1999 the OSCE Parliamentary Assembly established an Ad Hoc Working Group on Belarus chaired by the former Romanian Foreign Minister, Adrian Severin. The Group gradually got more and more involved in Belarus and the country's burdensome democratisation process. This was done in close co-operation with the OSCE Mission. The Group recommended to the Parliamentary Assembly of the OSCE that it should continue to consider the thirteenth Supreme Soviet as the legitimate (because democratically elected) parliamentary body for Belarus. This proposition was adopted. At the same time the Group was charged with the task of promoting the development of democratic institutions in Belarus and supporting the activities of the AMG.

Mr Severin established, together with the Chairman of the European Parliament's Subgroup for Belarus, Ukraine and Moldova, and the Parliamentary Assembly of the Council of Europe, a Parliamentary Troika to support the democratisation process in Belarus. This Troika visited Belarus regularly from 2000 onwards and formulated important recommendations for their parliamentary bodies, ensuring a co-ordinated and well-thought-through strategic approach to the politically unsatisfactory situation in Belarus.

2. The President's term of office expired in July 1999, according to the 1944 constitution. But Lukashenko had prolonged his term of office by two years on the occasion of the imposition of his constitution in November 1996. The opposition failed to organise successfully an alternative presidential election, but in spring 1999 several impressive demonstrations were held. The presidential administration and the President himself feared a *coup d'etat*. This led the authorities to take harsh repressive measures. It is in this period that the leading political figure and potential presidential challenger Genady Karpenko died suddenly, and three others disappeared: the former Central Bank Director Vinnikova, who was under house arrest due to criminal investigations against her; Yury Zakharenko, former Minister of the Interior; and Viktor Gonchar, Chairman of the Electoral Commission of the thirteenth Supreme Soviet and a gifted public speaker. Up to now the government has failed to dispel rumours and suspicions that it was deeply involved in the disappearance and probable death of these personalities. Only Ms Vinnikova has re-appeared on the stage, in the United Kingdom. Lukashenko refused to organise fresh elections in 1999.

Given the tense internal situation in Belarus, the AMG and the Ad Hoc Working Group of the OSCE Parliamentary Assembly engaged government and opposition more and more in dialogue, among other things by organising a brainstorming conference near Bucharest in June 1999. This exercise led eventually to an agreement between the OSCE and President Lukashenko to hold negotiations with the opposition on limited democratic reform. The negotiations were to concentrate on issues related to:

- the functions of parliament;
- opposition access to the media and media freedom;

- the electoral law; and
- confidence-building measures such as an end to the prosecution of political opponents in the criminal and administrative courts.

The thirteenth Supreme Soviet authorised the Advisory Council of Opposition Political Parties, which had been set up by eight political opposition parties, to conduct these negotiations.

The negotiations started in September 1999 on the issue of regular opposition access to the electronic and print media. An agreement was negotiated and signed on 5 November 1999 by Mikhail Sasanov, trusted aide to the President, who had been in charge of negotiations with the Russian Federation on the Union Treaty, and Mikhail Pastukhov, principal advisor to the Advisory Council of Opposition Political Parties for media matters. The 'Protocol of Agreement on the Conditions of Access for the Political Opposition to the Media for the Period before the Negotiations' would provide the opposition with regular and uncensored access to the official electronic and print media. Weeks later, Lukashenko withdrew his consent and dismissed Sasanov without appointing a successor. He replaced the negotiations with a 'Public Political Dialogue', but reserved his position on the results of this dialogue. Thus he abandoned the idea of negotiations with the opposition and reduced the notion of a dialogue between equals to a purely advisory dialogue. This new concept was of course rejected by the opposition parties and by most of the independent NGOs. The discussions brought about some, albeit minimal, results, which were incorporated into the new electoral code for the parliamentary elections in October 2000 and the presidential election in 2001. The President and the head of the AMG clashed publicly at the final session of the Public Political Dialogue on 30 May 2000 in the presence of representatives of 110 political parties and NGOs, and of course core elements of the presidential and governmental administrations as well as parliament.

3. In the absence of a promising platform for meaningful dialogue and negotiation between government and opposition, the AMG activated the Parliamentary Troika of the European institutions (OSCE, European Union, Council of Europe) in an attempt to bring about substantive improvements in the legal and administrative framework for the forthcoming parliamentary elections – but to little avail. Because of the unsatisfactory conditions for the

elections (electoral law, media access, discrimination against political opponents, lack of improvement in the functions of the parliament to be elected) the European institutions decided in August 2000, after several rounds of consultations, not to organise a long or short term official international election observation mission, as usually organised by the European institutions with technical and professional support from the OSCE's Office for Democratic Institutions and Human Rights (ODIHR). However, the Parliamentary Troika decided to be present during the elections, together with – though only up to the elections, not on election day itself – a technical assessment team from ODIHR.

The elections were conducted under non-democratic conditions. The opposition parties were not represented on the electoral commissions, except for some political parties on the Central Electoral Commission. The registration process for candidates and the counting of the votes were manipulated. This was established beyond doubt by the network of domestic election observers recruited and trained, with the support of the AMG, by NGOs such as the 'Belarus Helsinki Committee', the 'Republican Club of Voters' and 'Sapiega Foundation' (an NGO named after a ninteenth century Belarusian reformer). They registered violations of the legal and administrative rules, submitted complaints and appeals, and properly documented the whole election process. It was shown that a great number of constituencies had not managed to achieve the 50 per cent turnout of registered voters which is a precondition for valid elections under Belarus law. The official side established such failure in only 13 constituencies.

Despite national and international non-recognition of the parliamentary elections as democratically conducted, President Lukashenko rejected any further changes to the legal and administrative framework for elections. He denounced in very strong terms the international, mostly OSCE-based, financial support for the domestic observation network. Because of this, and on account of a number of other controversial issues in the OSCE, e.g. related to Chechnya, the Russian Federation and Belarus blocked the adoption of a joint statement at the OSCE Ministerial Conference in December 2000.

4. Constructive co-operation between the AMG and governmental institutions became almost impossible. Nevertheless attempts were made to bring about technical improvements in the framework conditions for the forthcoming presidential election. These attempts also failed. Worse, the President imposed a number of negative changes by presidential decree, banning all international financing for the domestic observation network, imposing new restrictions on financial support for NGOs, restricting demonstrations and obliging candidates in the election not only to present a financial statement about their own income and financial status, but also that of a large number of family members, including grand-parents and grand-children.

The AMG offered help to both sides, government and opposition, in preparation for the presidential election:

- participation in ODIHR-organised international election observation teams in other countries (Yugoslavia, Bulgaria, Slovakia);
- training and equipment of domestic election observation organisations and training for political parties.

The governmental side made little use of this offer.

Conduct of the presidential election

Given the importance of the presidential election and the fact that the opposition planned to participate, the European institutions decided on 5 July 2001 to send a long and short term election observation mission to Belarus involving more than 150 persons. The Belarusian authorities were taken by surprise and took more than a month to issue proper invitations.

15,000 independent domestic observers had also been recruited, trained and registered. Some 3-4000 observers gave in to direct or indirect government pressure not to participate. Others were deregistered on the eve of the election. The election results themselves were manipulated in a variety of ways before the results were even announced by the polling stations.

On 10 September 2001 the European institutions stated in their preliminary assessment that the election had not met OSCE standards.

However they noted also that a more politically mature civil society had emerged in connection with the election, establishing democratic structures of their own. This referred to the fact that a broad civil coalition, including most of the official trade unions, most of the youth organisations and all the democratic political parties, had managed to agree on a single candidate. According to opinion polls taken before and after the election, 30-40 per cent of the electorate supported the candidate of the broad coalition, Vladimir Goncharik, Chairman of the Federation of Trade Unions.

On the same occasion, the Parliamentary Troika and ODIHR stated that isolation was not conducive to the development of civil society. This message was misinterpreted by large parts of the public, including the government in Minsk, who expected that the European institutions would now reverse their position on the four conditions whose fulfilment was considered essential, even if taken in steps, before there could be any change in the political and legal attitude of the European institutions towards the regime in Belarus.

Emancipation of civil society from the authoritarian regime

Before the presidential election Lukashenko promised liberal reforms of the political structure (the powers of parliament) and the economy. None of these promises was met. On the contrary, after the election there was a huge purge of officials, notably among the state-appointed managers of industrial complexes. They were charged with alleged economic crimes and abuse of power.

Conflict with the OSCE about the mandate of the AMG, which the government wanted to curtail, continued unabated in connection with the nomination of a successor to the head of the Mission, Ambassador Wieck, who decided to retire at the end of 2001 after four years in office.

At the OSCE Parliamentary Assembly session in Berlin in July 2002 the Standing Committee referred to its winter session in February 2003 a decision on whether to seat a delegation from the National Assembly of Belarus. Some delegations claimed it was no longer possible for the thirteenth Supreme Soviet of Belarus to challenge this claim. Opponents insisted the National

Assembly could only be seated once there were positive developments relating to the AMG's work in Belarus and to other international demands for substantive democratisation in Belarus.

The Parliamentary Assembly also adopted a resolution criticising the Belarusian authorities for repressive measures against the independent media and opposition forces and urging the government of Belarus to co-operate with the OSCE and its institutions, including the AMG, in facilitating compliance with OCSE commitments.

Meanwhile the activities of the AMG in Belarus have practically come to a standstill. Only one or occasionally two members of the international staff remain in Minsk, and even they are not in a position to engage in any mandate-related activities. The acting head of the group and other members of the international staff remain in Vienna.

The Chairman-in-Office appointed Ambassador Eberhard Heyken, the head-designate of the AMG, as his Special Envoy for Belarus. He was charged with explaratory talks with the Belarus OCSE delegation in Vienna to identify specific issues for the mission to pursue on the basis of the existing mandate. These talks did not lead to any early concrete results.

Although no meaningful progress has been achieved with regard to the development of democratic institutions in Belarus over four years of very strong engagement by the OSCE, both alone and in co-operation with the other European institutions, substantial changes have taken place within civil society. As shown by the presidential election, the idea that change should come about through elections and dialogue if possible is generally accepted by broad sections of civil society. The Advisory Council of Opposition Political Parties established in 1999 has proved to be a functioning organ for consultation and consensus-building. Regularly reviewed and updated documents on an alternative strategy for Belarus have been developed on a broad basis within civil society. Some of the state-controlled social structures, notably the trade unions and youth organisations, have split, with part supporting a democratic alternative to the authoritarian non-democratic Lukashenko regime in Belarus. The prerequisites for effective democratic government are in place.

The OSCE and the Council of Europe have contributed to this development in a substantial way. However their support for dialogue with and between the two sides in the conflict in Belarus and for the further strengthening of the democratic alternative within Belarus remains indispensable.

The Union of Belarus and Russia in the European Context

Heinz Timmermann

Unfavourable starting conditions for Belarus

Many reasons can be given for the problematic situation in Belarus, one of which – and not the least important – is the country's lack of national identity and national self-awareness when it became an independent state in late 1991. This handicap was exacerbated by two further factors which made initial conditions in Belarus much more unfavourable than those in all the neighbouring countries in transition. One was the almost total lack of a local reform-minded elite of reformist communists and alternative forces which could have given the country fresh initiatives. Much of the country's brain-power had drained to Moscow during the Soviet era and did not come back after the change.

The second factor is that Belarus remained under the lee of history. The West maintained intensive contacts with Poland, Ukraine and the Baltic states, but paid little attention to Belarus. This may be due to the persistent perception in the West (and also in Moscow) that Belarus is actually nothing but a Russian province. But this is not the case. Belarus is by no means an appendage of Russia, but an independent state of a European type and with a European history, and will in the near future, after Poland joins the EU, be a direct neighbour of the EU. That is why EU member-states cannot be indifferent about the country's future. Developments in Belarus will affect events in the whole region in one way or another.[1]

Meanwhile, the supression of European values and principles in Belarus under Lukashenko has so far been an obstacle to fruitful relations with the EU and finally resulted in the country's self-isolation. Thus the Partnership and Co-operation Agreement (PCA) signed in 1995 could not be ratified after Brussels restricted its relations with Minsk in September 1997 as a consequence of the manipulated referendum and the dissolution of parliament in November 1996 under pressure from Lukashenko. However, the EU, despite the fact that the parliamentary elections of October 2000 and the presidential election of September 2001 were not rated free and fair, remains ready for dialogue. It does not expect full and immediate fulfilment of the demands of democracy as a precondition for a positive reaction, but must see substantial and visible steps in that direction. According to a statement by a senior German diplomat, the EU will 'respond to concrete positive steps by the Belarusian leadership with corresponding positive steps. At the end of this step-by-step rapprochement we may see the normalisation of relations between the EU and its member states and Belarus.'

In this context the EU is pursuing a dual strategy in conducting the dialogue: on the one hand broad support for the democratic opposition and civil society, on the other hand purposive contacts in the framework of EU resolutions with representatives of the regime. To exclude official representatives would be to misjudge the realities created by the presidential election, and would deprive the EU of an important opportunity to influence developments in Belarus.

In turn, relations with the democratic opposition and civil society are, as evidence of international solidarity, an appropriate means of promoting competence and proficiency in politics, business and society and motivating the people of Belarus to engage actively with European values, norms and standards. The combination of external incentives and greater efficiency within the country will give Belarus a chance to lay the foundations for an evolution towards democracy, economic reform and civil rights even in conditions of political repression and economic regression. In the event of internal change, this could serve Belarus as a basis on which the country could be included as an active partner in the European integration process.

For all their differences, Poland and Hungary may well serve as models. It is not coincidental that both countries are now among the leading transition states in Central and Eastern Europe. Even under their communist regimes a national elite of reform-minded communists and dissidents was formed and contacts established between youth organisations, churches and cultural organisations with support from parties, foundations and trade unions abroad. This made a substantial contribution to the process of directing systemic change reliably towards democracy, pluralism, economic reform and European concepts of order.

From this point of view it is very important to promote access to professional qualification in Belarus itself, through higher education, training programmes, scholarships, etc, thus contributing to the formation of an effective national elite. This is the only way to enable Belarus, in the event of internal change, to make full use of the wide potential of the PCA. It would also, at the end of the day, benefit Russia too: it would turn Belarus, with its modern industry and efficient service sector, from a burden requiring subsidies into a high-performance partner. Like Russia, Belarus would become in the long run an integral part of the 'European economic area' and could thus fulfil its role as a link between Russia and the EU.

The European dimension will be discussed further below. But let us first focus on one aspect of Belarusian policy which is little known in the West but is considered a priority by the leadership in Minsk, namely the Union of Belarus and Russia.

A sequence of bilateral treaties between Russia and Belarus

Under the auspices of a growing sequence of treaties between Russia and Belarus, the two states are moving closer and closer together. The Friendship Treaty of 1995 was followed one year later by a treaty on the creation of a 'Community' of Russia and Belarus, which was advanced in 1997 into a treaty on a 'Union'. The latest stage is the formaton of a 'Union state', the contractual foundations of which were signed in the Yeltsin era and ratified at the beginning of the Putin era (8 December 1999 and 26 January 2000).

On this basis Belarus was given a prominent place in the July 2000 'Foreign Policy Concept of the Russian Federation', the only country to be explicitly mentioned in the section on the CIS which, in turn, is given priority in the regional ranking of Russia's international relations. The words in the Concept are: 'A priority task is to strengthen the Union of Belarus and Russia as, at this stage, the highest form of integration of two sovereign states.' Belarus is, indeed, Russia's only remaining ally, as President Lukashenko has good reason to emphasise constantly. He knows that the relationship with Minsk is important to Russia not only materially but also emotionally, thus considerably raising his political standing vis-à-vis Moscow.

In early 2000 the basic institutions of the Union state were established, in particular the Supreme State Council (first alternating chairman: President Lukashenko of Belarus) and the Council of Ministers (first alternating chairman: Prime Minister Kasyanov of Russia). As the basis of the Union state, a 'Constitutional Act' is to be elaborated and then approved by referendums in Russia and Belarus as a constitutional amendment. A parliament of the Union, consisting of elected representatives of both countries, will be in charge of the legislation of the Union state and control of its executive power.

While at first glance this seems to be a well-balanced overall solution, a clear Russian dominance can be seen in the Union institutions. Lukashenko's presidency of the Union is of hardly more than symbolic significance. The real constellation of power is demonstrated by the appointment of Pavel Borodin as the secretary of the Union state, an appointment which was evidently made by Putin without consulting Lukashenko and accordingly met with harsh opposition in Minsk.

Borodin is the controversial former head of the Kremlin's finance department who in 2001 was temporarily under arrest in the USA. He is well acquainted with Putin who served for two years as his first deputy in the Kremlin's finance department. A confidant of Putin, Borodin is in charge of the operational policy of the Union and organises – particularly important in the initial stages – the personnel composition of the political executive and its staff of civil servants. This guarantees that staff in the executive bodies of the

Union are loyal to the Putin regime, and creates good conditions for a policy which is in line with Moscow and corrects the caprices of Minsk.

The 'integration' of Russia and Belarus is quite popular among a broad spectrum of the population of both countries. In Russia, however, it enjoys rather passive support, which would be hard to turn into an act of constructive state-building. Moreover, people are becoming increasingly aware of the sacrifices that Russia would have to make for Belarus.

The vast majority of the people in Belarus, for their part, support a close relationship – in terms of politics, security and the economy – with the Slav big brother, which is not surprising given the historical, cultural and family ties. 30 per cent of the people have close relatives in Russia, and many Belarusians have studied at Russian universities or started their political or professional careers in Russia. They have served with Russians in the Soviet army. All this creates special ties with Russia which no top politician in Minsk can ignore.

At the same time however there are a growing number of people who want to combine close relations with Russia with the preservation of their country's national sovereignty and a process of rapprochement with Europe. This applies in particular to the urban population, the younger generation, intellectuals, professionals and even parts of the nomenklatura, who are fed up with repression and mismanagement. It was certainly not by coincidence that Lukashenko's election campaign laid a strong emphasis on defending the country's national sovereignty against Russia.[2]

Converging and diverging interests

Given the close links between Russia and Belarus inherited from the Soviet era, it is only natural that, after the shock of the disintegration of the Soviet Union in 1991, Moscow and Minsk should have made efforts to intensify their relations. Already under Shushkevich/Kebich there was clear evidence of a common interest, but it became even more evident after Lukashenko was elected president in 1994. (Together with combatting corruption he had made close relations with Russia a central theme of his election campaign.)

The above-mentioned passage in the Russian 'Foreign Policy Concept' underlines this continuity. It manifests itself e.g. in regular joint meetings of the boards of key ministries (foreign affairs, interior, defence) and the central security agencies (Security Council, secret services), at which the strategic positions of the two sides are harmonised.

However, the dynamism of integration, which exists on paper in the form of ever more documents promoting unification, has now reached its political limits. Further progress is possible only if both sides unambiguously declare their readiness, following the example of the EU, to transfer clearly defined competencies to supranational legislative and executive institutions. But this is something neither Putin nor Lukashenko is willing to do.

Given the asymmetry between the two states as to territory, population and economic power, the Russian leadership cannot conceive of a supranational body with parity for the two sides, and is insisting on a single joint rouble emission centre situated in Moscow. Lukashenko, for his part, is sticking to his position of defending his country's sovereignty and conceding parts of it only if Belarus can participate in the relevant supranational institutions on equal terms. This divergence as to the character and perspectives of the Union state is the main reason why the unification process has staggered from one deadlock to another, to the two sides' mutual frustration.

Against this background it was of great symbolic significance that Putin made a stop-over in Minsk on 17 April 2000 en route to London and Kiev, making Minsk the first foreign capital he visited after his election. According to a Reuters report, he used this occasion to suggest to his host Lukashenko, for whom he personally seems to have little sympathy, that the time for florid rhetoric about Slav brotherhood, stage-managed symbolism and pointless declarations of intent were over. It was necessary, Putin stressed, to proceed in building the Union state without haste, carefully, and at the same time coherently. Integration could take place only in line with progress in adjusting the economic systems. (What he had in mind was the gradual reduction in the extreme Soviet-type state interventionism in Belarus.)

In late December 2001 Russia increased its pressure on Belarus. At their meeting in Moscow Prime Minister Kasyanov made a direct appeal to his newly-appointed colleague Novitsky to adjust his country's economic order to that of Russia. As Novitsky reported, Kasyanov urged him *inter alia* to harmonise legislation on banking, currency systems, customs regulations and budget planning, describing all this as a precondition for economic co-operation. After this a group of Russian consultants was sent to Minsk to help the Belarusian authorities with the harmonisation process.

Putin's line is characterised by pragmatism. He obviously intends to use the political, economic and military asymmetries between Russia and Belarus, more than his emotional and impulsive predecessor Yeltsin did, to take a harder line *vis-à-vis* the junior partner in the Union even if this retards the prospect of unification. The Putin regime is primarily interested in 'doing a proper job', rather than producing idle integration rhetoric.

Generally, Putin seems to be pursuing a strategy of getting Lukashenko into a situation which leaves him with no choice but to accept a process of convergence and unification on Russian terms. Examples for this strategy are the above-mentioned rouble emission centre in Moscow and the beginning of a takeover of Belarusian enterprises by Russian capital. How does Putin's line manifest itself in key bilateral fields and in the shaping of the Union state?

The Union state as a phantom

Due to the divergencies mentioned above, negotiations on forming a common Union state are proceeding extremely sluggishly. Representatives of the consultative Parliamentary Assembly (who are delegated by the national parliaments) are constantly complaining about its powerlessness. They say that no attention is paid to the 'model acts' passed by them and designed to standardise laws and legislation in the partner states.[3]

The elaboration of the Union state constitution is continuing, but there are still considerable differences between the two sides on the contents and scale of supranational competencies. The main reason for this is that no answer has yet been given to the question of the nature of the future state:

confederation or federation? What would this mean for the relationship between deeper integration on the one hand and national sovereignty on the other? And finally, since the classical concept of a federation does not allow its members sovereign status, wouldn't it be better to think about the creation of a 'federation of a new type'.[4]

Russian and Belarusian lawyers are right in stating that the multitude of partially contradictory draft constitutions is not the result of drafting problems, but of a lack of political consensus between the partners. As long as the respective political leaderships do not agree on the political course to be pursued, consultations about the future character of the Union state must be seen as nothing but 'kitchen talk'. A similar scepticism was expressed by the head of Russia's National Election Commission, Veshnyakov, who said that before thinking of passing the constitutional act one must 'elaborate a document fixing the powers, rights and obligations of the various institutions of the Union'. This is all the more true as even from the media one can see 'that positions on these questions are diametrically opposed and there is a general uncertainty about whether the build-up of the Union should start from politics or the economy'. Anyway, Veshnyakov emphasised, one must act prudently in order to prevent resulting 'conflicts or wars between parliaments'.[5]

Thus a Union state of Russia and Belarus endowed with significant supranational powers is not likely to become a reality in the near future, especially since it could be constituted only after a positive referendum result in both countries. The parliament of the Union will have little influence even after its direct election, which is planned for 2002, and will have even less influence on the already meagre Union budget, which is passed by the Supreme Council and the Council of Ministers (for 2002 a total of 3.3 billion roubles, with 34 per cent going to Belarus).

On the whole, in the tension between maintaining and conceding sovereignty between Russia and Belarus there will remain so many ambiguities, asymmetries and diverging interests that any attempt to outmanoeuvre them politically would do more harm than good. Given their mutually frustrating experiences, it is no surprise that in their 2002 New Year messages the two presidents mentioned prospects for the Union state only in passing (Putin) or not at all (Lukashenko).

Economic co-operation

Moscow gains great geopolitical and geoeconomic benefit from close interaction with Belarus. It minimises the potential risk of being isolated from Central Europe, it gives Moscow additional instruments in its policy towards Poland, Ukraine and the Baltic States, and facilitates communication with its exclave Kaliningrad.

In economic terms Belarus is Moscow's window into Europe. 80 per cent of Russia's trade with the EU (which is already nearly 40 per cent of its total foreign trade and after the accession of the states of Central and Eastern Europe will be more than 50 per cent) is carried via Belarus. The country itself ranks third (after Germany and Italy and equally with Ukraine, which has five times the number of people) among Russia's trading partners (6.3 per cent of overall imports in 2001). On the Belarusian side the figures are even more impressive: 60 per cent of its trade is with Russia, and it gets over 90 per cent of its energy supplies from Russia.

Therefore *any* Belarusian government would depend on a good relationship with Russia, for neither in foreign trade nor in energy supply is there a realistic alternative. Moreover, given the close economic interlocking inherited from the Soviet era, Moscow need hardly fear that a change of leadership in Minsk would lead to a change in Belarus's alliances.

Finally, Belarus plays an important role for Russia as a transit country for energy supplies to Western Europe. This role will be even greater in the future when new pipelines are built – according to Lukashenko 80 per cent of Russian oil exports and 20-50 per cent of gas exports to Europe will in future be transported via Belarus. Unlike Ukraine, Belarus has proved to be a reliable partner, which makes the country even more attractive for further investment in new transit infrastructure.

But at the same time there are a number of tensions relating to trade between the two countries, in particular with regard to energy prices (oil, gas, electricity), transport tariffs and customs. By promoting the Union state, the Lukashenko regime has primarily been pursuing the goal of securing energy supplies and transport services at the low Russian domestic rates. But Moscow has so far shown only limited readiness to grant such concessions, so that Belarusian products are losing their competitiveness on Russian markets.

Moreover, because of Belarus's unfair practices, Moscow has erected new customs barriers for certain products from third countries, which was criticised in public in May 2000 by the then Prime Minister Yermoshin as 'an unfriendly act in foreign trade', and in June 2001 by President Lukashenko even as measures 'to destroy the Union'. All this demonstrates that the Putin regime is less willing than the Yeltsin leadership to solve Belarus's domestic problems at the expense of Russia for the sake of a vague prospect of unification.

Standardisation of currency systems

Monetary and currency policy continues to be a subject of sharp controversy between Moscow and Minsk. To be sure, the Belarusian leadership seems to have resigned itself to the absorption of its weak national currency by the Russian rouble, but it vigorously opposes the idea that Moscow Central Bank should be the only emission centre, which would be tantamount to the downgrading of the Minsk National Bank to a branch office. In Minsk it has now become a commonplace that to accept these conditions would mean giving up a vital element of national sovereignty.

The Belarusian side made several alternative suggestions, such as creating a supranational Central Bank of the Union as the only emission centre, or a non-cash currency as a clearing unit between enterprises in the two countries. Anyway there will be no Union on Russian terms, Lukashenko said, referring to the clauses on preserving national sovereignty in the Treaty on the Union State.

For Moscow this is absolutely unacceptable. Given Russia's dominant economic and financial power, its leadership insists on retaining for itself unlimited control over monetary and financial affairs. Anything else (e.g. printing the common currency in Moscow and Minsk) would be 'economically hazardous', according to Moscow; it would be as if legal US dollars were printed in Washington, Mexico and Tokyo at the same time.[6] Reference is also made to an earlier step by Moscow: one of the main reasons for liquidating the rouble zone was that the former Soviet republics planned to establish their own emission centres (based on the rouble), thus gaining influence over Moscow's monetary and financial policy.

Thus the partners in the Union agree in principle on the Russian rouble as the common temporary currency beginning in 2005, to be followed by a common Union currency in 2008 which will be printed in a single common emission centre. But the nature and place of this emission centre remains in dispute between Moscow and Minsk, which is a major obstacle to the formation of the proposed Union state. The fact that payment of $30 million, the first tranche of a $100 million credit granted by Moscow to support the ailing Belarusian rouble, was delayed by several months and made only in late December 2001, was undoubtedly due among other things to Putin's policy of exercising pressure on Minsk over the emission centre.

Economic systems drifting apart

Another handicap in developing the Union state is the fact that the partners' economic systems are resolutely drifting apart. The two countries will not be able to play the same game if the rules are different. Putin has developed an impressive programme of economic structural reforms which have already been partially realised. Among them are tax reform, land reform, justice reform and regulations for the promotion and protection of investment.[7] Such measures, designed to create transparency, predictability and efficiency, are important preconditions for a domestic boom and for Russia's integration into the world economy and its partnership with the EU.

In Belarus the situation is quite different. It is true that Lukashenko was quick to order the newly-appointed government under Novitsky to issue a similar bundle of reforms comprising price liberalisation, new tax legislation, reduction of subsidies and control of tariffs, which along with privatisation, determined pursuit of WTO membership and the development of small and medium-size businesses are essential instruments and goals of this policy.[8]

But so far this programme exists only on paper. Even in the House of Representatives, which is loyal to the regime, it has met with little approval. One Deputy, Morozov, referring to the majority opinion of his colleagues, noted sarcastically that there was no government programme at all: 'All that was presented was a number of commonplaces such as you can find in economic textbooks for first-year students.'[9]

Indeed, we can hardly expect Novitsky's reform programme to be implemented under the present regime, because this would undermine two essential pillars of the Lukashenko system: the right to appoint managers of top enterprises (80 per cent of which are still state owned) and the continuation of the social contract for employees (which requires continual massive subsidies to uncompetitive and inefficient industrial and agricultural enterprises). Excessive state interventionism, combined with stubborn resistance to reform in the economic and financial field, is all but essential to the survival of the Lukashenko regime. 'While Russia is developing a market economy, Belarus is perfecting socialism', as the opposition politician Sinitsin, a man of the nomenklatura, has pointed out.

Lukashenko, for his part, has threatened to call a halt to the Union if Moscow goes ahead with its plans to liberalise foreign trade without Belarus's approval. The question is whether Moscow will really allow its accession to the WTO to depend on the (extremely low) willingness of its partners in Minsk to liberalise their own trade regime. Thus, the growing divergencies in the economic systems are, like energy prices, transport tariffs and the rouble emission centre, a major obstacle to the development of the Union state. For Russia the harmonisation of general economic conditions and standardisation of regulatory instruments are indispensible, because, according to Prime Minister Kasyanov, this is the only thing that will provide 'uniform conditions for economic activity and business'.[10]

Meanwhile Lukashenko's strategy of perpetuating state control of the economy as a means of safeguarding his authoritarian power is being undermined in another field. Russian enterprises are increasingly purchasing the most competitive Belarusian enterprises, such as refineries, chemical plants, synthetic fibre factories and the Minsk Automobile Works. This economic engagement, which has not however yet been legalised by formal transfer, must apparently be seen in the context of Russian loyalty during the Belarusian presidential election. The Russians supported Lukashenko during the election, while he promised Moscow and Russian business a stake in the Belarusian economy. In any case it is in line with Putin's pragmatic approach, which can also be seen in other contexts. He seeks, much like Ukraine, to gain political influence through a strategy of 'soft integration', by penetrating important enterprises and plants, rather than by the pursuit of risky and vague designs such as the proposed Union state.

Here, as in the case of the economic system and the emission centre, it is evident that Lukashenko's room for manoeuvre is getting narrower as his country's economic and political situation deteriorates. Thus the independence and sovereignty of Belarus, explicitly recognised in the Treaty on the Union State, may wither away almost unnoticed.

Military co-operation

Along with economic relations, there is another field in which Russia and Belarus have a high degree of co-operation, namely military co-operation. In a way this has a kind of pilot function, for integration in the military field – not least due to extensive common infrastructures inherited from the Soviet era – has advanced more than in most other fields, and the same is true for the intermeshing of the military-industrial complexes of the two countries.

The policy of deepening integration in these fields reflects a convergence of interests. Russia is primarily interested in geopolitical advantage and in a military-strategic safeguard for its Western glacis, as Putin emphasised at the ratification of the Treaty on the Union State. He said the treaty was in full accord with the 'military and political interests' of Russia and appropriate 'to strengthen its own strategic and military potential'. The Belarusian leadership, for its part, puts the accent on the political and economic benefits: it hopes to gain from military intermeshing and its profile as Russia's closest brother-in-arms.

A strong indication of the degree of military integration is the new Russian Military Doctrine, signed by Putin in April 2000. It says: 'Russia is developing a common defence strategy with the Republic of Belarus, co-ordinating activities in the field of military build-up, development of the armed forces of the member-states of the Union and the use of military infrastructure, and will take further measures to support the defence capability of the Union state.' This passage in the Military Doctrine is not only remarkable for its substance but also deserves attention as illustrating a certain tendency. In the draft of October 1999 there was no passage on Belarus in the text. It was added into the final wording only relatively late – undoubtedly after consultations with Minsk.

This integration tendency is clearly expressed in various provisions, in particular:

- Elaboration of a common military doctrine for Russia and Belarus.
- Extension of the Russian nuclear shield to Belarus – but without any new deployment of nuclear weapons on Belarusian territory.
- Formation of a joint armed forces group of 300,000 men in the west of the Union state, though not as a newly-formed army along the border with Nato, as Lukashenko originally announced, but in the form of closer co-ordination between the forces already in Belarus and the Moscow and Leningrad military districts (Russia: 220,000, Belarus: 80,000).[11]
- Modernisation of the Russian early warning system in the west of Belarus. The first installation will be carried out by the Russian Strategic Missile Command and will be the latest version of the Russian missile intelligence system.
- Development of the 1996 common air defence system into a joint air defence system with a joint command and, it seems, the deployment of Russian combat aircraft on the territory of Belarus.
- Joint exercises on the model of the 1999 strategic exercise 'Zapad' (West) which involved some 7000 men (though originally announced as 50,000) and simulated the repulse of an attack on Belarus and Kaliningrad.
- Finally, increased inclusion of Belarusian arms factories, particularly those making electronic and optical instruments, heavy trucks and land-based missiles, into the Russian military-industrial complex. A total of 280 organisations and enterprises in the two countries, with about 400,000 employees, are engaged in carrying out 19 joint large-scale projects.[12]

It remains to be seen whether Moscow's interest in ever-closer military and arms co-operation with Minsk will last after September 11 following Russia's repositioning *vis-à-vis* the West in general and Nato in particular.

The presidential election

Moscow's repositioning in the context of the anti-terror alliance could not affect the presidential election in Belarus held on 9 September 2001. But even before this the Putin leadership was in something of a dilemma regarding its relationship with the Lukashenko regime.

On the one hand Lukashenko is still seen by the Kremlin as the person who can best guarantee a close alliance between Russia and Belarus and prevent his country drifting towards the EU. On the other hand Moscow is afraid of the potential political and material cost of the reform-resistant regime and its unpredictable President. Moreover, Lukashenko's fundamentally anti-Western attitude does not fit into Moscow's policy of establishing a strategic partnership with the EU and giving Europe priority in its international relations. The EU's persistent discussion of the 'Belarus issue' and its emphatic calls on Moscow, presented at the highest level, to exert a moderating influence on the Lukashenko regime in order to guarantee free and fair elections – all this makes Lukashenko an uncomfortable partner from the international point of view.

In this complicated situation, Putin avoided expressing clear support for Lukashenko's candidature until summer 2001, and seemed to want to stay neutral in some way. If Lukashenko had hoped that the CIS summit in June in Minsk would secure him substantial backing from Moscow for his re-election, he was frustrated. He even seems to have feared covert action by Moscow, as shown by his allegations against the Russian secret service and their 'extensive operations against Belarus' in the context of the election.[13] Such fears may have been exaggerated, and owed something to Lukashenko's fear of the risks involved in losing power. But there were indeed high-ranking politicians in Moscow who suggested Russia should draw a lesson from the disaster of its biased support for the Serb leader Milosevic, and make early contact with the Belarusian opposition (e.g. Dmitri Rogozin, chairman of the State Duma committee on international relations).[14]

Against this background it could not be ruled out that Moscow might have found trade union leader Goncharik, on whom the opposition had agreed as their common candidate, an acceptable alternative to Lukashenko. As a politician of the nomenklatura loyal to Moscow, and having excellent contacts with the Russian trade unions, Goncharik had gained the profile of a politician who seeks a balance of good relations with Russia *and* Europe and the EU.[15] A neutral position from Moscow would have been an important hint to parts of the Belarusian ministerial bureaucracy and the directors of state enterprises to adjust themselves to a democratic alternative. In this way Moscow could have acknowledged that even with a change of leadership the democratic power in state and business could have relied on a stabilising level of efficiency – in contrast to 1991 when the country unexpectedly and without preparation became independent in the wake of the disintegration of the Soviet Union.

However, in the last few weeks before the election Putin switched to unequivocal support of the incumbent President. This support was emphasised by a multitude of visits by high-ranking Russian politicians to Minsk, among them the Chairman of the State Duma, Seleznev, Moscow's Mayor Luzhkov, Communist Party Chairman Zyuganov and LDPR Chairman Zhirinovsky. The two Moscow TV stations and Russian independent television, which can be received in all or part of Belarus, devoted 80-90 per cent of their election coverage to Lukashenko; the climax of bias was the propaganda film 'A Day in the President's Life'. The opposition, by contrast, was given less and less attention as the election approached.[16]

Subsequently, Putin welcomed Lukashenko's victory, which in the opinion of Russian observers had been achieved correctly, but in fact, as the official observer mission from European organisations reported, with massive manipulation. All the more remarkable is the subsequent judgement of the head of Russia's Central Election Commission, who stated that the election was 'far from setting an example to Russia and other countries that have chosen the path of democracy'. Although the election had been conducted in accordance with Belarusian election law and to a certain extent even with international standards, Belarusian colleagues must nevertheless be given 'serious advice on how to guarantee that future elections meet the standards fully and not only to a certain extent'.[17] However, official Moscow has not so far taken any notice, in its political conclusions, of this harsh criticism, which comes close to the negative judgement of the European observer mission.

Moscow's new international positioning and its consequences

Russia's repositioning after September 11 can be seen most clearly in the intensification of relations between Moscow and the Euro-Atlantic community in general and Nato in particular. To be sure, there has been no fundamental change in the relationship between Russia and the West. After the end of the Yugoslav war, Moscow resumed its normal businesslike relations with the USA and Nato and even gave relations with the EU a certain priority, but after September 11 these first steps towards co-operation got a renewed impetus going far beyond a pragmatic day-to-day policy based on national interests.[18]

The new dynamic became most evident in Russia's relations with Nato. Until now Russia has been confronted, in the Permanent Joint Council ('19 plus 1') with positions already agreed in advance by the Alliance, and treated – as Moscow has complained – as a marginal figure in a political game the rules of which are determined by others. With the establishment of the 20 partners' Nato-Russia Council, which the heads of state and government agreed upon with President Putin in May 2002, Russia will now be included in the consultations and decisions of the Alliance 'on equal terms and as a partner'. This applies to tasks which do not come under Article 5 (collective defence). These tasks include – in addition to combating international terrorism – new initiatives on arms control and disarmament in the strategic and conventional field, missile defence, strengthening the global non-proliferation regime for nuclear, chemical and biological weapons, and crisis prevention and management.

For the Lukashenko regime Moscow's repositioning, particularly *vis-à-vis* Nato, is a shock, because its concept of the enemy focuses primarily on the dangers allegedly threatening Belarus and Russia from the West. Obviously the era in which Minsk might benefit from tension between Russia and the West is over. How should Minsk react to this turn of events, where should it find its place in a changing world? Could Lukashenko hope that the new position would meet with vehement opposition in Russia itself and that Putin would not be able to enforce his new policy towards the West against the conservative establishment? Were there not fierce protests from influential groups in the military and the military-industrial complex, from the state bureaucracy, from the 'national patriotic' camp of Zyuganov's Communist Party, from certain intellectuals in political consulting, journalism and science?

In this troublesome situation Lukashenko showed enough realism to go on betting on Putin rather than seeking (as in 1998/99 prior to the Russian presidential election) a profile as a point of reference for the communist-nationalist opposition.[19] He changed his rhetoric in much the same way as he did on the question of the economic order, pointing out the necessity of co-operating with Nato in the context of the Partnership for Peace programme and the Euro-Atlantic Partnership Council. However, he did not omit to state that relations between Belarus and the Atlantic Alliance were essentially unchanged.

As part of this tactical correction to his course, Lukashenko instructed his foreign minister to improve Belarus's relations with the European organisations and start exploratory talks with EU ambassadors in Minsk about the possibility of intensified political and economic co-operation. He said: 'The build-up of – in the full sense of the word – friendly relations with the united Europe is a vital interest for our country',[20] playing down the fact that the presidential election had not been recognised by the OSCE, the EU and the Council of Europe because of massive manipulation and fraud.

But in this case too, as in the case of the economic order, there is a gap between words and action which has so far not allowed any modification, let alone revision, of the EU decisions of September 1997 on the limitation of relations. To be sure, after the election Lukashenko declared his readiness to bear in mind minority positions because 'we are living in one country and there is no reason to divide us',[21] but no action followed. Thus, the meeting with EU ambassadors never took place, and there was no concrete reaction from the regime to the EU's offer to open itself to Belarus on a step-by-step basis as the regime for its part gave the opposition leeway to participate actively in the state, the economy and the media. This should include, as had been demanded before in the context of the parliamentary elections of October 2000 and the presidential election of September 2001, a period of political peace and an end to repression of the Belarusian opposition, electoral legislation meeting European standards, a transparent election procedure, access for all parties to the state-controlled electronic media, and extension of the rights of the toothless parliament appointed by Lukashenko.

Western representatives are right in pointing out, in the words of the German diplomat quoted above, that this has nothing to do with 'arbitrary demands which apply only to Belarus. On the contrary, these are standards which we also accept for ourselves, and to which Belarus has committed itself in the framework of the OSCE. This is something the Belarusian leadership tends to forget while blaming the West for double standards'. Paradoxically, in demanding the fulfilment of such democratic essentials the community of European states could even refer to the text of the Treaty on the Union State, which in its introduction refers to the intention to build a 'democratic constitutional state', observing 'human and civil rights and freedoms in accordance with the common principles and norms of international law'.

So far the regime has not complied with any of the demands presented by the Western organisations. On the contrary, since the election the repression of dissidents in politics and the economy has become even harsher and the independent press have been subject to intensified harassment. The regime has restricted substantially the activities of the Minsk OSCE mission, which has made every effort in a dialogue with the government and opposition to support fair elections and the gradual democratisation of the country.

There are many indications that the Lukashenko regime is feeling deeply insecure about Moscow's repositioning, but by its very nature it is hardly able to make the necessary adjustments and give the proper answers. This is likely to evoke increasing criticism in Moscow and to reduce even further Russian readiness to make substantial concessions to Belarus in building the Union state.

Russia, Belarus and the European Union

In a multitude of special missions and with the help of its permanent observer group in Minsk, headed by the German diplomat Hans-Georg Wieck, the OSCE made many attempts to induce Lukashenko to keep the promises he made at the Istanbul summit in November 1999, namely to create the preconditions for free and fair elections by entering into a dialogue with the opposition. Moscow, in turn, has called upon Western governments to appreciate properly Minsk's policy of 'opening' and to normalise relations with Belarus.[22] Such appeals would provide an opportunity to overcome the deadlock if they were accompanied by appeals to Lukashenko to keep the promises made in Istanbul. This is what Adrian Severin, Chairman of the OSCE Parliamentary Assembly, had in mind when he called upon Moscow to take the appropriate initiatives. As a strategic partner of Belarus, he said, Russia exerts great influence on developments in Minsk. Therefore Russia, which is itself approaching European standards of democracy, must be greatly interested in the realisation of democracy, pluralism and freedom of the media in its partner-state Belarus.[23]

The EU has repeatedly brought up the issue of Belarus at the EU/Russia summits held in the context of the Partnership and Co-operation Agreement, and asked Moscow to exert a moderating influence on the Lukashenko regime in the interest of promoting democracy. The same is true for the European Parliament. In an appeal it urged President Putin 'to support a democratic multi-party system and pluralistic development in Belarus'. Though there is little scope at present for Brussels to exert much influence, this will grow as the EU becomes more important for Russia as a partner in policy formulation and economic modernisation. In this context, in future talks with Moscow Brussels could argue along the following lines:

- Russia's close alliance with the eccentric autocrat Lukashenko and his Soviet-style conception of the world is not beneficial to Putin's reputation as a Russian moderniser. The close relationship between Russia and Belarus in the Union state imposes a certain responsibility on Russia to promote democracy and pluralism in Belarus in accordance with the norms of the OSCE and the Council of Europe.
- Belarus's domestic constitution and the nature of its foreign relations are an obstacle to the European integration process in general and the partnership between the EU and Russia in particular. For instance, how would the Partnership and Co-operation Agreement be implemented if Moscow, as a partner of the EU, were moving ever closer to a partner in Minsk who was authoritarian in his policy and resistant to economic reform? What would happen if Russia were to accept EU standards and norms in the economy, environment and technical production, while its integration partner Belarus refused to accept them? The incompatibility of the liberalised economic order

in Russia and Lukashenko's model of a state-controlled economy might in future become a problem for the partnership between the EU and Russia.

- It will be hard to create the 'integrated economic area' envisaged by Moscow and promoted by the EU with a Belarusian regime which is resistant to reform. Transparency, predictability and efficiency are essential not only for fruitful relations between Russia and Belarus, but also for the parallel integration of the two countries into the common European economic area.
- Belarus should maintain a balance in its foreign relations, and as an independent state play a role as a bridge and hinge between its eastern and western neighbours. Firstly, this would promote domestic harmony: since the elite and the people have diverging preferences for either the Russian or the European direction, coming down on one side or the other would evoke resistance on the losing side. Secondly, the country's economy is vitally dependent on both neighbours, the EU and Russia. For Belarus, which is suffering an economic recession, the EU is the more effective partner in expanding trade relations, direct investment and the short-term supply of modern technology. Russia, on the other hand, is an indispensible partner as a reliable supplier of Belarus's energy requirements and market for Belarusian products.

The EU's intention is not to separate Belarus from the Union with Russia and eventually integrate it into the EU, as is widely feared among the elite in Moscow. The EU and the USA have repeatedly underlined that they are ready to accept a decision of the Belarusian people to go ahead with the Union, provided that this decision is the result of a free and fair vote.

However, as we have seen, for many reasons Belarus needs both sides as partners. In fact, the primary interest of the EU and its member states is to have basic European values and principles prevail in Belarus as they do in Russia. This is one of the essential preconditions for the shaping of the 'common European house' for which Putin has appealed, referring to Gorbachev's well-known vision.

Notes

[1] See: 'The Forgotten Neighbour – Belarus in the Context of EU Enlargement,' Batory Foundation, *Policy Papers 4*, Warsaw 2001. See also: Heinz Timmermann, 'Belarus und Russland. Kontroversen über den zukünftigen Charakter der Union,' in: R.Lindner/ B.Meissner (eds.), *Die Ukraine und Belarus in der Transformation*, Cologne 2001, pp. 235-246; and A.Moshes, *Russia's Belarus Dilemma.* Council on Foreign Relations: Policy Memo Series No. 182, Washington 2000.

[2] Cf. *e.g.* his election programme 'Za silnuyu i protsvetayushchuyu Belarus!' [For a strong and flourishing Belarus!], in: *Sovetskaya Belorussiya* (Minsk), 9 September 2001.

[3] *Rossiyskaya gazeta*, 1 March 2001.

[4] See N. Pastukhova, 'Ot soobshchestva k soyuznomu gosudarstvu. Rezultaty etoy 'pyatiletki' mnogoznachny [From a community to a union state. The results of the current 'five years plan' are equivocal],' in: *Nezavisimaya gazeta* (Moscow),29 March 2001; cf. also V. Yefanov, 'Soyuz Belarus-Rossiya,' in: *Rossiyskaya gazeta*, 1 November 2001.

[5] *RIA Novosti* (Moscow), 15 February 2002.

[6] S. Novoprudsky, 'Derevyanny, olovyanny, steklyanny [Made of wood, of tin, of glass],' in: *Izvestiya* (Moscow), 24 February 2000; cf. also the same author, 'Soyuz sovetskikh sotsialisticheskikh rubley [Union of Soviet socialist roubles],' in: *Izvestiya*, 12 December 1999.

[7] Cf. for this in detail R. Götz, *Präsident Wladimir Putins Wirtschafts- und Gesellschaftsmodell. Konzeptionen, Einflüsse, Realisierungschancen*, Berlin 2001 (SWP-Studie)

[8] Economist Intelligence Unit, loc.cit., p. 16-18.

[9] *BelaPan*, 6 December, 2001.

[10] Cf. K. Fokina, Minsk – tsentr integratsii [Minsk – centre of integration], in: *Nezavisimaya gazeta*, May 24, 2000.

[11] Defence Minister S. Ivanov, then Secretary of the Security Council, in an interview with *ORT* on 24 April 2000.

[12] Cf. in detail: 'Belorussiya obyedinilas [Belarus has unified],' in: *Kommersant* (Moscow), 1 July 2000; and V. Yegorov, 'Integratsiya stala realnostyu [Integration has become reality],' in: *Nezavisimoe voyennoe obozrenie* (Moscow), 47, 2001.

[13] For more details see A. Polevoy, 'Lukashenko opasaetsya rossiyskikh spetssluzhb. Prezident Belorussii budet protivostoyat vragam do kontsa [Lukashenko is afraid of Russian secret services. The President of Belarus will resist the enemies until the end],' in: *Nezavisimaya gazeta*, 17 March 2001.

[14] ITAR-TASS (Moscow), 30 January 2001.

[15] See Goncharik's electional programme 'Dobro vashemu domu! [Well-being for your house!],' in: *Sovetskaya Belorussiya*, 31 August 2001. Cf. also E. Korotkova, 'Belorusskiy Lekh Valensa [The Belarusian Lech Walensa],' Interview with Goncharik, in: *Moskovskiy komsomolets*, 22 July 2001.

[16] Cf. *The European Institute for the Media, Preliminary report on Monitoring of Media* Coverage during the Presidential Elections in Belarus September 2001, Düsseldorf/Paris 2001.

[17] *BelaPan*, 5 November 2001.

[18] Cf. Ch. Meier/H. Timmermann, *Nach dem 11. September: Ein neues deutsch-russisches Verhältnis?*, Berlin 2001 (SWP Aktuell 22).

[19] Cf. my study: 'Lukaschenko: Griff nach der Macht in Moskau?,' *Aktuelle Analysen des BIOst (Cologne), No. 34*, 1 September 1998.

[20] Speech in the House of Representatives, in: *Sovetskaya Belorussiya*, 11 October 2001.

[21] Press release of the Embassy of the Republic of Belarus in Berlin, No. 31, 9 November 2001.

[22] See *e.g.* Foreign Minister Ivanov, ITAR-TASS, 25 February 2000.

[23] Interview with *Nezavisimaya gazeta*, 22 June 2000.

4
The EU and Belarus

The EU and Belarus: Time for a Fresh Start

Sergei N. Martynov

The European Union and the Republic of Belarus are currently living through a particularly important period in their relationship. Many factors converge to indicate that it is not only advisable, indeed necessary, to vastly improve their relations, but also that this can be achieved. It is time to make a bold move to leave behind the mistakes and myopic policies of the recent past, which were a drag on relations and a drag on prospects for a New Europe settling in for real in the Central and Eastern parts of the continent.

There is a window of opportunity here and now. Change is in the air.

The Belarusian angle

The key watershed event for Belarus's relationship with the outside world was the presidential election of September 2001 and the convincing victory of the incumbent President, Alexander Lukashenko, over his rivals. International election observers led by the OSCE were invited by Belarus to monitor the elections. Observers from the European Parliament, the Parliamentary Assembly of the Council of Europe and the Parliamentary Assembly of the OSCE took part in the observation mission. These observers, while expressing unhappiness with regard to the implementation of the 1990 Copenhagen Document, recognised the emergence of a pluralist civil society in Belarus and reached a truly ground-breaking conclusion: 'Isolation of the country is not in the best interest of the Belarus people and is not conducive to strengthening democratic development'.

This conclusion deserves very special attention from EU decision-makers, since it contains a core principle: it is not isolating Belarus but its opposite, engagement, that can best help strengthen European values in the country.

The conclusion was followed by an explicit recommendation, that 'the international community at its highest levels should reassess its policy towards Belarus.'

It is worth noting also, albeit in passing, that while criticising aspects of the electoral process, the international monitors recognised that voters in Belarus had been offered a genuine political choice. They also rejected allegations that the government had 'falsified' the election results.

The election made it abundantly clear to all, whether well or ill disposed towards President Lukashenko himself, that he is indeed the indisputable leader of the vast majority of the Belarusian people and will continue to be so for at least the next five years.

A political line was thus clearly drawn in the sand inviting a realistic rather than illusory, long-term rather than myopic policy towards Belarus, a middle-size European country strategically located in the heartland of our continent.

The presidential election of 2001 was also an important watershed in Belarus's internal development. After the election the President proclaimed the need for a new course towards the liberalisation of the economy and the consolidation of civil society. He also made it publicly clear that the country was open to much closer co-operation with the EU.

Belarus appreciates the emergence of a united Europe as one of the major global centres of political and economic power. We are of the view that the EU and its enlargement will have a more powerful impact on Belarus than Nato enlargement. This is because Belarus, unlike the majority of former Soviet Union countries, has a viable, export-oriented manufacturing economy with an emphasis on sophisticated high technologies. Belarus exports more than 55 per cent of its GNP and 80 per cent of its industrial output.

Closer co-operation with the EU is therefore increasingly vital for Belarus. In 2001 Belarus's trade turnover with the EU amounted to 37 per cent of its total turnover with non-CIS countries and the share is still rising. The EU's share in Belarus's imports from non-CIS countries has risen in recent years to 52 per cent.

The European Union angle

The international monitors' conclusion that isolating Belarus was counter-productive was ground-breaking not only in theory but, hopefully, in practice too. In its declaration after the presidential election the EU endorsed the international monitors' conclusions in their entirety. In its subsequent statement the EU went a step further and specifically upheld the notion that isolating Belarus was counter-productive. There was also a noteworthy new element in the second of these statements: recognition of Belarus's role in regional stability. This obvious statement was long overdue.

The conclusions and recommendations of the international observers prompted the EU to look again at its 1997 decisions. Those decisions, taken by the EU Council on 15 September 1997, were the basis for the isolation of Belarus in European politics. They included suspension of the process of ratification of the Partnership and Co-operation Agreement (PCA) between Belarus and the EU, which was concluded back in 1995, and the freezing of the Interim Trade Agreement, intended as a bridge to cover the long-drawn-out process of ratification of the PCA by all the fifteen EU member-states. The 1997 decisions also restricted contacts between the EU and Belarus to below ministerial level, and ended virtually all technical assistance and co-operation programmes except for those that were regionally based. The 1997 decisions left open the possibility of contacts between the EU presidency and Belarus, but this lever was never used by the EU.

By 2000-2001 it had became abundantly clear to everyone closely involved in EU/Belarus relations that these decisions had been a mistake. They were a mistake not because they were not to the liking of Belarus, which is self-evident, but because they were ineffective from the point of view of the goals set by the EU in its relationship with Belarus.

The need for a fresh look

In revisiting its relationship with Belarus and in reassessing its policies towards our country it is essential for the EU to look into two basic questions:

1. What, actually, is Belarus?
2. What would be the best, most effective EU policy towards Belarus?

Reality versus perception

Belarus, as a country in transition with a Soviet past extending back over seventy years, has of course many hurdles to overcome to bring its civic standards up to the European level. At the same time it has many social and civic assets inherited from that same past, especially in terms of the social safety net, education, medical care, etc. This situation does not differ in principle from that in other post-Soviet states.

But for a number of reasons there are rampant preconceived notions and misperceptions in the West, including in EU countries, about Belarus. This is borne out by the simple fact that almost everyone from the West who visits Belarus for the first time is surprised. Pleasantly surprised. While the difficulties of the transition period are obviously present in day-to-day Belarusian life, visitors register the very European look of the cities, the charm of the people, the very high level of education and culture, and the sophistication of science and industry. Paradoxically, or not so paradoxically, the less a country is involved with Belarus, the more sombrely it views the country. People who know Belarus, who are actively involved with the country, live there or have frequently visited, while critical of aspects of Belarusian life, usually have much more respect for the country than the ignorant.

It is important therefore for European decision-makers to take stock of some of the facts about the real Belarus, to go beyond the stereotypes implanted by the usual sensationalist and patronising press reporting.

Belarus had the highest living standards in the Soviet Union. This is why a substantial number of Belarusians still have a certain nostalgia for Soviet times and quite often have a cooler attitude towards dramatic reforms.

In the period of transition Belarus opted to go its own way, avoiding the 'shock therapy', ill-thought-through reforms and corrupt privatisations which led in many neighbouring countries to the destruction of the national economy and to violations of elementary social justice. This does not mean that Belarus is alien to the spirit and goals of reform. Not so. But the leadership of Belarus chose to try to ensure a smooth, easy transition from the administrative command economy to a market-driven economy and to preserve the basis of the social safety net, which became even more vital to the population in the difficult transition years. To ensure that, the government was compelled to use 'administrative resources', rigid discipline and a very demanding policy at all levels of the executive. The need for such an approach was based on a clear understanding that productive economic liberalisation is possible only after a sound economic and legislative basis has been laid down for normal, civilised market relations.

The government's course proved to be right, as is borne out by the facts. For the last four years Belarus has registered stable GNP growth. Our country, which has about 3.5 per cent of the population of the former Soviet Union, is now producing anywhere from half to two thirds of the total output from the whole of the former USSR across a broad range of sophisticated technical products. We are talking here about such products as large dump trucks, other types of truck, computing and communications equipment, microelectronic equipment, optics, lasers, watches, refrigerators and television sets. Microelectronics, nanoelectronics, computer programming, laser physics, nuclear physics and composite materials are among the strongest sectors of Belarus's R&D complex and industry.

Needless to say, the IMF and the World Bank were the most rigid critics of Belarus's economic policy. Nevertheless, in a report issued in 2000, *Transition: the first ten years. Analysis and lessons for Eastern Europe and the former Soviet Union*, the World Bank draws notable conclusions about Belarus's experience. In particular, the World Bank concludes that Belarus has become one of the 'most resilient economies in the Commonwealth of Independent States. GDP in 1999 reached 89 per cent of its 1990 level, well above the CIS average of 62 per cent' and refers to 'the country's relatively favourable growth performance'. Observing that 'Belarus has largely abolished the Soviet command system' and 'international trade has been liberalised', the World Bank suggests that 'continued state ownership and control of large enterprises, as well as preferential treatment by Russia, have played a key role in maintaining industrial production and bolstering economic growth'. Noting that Belarus has been able 'to avoid some key mistakes in the early stages of transition', the World Bank emphasises that 'Belarus's experience suggests important lessons about transition'. Summing up its conclusions, the World Bank notes that 'the ability of the state to prevent a collapse of its capacity and control early in transition appears to have saved the Belarusian economy from the rapid decline felt elsewhere in the region' and 'if Belarus were to change course now and embark on economic reform, its initial conditions would be far more favourable than those of the other CIS countries in the early 1990s'.

This is exactly what the new government is working on after the presidential election. The government is preparing a number of documents intended to liberalise small and medium enterprises and reform the agricultural sector. Belarus's leadership is set to expand economic freedom and release entrepreneurial initiative. The emphasis in economic policy will be on the promotion of effective ownership. The government wants to switch to exerting influence on the economy through economic rather than administrative means.

A wider look at the situation in Belarus will show that according to the UN generalised index of human development Belarus has risen over the last five years from about seventieth to fifty-third place out of the 162 countries covered by the index. Belarus is ahead of all the other CIS countries on this index. That puts her at the top of the countries with a medium level of human development. It is worth mentioning also that Belarus is internationally recognised as one of the ten least corrupt countries in the world. Belarus takes pride in this given the rampant corruption in many other post-Soviet countries. Another important (and perhaps the most reliable and comprehensive) indicator of life in Belarus is that twice as many people come and settle in Belarus as emigrate.

All this does not mean that Belarus does not wish or need to improve itself. As a society we have many deficiencies, like any other country in the post-Soviet world. We all have much the same problems and hurdles to overcome.

But if one looks at the nature of the relationship between the EU and Belarus on the one hand, and, for example, the EU and Russia, Ukraine, Kazakhstan, Azerbaijan or Uzbekistan on the other, then the contrast in the nature of these relationships is evident. But is it really warranted? The answer is certainly no.

The European Union's policy options

The EU is of the opinion that many changes are needed in Belarus to bring it up to full-blooded European standards. The leadership of Belarus also sees the need to work for important transformations in the country. Belarus needs to develop and change. It is here that the core problem arises: how can the EU best promote further transformation in Belarus? What is the best, most effective policy for the EU to pursue to influence the transformation unfolding in Belarus?

There are two primary policy options for the EU: an easy one and a less easy one.

The easy one is the standard approach. It could be summarised briefly as follows: Belarus should change first, and only then will the EU get involved.

This option will not work.

It will not work because such policies would be a rerun of the 1997 policies which, as everybody now recognises, were a failure. The verdict on these policies was passed by the hundreds of international observers in their conclusions after the presidential election.

This option would, furthermore, lead to a vicious circle in the relationship between the EU and Belarus, to an entrenched stalemate casting a shadow over the future. Operationally, however well-packaged and nicely-worded, this policy would amount to presenting Belarus with a set of conditions to be fulfilled before the EU will engage in a meaningful relationship. Needless to say, such an ultimatum would not be acceptable to Belarus. Most probably Belarus, in its turn, would respond with the same proposition to the EU: reverse your policies and then Belarus will respond. This would lead nowhere.

The meager results of the 1997 policy should, hopefully, have proved to EU policy-makers that Belarus does not act under pressure. This was amply demonstrated in the most difficult of all imaginable circumstances: by the unprecedented resistance of the Belarusians in the Second World War, which led them to lose one third of their brethren and eventually to emerge in 1945 as a UN founding member, recognised by the great powers for their contribution to the defeat of the Nazis in the bloodiest conflict in the history of the world.

This does not mean that Belarus does not want to or will not move in many of the areas which are of interest or concern to the EU. It is already doing so. But it is important to understand that Belarus is acting on its own behalf in taking steps to transform itself. We are doing it for our own benefit, guided by our own concerns. We are not doing it for the outside world.

It is also important to understand that in transforming itself, Belarus will not opt for revolutionary change. Belarusians have had enough of that. They are cautious and conservative by nature.

Changes are under way in Belarus, and they will continue to unfold. But these will be gradual, evolutionary changes. Changes in the right direction. Belarus will not jump through hoops to get to any 'benchmarks' just to earn applause from the outside world.

Thus, the setting of preconditions is not a viable option. Above all, it will not provide leverage for the EU to change Belarus. As a result, if such policies were to be adopted, or rather slipped into, the result is clear: nothing will happen. This is a sterile option. As is often the case, the easiest option is not the best.

The other option for European policy towards Belarus is to engage the country in interaction on as many topics as possible which are of real and concrete importance to Belarus. Engagement will bring leverage for the EU in Belarus. No engagement – no influence.

Of course, this requires a non-standard approach for a large union making policy towards a medium-size country living through hard times. It requires creativity. It requires political boldness.

But the rapid coming of age of the European Union, its maturing and its growing importance may lead its decision-makers to be more open to an unorthodox approach which would give the EU a more positive role in the eastern part of Europe.

This option may be a difficult one for the fifteen governments to take, especially given the diversity of their views on the situation in Belarus.

But the prize for such an unorthodox, wise decision would be an effective EU policy towards Belarus. The prize would be a breakthrough in the stalemate affecting its relationship with a country located at a strategic crossroads in Europe.

Key factors

What factors should European decision-makers bear in mind when making a choice between these two different options in their Belarus policy? Several should be mentioned:

a) The EU and Belarus are fated to become close neighbours. EU enlargement is no longer a theoretical notion but a fast-approaching reality. By the end of 2004 the EU and Belarus may be direct and immediate neighbours with a shared border of more than a thousand kilometres. Belarus wants this border to unite rather then divide us. There is much more to our neighbour status than mere physical proximity.

b) Belarus is the major ground transit route from the EU to Moscow and Russia. If one were to draw on a map a line from Berlin to Moscow, this line would pass through Minsk, the capital of Belarus. Not Kiev or Riga, but Minsk. Any transit route bypassing Belarus will be at least 50 per cent longer than via Belarus. That makes no sense commercially. Also, Belarus has a much better transit infrastructure than many other countries of the former Soviet Union. Does it make sense to invest the European taxpayer's money in vastly upgrading the border-crossing infrastructure on the western side of the Belarus border without the same investment in the infrastructure on the Belarus side of that border? This would be to invest in creating bottle-necks.

c) There are other important commercial opportunities at stake. As a member of the Eurasia Economic Community with Russia, Kazakhstan, Kyrgyzstan and Tajikistan, Belarus can give an EU entrepreneur with production facilities in Belarus direct access not only to its own market of ten million people, but also to the 200 million people in the combined market of the customs union of the five. Further, Belarus has several free economic zones. One of these is located at Brest, the most western and most important railway and highway hub in the former Soviet Union and now in Belarus. After EU enlargement the Free Economic Zone Brest will probably be the only free economic zone sitting right on the EU border. It does not take much imagination to fathom the commercial opportunities this opens up.

d) The EU is trying to build an energy partnership with Russia. The EU's dependence on Russian energy supplies will become ever greater and more strategic. Belarus, Poland and Ukraine are clearly the most important countries for the EU in terms of energy transit. Moreover, Belarus is the only country which was mentioned three times in this context in the statement on the further direction of the energy dialogue between the EU and the Russian Federation at the EU-Russia summit in Brussels on 3 October 2001. Belarus already hosts the strategic Yamal-Europe gas pipeline network. It also hosts a major oil transmission system 'Druzhba'. A new gas pipeline, Kobrin-Velke Kapoushany, is in the offing, going via Belarus and Poland to the EU. The October 2001 summit between Russia and the EU also recognised the parties' common interest in connecting up their electricity networks. How, without Belarus, can one secure the whole new energy transport infrastructure, which is obviously in the interest of everybody involved? How can one ensure the physical security of the gas and oil pipelines between Russia and the EU without Belarus, especially after the events of September 11, 2001? Which is the EU more interested in: stability or instability in Belarus, which carries the major energy arteries to the EU?

e) The European Union intends to create a common economic area with Russia. Can one realistically imagine a functioning and effective common economic area between the EU and Russia with Belarus sitting in between and not playing a meaningful part in the same economic area? Furthermore, Belarus is Russia's number two trading partner, almost on a par with Germany. Russia has a trade turnover of $11 billion with Belarus, with its ten million people, against $10.5 billion with China, with its more than 1 billion people.

f) Western Europe in general, and the EU in particular, are extremely concerned, and rightly so, about the influx of illegal migrants. But few people take account of the fact that the wave of illegal migration from Asia is to a large extent being prevented from reaching Western Europe by Belarus, at its border with Poland. With the de facto absence of borders within the CIS, ten of thousands of illegal migrants from terrorism-prone countries in Asia are penetrating the south-eastern borders of the CIS countries and attempting to move on to the West through Belarus. Until the fateful events of 11 September the Belarus-Polish border was the first real barrier these waves of illegal migrants encountered on their way to Europe from Afghanistan, Pakistan, Bangladesh and other countries. According to conservative estimates by the Belarusian border control and law enforcement agencies, there are currently between 100,000 and 200,000 illegal migrants in Belarus trying to penetrate further to the West. Thus Belarus, through its own efforts and using its own resources, is holding back a huge surge of illegal migration targeted on EU countries. This effort clearly serves the interests of the EU. Unfortunately, the EU has not so far given Belarus any help with this.

g) For much the same reasons the international fight against terrorism is inconceivable without the active participation of Belarus, located as it is on a key route between Europe and Asia. Let us note in passing that the notion of a world changed by the events of 11 September is already a commonplace in political jargon, but clearly no practical conclusions have been drawn from this as regards EU co-operation with Belarus on these priority issues. For example, the EU has invested and continues to invest substantial political and financial resources in closing the Chernobyl nuclear power station in Ukraine and encouraging the closure of the Ignalina nuclear power station in Lithuania. Both sit right on the border of Belarus. Is it possible in the dangerous, terrorism-prone world of today to ensure the physical security of these nuclear power stations, especially from the air, without the participation of Belarus? It is time to think more about this problem, including the possibility of multilateral arrangements involving the EU to provide co-operative physical security for these nuclear power stations. Neither the world nor Europe wants any more Chernobyls.

h) Belarus is a very stable country. It has no territorial disputes with or territorial claims against any of its neighbours. Belarusian society is free of inter-ethnic or inter-confessional strife, although we are a multi-national and multi-confessional country.

i) Belarus also makes an extremely important contribution to our common European security. Belarus was first among the Soviet Union's nuclear heirs to renounce, without preconditions, its nuclear weapons. It was this decision by Belarus that tilted the balance towards the successful handling of the nuclear succession. One cannot overestimate the importance for the security of Europe and the world of the safe resolution of this ominous issue. Belarus also plays a principled role in eliminating conventional armaments under the CFE Treaty. Belarus has destroyed more conventional weapons than, for example, the United Kingdom, France and the USA together. Belarus delivered on its commitment to eliminate huge amounts of conventional weapons inherited from the USSR and did so without any foreign assistance, although we requested help with this vital security measure. Belarus was also the first country to ratify the adapted CFE Treaty signed in 1999 in Istanbul by the heads of states of the militarily important European countries.

j) By virtue of these actions Belarus is a net contributor to stability and security in its subregion and thus in Europe. Europe, having very recently paid a heavy price for regional and local conflicts, should be more appreciative of Belarus's role and achievements.

k) Belarus's significance on the post-Soviet political stage is greater than its size would suggest. Throughout the twentieth century Belarus has more often than not been a make-or-break country for the area. Suffice it to mention that it was in Belarus in 1898 that the Bolshevik Party of Russia was established, which nineteen years later, in 1917, led the October Revolution that 'shook the world'. Belarus was among the four republics that established the Soviet Union in 1922. It was in Belarus that in December 1991 the leaders of Russia, Ukraine and Belarus put an end to the Soviet Union. Belarus has since then been the seat of the headquarters of the new formation of former republics, the Commonwealth of Independent States. Belarus is at the core of all the integration efforts in the area of the former Soviet Union. So far, the most advanced of these are the Belarus-Russia Union and the Eurasia Economic Community, which brings together Russia, Belarus, Kazakhstan, Kyrgyzstan and Tajikistan.

l) Finally, the existence of an independent and viable Belarus is an important factor for regional stability at a geopolitically strategic crossroads. All of its neighbours, and the EU in particular, have a stake in making sure that Belarus continues on this path.

The importance of many of these factors and the significance of Belarus's contribution to them will only continue to grow over time.

Time for a fresh start

Summing up, it is time for the EU to take a closer look at the realities of today and tomorrow and to resolve for itself a stark option: whether to continue, with variations, its 'politically correct' but ineffective policy or to embark on a new policy, engaging Belarus on an equal footing and making it a reliable partner in the new Europe.

Of course, in international politics things rarely happen in the blink of an eye. It will take time to improve substantially the relationship between the EU and Belarus. A step-by-step, give-and-take approach is what is needed.

Step-by-step involvement and engagement between Belarus and the EU could take different forms. But engagement has to be tangible, not just lip service. Meaningful steps might include in-depth co-operation and assistance on issues of illegal migration and counter-terrorism; joint exploration of the consequences of EU enlargement for Belarus and ways of maximising the positive and minimising the negative consequences in trade flows and other sectors; finding practical ways of facilitating continued free travel for law-abiding citizens when the Schengen regime is introduced by EU candidate countries in Central and Eastern Europe; abolishing outdated EU quotas on textile exports from Belarus; unfreezing and bringing into force the Interim Trade Agreement; and ratification of the Partnership and Co-operation Agreement between the EU and Belarus.

If engaged, Belarus will respond positively. President Reagan was right when he said that it takes two to tango. Normalising EU-Belarus relations would be an important and lasting contribution to the creation of a truly united Europe.

One final point in conclusion. Belarus, situated at a historic crossroads and both a beneficiary and a victim of its geostrategic location, vitally dependent on European trade flows, is concerned not only about the short and medium but also the long-term perspective. We are concerned that the independently developing integrationist processes in the West and the East of the European continent, i.e. the European Union and the Commonwealth of Independent States (or whatever other formation there might be in this area), could eventually lead to the creation of new closed blocks – economic blocks now rather than the military blocks of the past. We do not think this is the right future for the European continent. Belarus would like to see in due course an integration of integrations, combining the two major integration processes in the West and East of our continent in one single evolution. We are sure that such a super-integration would serve the common interests of all the European peoples.

The time has come to give a fresh impetus to EU-Belarus relations for the sake of our common future.

The EU and Belarus: From a Zero to a Positive Sum Game

Catherine Guicherd

Over the past few years, relations between Belarus and the European Union have come to a dead end, from which the parties do not quite know how to extricate themselves. Both have to share part of the blame. By resisting any meaningful democratic and economic reform, and placing all its bets on Russia, Belarus has isolated itself from the European 'mainstream' driven by the EU. Among the countries of Central and Eastern Europe, it is the only one not to have bid for membership and its desire for rapprochement with the Union remains ambiguously expressed. Belarus's self-isolation has been compounded by its quasi-total boycott by EU countries since 1997 – a policy that has notably failed to bring about the intended change of regime, as is usually the case with policies of isolation. Enlargement, the rapid development of the EU-Russian partnership and the inherent limitations of both sides' approaches, however, are forcing them to review their strategies. Beginning with a brief overview of EU-Belarus relations since the latter's independence, this chapter explores the possibility of a partnership between Brussels and Minsk that would measure up to the requirement of their soon-to-be neighbourhood, and to the intensification of economic and political relations across the continent.

From benign mutual ignorance to 'cold peace'

Relations between the EU and Belarus have never been close. However, even before the two sides became aware of each other's existence and peculiarities, tensions began to escalate, leading, since the mid-1990s, to a 'cold peace' that somehow looks out of place in the integrating Europe of the twenty-first Century.

A low degree of mutual interest

Among the Newly Independent States (NIS) located in Europe, Belarus has demonstrated the least enthusiasm for a possible 'Western' orientation. The Western-leaning component of its political spectrum – mostly represented by the Belarusian Popular Front (BPF) – never gathered more than minority support in public opinion and, unlike in Ukraine and Moldova, there was never any fear that the country would implode under the pull of centrifugal Western and Eastern tendencies. Although, like Ukraine, Belarus presented itself as a 'bridge between East and West', proclaimed the adoption of a 'multi-vectored' foreign policy, and declared its neutrality in the early 1990s – at the same time as it was abandoning nuclear weapons under strong Western pressure – pro-Russian political and economic choices soon gave the lie to that policy of equidistance. Minsk's adhesion to the 1992 CIS security treaty (Tashkent Treaty) and to the first CIS monetary union in 1993 were clear signals that Belarus saw its future in arrangements reminiscent of a reconstituted Soviet Union. That the EU, which then mainly functioned as an economic grouping (the Union was just making its first hesitant and rather unsuccessful inroads into foreign and security policy), should have figured rather low in Belarusian priorities at the time should not be surprising.

The EU, for its part, was too busy re-tailoring itself (through the Maastricht Treaty on Political and Monetary Union) and trying to attend to pressing security questions (the Balkans) to pay detailed attention to developments in the NIS, beyond its general concern about a possible further disintegration of Russia and Ukraine. Until the late 1990s Brussels did not develop an active policy towards Eastern Europe, except vis-à-vis the enlargement countries. With its lack of clear identity, doubts about its real desire for sovereignty, and its apparently low degree of 'europeanness', Belarus was not a likely candidate for EU attention. As it expressed no particular European aspirations, nor presented particular signs of instability, it did not call either for specific treatment. The EU's offer to Belarus at the time therefore reflected its rather undifferentiated approach to the NIS, taking the form of a Partnership and Co-operation Agreement (PCA), which was signed in 1995.

A gradual estrangement

Instead of a progressive rapprochement on a trial-and-error basis, as was the case with Russia and Ukraine, a situation of mutual estrangement gradually evolved between the EU and Belarus, escalating into open hostility.

That deterioration was triggered by President Lukashenko's authoritarian ways domestically and his often openly adversarial attitude to Western partners. As the President (elected in 1994) moved to secure unchallenged political control through the gradual curtailing of civil and political freedoms, the organisation of a controversial constitutional referendum (November 1996) and the ensuing replacement of parliament by a hand-picked legislature, it became clear to the EU that 'business as usual' was no longer possible. In February 1997 Brussels virtually broke off contacts with Belarus, postponing ratification of the PCA and the entry into force of its Interim Agreement, suspending bilateral contacts at ministerial level, and freezing assistance programmes with the exception of humanitarian aid, regional programmes (involving not only Belarus) and programmes directly benefiting the democratisation process (Tacis assistance for the media, NGOs and young people). These measures were temporarily tightened by a policy of sanctions in the summer of 1998, with Belarusian senior officials being banned from entry onto EU territory following the President's unilateral decision to expropriate Western embassies in Minsk.

As a consequence of and counterweight to this self-imposed, Western-reinforced isolation, from 1996 Belarus turned almost exclusively to Russia and the CIS. This process of Eastern re-integration culminated with the signing of a 'Treaty on the Formation of a Union State' between Russia and Belarus in 1999. The Union Treaty provides for the establishment of a set of common institutions and the gradual implementation of common policies (often on the EC/EU model), including a single citizenship; equal rights of residence, economic activity and access to social services; and an ambitious plan for economic and monetary union up to currency unification, due to occur in 2005. Co-operation in the field of security and defence, which is already intense both in the context of the CIS and bilaterally, is slated to be upgraded into a common foreign and defence policy, a reassurance Belarus has sought in the context of Nato's enlargement and its intervention in Yugoslavia.

The cultivation of close political and economic ties with Russia has provided Minsk with a political home in the absence of links with the West, and served as an 'insurance policy' against the kind of reforms normally required as a condition for partnership with Western institutions, the EU in particular. Thus, thanks to cheap energy imports, debt cancellation, advantageous credits and the chance to continue basing a large part of its trade on barter, Belarus has been able to postpone painful structural economic reforms (for example, privatising large state firms, which continue to account for 80 per cent of GDP), and to maintain the socialist-style welfare state which its neighbours have long ago had to dismember.

Despite some misgivings about the implications of the Russian-Belarusian Union, Belarusians have been broadly supportive of the course followed by their government. Indeed, according to opinion polls, two-thirds of them readily agree that 'Russians and Belarusians are historically one people, they are spiritually close, and they have similar languages, cultures, and traditions'. Economically, people are sensitive to the government's argument that Russian-Belarusian integration will ensure economic growth, maintain employment and preserve their social benefits. As a result, integration with Russia in one form or another is approved by the majority of citizens (62 per cent according to a November 2001 independent survey), contrasting with a low level of interest in integration with the EU (15-18 per cent).[1] Even President Lukashenko's opponents, who would like to strike a different course in domestic policy and relations with the West, make a point of stressing their commitment to close links with Moscow.

In this context, criticism by the EU of the conduct of Belarus's elections and of the Lukashenko government's behaviour falls flat with the majority of politically inactive Belarusian citizens. This does not mean that Belarusian opinion is on the whole hostile to the EU. But they tend to perceive the EU as something distant and somewhat inaccessible. In this respect, the statement by a high-ranking Foreign Ministry official, Oleg Latpyonok, that 'the European Union... cannot realistically constitute a 'common home' for all European peoples in the medium term'[2], probably reflects the majority view in the country.

Two policies in need of reassessment

For a few years (approximately 1997-2001), the coincidence of Minsk's drive for integration with Russia and the EU's isolation of Belarus led to a tense status quo, but a status quo nevertheless which relieved the two partners of the burden of thinking about their future relationship. However, by the end of 2001 this situation seemed no longer tenable for a number of reasons linked both to the limitations of each side's policies and to larger contextual events.

Broadly speaking, from the EU's side the freeze in EU-Belarusian relations was becoming too onerous a constraint in view of Brussels's two top priorities in Eastern Europe: ensuring the success of enlargement and of the partnership with Russia. Belarus, for its part, is gradually realising that its policy is leading to political marginalisation, economic irrelevance, and a burdensome one-way dependence on Russia, and that, as a simple matter of survival, it will need to recreate a 'breathing space' for itself by establishing contacts with other European and international actors.

New requirements: EU policies

The first and most obvious reason why the EU should want to change course *vis-à-vis* Belarus is its failure to bring about the hoped-for democratic changes through isolation and pressure. Actually, EU members (some more than others) have never been fully comfortable with the isolation policy, and have earlier sought to relax it. Thus, following the climax of the embassies episode in 1998, a détente was attempted in 1999. Modest 'carrots' were provided in the form of a rise in the Belarusian quota for the duty-free export of textiles to the EU market, the revocation of visa restrictions for Belarusian senior officials, and a slight increase in aid. However, the EU's approach remained highly conditional, with the yardstick for normalisation being set by a series of benchmarks worked out by the OSCE in the context of the forthcoming parliamentary elections. However, this policy, intended to support the fragile dialogue between government and opposition in the run-up to the elections, was scarcely more successful than the previous one in eliciting a change in the government's attitude. Neither the autumn 1999 parliamentary elections, nor the presidential election two years later were deemed free and fair by the OSCE.

On the other hand, what these elections, and in particular the latter, demonstrated is that President Lukashenko continues to have genuine political support in the country. Most independent analysts agree that he would have won a democratic election in autumn 2001 despite the budding mobilisation of an opposition and the deteriorating economic conditions. An independent opinion poll commissioned by the US State Department during the campaign showed that a majority of 58-60 per cent of Belarusians had a positive opinion of their President and thought he had performed well enough to deserve re-election; and in polls setting him against other candidates, Lukashenko regularly gathered 47-62 per cent support (depending on the polling agency), contrasting with the mere 5-19 per cent endorsement of opposition forces.

Thus, as the Belarusian leader appeared firmly in the driver's seat for another four years at the end of 2001, European capitals began quietly to consider a return to *realpolitik* in their relations with Minsk. An end to mutual ignorance looked all the more essential in that enlargement and the rapid development of EU-Russian relations made contacts with Belarus inescapable.

Enlargement

With Polish, Lithuanian and Latvian membership, by 2004-2005 the EU will have 1250 km of common border with Belarus. This proximity offers opportunities, but it also carries risks. The opportunities include the chance to strengthen economic and human interaction at all levels, in other words to develop a positive dynamic of interdependence regardless of the specific legal relationship between Belarus and the EU. The risk is one of growing asymmetries developing between Poland, Latvia and Lithuania on the one hand, and Belarus on the other, as the former pursue their institutional, legal and economic adjustment to Western standards, while Belarus continues to function as a sovietised society, economy and polity. And asymmetries, as peace research and empirical experience demonstrate, create a potential for instability and conflict. Above all, proximity creates its own demands: with Poland, Latvia and Lithuania adopting the EU acquis, a large number of issues that used to be bilateral matters in their relationship with Belarus, from health and environmental regulations for chemical imports to technical regulations for electronic components, to customs rules, to the crucial issue of visas, will become EU-Belarus issues, requiring at least a minimum of interaction and co-operation between Minsk and Brussels.

In practice, the two sides are ill-equipped to deal with these new challenges. Belarus's exports to the EU are likely to diminish as a result of its inability and/or unwillingness to adapt to EU regulations and standards, and the fact that its preferential trade agreements with Central European partners will have to be cancelled as they enter the Common Market. Growth on one side of the border and stagnation on the other will create additional incentives for Belarusians to seek work illegally in Poland and Lithuania, and from there, in other EU countries. This incentive will be all the stronger in that, with the new members entering the Schengen zone, the loose cross-border movements that have remained possible between Belarus and its western and northern neighbours over the past few years will have to give way to a much tighter, centrally-controlled transit regime. Latvia and Lithuania, which imposed visa obligations on their former compatriots in the early 1990s, are gradually bringing them into line with Schengen requirements. Warsaw, for its part, tightened its entry regulations for Russians and Belarusians in 1998, but citizens of both countries can still enter Poland with a voucher obtainable from the local administration. By the end of 2002, or mid-2003 at the latest, these arrangements will be revoked.

The negative implications of the Schengen visa policy are obvious. For one, it will affect the ethnic minorities of some 250,000 Belarusians in Poland and some 2-500,000 Poles in Belarus (depending on whether any Catholic in Belarus is considered a Pole or not), who may want to continue to have close relations with their kin on the other side of the border. Second, it will curtail the informal economic activities associated with easy border transit ('suitcase trade', daily employment, etc) which are important in the border regions, not only on the Belarusian side but in the eastern regions of Poland, which are the poorest in the country. But perhaps even more important are the political-psychological-cultural implications of the Schengen border. While the end of the Cold War made it theoretically possible to create a 'single Europe whole and free', the Schengen border will deepen the sense of division already created by the distinction between EU candidate countries and the others. As Polish officials and analysts often stress, the visa-free travel their citizens and other Central Europeans have enjoyed since 1991 has made a tremendous contribution to the modernisation and 'europeanisation' of the country, as millions were able to see for themselves what life in 'the West' looks like, learn about its requirements, and occasionally acccumulate some starting capital that they were later able to invest at home. This openness has also greatly helped the reconciliation process with Western neighbours, in particular Germany. Should the same options be denied to Belarusian (and Ukrainian) citizens, this would undermine the EU's own efforts to promote modernisation and opening in those countries.

EU officials claim that Schengen must not mean erecting new walls in the East. But for this to be true, flexibility in the EU's attitude and co-operation with Belarus (and others) is necessary. Flexibility, in this case, means a readiness to examine, together with the three candidate countries concerned (Poland, Lithuania and Latvia) and the Belarusian government, the possibility of working out special visa and transit arrangements to allow for smooth and uninterrupted border-crossing by frequent travellers and local populations. Analysts have developed proposals in this sense for some time, but the EU has demonstrated a particular reluctance to consider them, for fear this would weaken the commitment of candidate countries to Schengen, and it would certainly not begin with Belarus. Co-operation is also required in two other areas. First, so that Schengen does not hamper the transit of honest and law-abiding citizens, the EU and Belarus must work together to combat illegal immigration and organised crime. Certainly, the Belarusian police and intelligence services are not the kind of partners the EU would readily embrace; nor does the fact that the border is jointly policed by Belarusian and Russian border guards facilitate the EU's task. Nevertheless, it might be worth looking more closely at the interior ministry to see whether there would not be partners there with whom the EU could work without betraying its principles. In addition, Brussels should try and make maximum use of the relatively good relations the Polish and Lithuanian authorities are said to enjoy with Belarusian counterparts at the local level to 'civilise' border control. And a dialogue with Belarus on possible legal (and probably temporary) work migration to EU countries would allow for differentiation between Belarusian citizens and those who use Belarusian territory as a transit point to the EU, thus clearing the atmosphere for a more ruthless EU attitude to illegal migration across its eastern border. Second, in order to facilitate transit of merchandise, not least to take account of Belarus's geographical situation on the most direct transit route between Western Europe and Russia, it is essential to make technical improvements to border posts and streamline customs arrangements on the Polish-Belarusian border. Here again, many of the impediments come from the Belarusian side in the form of over-regulation and bureaucratic dysfunction. However, progress in the physical improvement of facilities and the training of Belarusian administrative personnel has also been hampered by the limitations on Tacis assistance due to the sanctions policy. The channelling of funds to Belarus through cross-border and regional programmes has only partly compensated for these shortcomings and has left stumbling- blocks which will increasingly hinder the development of the EU-Russia partnership.

A crucial contextual factor: the EU-Russia partnership

Russia and the EU are aiming at a 'strategic partnership'. This partnership has a strong economic component, gradually slated to evolve into a 'Common European Economic Area', a sort of pan-European equivalent of NAFTA. Since October 2000 it has had an energy component with economic, environmental and security dimensions. At the same time the partners also decided to reinforce their political dialogue, with the aim of developing security co-operation between them. This 'strategic partnership' has progressed at remarkable speed since President Putin's arrival in the Kremlin; it is strongly willed by both sides and has received additional momentum in the wake of the September 11 terrorist attacks. This will have an impact on Belarus's relations with the EU in several ways, and to some extent force Brussels to review its Belarus policy.

At first glance, the greater focus on Russia will mean less interest in the smaller NIS countries (not only Belarus, but also Ukraine) i.e. less political attention and a further decline in interest on the part of Western capital, which will invest primarily in Russia. By contrast, Russian capital will continue to invest in Ukraine and Belarus, a movement that has clearly accelerated since 1999. Given the lack of adequate conditions for Western investment in those countries, EU governments will probably cast a benevolent eye on this process on the assumption that there is no immediate alternative, that by contributing to economic growth Russian investment will also foster stability in those countries, and that Russian management, even if it has not reached Western standards of transparency and efficiency, can nevertheless assist the modernisation of their economies. There is embryonic evidence of the latter in Ukraine, and signs that Russian companies are seeking assurances that they will enjoy sufficient management freedom if they invest in Belarus, which is beginning a careful privatisation process.

Overall, for Belarus economic integration with Russia appears to be a factor for modernisation and change, and in the context of developing EU-Russia relations a factor for rapprochement between Belarus and the EU. Belarus has already had to adjust its customs regulations to Russia's as part of the planned customs union between them. It has also had to amend its monetary policy as a consequence of the currency unification process. The gradual development of the 'Common European Economic Area', plus the parallel use of the euro in EU-Russian transactions, will intensify the movement. Russia's efforts to enter the WTO – a mutually reinforcing process with economic integration with the EU – will create additional pressure on Belarus to follow suit. Even though Minsk also aims for membership in the WTO, it is much further even than Moscow from fulfilling the conditions of fair competition and transparency in economic regulation that would make WTO membership possible.

Two questions that may arise for the EU in this context are whether to (i) provide Belarus with technical, legal and financial assistance so that it can take the measures required for WTO membership in step with Russia; (ii) help Belarus with the social consequences of its economic liberalisation policies, should the latter gain significant momentum. A critical period in this respect could begin in the second half of 2003, when President Lukashenko is still in power, preventing bold political moves, but the effects of liberalisation could begin seriously to be felt.

A second factor with potentially far-reaching consequences for EU-Belarusian relations is the development of the energy dialogue between the EU and Russia. This dialogue will objectively benefit Belarus (partly at the expense of Ukraine) and circumvent the EU's political reservations about relations with Minsk. Indeed, policy decisions since the end of 2000 demonstrate that energy policy regarding Eastern Europe in EU capitals is determined more by oil and gas interests and EU-Russian geo-strategic and economic interests (the EU's desire to diversify its oil and gas supplies as its consumption increases; Russia's need to attract Western capital to modernise its oil and gas industry), than by the particulars of its relations with 'smaller' nations. Already, Belarus is the main transit route for Russian oil coming to Western Europe by land; this position is being reinforced as it becomes a major transit route for gas as well. Thus, EU governments have demonstrated full understanding for Gazprom's intention to build the new Yamal-Western Europe gas pipeline, and perhaps also a secondary conduit, through Belarus, rather than using the Ukraine route, which has traditionally carried 90 per cent of Russia's gas to the West. EU gas companies, including Gas de France, Snam (Italy) and Ruhrgas (Germany) are involved in the project. In that equation, Belarus not only has the geographical advantage of offering shorter transit, but it charges lower fees, is not suspected of pilfering gas on the way, and is a much more predictable partner than Ukraine for both Europe and Russia.

A third factor in EU-Russia relations that could have an influence on Belarus is the EU-Russia political dialogue. There, the advantage could be for the EU provided it plays smartly. Certainly, there are things that Brussels cannot expect, such as Russia campaigning for democracy in Belarus. Besides, President Putin's course in domestic economic policy and international affairs is ruffling enough feathers at home, and he would not want to antagonise even further the oligarchs and local bosses who are the strongest supporters of Lukashenko. Thus, he has so far characteristically failed to disavow the Belarusian autocrat despite his known aversion to the man. What would seem possible, however, would be to induce Russia to use its economic leverage to try and speed up economic liberalisation in Belarus. This would not only help breach Belarus's isolation from world economic trends, but also weaken the regime's control and gradually pave the way for political change. Stressing the economic factor in EU-Russia discussions about Belarus would seem desirable in many ways as it would: (i) focus the debate on one area in which the two partners objectively have a common interest; (ii) touch a less sensitive chord than addressing the political question of the behaviour of the Lukashenko regime; and (iii) avoid creating a sense in the Kremlin that the EU would accept Belarus's reintegration into Russia's sphere of influence – if only Moscow made sure its vassals were presentable!

New requirements: Belarusian policies

Beyond the obvious intensification of the EU-Russia relationship, two factors are stimulating Belarus to open up to the European Union.

The first is a gradual realisation that the Russia-Belarusian Union may be leading to a greater degree of loss of sovereignty than is desirable. Indeed, rather than being a process of convergence on equal terms, or at Belarus's behest, it is becoming more and more a process of adjustment by Belarus to Russian norms, on Russia's conditions. As alluded to above, Belarus has already had to reform its customs regulations, VAT procedures and monetary policy to increase their compatibility with those of Russia. Adjustment in the tax domain is expected to follow, as has been made clear by Russian Economic Development and Trade Minister German Gref. President Putin, for his part, has clearly signalled to his Belarusian colleague that political and institutional aspects of the Union will have to take second place, while Belarus is expected to carry out the economic reforms required before integration can proceed. And certainly, President Lukashenko's ambition, when he initiated the process in 1996, of finding himself one day in the driver's seat of the Union, has been destroyed by Putin's arrival.

In that context, contacts with the EU would be a way for Minsk to unlock what appears to be a unidimensional and stifling foreign and economic orientation, and to recreate for itself room for manoeuvre, even if it maintains privileged relations with Russia.

The second factor calling for change is the gradual realisation in Belarusian government circles that the state of the country will not afford it the luxury of postponing economic reform indefinitely, and that economic modernisation will require Western advice and capital input. Although the full implications of this may not yet have been grasped by the President and his close circle of advisers, it is progressively permeating through the bureaucracy of the foreign and economic ministries. Belarus's bid to join the WTO can be seen as a manifestation of this growing awareness.

Belarus's overtures

Minsk's half-hearted overtures have been conspicuously timed to coincide with periods of reassessment by the EU of its Belarus policy. Thus, the first signals were given in 1999, with Belarus rekindling the theme of the 'multi-vectoredness' of its foreign policy, an orientation it had set aside almost immediately after adopting it in the early 1990s. Domestically, the new orientation has been advertised under the slogan 'together with Russia in Europe', which is a way of reconciling popular aspirations to the maintenance of a special relationship with Moscow and the attraction of the higher living standards associated with the EU.

More direct messages were conveyed to the EU following the election of President Lukashenko to a second term of office in September 2001. In the late autumn of 2001 both the new, reportedly relatively open-minded Prime Minister, Gennady Novitski, and the Foreign Ministry highlighted the role that the EU could play in the future in Belarus's external political and economic relations, suggesting that Minsk might be interested, at some point, in concluding an Association Agreement. At the same time the President announced that he had instructed the government to rejuvenate contacts with Minsk-based EU ambassadors. The appointment as Belarusian Ambassador in Brussels of Sergei Martynov, who is not only a 'heavyweight' (he has been Ambassador to the EU and to the US) but is well-versed in EU matters as former Vice-Minister of Foreign Affairs in charge of the EU dossier, can also be interpreted as demonstrating a desire to upgrade relations. That said, several months later, few concrete follow-up moves had been taken and the general context of continued tensions with Western countries over the OSCE mission, plus moves to crack down on allegedly corrupt oligarchs, did not bode well for the resumption of relations at a high political level.

Steering the EU's Belarus policy onto a new course

Having taken stock and realised that their policy had failed to achieve the desired ends, by late 2001 EU capitals were progressively rallying to the conclusion of a Polish expert that 'in a centralised and sovietised country like Belarus, revolution can only come from above, and therefore it is at that level that change has to be fostered.'[3] The problem for the EU, however, was how to re-open channels to Minsk without sending the 'wrong' political signal, i.e. how to justify a change in policy without appearing to reward President Lukashenko when he had satisfied so few of the demands placed on him. This, it seems to the author, could best be done by combining careful bilateral measures and the development of a regional EU 'Eastern Dimension'.

Bilateral EU-Belarus relations

The twin declarations following the presidential election of September 2001 and the ensuing change of government in October testify to the EU's search for new ground in its relations with Belarus. While they maintain the critical line of previous years on the lack of democracy in the country, these statements contain two new elements: one is a reference to 'the emergence in Belarus of a degree of pluralism and of a civil society'; the other expresses a policy intention: the EU 'does not wish Belarus to be isolated' and 'it would like to see Belarus in time regain its place within the international community'.

This did not yet amount to a new policy. The reservations of some members (primarily Britain and the Nordic countries) on human rights grounds did not permit that so soon after the election. What seemed to be emerging toward the end of 2001, though, was a kind of 'permissive consensus' enabling those EU governments that wanted to do so to re-establish contact with the Belarusian authorities, up to ministerial level but excluding the ministries and agencies suspected of being involved in repression (Ministry of the Interior, intelligence services) and of course ruling out contact with the

President himself. Channels could be created or exploited to use this opportunity in a discrete manner, such as Italy using the meeting of the Heads of Government of the Central European Initiative in Trieste in November 2001 for consultations with Prime Minister Novitski, or the Swedish Social-Democratic Party, the main force in the government coalition in Stockholm, inviting Foreign Minister Mikhail Khvostov to open a seminar on developments in Belarus the following month.

The next step could be to transform this informal approach into a policy permitting the EU in particular to move beyond Tacis's exclusive support for NGOs of the past few years and to resume technical assistance to Belarusian government agencies. This would, after all, only re-align EU programmes with those of the EBRD, which never ceased to entertain a 'critical dialogue' with the Belarusian authorities. Measures of this kind were being pondered at the beginning of 2002, with small businesses also being identified as potential beneficiaries of EU funding. These measures, however, would only be significant if Tacis support for Belarus were raised from the paltry 10 million euros planned for 2000-2003 to an amount of, say, at least the 50 million euros earmarked for Moldova. (Belarus has more than twice the population of Moldova and its territory is six times as large.) A possible low-key way of increasing Belarus's share under Tacis would be to channel more funds to the country through the multinational regional, cross-border and nuclear safety programmes. By doing this, the EU would help Belarus, but it would also increase its own security and alleviate social and economic pressures in the easternmost regions of its new members, Poland, Lithuania and Latvia.

In order to avoid the risks of political exploitation of increased EU assistance, it would be preferable for any new start in EU-Belarus relations to be made with as little publicity as possible. In the period leading up to enlargement, which corresponds approximately to the lifetime of the Lukashenko regime (assuming the constitution is respected) the EU could also make active use of Poland and Lithuania as quiet channels of communication and partners in co-operation with Minsk. Poland is particularly keen to offer the help of its experts, businessmen, NGOs, local officials, etc, who can share their experience of systemic transformation with Belarusian counterparts. The EU should support these initiatives as actively as possible.

A policy of greater engagement, with a significant increase in Tacis funding, EIB loans, etc could possibly follow the EBRD's and World Bank's two-option scenarios, which foresee scaled support programmes depending on the degree of economic reform carried out by the government. Should Belarus genuinely move towards structural economic reform, it would be in the EU's interest to help cushion its social consequences and assist in steering the process at the same time. But as this would imply a qualitative change in the EU's approach and reinstate a clear political component in the relationship, Brussels should presumably more clearly include elements of democratic conditionality in its criteria than the EBRD or the World Bank.[4] Until Minsk decides to pursue membership of the EU, however, there would be a logic in Brussels being less stringent than it is with those countries that wish to join the Union, such as Ukraine and Moldova. Finally, integrating Belarus into the EU's Northern Dimension could also be part of the re-politicised relationship. Involving Belarus from the outset in a new 'Eastern Dimension' would be an alternative or additional option, but with less political visibility as this would not identify the country as a special case.

A regional EU 'Eastern Dimension'

Developing an EU 'Eastern Dimension' that would encompass Belarus, Ukraine, Moldova and Russia would have significance for the region as a whole, but for Belarus in a particular way, given its present isolation.

An Eastern Dimension would have three main aims. The first would be to take stock of the impact of enlargement on neighbouring eastern countries in a comprehensive manner in order to develop a set of policies that would (i) mitigate and compensate for the asymmetry-creating effect of EU expansion to Central Europe; and (ii) counter the sense of isolation engendered by enlargement. This would also help remove the contradiction between the discourse of openness being pursued by the EU heads of government and foreign ministers and the restrictive policies of their interior ministers. The second aim would be to overcome the limitations of EU bilateral policies vis-à-vis Ukraine, Belarus and Moldova, which are shaped almost exclusively in the light of domestic developments in these countries, whereas, as we have highlighted for Belarus, the state of their politics, economy and society is strongly influenced by the contextual factor of EU-Russia relations. Finally, an Eastern Dimension would be a propitious vehicle for the EU to convey a more positive message to Kiev, Minsk or Chisinau than bilateral relations, which are often occasions for Brussels to point the finger at their democratic shortcomings and slow pace of reform.

Conceptually, just like the Northern Dimension (and to a large extent the Stability Pact for South-eastern Europe) the Eastern Dimension would not seek to imagine a completely new set of policies. Rather, it would place the policies that are being developed in a single framework, so as, first, better to identify weaknesses and gaps, and, second, to foster a regional dynamic. The emphasis would be on neighbourhood policies and regional co-operation – the two being often linked – in the following fields:

- visa and transit arrangements, with the objective of encouraging co-operation so as to foster transit and human interaction rather than choking them, as tends to be the case at present. The policy would aim to increase and rationalise EU funding directed at helping candidate countries meet their Schengen requirements, and to ensure the conditions for proper border control and transit on the other side. It would foster tripartite EU-candidates-neighbours collaboration in this field;
- cross-border and regional economic co-operation and trade. This could involve: (i) support for the development of cross-border economic inter-action, notably through the promotion of small and medium size enterprises (partly in connection with the EU's structural policies to help the least developed regions of the candidate countries, which often happen to coincide with their eastern border areas); (ii) a systematic review of existing bilateral economic agreements between candidate countries and their eastern neighbours in order to keep as much as possible of these agreements in place, adapting them to EU requirements where appropriate; (iii) the search for a synchronisation of existing regional trade development schemes and EU bilateral and regional plans for trade expansion;
- trans-border and regional environmental issues, whether they are of regional magnitude (for example the effects of Chernobyl, in particular in Belarus) or local, such as problems of water contamination, industrial pollution, etc;
- the development of regional infrastructure: here again the goal would be to foster interaction between new members (and by extension the EU as a whole) and neighbours. Particular attention should be devoted to the energy sector, both as regards electricity networks, in

the context of broad-ranging changes in the configuration of electricity grids in Central and Eastern Europe, and the oil and gas sector. The Eastern Dimension should be used as a tool to establish a political, economic and strategic coherence between the EU-Russia energy dialogue, developments in the gas and oil industry in neighbouring countries, and the INOGATE (Inter-State Oil and Gas to Europe) programme, which have remained largely unconnected so far. In all sectors the guiding principle should be to seek to increase East-West interdependence and the diversification of sources of energy for the candidates as well as the Eastern partners in order to enhance their security;

- the fight against organised crime and illegal migration – problems which, by nature, cannot be resolved on a bilateral basis. In conjunction with this, an agenda could be developed to define conditions for the legal migration of NIS citizens to EU countries, be it for the purpose of business, seasonal or expert work, or training. The point of such an agenda would be progressively to elaborate a set of measures that would help foster human and economic development in the NIS, in partnership with the EU. Belarus would not be the last to benefit from it;
- in the same spirit of awareness-raising, an information component, as there is a dire need in all the countries of Eastern Europe to increase understanding of what EU integration, and even a more modest 'partnership' with the Union, implies in practice. Regardless of Belarus's future intentions, it would be in Brussels's interest that its citizens be better informed of the EU's nature and functions.

Involving Belarus in an Eastern Dimension would be a way to overcome the limitations arising from the zero sum game in which Minsk and Brussels have been engaged. Without singling out the country as a special case, it would lift it out of its isolation and hopefully contribute to its government letting itself be drawn into the positive sum game represented by European integration.

Notes

[1] Sources: Centre for Sociological Research, Moscow, May-June 1999; Independent Institute of Social-Economic and Political Studies (NISEPI), Minsk, November 2001.

[2] Oleg Laptyonok (Director of the International Organisations Department, Belarusian Foreign Ministry), 'Plurality of the Foreign Policy Vectors of Belarus in the New International Setting', *Belarus in the World*, 4(4), 1999, p.44.

[3] Interview with a representative of the Polish Policy Planning Staff by the author, Warsaw, December 2001.

[4] The EBRD is required by its statutes to apply an element of democratic conditionality; the World Bank is not. In practice, the policies of the two lending agencies do not differ much.

The European Union and Belarus: A View from the European Parliament

Rob van de Water and
Jan Marinus Wiersma

Belarus is a country in the heart of the European continent, and its very geographical situation makes it important to the European Union. At the same time it would, because of this geographical situation, be only natural if the European Union were considered of major importance to Belarus. But this seemingly self-evident situation of mutual importance has never managed to translate into a good working relationship between the two.

Belarus is from all perspectives a truly European country. It has never, however, been part of mainstream European history. In a way the country always seems to have been hidden behind Moscow, even though it lies further to the west. And it would probably not even be correct to describe Belarus as a nation because of the 'Russianness' of the country and its people.

It is difficult to identify the country's specific characteristics. Its historical record is rather nondescript. It does not have any clear and historically-established frontiers. And above all, Belarus and its people lack a long-established cultural identity. It has even proved to be difficult to establish Belarusian as a national language. It is therefore easier to say what Belarus is not, than what it is. Or maybe one could describe Belarus as the only post-

Soviet state that never met the challenge of economic and political reform or made a start in the direction of the necessary change.

Belarus became independent in 1991, almost by chance. Its independence was not the result of a struggle of many years, but was the consequence of external events, after a coup attempt in Moscow failed. The country did not have a significant national movement, capable of guiding the people into a different era – to a newly-acquired independence with a new national identity. In the early years there was a short window of opportunity for independent politicians to build a new independent state, part of the new developments taking place in Central and Eastern Europe. But they soon lost their influence and momentum, as they could not build on a groundswell of reformism or national feeling amongst the population.

The old system was never actually in real danger. It was able to emerge again a few years after independence because most voters did not know how to deal with their new-found freedom. The Belarusians showed themselves to be the most nostalgic of all the people in Central and Eastern Europe. Many Belarusians would probably have felt safer remaining Russians whatever that country might stand for. One wonders whether there was much real support for the dissolution of the USSR. Alexander Lukashenko was at that time the only member of parliament to vote against it! Deep in their hearts the people of Belarus have always remained part of the USSR and measure up better against old soviet than 'European' standards.

Within the Soviet Union Belarus was a model republic. In present-day Europe it ranks very low. We would call this a conservative evaluation of Belarusian society based on certain historical factors. Up to now Belarusians have judged their situation from the perspective of their past experience rather than their hopes and prospects for the future. Against this, the people of Belarus have never had a genuine choice, or seemed prepared to help create the conditions to be able to make a real choice, about the future development of their country. This moment must however come one day because, like any other people, the Belarusians can and will change their ways.

We believe that the European Union's policy towards Belarus should be based on the distinct possibility of, or maybe hope for, change. It should assume that Belarus will be a viable independent state that should and will one day become part of the large European family of democratic nations. That Belarus will eventually become a nation able to formulate its own options for its own future.

We believe that in the end the people of Belarus will themselves demand the right to decide in a democratic way the future direction of their country. It is too easy to deny Belarus this capacity for development and place it for all eternity in the Russian orbit, as if it could never develop a democratic will of its own.

Belarus is a relatively small country and the lack of real historical determinants makes it easier for the people to be flexible. This can work in its favour. Belarus is not China, where it will take an enormous amount of time for the stream of change to trickle down into every corner of the nation.

If, within the context of an open society, the Belarusians should decide to stick with Russia instead of opting for closer relations with the EU, that would be acceptable. Right now the Union between Belarus and the Russian Federation is a forced one, an affair between elites without real substance. But given the total impossibility of debate in Belarus about these matters, it is difficult to know exactly how people feel about it. This is in stark contrast with Ukraine or even Moldova, where the issue of the nature of relations with the big neighbour remains very high on the agenda. Those in Belarus who express themselves in favour of closer ties within the framework of the Union are the same people who vote for President Lukashenko. And they vote for him because he promises protection against the kind of economy and the kind of chaos that have developed in Russia. President Lukashenko presents himself as the representative of the old paternalistic traditions. The President as the patriarch who protects his people. These same people who feel protected by the policies of President Lukashenko are probably also afraid to get closer to the EU because of the drastic reforms needed for a closer relationship.

The advantages of a closer relationship between Belarus and the European Union, including the pressure for more democracy and for economic reform, may be more appealing to other sections of the population, in particular the younger generation.

The European Union's calls for political reform, respect for basic human rights, the holding of free and fair elections and the establishment of democratic institutions in Belarus is not free of a certain degree of self-interest. The intensity and seriousness of the European Union's approach to Belarus and its regime are partly based on the simple geographical awareness that the EU will soon – after successful completion of the enlargement process – have common borders with Belarus. When, for instance, a country like Poland becomes a member of the EU. We should avoid letting the new borders of the EU become new walls or create a new divide on the European continent. The new member states will exert increasing pressure to develop effective approaches to avoid that, for instance through creative implementation of the provisions of the Schengen Treaty.

But there are also economic interests to consider. Important energy transport systems, such as the gas pipelines between Russia and the countries of the European Union, run through Belarus. Their long-term security is closely linked to political developments and the possibility of creating lasting democracy and stability in that country.

And finally there is the human element. The European Union has a moral obligation to reach out to a people that has suffered so much during the last century and that in more recent times was severely hit by the Chernobyl disaster.

Give Belarus and its people a chance. That should be our slogan and that must, above all, be the European Union's basic attitude to the country. But that is easier said than done. What we believe to be good for Belarus is based on our own, quite general, assumptions about what we believe is good for any country in the world. We have never been able to assess the real wishes and intentions of Belarus's people. We do not know how they would react if they were given the opportunity to determine the future development of their lives under democratic conditions. We have no idea how their fear of the present relates to their understandable fear of an unknown future.

Do the people of Belarus want revolution, gradual change or nothing at all? Under the present conditions elections are certainly not a reliable indicator of the political feelings of the people of Belarus. Nor are opinion polls.

Without gradual change and a sincere start on political and economic reform, revolution seems to be unavoidable. The country's economic system is not sustainable; neither in Europe nor in any other part of the modern, globalised world. This must be President Lukashenko's nightmare. To lose power and control in the same way Milosevic lost power and control over developments in Yugoslavia. The whole of Lukashenko's repressive machinery is directed to suppressing such unwanted and uncontrolled events. His reaction to the events in Yugoslavia in October 2000 make this clear. In fact his fear of this eventuality is encouraging because it implies a lack of belief in his own policies.

Belarus cannot be considered in isolation from Russia. Russia and the European Union have different agendas for Belarus. And Russia's agenda is a cynical one. The Russian political class does not want to take any responsibility for the economy of their neighbouring country. But many Russians play with the romantic idea of a complete reunion between the two countries; of a return of Belarus to Mother Russia. And Belarus is considered by many Russian politicians to be a vital element in the *cordon sanitaire* against 'the evil forces of the West' and in particular against Nato. These feelings are especially strong in the Duma, the Russian Parliament, where many dream of restoring at least part of the old empire. Belarus is their obvious candidate and Lukashenko the perfect instrument to accomplish that dream. So he had to be re-elected. Russia has maintained over the years a strong economic, political and cultural influence on Belarus, and is using it. Neither democratic ideas and principles nor the concept of independence and equality play an important role in the relationship between the two countries. Russian politicians accept Lukashenko because of his loyalty to the powers that be and because he offers a certain kind of stability to Russia's most western frontiers.

The Russian political system sees no serious alternative to Lukashenko, but this should come as no surprise because it never seriously considered the existence of a viable alternative. Russia is a full member of the OSCE and the Council of Europe, but when it comes to Belarus the founding principles of both organisations are completely ignored. When talking to our Russian interlocutors we are always told to be patient and to accept standards which they themselves would find absolutely unacceptable in Russia itself. So Russia's role in the development of Belarus cannot be considered very helpful. The decision-makers in Moscow do not seem to accept the principle that the people of Belarus should be free to choose their own destination.

The United States has in the recent past taken a completely different line. They chose to isolate Belarus, thus hoping to force the regime to accept a rapid and drastic change in the political and economic system. They did so however without considering the viability of such a radical change in the context and the realities of Belarus's society. The United States chose to give the major part of their support to the radical nationalist opposition. But this radical opposition did not succeed in making any impression during either the parliamentary or the presidential elections. Over the last two years the United States has become aware that this strategy was not working, and they have started to contribute – in closer co-operation with the EU – to support for a broader-based democratic alternative to Lukashenko's autocratic regime. The events of September 11 have also changed the world. Russia has become one of the United States' strongest allies in the fight against terrorism. And even Belarus has joined the international coalition against terrorism, being very eager to be part of at least one international something. And it is in turn using its participation in this international coalition to impress the European Union with the country's international solidarity.

After the collapse of the Soviet Union the EU tried to develop good and stable relations with all the newly independent states. This was the case with Belarus, as with other western CIS members like Ukraine. The EU never gave up its attempts to establish good relations with Belarus and to engage it in the continuing process of European integration.

The EU did offer Belarus a Partnership and Co-operation Agreement (PCA), aimed at creating stronger ties in many different areas, in particular trade and co-operation in the development of agriculture, industry and services, etc. But these PCAs also include provisions concerning democracy, respect for basic human rights and respect for the rule of law. A PCA is the first step in a series of arrangements that may lead to EU membership. Thus, the implementation of the PCA with Ukraine is the basis for a lively discussion about that country's possible future membership of the EU. The PCAs do in practice establish a clear European perspective for all countries concerned. The absence of such an agreement between the EU and Belarus explains the lack of such a European perspective today in Belarus. Instead there is the Union with Russia.

One can hardly blame the EU for this impasse, for not persisting in reaching an agreement. After the internationally heavily criticised constitutional referendum of 1996, used by Lukashenko to prolong his term of office and to abolish the remainder of the last democratically-elected parliament, the EU had no choice but to freeze the process for conclusion of the Interim Agreement as the first step towards the full ratification and implementation of the Partnership and Co-operation Agreement.

President Lukashenko's regime became a pariah with Europe's democratic nations and institutions. Official political contacts were strictly avoided and limited to efforts to improve the authorities' understanding of democracy. Diplomatic activities were also restricted to the absolute minimum. The EU's Tacis programme could not be applied as in the other CIS countries and economic assistance and co-operation therefore became impossible. Eventually the EU was only able to agree to a limited programme of activities in the field of civil society development.

It was not only the EU that had problems with the Lukashenko regime. The OSCE and the Council of Europe also refused to treat Belarus as a democratically-functioning state. The OSCE even decided to open a special office in Minsk with the single goal of monitoring the democratic process in Belarus and giving advice on possible improvements. The regime grudgingly accepted this (as they called it) 'foreign interference', thus avoiding becoming completely isolated within the OSCE. Here too one suspects the guiding hand of Moscow, which has never allowed Belarus to become a complete dictatorship.

As a consequence of the 1996 constitutional referendum a parliament was 'elected' which was not really worth the name and was therefore not accepted by international parliamentary institutions. This meant in practice that only members of the previous parliament, the last Supreme Soviet of Belarus, were invited to international meetings to represent their country.

In the absence of a respectable counterpart, and refusing to conclude even the Interim Agreement in preparation for ratification of the PCA, the European Parliament was not able to establish a normal parliamentary relationship with Belarus as it has done with all other newly independent states. The delegation which is also responsible for relations with Ukraine and Moldova was nevertheless also given the responsibility of monitoring specifically political developments in Belarus. After the events of 1996 the only thing the Parliament could do was launch repeated calls on the Belarusian authorities to accept international democratic standards and express its support for the democratic opposition to the regime.

In 1999, directly after the European elections, the newly-appointed European Parliament delegation for relations with Belarus was confronted with the question of what to do about the upcoming parliamentary and presidential elections.

On the basis of signals that the Belarusian regime was seeking a certain degree of international recognition for these elections, the decision was taken to try for greater European involvement in political developments in Belarus. Since it is only normal that parliamentarians monitor electoral processes, contacts were made with the parliamentary assemblies of the OSCE and the Council of Europe. This initiative led to the creation of the Parliamentary Troika for Belarus that was to play a crucial role in the evaluation of both elections.

The Troika, with the support of the institutions it represented and of the OSCE's Advisory and Monitoring Group in Minsk, started a process of discussion and consultation with all relevant actors in Belarus's political life, including extensive contacts with the regime. These actions were undertaken on the basis of a clear belief that the complete isolation of Belarus would not be in the best interests of its people or conducive to strengthening democracy. The three institutions attempted to establish a formal dialogue between the government and the opposition, hoping to create a more acceptable climate for the organisation of the parliamentary elections. It tried to persuade the President and the Belarusian authorities to adopt an unbiased electoral law, to stop their harassment of the opposition, to create a level playing field and guarantee equal access to the media, in particular to the electronic media, and to give the newly-elected parliament meaningful powers. Though some concessions were made, in particular as regards some of the legal provisions for the organisation of the elections, they were not enough to convince either the opposition or the international community that the regime sincerely wished to create the conditions for the parliamentary elections to be recognised as free and fair. Except by Russia of course.

Some of the opposition parties even opted for a boycott of the elections. In the meantime Lukashenko became more and more critical of the Troika's efforts to assist in the reform of Belarus's political climate when he became aware of the very high price he had to pay for international legitimatisation of the country's political system. Together with the OSCE's Minsk office, the Troika was depicted as part of some Nato conspiracy to weaken and in the end destroy Belarus and its values, thereby making it unacceptable to adopt their proposals for democratic reform.

It cannot have come as a real surprise to President Lukashenko when the Troika presented its conclusions immediately after the election: that the four basic requirements for free and fair elections had not been met and that the electoral process had therefore failed to produce an acceptable result. The elections had been more or less 'fixed' by those in power. The new parliament therefore lacked democratic legitimacy, according to the representatives of the European parliamentary institutions. The Troika at that moment expressed its hope that the upcoming presidential election would give Belarus a new chance. The conclusions of the Troika were contested by the regime and not supported by representatives of the Russian Federation. But all parts of the EU, OSCE and Council of Europe institutions, as well as the US State Department, shared the conclusions of the Parliamentary Troika.

The story would repeat itself again about a year later, on the occasion of the presidential election in September 2001. Once again the Parliamentary Troika wanted to demonstrate its clear commitment to political development in Belarus. This time none of those in opposition to Lukashenko and his regime were boycotting the elections. All the opposition forces decided on this occasion to put their differences aside and unite behind a single presidential candidate. In principle the voters were offered a simpler choice, but the way the campaign was conducted made it extremely difficult for voters to be fully informed about the alternatives. Again there was no level playing field for the different candidates. The media were totally biased in favour of the incumbent candidate and throughout the election campaign there was an atmosphere of intimidation in the country, directed at opposition activists, domestic independent election observers and the independent media.

As always during elections in Belarus, few incidents were reported during the actual casting of the votes. But there were also clear indications that the voting results were manipulated, in particular through an extended use of early voting and through successful efforts to block wide-spread monitoring of the counting process.

This time an official but limited observation mission under the auspices of ODIHR, the OSCE's specialised organisation for electoral processes, was present in Belarus to monitor the election and the last three weeks of the election campaign. This had not been the case a year earlier during the parliamentary elections. The opposition had also urged the international democratic institutions to reinforce this election observation mission by sending a parliamentary delegation. There had been improvements compared to the parliamentary elections, but these were insufficient to overshadow the fundamental flaws in the electoral process.

Again Russia congratulated Lukashenko on the outcome of the election. The rest of Europe, including all the candidate countries, agreed the conclusions of the Parliamentary Troika that 'the 2001 presidential election process failed to meet the OSCE commitments for democratic elections formulated in the 1990 Copenhagen document and the Council of Europe standards'.

It took the Troika a long time to formulate its final conclusions. Not because of its judgement on the electoral process as such – on this point opinions were unequivocal. The ODIHR assessment of the election campaign spoke for itself. No, the real difficulty was what to add to this first negative conclusion. The representatives of all the Troika institutions were aware of the need to formulate an opening, a possible continuation of efforts to stimulate the democratic process in Belarus. For the next few years there would be no new focal point in the form of elections to test political developments.

A kind of agenda had to be developed for the parliamentary institutions concerned as well as the international community as a whole. The guiding principle had to be to continue support for the Belarusian people in one way or another. It was therefore emphasised that the existing democratic deficit should not result in a further isolation of the people of Belarus. And the international community was urged to show a willingness to reassess its relations with the country in the light of any political progress, in particular as regards the development of a more pluralistic political environment in the country. It was decided to lay particular emphasis on certain positive developments such as the development of civil society, illustrated by the united approach of the democratic opposition and the creation of a network of many thousands of domestic election observers.

The Parliamentary Troika committed their institutions to continue to help promote a constructive dialogue across the political spectrum of civil society and between the authorities and the international community, with a view to facilitating the process of democratic transition in Belarus and its integration into European democratic structures.

The Minsk authorities were of course not very pleased with the Troika's final conclusions on the presidential election because the election had not succeeded in bringing about any change in the President's pariah status. It also meant that relations with the EU would not improve for the time being because all EU institutions accepted the recommendation of the European Parliament's observer delegation not to change their policy towards Belarus.

The European Parliament committed itself to a reassessment of its position on Belarus. This, linked to the notion of no isolation, was interpreted in Minsk as a kind of opening and therefore welcomed and presented as the Troika's main conclusion. One always wonders, given the total state domination of the media, whether any part of the real message has ever reached the ordinary Belarusian. In Minsk maybe, but certainly not in the rural areas which form the basis of Lukashenko's power. The President can always sell stories to his own people, but it is more difficult to fool the international community. The hard fact remains that even if it is not our intention to isolate the country, its regime is fully capable of continuing to isolate itself.

And, yes, we are prepared to reassess our relations with Belarus, but this presupposes that there are real and recognisable signs of change, transparency and reform in Belarus's political environment.

It is the regime in Minsk that will have to move and accept the need for gradual change. Not to please the individual members of the Parliamentary Troika, the European Union or the international community. But because democracy, respect for basic human rights and respect for the rule of law have become accepted values in the Europe of today. By not accepting these basic values, President Lukashenko continues to sow the seeds of a revolution that will oust him at the appropriate moment, just as happened elsewhere. The only alternative is to accept a basic degree of democratic normality, such as the fact that in a democracy institutions are a certainty but the outcome of elections is not. The EU will never do real business with a neighbour that is only partly a democracy.

The European Union does have a lot to offer in the framework of an eventual reassessment of its relations with Belarus:

- Reopening of the process for the conclusion of an Interim Agreement, leading to the creation of completely new opportunities for trade and economic development. Such new opportunities constitute in themselves a driver for economic reform, which is absolutely long overdue. Belarus cannot maintain the present economic status quo. Even the Russians tell Lukashenko so. The relative poverty of the average Belarusian will become absolute if no action is taken in this field very rapidly.

- Reopening of the process of ratification for the full Partnership and Co-operation Agreement (signed on 6 March 1995). The eventual ratification of this agreement will offer Belarus the same status as countries like Ukraine and Moldova or the Caucasus states, and will above all signal Belarus's ambitions to integrate and participate in Europe's democratic structures
- A significant increase in Tacis aid, far beyond the present support for elements of civil society, not only directed at increasing the economic capacities and legal structures of Belarus, but also paying serious attention to the development of health programmes.
- Cross-border co-operation with the future EU member-states on Belarus's northern and western borders. If the regime continues its policy of deliberate refusal to accept basic European values, it will further isolate itself from its direct neighbours when these become members of the European Union and part of the EU's single market and Schengen regime.
- Participation in European political co-operation. At a moment when almost all European states are members of the OSCE and the Council of Europe and participate in joint discussions with the European Union, it is no help to remain on the sidelines.

For this agenda to become real, Minsk must offer more than some half-hearted concessions in the field of economic development or loud propaganda about its 'important' contribution to the fight against international terrorism. It must stop confusing international engagement with unlawful interference. It must improve its human rights record, starting with a serious improvement in its very bad record on disappeared persons. It should stop accusing the European Parliament of being biased, because there are few countries in the world which are worse.

A clear commitment to democracy and the rule of law and a clear commitment to the future of its people would not only earn President Lukashenko the world's respect, but would for the first time in history offer Belarus a peaceful, stable and prosperous future.

The Change is Yet to Come: Opposition Strategies and Western Efforts to Promote Democracy in Belarus

Vitali Silitski

Introduction

Europe approached the end of the twentieth century with two countries still largely regarded as undemocratic. Presidents Slobodan Milosevic of Yugoslavia and Alexander Lukashenko of Belarus shared the dubious reputation of being the last dictators on the continent. Milosevic's regime collapsed in 2000 after he lost the presidential election. Events throughout Serbia were met with jubilation by the Belarusian opposition, which began to contemplate a 'Yugoslav scenario' for the presidential election scheduled in their own country for September 2001. The Belarus vote, however, confirmed the autocrats' sustained ability to vindicate their rule through manipulation of the electoral process. Saddest of all for Belarus's democrats, Lukashenko appeared to score a genuine majority in the election (though not nearly as large as the election authorities claimed) notwithstanding the vote-rigging and electoral violations.

Popular endorsement of the leader is not sufficient to make a country a democracy. Massive human rights violations, restrictions on press freedom, electoral irregularities, political censorship and violence and oppression towards opponents are endemic to political life in Belarus. Yet the ability of its autocratic ruler to claim a legitimacy any democratic leader would love to enjoy (and to transform it into the vital building-block of his regime) is what distinguishes the current situation from the Soviet totalitarianism of the past. Belarus's dictatorship is authoritarian rather than totalitarian. This implies that some of the basic Soviet-era mechanisms of control and coercion are defunct, whereas there is a political pluralism, albeit limited, which leaves room for political opposition and a relatively autonomous civil society. These facts have far-reaching implications for the democratic opposition and the international community, the players most interested in bringing Belarus back to the path of freedom and democracy.

Traditional explanations for Lukashenko's remarkable resilience and stability hinge on three factors: the severity of the government's repression of opponents and its unchallenged domination over all aspects of political, economic and social life; the people's conservatism and lack of feel for democracy; and Russia's sponsorship of the regime. These factors are relevant and important, but not sufficient. Repression can buy compliance but not grassroots support, a valuable asset which strengthens Lukashenko's grip on power. His hardcore constituency of elderly, retired, rural and poorly-educated supporters has not had its political attitudes and values formed within the last couple of years. It constitutes a large part of society, but not the majority. Increasing support for democracy, the market and national independence has been registered over the last few years by Belarusian and Western researchers alike. Just before the September 2001 election, more than half the electorate were ready to back a candidate who would promise a radical shift away from Lukashenko's policies and put the country on a democratic track. Russia backed Lukashenko when his authority was challenged. But the Russian media also broke the government's monopoly on information, while President Putin's policy of economic liberalisation endangered the long-run survivability of the Belarusian state-run economy and could eventually destabilise the political foundations of Lukashenko's authority.

Opposition strategy: to promote change or adjust to the status quo?

The strength of Lukashenko's autocratic regime is a mirror image of the weakness of his opponents. Even when popular demand for political change emerged, it was not met by a credible democratic alternative. The internal opposition and its sympathisers outside Belarus have long ignored this fact. After being violently ejected from government structures in 1996, the opposition pinned its hope for a return to democracy on three major factors: the collapse of the economy, giving rise to popular discontent; increased political activism among the younger generation leading to a strong challenge on the streets, especially in Minsk; and external pressure and international isolation, which would destroy the legitimacy of the Belarusian regime and force it to succumb to more civilised standards of behaviour. Even before the 'Yugoslav scenario', the vision of a velvet revolution captured the imagination of the opposition and its leadership.

A straightforward comparison between Belarus and totalitarian regimes of the past proved of little use in drawing up a route map for democratic change. However bad the economic situation, it did not deteriorate sufficiently to produce massive public protest. There is little evidence to support official claims that living standards rose 70 per cent in 1996-2001. However, even international statistics rank living standards in Belarus above those in Ukraine or even Russia, while in the World Bank index of human development, Belarus ranks above all the CIS countries and some Central and East European countries. The public's most common response to worsening economic conditions was exit rather than protest. Produce from the plots owned by virtually every Belarusian family and extensive engagement in the informal sector provided a vital addition to official wages. In these conditions, little could be expected to happen without action by protagonists of change. Ironically, polls showed the strongest support for Lukashenko coming from those with the lowest incomes, which may suggest that economic hardship only strengthened his hold on society. However strong the antipathy towards Lukashenko among the younger generation, young people are also the most apathetic and politically inactive. The relatively relaxed social atmosphere gave young people a more attractive alternative to political activism in the form of rock concerts, partying and the internet.

Lukashenko's opponents, underestimating the stability of Lukashenko's regime and naively expecting a rapid, radical transition from his authoritarian rule through a local 'velvet revolution', spent five years after their expulsion from parliament in a 'parallel society.' This was organised as a dissident micro-world that lived by its own rules and had little impact on life outside. It had its own parliament, the rump of the last Supreme Soviet, whose legitimacy was recognised by the international community but whose members' activities were largely restricted to travelling abroad and denouncing Lukashenko in international fora. The 'shadow government' of the opposition, the National Executive Committee formed by the Supreme Soviet and opposition parties, was given the task of developing alternative programmes of social and economic reform to challenge the official vision of the country's development. Finally, alternative presidential elections were called in spring 1999 to elect a 'parallel president', using ballot boxes carried from door to door to allow the public to vote. This last campaign proved a major embarrassment to the opposition. One candidate withdrew from the race just three days before its official end citing 'irregularities' in the voting process, while the other was arrested on charges of corruption before the campaign even started. The 'parallel' election commission claimed that over half the population participated in the vote, whereas independent research put the number at a tenth of that. The scale of vote-rigging seems to have exceeded that admitted by Lukashenko in the 1996 referendum. This lost the opposition the high moral ground, and showed how desperate it was to impress the outside world with a strength it had yet to accumulate.

There were two reasons for the switch to a 'parallel society': Lukashenko's intention to remove opponents from the mainstream political and decision-making process, and the opposition's own fear that participation would lead to its incorporation by the authorities and thus legitimise Lukashenko's rule at home and abroad and take the steam out of popular protest. Operating as a political subculture, however, the opposition lost all chance of winning broad popular support and mounting a credible political challenge. First, it did not establish a nationwide political organisation to extend its influence beyond its political base, thereby failing to communicate its programme and values to a broader audience. Anticipating mass popular protest, the opposition concentrated its activities heavily on the capital city. But since support for the President was lowest in Minsk and other large cities this was preaching to the converted. The opposition ended up without a strong political base in the periphery, where support for Lukashenko remained strong. Second, attempting to stimulate a mood of protest, it carried out largely negative campaigns focused on political issues, and failed to address matters of concern to the majority of the population, such as living standards and personal and social security. Meanwhile, the authorities carried out ever nastier defamation campaigns against their opponents. Official propaganda spared no effort to spread fear of imminent economic collapse, and of rising prices, unemployment and enrichment of the few at the expense of the many if the opposition should take over. Third, it chose to reject participation in the political and social life of 'official' society (including elections). In so doing, the opposition failed to represent the social groups and interests that formerly provided their grassroots support. The traditional democratic constituency of students, the intelligentsia, businessmen, etc. had a substantial stake in decisions taken within the existing political system. The absence of democratic political parties and social movements from the mainstream political process, and their conspicuous lack of interest in it, resulted in the declining relevance of the opposition to its core potential constituency. The fact that the President's opponents mistrusted nearly all opposition-controlled institutions even more than his supporters did demonstrates how far the democratic elite was divorced from the democratic public.

Its organisation as a 'parallel society' achieved one goal for the opposition. It allowed it to challenge Lukashenko's legitimacy at the international level and enabled opposition institutions to represent Belarus in important international fora such as the Council of Europe and OSCE Parliamentary Assembly. However, lack of recognition by US and European institutions did nothing to destabilise the regime. Belarus did not have a high level of foreign debt, nor was it sufficiently exposed to Western markets to feel economic pressure from the suspension of the trade agreement and the blocking of financial assistance. Unlike Milosevic, the Belarusian president had no record of war crimes or ethnic cleansing, so there was no case for stricter sanctions or military intervention. The country's strong ties with Russia, which gave Lukashenko unconditional endorsement, and growing links with rogue states minimised the impact of isolation from Europe and the US. It turned out that sources of domestic and Western standards of legitimacy were different. Domestic support for the regime and acquiescence in its style of government derived not from its respect for democratic norms and procedures but from its ability to address matters of day-to-day concern. The opposition's over-investment in overseas activities and efforts to thwart regime representatives at every international meeting were no substitute for political work at home. In this respect, the domestic legitimacy problem became more acute for the opposition then for the government. In spite of Lukashenko's declining popularity in the late 1990s, his opponents' approval ratings barely grew, which still left the President the most popular political alternative.

The opposition approached the election season of 2000-2001 weakened and divided. It included a large number of political parties, many locked in rivalry in spite of being barely distinguishable. For example, there were two nationalist parties (Belarusian Popular Front (BPF) and Conservative Christian Party), two liberal parties (United Civil Party (UCP) and Yabloko), and at least four social democratic parties (Belarusian Social Democratic Party (BSDP), Belarusian Social Democratic Assembly, Labour Party, Women's Party). Their popularity was astoundingly low, most of them failing to clear the 5 per cent barrier. (In Serbia, the aggregate rating of major opposition parties exceeded the Milosevic bloc's as early as a year before the presidential election.) Political parties were consistently the country's most mistrusted institutions. Membership of the three largest parties is less than 3,000 each (By contrast, the Democratic Party of Serbia alone had 40,000 members in 1994.)

The lack of popular and authoritative personalities in the Belarusian opposition also reduced its chance of connecting with the public. Remarkably, since Lukashenko's advance to political power in 1994 there had been little change in the democratic elite. Most newcomers were defectors from the president's office or the former Communist Party nomenklatura. When the most notable and charismatic opposition personalities tipped to challenge Lukashenko in the presidential election died or disappeared in 1999, no-one emerged to fill their shoes. The new group of young political leaders known as the 'New Wave' which emerged in 1999 were unwilling to take the political risk of seriously opposing the President.

Divisions within the opposition were mostly caused by personal rivalries and political differences between its 'nationalist' and 'liberal' wings (represented by the BPF and the parties of the centre and left respectively). A major attempt to overcome fragmentation was undertaken in early 1999 with the establishment of the Coordinating Council of Democratic Forces (CCDF). However, this unity proved to be short-lived. It collapsed over the issue of participation in the House of Representatives elections called by Lukashenko in 2000. The Supreme Soviet, a rump parliament still recognised in the West as Belarus's legitimate legislature, and the most prominent opposition parties, such as BPF and UCP, decided to boycott the elections because the government had failed to meet the four demands put forward by the opposition and supported by the OSCE (opposition access to the official media; release of political prisoners; broadening the prerogatives of parliament; and inclusion of the opposition in election commissions). At the same time a number of democratic organisations declined to boycott the elections and opted to participate. Groups of activists from the boycotting parties also joined in the election campaign. The issue of boycotting/participating in the election reflected a fundamental difference in vision of the future within the democratic opposition. The pro-boycott forces insisted that a radical change in the political system was imminent, possibly brought forward by the 'velvet revolution' they were trying to organise through mass rallies and civil disobedience campaigns. They considered that opposition participation in the elections would legitimise Lukashenko's regime. The pro-election faction thought a boycott would lead to the opposition's isolation in society and conversion into a sect, which might strengthen Lukashenko's grip on power. The dispute over strategy and tactics grew into a campaign of mutual attacks and accusations, which, predictably, resulted in a landslide victory for pro-Lukashenko candidates, helped by massive falsification of the election results.

The OSCE technical assessment mission refused to recognise these elections as free and fair, quoting widespread manipulation, as admitted by the authorities. Supporters of the boycott claimed victory for their initiative, maintaining that only 45 per cent of the eligible electorate voted in the first round of elections. Some even declared an 'electoral revolution,' apparently counting those who did not vote as opposition supporters. The cheers were clearly premature, as the two most pressing problems for the opposition, lack of unity and weakness of public support, only worsened. According to a poll taken a month after the vote, about 58 per cent of respondents admitted participating in the elections, and only seven per cent of those who did not vote claimed to have boycotted them.[1] The same poll recorded an increase in Lukashenko's approval rating from 33 to 41 per cent, while the composite rating of all the potential democratic candidates fell from 13 to 9 per cent.[2] Ironically, the opposition now had to go into the presidential election of 2001 in even less favourable conditions than the parliamentary vote it had boycotted. The President twisted the rules of the game even further by barring foreign assistance to most NGOs and to election-related projects such as training of observers. By the time the presidential campaign began, the unity of the opposition had ended with the collapse of the CCDF in winter 2001, when the leader of the BSDP was expelled for participating in the parliamentary elections. Other social democratic parties left one by one, suspecting that the right-wing parties, BPF and UCP, were trying to usurp the leadership of the Council. They established their own coalition 'For Social Change' in July 2001. As a result, no mechanism for nominating a single opposition candidate existed by June 2001, when the presidential election was called.

2001 election

The most prominent opposition politicians to run for the presidency were Semion Domash, former Governor of Grodno region; Vladimir Goncharik, head of the Federation of Trade Unions; Mikhail Chygir, former Prime Minister; Pavel Kozlovski, former Minister of Defence; and Sergei Kaliakin, leader of the Communist Party. Remarkably, with the exception of the Communists, the major opposition parties not only failed to nominate their own candidate but refused to declare their support for any of the democratic nominees. Participation in the election campaign thus became a personal business for rank-and-file activists. In April Kaliakin, Kozlovsky, Domash, Chygir and Goncharik signed an agreement eventually to nominate a single candidate of 'the five.' Many opposition activists, however, joined the campaigns of other candidates (of whom there were 22 initially) to collect the 100,000 signatures needed to support a nomination. Signature collection was a mess, with the same household suffering visits from up to a dozen opposition activists, frequently denigrating each other. Many refused to sign anyone's petition. As a result, only two opposition candidates, Domash and Goncharik, managed to get over the 100,000 threshhold. The promise to nominate a single candidate for the five was eventually fulfilled on 21 July, the day after signature collection closed. The choice fell on Goncharik. Domash then withdrew from the race, reducing the field to only three candidates: Lukashenko, Goncharik and Sergei Gaidukevich, leader of the Liberal Democratic Party (a Belarusian clone of Zhirinovsky's party in Russia).

The failures and distortions of the electoral campaign and voting procedures are dealt with elsewhere in this volume. According to the official results, on an 83.86 per cent turnout Lukashenko won with 75.65 per cent of the votes, with Goncharik gaining 15.65 per cent and Gaidukevich 2.48 per cent. Even most of the opposition press recognised Lukashenko's victory, challenging only the validity of official claims about its size.

Given the controversial nature of official claims, I turn to independent research data to help interpret the results. Polls confirmed that Lukashenko enjoyed a high level of public support throughout the year prior to the election, reaching 46.8 per cent the day before the vote. Importantly, these were not all committed Lukashenko supporters. In April 2001 only 18.3 per cent of the total electorate was satisfied with his performance in office, with 33.8 per cent dissatisfied and 46.9 per cent uncertain.[3] The same month, committed supporters (those who would vote for the incumbent President no matter what) stood at a mere 17.1 per cent, whereas committed opponents made up a third of the total electorate, with half of the electorate falling into the category of 'hesitant majority'.[4] Furthermore, at the beginning of the year, half the voters expressed a desire to support a presidential candidate who would promise a radical change from Lukashenko's policies, whereas those who favoured continuity accounted for less than 40 per cent.[5] On most political issues (promotion of democracy and the rule of law, transition to a market economy, etc.), the electorate expressed a clear preference for reformist initiatives and proposals over preservation of the authoritarian *status quo*. This fact is important in view of the claims of some opposition analysts who cited insufficient demand for democratic change as the reason for another

Lukashenko landslide. Although the demand was probably not enough to assure the opposition's victory, it would have provided a ready platform for a credible electoral challenge. The fact that this demand was again not met by an adequate political alternative can therefore be considered a primary reason for the opposition's dismal performance as well as for Lukashenko's easy victory.

Against the background of a sizeable groundswell in favour of change, committed opposition support remained marginal. The composite rating of 'the five' stood at 17-20 per cent just a few weeks before the election. Furthermore, supporters of one candidate were not very likely to vote for another. As a result, when Goncharik was named as the opposition's single candidate, his support barely increased. This forced Goncharik's team to spend precious weeks consolidating the core democratic vote rather than making an impact on the large body of uncommitted voters. Goncharik's rating did begin to pick up just before the election, but this was too little too late. According to a poll taken just before the election, he enjoyed the support of only 26 per cent of the population, which should have translated into 33 per cent of the vote on the eventual 82 per cent turnout. Lukashenko's predicted vote stood at 46 per cent of the total electorate, or 55 per cent of those who voted. In other words, Lukashenko managed to maintain the loyalty of his supporters and to translate it into the majority on election day. By contrast, the opposition candidate secured just half of the potential democratic vote.

After Milosevic's downfall in Yugoslavia, it is clear that defeating a dictatorship in an election it has organised is not impossible. But the opposition has to secure a democratic majority beforehand. Unlike democratic states where a last-minute swing of a fraction of a percentage point can decide the vote, the opposition can win elections under a dictatorship only if it has a solid popular majority well before the election. This was the case in Yugoslavia, where the democratic parties secured commanding support from society long before the historic 2001 elections. Unfortunately for the Belarusian opposition, it started preparing for the elections only when they were called. To have even a remote chance of winning, it had to (a) forge and maintain internal unity; (b) establish an efficient mechanism for communicating its message to the voters; (c) formulate a credible democratic alternative to the autocratic status quo; and (d) break up the ranks of the ruling regime by attracting support from at least part of the government bureaucracy. Failure to do this produced a disastrous campaign and, consequently, defeat.

(a) (Dis)unity of the opposition

The opposition officially united for the presidential election, but this unity was achieved too late to allow a concerted and effective opposition campaign. Without clear mechanisms to resolve internal disputes or clear criteria for nominations, the choice of a nominee turned into a process of bargaining between candidates. Goncharik's nomination emerged from a private meeting of 'the five', left many dissatisfied and caused upheaval in those parties supporting Domash. Some called on Domash to disregard the decision and continue the race. Within days, Domash and Goncharik, as well as their campaign team members, publicly exchanged attacks in the media, at opposition gatherings and on the internet. This was followed by bargaining between Goncharik and other party leaders, who now demanded political guarantees in exchange for their support. Negotiations were completed only three weeks before the election. Goncharik promised to appoint Domash Prime Minister and to carry out political and economic reforms, including fresh parliamentary elections, constitutional changes and privatisation.

A further round of political bargaining followed, now at local level, and was completed only at the end of August, effectively leaving only a fortnight for the opposition's campaign. Even this eventually degenerated into several separate mini-campaigns run by individual organisations, some of which refused to co-ordinate their activities with the candidate's headquarters. Overall, independent campaigns did little to promote the candidate and inform the population about his platform. Most materials distributed contained criticism of Lukashenko and revelations about corruption, government involvement in the disappearance of opposition figures, etc. Sometimes, the messages offered were in direct contradiction to the candidate's platform. Official propaganda spared no effort to convince the population that violence and civil war would follow an opposition victory. The opposition's negative campaigning worked in Lukashenko's favour, helping to strengthen the widespread perception that there was no alternative.

Overall, the 'unity' of the democratic opposition on the eve of the 2001 election was an illusion which did not translate into a concerted effort by all its nominal supporters.

(b) Organisation of the campaign

One result of the opposition's self-isolation was a weak organisational structure that barely touched the countryside and small towns. This produced catastrophic conditions for the 2001 campaign, when a countrywide effort to challenge Lukashenko failed to materialise. Of 6,000 volunteers working for Goncharik's campaign, some 2,000 were concentrated in Minsk. This network, as well as the overall campaign, suffered from poor management and an inefficient distribution of resources. Leaflets and information materials kept arriving late, and stockpiles were left undistributed in regional headquarters after the election. At the grassroots level, the campaign revealed the weak commitment of many democratic activists. The slothful approach of some was at least in part due to the fact that they treated their activities as a part-time job generating extra income.

(c) Failure to present an alternative

What the opposition presidential campaign lacked was a clear message to the voters, a vision of the future and a coherent explanation of what would happen after a victory for the democrats. Although Goncharik himself repeatedly promised political and social stability, 'change without turmoil', this message was not sufficiently substantiated. The election manifesto, only a few pages long, addressed general issues such as the rule of law, economic reform and overcoming international isolation, and was generally well received wherever it was read. But the message began to be heard too late and was spread too narrowly. Some important constituencies, such as pensioners, young people and rural dwellers, were not adequately addressed. The absence of a committed democratic following drove Goncharik to seek support from undecided voters. His platform was filled with ambiguous promises: market reform while preserving Soviet-era social guarantees; equal treatment for private and public companies instead of privatisation: increased support for education and health plus lower taxes; and strengthening Belarus's sovereignty without breaking union ties with Russia. Lukashenko engaged in the same kind of doublespeak, making the economic and social part of his election platform almost identical to Goncharik's. The two programmes differed radically only on political issues. This gave credibility in the eyes of an ill-informed public to Lukashenko's claims that power was the opposition's only goal. At one point, Goncharik made the disappearance of leading political figures a main theme of his campaign. But this failed to generate much public interest. It mattered only to those who already mistrusted Lukashenko, turned the President's supporters even more strongly against the opposition, and left the undecided indifferent. Its elevation to a central theme of the campaign prevented the candidate from concentrating on the electorate's major concerns: socio-economic conditions and the problems of day-to-day life.

Meanwhile, Lukashenko built his election message on the achievements of his seven-year rule (including preservation of the social safety net and equality, avoidance of abrupt economic reforms and mass unemployment, and claimed continuous economic growth since 1997), and deliberately encouraged fear of the opposition. A gloomy picture of imminent layoffs, price rises, property sellouts and other disasters was systematically painted in the official media. The opposition, with limited access to the mass media, had little chance to counterattack, and wasted even this chance by negative campaigning. At the same time it should be admitted that Lukashenko addressed more actively the day-to-day concerns of most voters, and put socio-economic issues (wages, prices, social guarantees, etc.) at the forefront of his campaign message.

In the end, Goncharik's campaign failed to reach the largest block of voters, the uncommitted, i.e. those who had doubts about Lukashenko but were still not prepared to vote for the opposition. Some of these apparently abstained, some voted for Lukashenko. Lukashenko also managed to boost his support by sharply raising public sector pay, which grew 23 per cent in the first nine months of 2001. Though this increase was offset by drastic price rises immediately after the election, it helped him woo some undecided voters on the day.

(d) Silence of the insiders: the behaviour of the nomenklatura

The presidential campaign brings to mind Stalin's dictum: 'It doesn't matter who votes, what matters is who counts the vote.' To be more precise, both vote count and voting *per se* were important in deciding the election. The position of the ruling elite, still known as the nomenklatura, was central to ensuring the fairness of the electoral process. Here the opposition had high hopes: according to independent analysts, up to 80 per cent of state officials mistrusted Lukashenko and wanted him out. Nevertheless, very few civil servants involved in the election commissions resisted vote-rigging or co-operated with the opposition and independent observers. One possible explanation for their behaviour is that disobeying orders from the regime required a certain degree of assurance of security if the regime changed. Goncharik repeatedly promised this in his campaign speeches. However, the message was somewhat diluted by the elite's fear that radical opposition activists would want to settle scores, and their fear of the President, who threatened to remove local officials if they failed to achieve the required vote in their localities. Their fear was strengthened by a widespread perception that Lukashenko would win anyway and that resistance to electoral violations would be pointless. According to a poll of the elite (conducted separately for the nomenklatura and the opposition elite), only 3 per cent of state officials admitted voting for Lukashenko while 50 per cent voted for Goncharik and 28 per cent refused to answer the question. 53 per cent considered the elections not to have been free and fair, with only 14 per cent thinking otherwise. 46 per cent of officials polled noted that the official election results could not be trusted, with only 25 per cent taking the opposite view. Still, 61 per cent of them considered the irregularities to be insufficient to influence the outcome of the election. Indeed, while the nomenklatura voted for Goncharik, it failed to make him president in the face of resistance from both the President and the electorate.[6]

The democratic elite sought the support of the old party apparatchiks before the campaign. This decision was confirmed at the meeting of the CCDF in December 2000, when it recommended three representatives of the old guard (Domash, Chygir and Goncharik) for consideration as presidential contenders. The fact that the field included none of the leaders of democratic parties or veteran opposition activists showed a lack of confidence in their ability to mount a serious challenge in their own right. The attitude of the Belarusian opposition towards the ruling elite had evolved from total confrontation in the early 1990s, when the nomenklatura was omnipotent and an independent political player, to counting on it as a saviour in the last few years, when it was entirely stripped of its autonomy and subordinated to the President's will. Both approaches proved to be self-defeating. It was naïve to expect the nomenklatura to undermine the President's authority, at least until his public support had waned further. The most that could be expected was that moderates among them would facilitate the transition to democracy and help to avoid violence. It was even more naïve to believe in the omnipotence of the government apparatus when the political regime gave the President unlimited authority to identify and immediately remove dissenters. Moreover, the opposition allied itself with members of the old elite who had already been sidelined and who had a minimal influence on the effective government bureaucracy. The 'old guard' had to confront the current state bureaucracy, much of which originated from the lower ranks of the nomenklatura and owed its bureaucratic advancement to Lukashenko. All this does not negate the need to co-operate with the reform-minded part of the state apparatus. Effective co-operation, however, depends upon the degree of institutional autonomy of the elite, which can only come with substantial political liberalisation, as well as upon the commitment of both sides to partnership.

The West: why has it failed so far and how can it help in future?

Western involvement in Belarus has been reduced to a minimum since the country slipped from the democratic path of development. Still, the US and European governments, inter-governmental institutions and a variety of Western-based NGOs have attempted to influence Belarusian politics through a variety of mechanisms, including pressure on the government, sanctions and democracy-building assistance to civil society. These actions have, however, so far been poorly co-ordinated, sometimes contradictory, and often failed to target the most significant bottlenecks on Belarus's road to democracy.

The United States government adopted in 1997 a new policy of 'selective engagement' towards Belarus. This involved limiting contacts with the government and state sector to the essential minimum, exerting pressure on the Belarusian authorities to liberalise the political system, and supporting the democratic opposition and non-governmental sector in a bid to promote democratic change from below while suspending all direct assistance to the state sector. Under this policy, the United States emerged as a principal sponsor of the 'third sector' in Belarus. USAID's annual budget for Belarus in 1997-2001 was $7-11 million and was allocated for programmes aimed at 'increased and better-informed citizen participation in civic and private economic activities', and for transfers to grant-making institutions (e.g. National Endowment for Democracy, International Republican Institute).[7] Support from private foundations further increased this amount. Not all, or even most, of this money has benefited the opposition. Direct assistance to political parties is prohibited under both US and Belarusian law. It is noteworthy, however, that most of this money was channelled to NGOs, many of which operate as a life support system for the opposition parties and their leaders. It is common in Belarus for a political party to establish around itself a network of NGOs to which it is linked by close cross-membership ties. Most of the independent press survives on foreign grants as well, since discriminatory pricing for publishing, distribution and paper purchase otherwise drives them out of existence.

The Council of Europe (CoE), an institution set up to promote democracy and human rights on the continent, responded to the stifling of democracy in Belarus by expelling it from its ranks in 1997. The Parliamentary Assembly of the CoE has provided a forum for representatives of the opposition, particularly the Supreme Soviet, to voice criticism of the abuse of democracy by the authorities. The CoE was instrumental in denying legitimacy to Lukashenko's regime through its insistence on recognising the Supreme Soviet as the true representative body. The CoE's presence in Belarus was maintained through visits by the troika to assess progress towards democracy and communicate the results to the Assembly. Otherwise, the CoE's direct leverage was limited to granting or denying membership.

The OSCE maintained a high profile in Belarus after its Advisory and Monitoring Group (AMG) was established in Minsk in 1997 with a mandate 'to assist the Belarusian authorities in promoting democratic institutions and in complying with other OSCE commitments; and to monitor and report on this process.' This clearly implied a more co-operative relationship with all sides in the political process, including the government. Aside from monitoring political events and human rights, and consulting on electoral law, the AMG tried to bridge the existing political divides and work out a political compromise that would lay the foundations for progress towards a more democratic form of government. Negotiations between the opposition parties and Lukashenko's government in 1999-2000 were intended to provide a framework for free and fair parliamentary and presidential elections. This effort collapsed, as it appeared that neither side was ready for dialogue. The Lukashenko administration reneged on its promise to enter talks and instead arranged in spring 2000 a 'dialogue' with pro-government organisations, which unconditionally endorsed its policies. Moderates inside the government who had been pressing for talks with the opposition and advocating at least a partial liberalisation of the electoral law were removed. The opposition, meanwhile, at first greeted the AMG's initiatives with suspicion, fearing to legitimise Lukashenko's regime. The independent media and the most radical political parties even accused Hans-Georg Wieck, head of the AMG, of executing the orders of the German government to strike a deal with Lukashenko and bring Belarus closer to Russia's orbit. This, they insisted, would serve the interests of Germany's multinationals, particularly the 'gas lobby,' which were involved in trade with Russia and dependent on its gas. Ironically, Lukashenko in turn denounced Wieck as the sponsor of his opponents and the AMG as the opposition's major think-tank and command headquarters.

The European Union's involvement in Belarus has been minimal. Relations with Belarus were curtailed after the November 1996 referendum and reduced to humanitarian and regional projects and those which directly support the democratisation process. It was not until 1999 that the EU formulated a new policy towards Belarus, which came to be known as the 'step-by-step approach.' Under it, improvements in relations between the parties depend on the Belarusian authorities reaching essential benchmarks in political and economic reform.

As this brief overview suggests, there were numerous strategies pursued by various Western actors – governments and institutions – as well as a wide diversity of ideas about how best to promote democratic change in Belarus.

Thus, US and CoE policies emphasised pressure and selective engagement, whereas the OSCE and EU left room for compromise. As a result, some shifted to unconditional support for the opposition, while others sought dialogue and co-operation with the government. There was insistence on a return to the 1994 Constitution from one corner, attempts to work out a liberalising solution within the Lukashenko-drafted basic law from the other. This pluralism induced splits within the opposition, where internal disagreements led to a major internal fight in 2000-2001. Those who supported a boycott of the parliamentary elections developed stronger ties with US political and grant-making institutions, whose government was sympathetic to the boycott initiative. Those who opted to participate in the election sought endorsement from the OSCE mission, which had nudged the opposition in that direction. Regardless of the rights and wrongs of the dispute, the fact that an internal disagreement in the opposition turned into a 'two-level war' could only lead to the simultaneous failure of both strategies. Such pluralism and unnecessary competition should be avoided in the future.

In a broader sense, governmental, inter-governmental and private democracy assistance practitioners alike often replace in-depth analysis of key political patterns in a specific country with highly schematic and often inadequate paradigms that dictate standard approaches. Thus, post-communist countries are always assumed to be 'in transition' even if many of them have barely started on the path to democratisation and market reform.[8] When it becomes obvious that 'transition' is non-existent or in abeyance (as in the case of Belarus), the existing paradigm fails to explain what is going on. Such thinking leads to a revival of images from the past (such as Cold War stereotypes) as well as recourse to old policy approaches, such as isolation and selective engagement. This tendency was most obvious in the proponents of a more confrontational approach to Belarus, who, like the opposition, underestimated the stability of Lukashenko's regime and misunderstood the sources of its resilience. The democracy assistance community demonstrated remarkable stubbornness in finding and funding Belarusian clones of Charter-77, Solidarity or the Popular Fronts in the Baltic States. Unlike Communist dictatorships in Central and Eastern

Europe, where these movements and groups emerged from national resistance to foreign-imposed regimes, Belarus's autocracy is essentially home-grown to the extent that it was initiated through a democratic process almost a decade ago when Lukashenko won a competitive and generally free presidential election. In the last two years, activities have changed to try to emulate the victorious 'electoral revolution' in Yugoslavia. Following this blueprint, a voter mobilisation campaign was generously funded and a Belarusian version of the student Otpor movement was promoted. But such assistance came without the groundwork for political change being laid by the opposition itself and without regard to local conditions. The mobilisation campaign was funded without taking into account that 85 per cent of the population were going to vote anyway; no assessment seems to have been made of the marginal efficiency of such a campaign if the turnout was already expected to be high. The policy of 'selective engagement' targeted the opposition as a dominant or even the sole partner in bilateral relationships. This often led to the adoption of particular leaders and movements and reinforced their position as a political subculture. It has produced more clients than responsible citizens and generated the problem of moral hazard: funding was accepted even when no tangible results were achieved. It is worth noting that most of the opposition's self-destructive political campaigns were underwritten by Western official and non-governmental donors.

International isolation failed to produce progress in restoring democracy and improving the human rights situation. To some extent, it lent credibility, in the eyes of the public, to the government's anti-Western and anti-democracy propaganda and helped to undermine the positions of those who embrace Western ideas of liberal democracy and use 'The West' as a symbol for change. Insistence on this policy may lead the West to occupy the low moral ground, as some of the most repressive governments in the world are currently considered valued partners in the international coalition against terrorism. The EU's more accommodating and flexible 'step-by-step' approach had its own limitations. Its implementation was dependent on the co-operation of the Belarusian authorities, but it lacked the ability to develop the potential for democratic change within the country without the good-will of the government.

Western strategy towards Belarus should not be a choice between selective engagement and a step-by step approach. Instead, it must accommodate and combine the two. Violations of human rights and state-sponsored repression should be denounced and confronted, while the seeds of democracy should be cherished in all corners of society and the state. Step-by-step tactics and conditionality should be explored in relations with the government to promote liberalisation. Engagement is important to building a consensus within Belarusian society on the need for democratic change.

Conditionality involves tit-for-tat bargaining between external actors and the authorities and promises tangible benefits for every credible step in opening up the political and economic system. Such a policy has little chance of succeeding as Lukashenko is unlikely to underestimate the potential danger of even half-hearted liberalisation. He seems to have learned from the collapse of communist regimes that giving an inch might lose him a mile. However, in spite of his convincing victory in the presidential election, he may not be up to the immense task of maintaining the status quo. He may be forced to introduce economic reforms in the face of mounting financial problems and increasing pressure from Russia to introduce market liberalisation and allow it to participate in the privatisation of state industries. However half-hearted and ill-designed these market reforms, they will seriously destabilise the political situation by forcing the government to curtail state regulation, cut down welfare spending and abandon the policy of full employment – policies which have won the compliance of a large part of society with the political *status quo*. In this situation, rising public discontent might be answered by intensified political repression. But this should not be treated as a pretext for withdrawal. Ironically, the alternative of increasing Belarus's international isolation, advocated by some Western politicians and human rights activists, might be welcomed by the regime, which for its part is doing all it can to minimise Western influence on Belarusian society. It is true that Belarus's international isolation is largely self-inflicted. But it will only help Lukashenko in his efforts to isolate Belarus from outside influences if the West reinforces his attempts to expel the OSCE mission, deny entry visas to European parliamentarians, or prohibit overseas educational contacts and foreign travel for government employees without high-level approval.

The policy of engagement avoids replicating the mistakes of the past, when Western policies towards Belarus were largely targeted towards (or against) two organised political forces, the government and the opposition, and failed to reach out to the majority in society who are beginning to favour democratic change but are not committed to the opposition. Most of these live and work within 'official society,' including middle and lower civil servants (central and local), the economic elite, the intelligentsia and millions of ordinary non-politicised Belarusian citizens, a constituency largely ignored by proponents of democracy in the last five years. Ultimately, the fate of democracy lies with them. 'Official society', operating under the auspices of the government, should be treated as a partner rather than an adversary. Even with the most radical political change, it will be impossible immediately to replace 100,000 government employees. And it would be good for the country's future for this important group to develop a better understanding not just of the need for reform but also how it should be pursued given the rich and readily-available experience of countries in transition.

Democracy assistance should aim to help Belarus to help itself. Ultimately, Belarusian citizens will have to generate the internal conditions for political change. Extending the pro-European and pro-democracy constituency inside Belarus, both among the general public and within the elite, is crucial. Contacts and co-operation between Europe and Belarus should not, therefore, be limited to a handful of opposition parties and NGOs. Democracy assistance should take into account that the proponents of democratic change have been a political minority throughout the decade, and no progress in democratisation can be achieved until this minority grows into a powerful force capable of securing the support of Belarusian society. The West can do a lot to assist this transformation through the transfer of knowledge, ideas and expertise to the pro-democracy camp, not to mention financial support. It is important to avoid maintaining independent initiatives as a subculture and preaching to the converted. Assistance to the third sector should reach out to the broadest social circles, building civic competence and professionalism, and incorporating the democratic alternative into Belarusian society rather then maintaining it as an alien phenomenon. In this respect, it is worth mentioning the remarkable success of the Tacis programme and also other projects such as those of the International Finance Corporation in developing civil society and a market economy in Belarus. Also crucial is encouraging public interest in Belarus's integration into European institutions such as the Council of Europe, and the upgrading of its relationship with the EU. On the domestic front, this will help to counter the commonly held view that 'Belarus is not welcome in Europe'. This will require a solid information effort and some shift in emphasis in engagement strategies.

Progress towards democracy requires liberalisation of the political climate in Belarus. It is important to promote zones of autonomy not only outside government structures but inside them. To achieve this, support for the development of parliamentarianism is of paramount importance. A legislature enjoying public backing and possessing a considerable degree of autonomy is crucial in establishing an independent political base for a pro-democracy constituency. The old choice between supporting the Supreme Soviet and working with the House of Representatives is no longer relevant. The policy of boycott has been abandoned even by those in the opposition who supported it two years ago. Participation in the parliamentary elections scheduled for 2004 is no longer in question. Consequently, it would be better for the opposition itself if the current House of Representatives could be encouraged to transform itself from a rubber-stamp into a more powerful legislature.

Last but not least, Belarus should be encouraged and assisted in pursuing economic reform. This might include a range of financial and technical assistance, education and training programmes, etc. Co-operation in this area should not be restrained by political factors, since market transformation will be instrumental in ensuring a transition to democracy.

These suggestions imply long-term solutions and may seem difficult to carry out. But big deals necessitate big efforts. That said, the chances of change in Europe's last dictatorship may not be as slight as the current situation suggests. The opposition will probably have to wait for its day until the next presidential election in 2006. By that time, a favourable combination of factors supporting democratisation may have emerged. The foundations of the state-run economy are set to crumble. The rapprochement between Russia and Europe, if its current momentum is sustained, will eliminate Belarus's importance to Russia as a bulwark against the eastward expansion of Western influence, just as Central and Eastern Europe lost its status as a Cold War frontline for the Soviet Union under Gorbachev's perestroika. The already emerging consensus between Western actors about the need for a new and coherent policy should increase the effectiveness of their joint effort. Finally, with the accession of Poland and the Baltic States to the EU, the Union will get the chance to take the lead in promoting democratic change. If (and only if) these factors are supported by the Belarusian people making their own choice in favour of democracy, will democratic transformation be inevitable and irreversible.

Notes

The author would like to thank the Central European University Special and Extension Programme for funding which made the writing of this paper possible.

[1] 'Zhizn' v nashe vremya' [Life in our time], *IISEPS (Independent Institute for Socio-economic and Political Studies) News*, no.1 (March 2001): 3-5.

[2] Ibid., 65.

[3] 'Zhizn' v nashe vremya' [Life in our time], *IISEPS News*, no.2 (June 2001): 3.

[4] Ibid., 56.

[5] 'Zhizn' v nashe vremya' [Life in our time], *IISEPS News*, no.1 (March 2001): 20.

[6] 'Elite and Past Presidential Elections,' available at IISEPS web site, http://www.iiseps.by/press-rel18.html

[7] USAID website, http://www.usaid.gov/pubs/cp2000/eni/belarus.html

[8] Thomas Carothers, 'The End of Transition Paradigm,' *Journal of Democracy* 13, no. 1 (2002): 5-21.

Barrier or Bridge on the Road to Europe? Justice and Home Affairs

Astrid Sahm

Belarus's geopolitical location and good rail and road connections not only offer it good trade opportunities, but also make the country highly vulnerable to challenges such as increasing migrant and refugee flows towards the West as well as organised crime and other illegal activities. Sharing borders with Ukraine, Russia, Poland, Lithuania and Latvia, Belarus is a cross-roads for a variety of transit routes going in all directions. Consequently, the country is an attractive transit zone for all kinds of illicit commodities from Russia and the Caucasus, as well as from Central Asia and Afghanistan, and also for illegal imports from Western Europe via Poland to the CIS countries. Therefore, there is also the risk that Belarus will become a state penetrated by powerful criminal organisations based in neighbouring states, mainly in Russia. Belarus's vulnerability to all these challenges has increased significantly since the introduction of the customs union with Russia in 1996, which eliminated the internal borders between Belarus and Russia. Because the Belarusian authorities stopped monitoring the border with Russia, there are in fact no control points for illegal activities and migrants from the Caucasus and Central Asia before the western border of Belarus, which will become the eastern border of the European Union in the near future.

In the light of all these problems, justice and home affairs (JHA) topics are of extraordinary importance for the European Union in the enlargement context. In general, co-operation in the field of JHA is the EU's most rapidly-growing policy area. As a consequence the candidate countries are constantly confronted with new JHA acquis developed by the EU on the basis of the new objectives and instruments introduced within the framework of the Treaty of Amsterdam. Consequently, JHA topics are also a particularly sensitive aspect of the accession negotiations between candidate countries and the EU. There are worries among EU citizens about the quality of the controls on the new external borders, and, related to this, about a possible increase in illegal immigration and international crime. At the same time the CEE countries are worried about the possible negative consequences of introducing 'hard' external borders and a restrictive European visa policy.

Theoretically, intensive bilateral co-operation in the field of JHA should therefore be in the mutual interest of both Belarus and the EU in order to reduce the risks of organised crime and illegal migration and trafficking, and to improve border management on both sides of the EU's new eastern border as a precondition for avoiding new dividing lines. However, due to the failure of Belarus's democratisation process, co-operation has in practice been very limited since 1996. In reaction to the controversial constitutional referendum of November 1996 extending the powers of President Lukashenko, the EU halted the ratification of both the Partnership and Co-operation Agreement (PCA) and the Interim Agreement. So as of now there is no institutional framework between the EU and Belarus for constructive political dialogue in general and co-operation in the field of JHA in particular. However, considering the importance of JHA issues in the enlargement context the EU was ready for closer co-operation with Belarus in this field than in other policy areas. Thus, although the Tacis indicative programme for Belarus was cancelled for 1996-1999, the country continued to be included in the Tacis cross-border co-operation programme. Co-operation in the field of JHA could therefore be a medium for improving the relationship between Belarus and the EU.

A shield for illegal migration?

The break-up of the Soviet Union led to a significant increase in migration to, within and from Belarus. The migration rate was at its peak in 1990-1991 with 167,400 persons leaving and 195,100 entering the country. Most of the immigrants were ethnic Belarusians not willing to live in other successor states of the former Soviet Union. In the following years the number of documented migrants fell steadily, from about 50,000 in 1993 to about 3,000 in 1999. For the whole period of 1990-2001 Belarus admitted more then 680,000 people, whereas about 500,000 people left Belarus.

In recent years the Belarusian authorities have elaborated a legal basis for dealing with the problems of refugees and asylum-seekers. Parliament adopted a law 'On Refugees' (1995) which *inter alia* provides for simplified citizenship procedures for ethnic Belarusians returning to the country, and a law 'On Immigration' (1998). Belarus also became a member of the 1951 Refugee Convention and a signatory of the 1967 Geneva Protocol in May 2001.

In 1997 the Committee on Migration set up under this legislation started hearings for asylum-seekers. By 1 January 2002 the Committee had granted refugee status to 604 persons, 461 of them from Afghanistan. The official approval rate is very high. Thus, for example, during 2000 the Committee received applications from 471 asylum seekers. The Committee issued 242 decisions granting refugee status to 200 persons. However the real situation is more complicated. According to the UNHCR-funded Refugee Counselling Services in Minsk and Vitebsk, the majority of asylum-seekers are rejected at the registration stage. The figure of 3,200 asylum-seekers and refugees in Belarus registered by the UNHCR differed by 2,490 persons from the official figures presented by the Belarusian authorities at the end of 2000. The difference can be partly explained by the 'safe country provision' included in the amendments to the refugee law. The list includes all countries bordering Belarus – Russia, Ukraine, Poland, Latvia and Lithuania. As a result, ethnic Chechens fleeing the war in Russia were barred from the asylum process.

However, the overwhelming majority of migrants staying in Belarus treat the country simply as an intermediate stop on their way to Western Europe. In 2001 the Ministry of the Interior reported that foreigners illegally in the country were estimated to number between 100,000 and 150,000 during the year. Other estimates of the number of undocumented migrants in Belarus ran between 150,000 and 200,000. The Belarusian authorities are only managing to deal with part of the problem of illegal migrants. Thus, in 1997 4,500 illegal migrants were arrested, and about 20,000 persons were not allowed to cross the border because of offences they had committed, including violations of the passport and visa regime. In 2000 about 600 illegal migrants were detained on Belarus's western borders, a number which increased to about 1,500 in 2001. Since 1995 the Belarusian authorities have closed 280 illegal migration routes and arrested about 140 organisers.

Increasing trafficking in drugs and persons

The problem of illegal migration is closely connected with that of drug and people trafficking. Illegal migrants in Belarus attempting to travel to the West often finance their trips through narcotics smuggling. International crime organisations involved in the drug trade are often also engaged in trafficking in persons. According to some experts people-smuggling is an even more profitable branch of international trade than drug trafficking. The price an illegal migrant has to pay to be taken to the West was about $5-6,000 in 2001.

In recent years drug use has became more widespread in Belarus. The number of registered drug addicts was about 5,000 in 2001, with an estimated growth of 7-800 new registrants per year, while the real number is estimated to be closer to 40,000. A trend towards a more varied menu of drugs can also be observed. Up to now opium derivatives like poppy oil have been the most popular drugs because of their relatively low cost. However, as the price of different drugs on the streets of Belarus has continued to fall in recent years, hashish, marijuana, cocaine and heroin have also become more frequently used. There is even a small market for synthetic drugs.

Despite these trends and the country's potential to become a major base for synthetic drug production, the international drug business has so far been interested in Belarus mainly as a narcotics transit corridor. The most important route is the one from Afghanistan. The second source of drugs arriving in Belarus is Moscow, which is the drug distribution centre for the regions of the former USSR. The Belarusian transport system is also used to bring narcotics from Central Asia, the Caucasus and Ukraine to the West. In addition, there are more and more cases of synthetic drug smuggling from Western Europe via Poland, indicating that drug trafficking via Belarus is not totally a one-way flow. Smuggling is also the most common drug-related crime. Other crimes include: stealing narcotic and addictive substances, organising or maintaining dens for drug-users, and forging medical documents to procure drugs. While total crimes recorded increased from 75,699 in 1990 to 130,540 in 2000, the official number of crimes associated with drug addiction rose from 372 in 1990 to 3,811 in 2000. The annual growth in drug-related crime was 30-40 per cent. According to Colonel Anatoly Gury of the Belarusian Interior Ministry, in 2000 the Belarusian police confiscated 63 times more drugs and arrested 29 times more pushers and users than in 1999. Although in general small-scale drug trafficking prevailed, there were also several cases of large-scale drug business.

Organised crime in general was by mid-1995 officially assessed to involve 138 criminal organisations headed by 151 leaders and ranging in size from 6 to 100 people, with an average size of about 20-25 members. In 2001 12 organised criminal groups were uncovered, and criminal proceedings were initiated against 286 leaders and common gangsters. Despite these successes the Belarusian authorities lack the necessary legal framework, equipment and training to combat organised crime effectively. However attempts are being made to address at least some of the problems. Thus, although the authorities do not release any statistics about cases of trafficking in persons – to which according to Belarusian NGOs several thousand Belarusian women have fallen victim – the new Criminal Code which entered into force on 1 January 2001 penalises trafficking in persons for the purpose of sexual or other kinds of exploitation, and the Ministry of Social Welfare has established a Gender Information and Policy Centre in partnership with UNDP.

In general, Belarus can be described as being relatively active in seeking international co-operation to deal with issues of crime transcending national borders. The country is a member of Interpol and is party to all relevant UN documents in the area of organised crime and trafficking. It has also joined in regional efforts at law enforcement co-operation and signed several bilateral co-operation agreements, for example with Germany, Lithuania and Poland. However, unlike Ukraine, Belarus is not a member of the Budapest Group, the only joint forum where immigration issues are discussed by specialists from EU countries, associated countries and CIS countries.

Fears of sealed borders

The challenges of illegal migration and organised crime make the border regime question a crucial one for the EU enlargement process. In order to create an area of freedom, justice and security within the EU, many EU decision-makers believe that a very strict border regime must be established on the future EU eastern frontier. However, this policy includes the risk that protection against imported illegal activities will lead to the introduction of obstacles to legal border-crossing, creating the impression that the borders are sealed to people from outside the EU. In addition, an effective EU border control regime will probably lead to an increase in illegal migrants into Belarus. One can already observe this tendency as a result of improvements in border control by Latvia, Lithuania and Poland as part of their preparations for accession to the EU.

The introduction of the Schengen system in the candidate states shows that the borders of the EU are real borders with the potential to divide countries. During recent years all the applicant states have introduced a visa regime for Belarusian citizens. Even Poland, which claims to be some kind of advocate for its eastern neighbours in their relationship with the EU, decided to introduce a visa requirement for Belarusian citizens in 1998, while Ukrainians still enjoyed visa-free travel to Poland. One must recognise, however, that the current Polish visa regime for Belarusian citizen is a very gentle one: in order to enter Poland one must either buy a voucher for a Polish hotel or show an invitation from Polish relatives etc. After Poland's accession to the EU this visa regime will undoubtedly become stricter.

Belarusian citizens are very worried about this forthcoming aggravation of the border control system, the most obvious consequence of EU enlargement for them. The Polish visa rules introduced in 1998 have already led to a significant reduction in border crossings. As a result of extensive protests by the Belarusian authorities and citizens, the visa system was somewhat simplified during 1998. However, the inhabitants of Belarus's western regions engaged in small-scale cross-border trade feel they and their opportunities to earn a living are especially threatened by the change in the border regime. In 1999, 42 per cent of all border crossings by Belarusian citizens were connected with small-scale business. Consequently, according to an independent poll conducted in the same year, 40 per cent of the people living in the western regions were even willing to accept a visa regime with Russia in order to get visa-free travel with Poland.

In theory, even with effective border controls, there are many ways of making legal border crossing easier for the inhabitants of Belarus. But such mechanisms as a simplified process for issuing multi-entry visas for the inhabitants of the border regions or the opening of new consulates outside the capital Minsk would be extraordinarily expensive for both Belarus and its neighbours. Belarus must also improve its legal provisions. Thus, Poland was forced to establish a visa system with Belarus in great part because Belarus refused to accept a readmission clause requiring Belarus to return illegal immigrants to Poland while Ukraine has signed such an agreement with Poland. Conclusion of a readmission agreement is also a precondition for the simplification of the visa regime by Latvia and Lithuania. In explaining their refusal, Belarusian representatives stressed in particular that Belarus could not finance camps for illegal migrants and had to sign similar agreements with CIS countries first.

The domestic impact

Independent opinion polls show that Belarusians with knowledge of other countries are more reform-minded than fellow citizens lacking such experience. The ability to travel is, therefore, of particular importance to the transformation process in Belarus. On the other hand, the strengthening of the border regime by applicant countries can be successfully exploited by President Lukashenko and his administration as an expression of the EU's hostile attitude towards Belarus in order to discredit Western democratic and market ideas.

The fight against corruption and crime is, like the fight against a hostile West, an important pillar of President Lukashenko's popularity and power.

On the one hand, it has to be admitted that it was indeed Lukashenko who started to deal actively with the challenges of organised crime and related illegal activities, whereas the Supreme Soviet neglected to adopt the necessary legal basis in the early years after independence. On the other hand, however, in many cases charges of corruption against leading state representatives and directors of large enterprises have clearly been used to create an atmosphere of fear within the apparatus and to get rid of (potential) political rivals. In addition, in a largely state-controlled economy the authoritarian style of policy espoused by President Lukashenko itself encourages the phenomena it pretends to combat.

In fact, there are a number of indications that the presidential administration has virtually privatised organised crime in Belarus. At the beginning of 2002 even Interior Minister Naumov stated that 'a process of merging of criminality, shady business and part of top officialdom is taking place.' Among the spheres most prone to criminal influence he mentioned the credit and finance system, the real estate market, the privatisation sector and also automobile, tobacco and alcohol businesses. One of the most prominent topics in 2001 had been the investigation by the State Control Committee into businesses involved with goods confiscated on Belarus's borders.

The security forces are also penetrated by corruption. In 2001 around 10,000 police personnel, or around 10 per cent of the total, faced penalties of various kinds. Mostly they were charged with the abuse of power, military crimes, bribery and causing road accidents. These problems are only likely to increase with the steadily deteriorating economic situation caused by the lack of economic reform. There is also a perceptible rise in the number of Belarusian migrant workers and asylum-seekers abroad.

The 'hole' in the Belarusian-Russian border

The open border between Belarus and Russia created in order to facilitate trade between the two countries makes it almost impossible for Belarusian border units to protect their country against illegal migration and smuggling from other CIS countries. However, the open border is also a significant source of profit for certain groups in both countries. Thus, at the end of the nineties the trade in second-hand cars imported from Western Europe was a source of profit to Belarusians due to the differences in customs and tax systems between Belarus and Russia. At the same time there was virtual war because the Russian Ministry of Transport created unfavourable conditions for Belarusian trucking companies carrying cargo from Western Europe to Russia in order to protect Russian companies from unwanted competition.

The Belarusian authorities have also been involved in business based on the lack of co-ordination of Russian and Belarusian customs policies towards third countries. In recent years President Lukashenko himself has granted special customs exemptions to particular foundations and enterprises. These were supposedly intended to cover only imports, in particular of alcohol, tobacco and sugar, for the Belarusian market. However, instead of selling them in Belarus, the foundations and companies exported them via the non-existent border to Russia, making a sizeable profit for themselves but causing significant damage to the state budget of both countries. One of the most prominent examples was Torgexpo, a company headed by members of the presidential apparatus.

In 1997, as a result of these problems, the Russian customs authority re-established a measure of control on the Russian-Belarusian border and demanded to take part in controls on the Belarusian-Polish border, evoking sharp protests from the Belarusian authorities. However, in late 1998 the Belarusian side itself erected police checkpoints on the border with Russia because state-controlled prices were making it profitable to resell Belarusian products in Russia, creating food shortages in Belarusian shops.

The 'hole' in the Belarusian-Russian border is, therefore, a source of (mostly illegal) profit for the Lukashenko regime, but at the same time it causes additional problems for the authorities to combat. One can assess the scale of the informal income to the presidential fund and other closed structures from the fact that, according to Belarus's official budget, in 1997 only about one per cent of the country's revenues came from transit services despite the country's optimal geopolitical location.

The EU strategy of selective engagement

Although Belarus continued to be included in cross-border and regional co-operation programmes despite the EU's restrictive policy towards Belarus after 1996, efforts undertaken within the framework of these programmes were very limited until 2000. The EU mainly subsidised improvements in border checkpoints and the demarcation of the Belarusian border with Lithuania. However, due to the EU's complicated internal structures, programmes started in 1996 began to show their first real practical effects only in 2000. All these projects are to be continued under the new Indicative Programme for Cross-Border Co-operation in 2002-2003. This includes in particular the following projects: (a) modernisation of Kozlovichi-2, where 35 per cent of all road freight traffic between Central and Western Europe and the CIS is handled; (b) continued demarcation of the Belarusian state border with Lithuania and a start on demarcation of the Belarusian border with Latvia (a Memorandum of Understanding on border demarcation between Belarus and Latvia was signed in January 2001); and (c) small facility projects.

With its forthcoming enlargement in mind, the EU has also decided to start co-operating with Belarus on other topics in the sphere of JHA. In fact all three JHA projects in the Regional Co-operation Programme for 2002-2003 include Belarus: (a) combating drug trafficking; (b) enhancing migration management in Russia and Belarus; and (c) improving asylum management in Belarus, Moldova and Ukraine. The main aim of all these projects is the creation of a 'filter system' to combat drug trafficking and reduce drug abuse in the partner countries concerned, to combat smuggling in human beings, and to reduce illegal migration both into the beneficiary countries and into the EU. The projects provide for legal assistance, the upgrading of equipment and related facilities, training in law enforcement and the enhancement of professional skills, and the encouragement of cross-border and national inter-service co-operation.

The new EU projects clearly cover problems of common interest to Belarus and the EU, and deal with the specific situation caused by the 'hole' in the Belarusian-Russian border. However, the strategy of selective engagement embodied in the new programmes will not be sufficient to create a real good-neighbourhood system on the future eastern frontiers of the EU, or to prevent the majority of Belarusians feeling they are being treated by the EU as unwanted outsiders.

Conclusions

After the events of September 11 2001, JHA issues became even more important to the EU. Belarusian representatives presented their country as an inseparable link in the anti-terror coalition at several international fora. However, this does not mean an automatic broadening of the basis of common interests between the Belarus and the EU, because the terror attacks in New York and Washington also strengthened the position of those within the EU in favour of stricter controls on the EU's external borders. The Belarusian authorities for their part seem to be convinced that the very fact that Belarus's western border shields many EU countries from a wave of unwanted migration should open the doors to closer co-operation with the EU and entitle them to receive solid support to deal with this problem. In other words, they consider their willingness to co-operate in the field of JHA should be sufficient compensation for the absence of adequate democratic standards and economic reform in Belarus. But some progress in these areas remains a precondition to the lifting of current EU restrictions on co-operation with Belarus.

In their assessment of the Belarusian presidential election results, the European organisations admitted that the policy of isolation and sanctions had not proved to be effective in relation to Belarus. The rise in imported illegal activities and the deteriorating economic situation in the country as discussed above create favourable conditions for a further increase in corruption in the state structures and thus further hinder democratisation and the establishment of the rule of law. Taking into account the relative willingness of the Belarusian authorities to engage in operational co-operation in the field of JHA, joint projects in this field can help to create the preconditions for changes in Belarusian policy by showing that the problem of illegal migration and organised crime can only be combated effectively through internal reform. The step-by-step abolition of EU sanctions might also encourage Belarus´s western neighbours to intensify their regional co-operation with Belarus, which would be a significant contribution to the transformation process in Belarus.

But in the end it is up to Belarus to change direction and make more active use of the advantages offered by its geopolitical location as a transit country in order to become not a barrier but a real bridge between East and West.

Notes

Facts and figures in this paper are taken from official and other public sources. Particularly useful references are:

Belarusian Ministry of Foreign Affairs (www.mfa.gov.by)
Charter 97 (www.charter97.org)
European Union (www.europa.eu.int)
Radio Free Europe/Radio Liberty (www.rferl.org)
United Nations in Belarus (www.un.minsk.by)
US Embassy Belarus (www.usis.minsk.by)
Worldwide Refugee Information (www.refugees.org)

Further reading

Margarita Balmaceda, 'Belarus as a Transit Route: Domestic and Foreign Policy Implications,' in Margarita M. Balmaceda, James Clem, Lisbeth L. Tarlow, eds., *Independent Belarus: Domestic Determinants, Regional Dynamics, and Implications for the West* (Cambridge: Harvard University Press, 2002), pp. 162-196

Belarus: The Foreign Aid Dilemma

Kenneth Charman

The international community remains reluctant to give aid to Belarus. Meanwhile the country's needs become ever greater. The need for a change in strategy is strong.

Introduction

The importance of Belarus to the European Union is undeniable, and an issue slowly raising its head. During the next decade, with the accession of the Baltic states and Poland, the enlarged Union will discover Belarus as its new neighbour. But the new EU will find its neighbour a country that is struggling, with an ageing industrial base, declining standards of living and social infrastructure, and with increasing health problems, including drug abuse and HIV. Furthermore the legacy of Chernobyl remains, leaving serious health-related and employment problems in the south of the country. If Belarus is to prosper, and to play an integral part in the new regional economy on the EU's eastern flank, then it needs assistance. Major humanitarian problems need to be dealt with, and Belarus needs at some point to turn away from the past and develop a new economic system, including trading links, private sector business and employment, new institutions, a two-tier banking system, and the legislative base to support a market economy.

Foreign aid can provide such assistance, and the EU can provide substantial support through a variety of programmes, the most significant being technical assistance. But, as with much of foreign aid nowadays, technical assistance is tied to progress in reform, especially democratic reform, and there have been few signs of that in Belarus since the mid-1990s. Consequently, foreign aid programmes have been withheld at a time when the country needs them most. This has left donors, and the EU in particular, with a dilemma.

History of EU aid to Belarus

Position of the EU and other donors

The EU has an interest in Belarus becoming a fully-fledged member of the international community, as it has with all other former centrally-planned states. Increased trade, co-operation, and educational and cultural links would all be part of this. One of the Commission's long-term objectives is to assist Belarus in its transition to a 'pluralist society and market economy' by reinforcing democracy, pluralism and respect for human rights and basic freedoms. The EU will provide developmental assistance to countries that adhere to these principles. For those countries where democracy is deemed to be taking hold and reforms are seen as significant, there is plenty of foreign aid available.

But it is the reform of political regimes that dominates EU policy on foreign aid provision. There are other objectives, such as fostering trade and economic links or alleviating poverty, but they are subservient. But where political relations are dire, as is the case with Belarus, aid programmes are restricted. The argument for this is quite reasonable. It is difficult to provide aid, particularly developmental aid, without a genuine political dialogue between the donor agencies and the government of the recipient country. The EU is not alone in taking this view. Almost all donors, bilateral and multilateral, have linked provision of aid to progress in reform, and have consequently restricted aid programmes to Belarus since the mid-1990s.

But the consequences of restricting programmes are serious, and lessons need to be learned. Ways need to be found of providing effective aid which do not support an autocratic regime but which help to build the institutional capacity which will be required when political relations are restored. Recent shifts by the World Bank and other multinational financial institutions to targeting poverty reduction provide further scope for proactive, non-politically-tied aid policies. It is not easy to design a foreign aid programme for a country like Belarus, but it can be done.

EU policy on aid since the 1990s

Belarus declared independence in 1991, the same year that Tacis (the EU's programme of technical assistance to the Commonwealth of Independent States) was established. At that time, technical assistance was not tied to political reform. But this began to change in the mid-1990s as provision of technical assistance became intertwined with political relations between the recipient governments and the EU and individual member states. Provision of aid through the Tacis programmes became closely related to, and later a 'strategic instrument' for, progress in political and economic reform.

The pivotal focus of both political relationships and (therefore) foreign aid has been the Partnership and Co-operation Agreement (PCA). PCAs were developed out of the desire to establish close links between the former centrally-planned states and the EU. A PCA is a ten-year bilateral treaty, a legal framework setting out the political, economic and trade relationships between the EU and the partner country. The PCA between the EU and Belarus was one of the earliest to be signed, in March 1995. Russia's was only signed in 1997. An interim agreement was signed between Belarus and the EU in March 1996, which was intended to speed up the trade-related components of the PCA.

PCAs formalise bilateral relations between the EU and individual partner countries, and implementation of the PCA is a major component of technical assistance programmes to former centrally-planned economies. The stated aims of the PCAs are to develop close political relations, to foster trade and development, and to provide a basis for mutually advantageous economic, social, financial, civic, scientific, technical and cultural co-operation. Conclusion of the PCA with Belarus was intended to support the country's efforts to consolidate its democracy and assist in completing its transition to a market economy. In the early 1990s programmes of technical assistance were lined up in support.

It was this tie to political and economic progress that led to the foreign aid programmes being suspended as fast as they had been established. The EU was unable to recognise the new 1996 Constitution, and political ties between the EU and Belarus were effectively suspended. Subsequently, in 1997, the EU Council of Ministers decided on a number of sanctions:

- The PCA was not to be concluded, nor was the 1996 interim agreement
- Belarusian membership of the Council of Europe was not supported
- Bilateral relations at ministerial level were suspended
- EU technical assistance programmes were frozen, with the exception of humanitarian aid, regional programmes and programmes directly related to democratisation.

PCAs have entered into force with all East European and former Soviet Union countries apart from Belarus and Turkmenistan. The EU's assistance strategy is based on adherence to the PCA, and clearly if the principles therein are not being adhered to, there is no basis for the provision of aid, particularly developmental aid. As the PCA with Belarus could not be concluded, the planned allocation of 37 million euros of Tacis assistance for the period 1996 to 1999 was frozen.

The EU position remains unchanged, and was summed up in a speech by Commissioner Chris Patten in a plenary session of the European Parliament on 5 July 2001, when he stated:

> 'The EU has a clear position – as long as the present intolerable situation remains, we cannot consider closer economic or political relations with Belarus. Unless and until there are significant improvements, our financial assistance will remain limited to direct help to those involved in promoting civil society and democracy and humanitarian assistance where needed'

The '2000 Regulation', a new policy for the provision of foreign aid to Eastern Europe and Central Asia, was approved by the Council of Ministers in December 1999, and governs the provision of aid to this vast region for the period 2000-2006. The Regulation encourages more 'dialogue-driven' programming, further promoting the role of co-operation between the EU and partner countries. Under this regulation, Tacis activities will focus on fewer areas, namely:

- Institutional, legal and administrative reform
- Private sector and economic development
- Consequences of changes in society, infrastructure networks
- Environmental protection

In each of these areas Belarus needs more assistance than most, but with political relations remaining cold, little is available, as aid statistics demonstrate. Total EU plus member states' provision of technical assistance to Eastern Europe and Central Asia under the Tacis programme between 1991and 1999 was 4226 million euros. The table shows how these funds were allocated to selected countries. Funds committed for 2000 to 2006 amount to 3138 million euros.

Tacis Country	1991	1992	1993	1994	1995	1996	1997	1998	1999	Total
Armenia	2.3	9.6	17.0	-	6.0	14.0	-	10.0	-	58.9
Azerbaijan	0.4	12.5	8.0	8.0	6.0	16.0	-	26.8	9.5	87.2
Belarus	8.9	14.6	9.0	7.0	12.0	-	5.0	-	-	56.6
Georgia	5.0	9.0	6.0	8.0	6.0	16.0	-	16.0	-	66.0
Kazakhstan	7.7	20.6	14.0	14.0	15.0	-	24.0	-	16.6	111.9
K rg z Republic	0.7	9.2	10.0	-	8.0	-	13.0	-	8.6	49.5
Moldo va	1.1	9.0	-	10.0	9.0	-	18.0	-	14.7	61.8
Russia	212.0	111.0	160.8	150.0	161.2	133.0	132.9	139.7	73.5	1,274.0
Tajikistan	-	-	-	4.0	4.0	-	-	-	-	8.0
Turkmenistan	0.9	8.8	-	8.0	4.0	-	11.5	-	6.7	39.9
Ukraine	28.7	48.3	43.3	50.5	72.5	76.0	59.0	44.0	38.6	460.8
Uzbekistan	1.7	18.8	-	15.0	10.0	28.0	-	29.0	-	102.5

Figures in million euros. Source: European Commission official figures

Summary of EU aid to Belarus

As shown in the table, considerable sums became available to Belarus soon after independence. Between 1991 and 1996, 54 million euros were made available under the Tacis programme. During this period, a further 22 million euros were provided under various EU multi-country, regional and nuclear safety programmes. Assistance within the Tacis programme was provided to support enterprises and further private sector development. Food production and distribution, energy and transport were also targets for assistance.

However, since 1997 the programme of foreign aid has been targeted but restricted, and this is still the case. After the cessation of the full technical assistance programme as a result of the 1997 Council of Ministers decision, the EU created a special programme of assistance aimed at those sectors not covered by the Council of Ministers ban. Programmes were planned for the development of civil society, under which a total of 5 million euros was targeted at the media, NGOs and youth organisations. This programme was agreed with the Belarusian Government in 1999.

In 2000 a further 5 million euros was allocated to small projects to assist in the development of civil society. In addition to technical assistance and civil society programmes, Belarus has received aid from a number of other EU programmes. These include the Tacis Cross-border Co-operation Programme, Regional Co-operation Programmes, and the Nuclear Safety Programme. These programmes benefit all states of the former Soviet Union. There have also been specific programmes to address the employment problems left by the Chernobyl disaster, and specific programmes under the European Initiative for Democracy and Human Rights (EIDHR).

In addition to all this, Belarus has received:

- A total of 10 million euros food aid from the 250 million euros food aid programme for the FSU
- A loan of 102 million euros for the purchase of food and medical supplies
- A loan of 55 million euros for macro-economic assistance in 1995, of which 30 million euros was disbursed in 1995; the remainder is frozen because of absence of progress in political reform.

However, the figures show that much of the assistance to Belarus occurred during the early part of the 1990s, with little made available since. Overall Belarus is in the lower quartile in terms of amount of foreign assistance given under the Tacis programme, and between 1995 and 1999 the country received less such assistance than Uzbekistan and Turkmenistan, other noted laggards in the transition-to-market process.

Future EU policy towards Belarus

The EU's long-term goal remains the same: to assist Belarus in its transition towards a democratic society and a market economy by reinforcing pluralism, respect for human rights and basic freedoms. Aid is intended to target areas where these objectives can best be met. However, the EU is constrained by the programming implications of the 1997 Council of Ministers decision. Tacis support will therefore continue to be restricted for the foreseeable future and will focus on civil society, education and training.

Provision of further aid will be determined under the 'step-by-step' approach adopted in 1999, which defines benchmarks that Belarus must achieve in order to receive further funding. Technical assistance programmes will be revised as Belarus achieves these benchmarks, which are closely linked to democratic reform. These benchmarks, set by the OSCE, are that

- substantial powers are returned to parliament
- the opposition is represented in the electoral commission
- there is fair access to the state media for the opposition
- electoral legislation conforms to international standards

Broadly speaking these conditions have not been met, although the endorsement by the Belarusian government of the Tacis Civil Society Programme in 1999 marked a step forward in relations. However, the EU has emphasised that it is ready to resume normal relations and full assistance programmes once the EU/OSCE criteria for free and fair elections are met.

Other donors and international financial organisations, including the World Bank, IMF and EBRD, have also adopted the benchmark system, choosing more economic criteria on which to judge progress. Of these, the most significant has been that of exchange rate convergence, something Belarus largely achieved in September 2000, and has struggled to maintain since.

Technical assistance to Belarus

Under a technical assistance project, Western experts work alongside locals, usually in key government ministries, the central bank and other key institutions, to provide advice, support and training to address a particular need. Typical areas of focus for technical assistance projects in transition economies reflect their specific needs in order to migrate successfully from centrally-planned to market economies. These would include:

- macro-economic policy
- price liberalisation, trade reform and exchange rates
- privatisation (large and small scale)
- governance and enterprise reform
- development of the civil service
- competition policy
- banking and securities markets development (e.g. stock exchange, non-bank finance)

Belarus's needs have been no different from those of its former centrally-planned neighbours. Foreign aid through technical assistance can contribute know-how to meet a range of needs. These include humanitarian and basic needs projects, the development of educational and cultural links and, to a considerable and growing extent, development of the country's institutional infrastructure to support democracy and the market economy.

An example of a technical assistance project: Belarus Economic Trends

Until recently the Tacis Policy Advice Programme funded the widely successful 'Belarus Economic Trends' (BET) project, providing statistics and economic analysis of developments in the Belarusian economy.

The Economic Trends publications, run by Tacis since 1994 in nine former Soviet Union countries, have provided comprehensive economic data plus expert analysis to both the local and international communities, and the publications have been widely used by governments, embassies, banks and academic institutions. In certain countries, including Belarus, the information has been the only internationally recognised source of economic data that has been produced locally. The publications have been heavily relied upon by those who study the region. Special policy and research papers have been published by BET economists and widely quoted.

In Belarus, as in most if not all countries where the Economic Trends project has operated, BET has not only been able to train and work with highly-qualified local staff and published reliable economic data, it has drawn in a wide local circle, including academics, students, businessmen and policy-makers. This has created a forum that has helped to raise the level of debate locally across a wide range of economic and transition issues. It has brought local and international analysts together and allowed them to communicate and share views. In a country such as Belarus, where there is little chance to do this, such a well-targeted piece of foreign aid has provided a valuable lifeline. Unfortunately, funding for BET ceased in January 2000 due directly to the decision to restrict funding for technical assistance to Belarus.

Civil society programme

Like most donors, the EU has targeted aid to 'civil society' since 1996. This fundamentally aims to promote democracy and a greater awareness of European democratic values and standards, especially regarding the rights of the individual. The Tacis Civil Society Programme, currently in operation in Belarus, targets the development of NGOs, the media and youth groups in support of this objective (e.g. encouraging 'active citizenship'). Further projects aimed at better education and training, and measures to promote small business and alleviate unemployment, will doubtless be a part of future programmes.

Under the Civil Society Programme, projects to support the independent media have included:

- Training in journalism and production for a terrestrial and cable TV station
- Training for young people in the production of school newspapers, to prepare them for a career in journalism (Gomel region)
- Training in news-writing skills for daily and weekly news reporting, photojournalism, newspaper design and distribution systems
- Internet training courses in Minsk
- Extensive training in magazine, radio, television and on-line journalism

Projects to support NGOs are based on the concept that a flourishing NGO sector greatly assists in the development of democracy, since NGOs can provide a voice for varying opinions. NGOs can give a balanced view of governmental activity, and play a vital role in helping address major social problems at the community level. EU programmes to support NGOs and to target social projects through NGOs have been particularly prominent in areas affected by Chernobyl.

Projects related to education and training have supported institution-building and 'twinning' arrangements, including strengthening the capacity of the European Documentation Centre. This involved the creation of a dissemination system for information on the activities of the European Communities and the promotion of European Studies in Belarus. Another project included capacity-building in management training at the Higher School of Management and Business, the State Economic University and the Institute of Privatisation and Management, major academic institutions in Belarus.

The Tempus programme 'twins' academic institutions and has been a powerful driver of development for local universities and academic institutions in transition countries over the last decade. The Tempus programme in Belarus has included

- Creation of course modules and curriculum development in European Studies
- Multilevel management and capacity improvement
- University management / student support programmes
- Dissemination, co-operation and university reform in teaching economics in Belarus
- Information and communications development in Belarus

All these programmes have been carried out through partnerships between European and Belarusian universities and academic institutions.

Other EU programmes

European Initiative for Democracy and Human Rights

The EU's European Initiative for Democracy and Human Rights (EIDHR) has also been targeted at civil society programmes. Included in this was a programme run in conjunction with the OSCE to train local election observers for the parliamentary elections in September 2001. There has also been a project working with the International Helsinki Federation to promote human rights advocacy. Projects have included training in support of local democracy, the strengthening of democratic media, penitentiary reform, monitoring of human rights compliance, and human rights training for law enforcement officers.

Projects have included the establishment of a system of public participation in elections, education programmes 'Toward Civil Society' at the Training Centre Foundation in Support of Local Democracy, and the opening of a department for electronic legal documents. There have also been programmes focusing on women in custody, children's rights, training for personnel in justice and law-making bodies, and the creation of a contact centre for NGOs, the media and trades unions. The total funded out of the 1999 and 2001 budgets (implemented 2000-2001) was 3.8 million euros.

However, Belarus is not amongst the EIDHR focus countries, so no specific sum has been allocated for 2000-2004. In principle, only regional projects to fight racism and discrimination against minorities are envisaged for those years.

ECHO

The European Office for Emergency Humanitarian Assistance (ECHO), set up in 1992, provides humanitarian assistance through partners, namely 200 NGOs, UN agencies, and other international bodies. These are linked to ECHO through a framework project. ECHO's activities cover disaster relief and children's needs. Its aims are basically to provide food, water, medicine, vaccinations, psychological support, clothes, shelter and rehabilitation.

In 2000, 2.8 million euros was provided for Belarus, Moldova and Ukraine. However, ECHO policy has been to reduce involvement in Belarus, Moldova and Ukraine on the grounds that the problems those countries are facing are structural, not humanitarian. However, recognising that humanitarian issues exist, funding was targeted at vulnerable groups such as the elderly, disabled, large families and children in institutions.

Cross-border co-operation

Cross-border co-operation projects address issues that affect a number of countries and that require some form of co-operation between countries to resolve them. Cross-border co-operation programmes focus on issues affecting neighbouring communities in different states. Recent foci of attention under the cross-border co-operation facility involving Belarus have included the environment, with river projects (5.5 million euros), border crossing and demarcation (10.5 million euros), and a small project facility (0.5 million euros) to promote small-scale cross-border co-operation (Poland, Latvia and Lithuania).

Regional co-operation programmes

Regional programmes are aimed at addressing problems shared by countries in a particular region, and focus on promoting co-operation between them. Themes include protection of the environment, telecommunications, energy and transport networks, justice and home affairs, and private sector investment. The Interstate Environment Project (5 million euros) includes measures for river protection, as well as Chernobyl-related projects for Russia, Ukraine and Belarus. Belarus currently participates in 3 regional programmes worth 2.3 million euros.

Nuclear safety and the response to Chernobyl

Although the Chernobyl disaster of April 1986 occurred in Ukraine, the radioactive fallout affected more than 40 per cent of the population of Belarus, primarily in the Gomel region in the south. This disaster, whose effects are still being felt today, required immediate foreign aid, and continues to require assistance in helping the most vulnerable groups in Belarus, particularly the young and the aged, to overcome the long term health, social and economic effects.

The EU's response was to provide assistance for the humanitarian effects of the fallout, the nuclear safety aspects of the reactors, and the local employment effects in subsequent years. A total of 6.7 million euros has been provided from the EU's ECHO programme for humanitarian assistance alone. A further 3.5 million euros has gone to develop employment opportunities in the southern region of Belarus, to help alleviate the unemployment and social problems created by the disaster.

Altogether a grand total of 340 million euros has been provided for Chernobyl and related projects since 1986. The majoirty of these funds have been spent in Ukraine, and have focused on three areas:

- The shelter and sarcophagus (entombment) of the destroyed Unit 4 at Chernobyl

- Damage assessment – over 100 research projects assessing the health and environmental impact, including assessment of the ground surrounding the reactor and investigations into the secondary medical effects of the disaster
- The decommissioning of the plant and energy replacement projects to compensate for the closure of Chernobyl.

Position of other donors

Aid from EU member states

Five EU member states have embassies in Belarus: France, Germany, the United Kingdom, Greece and Italy. Other EU member states also active in Belarus include Austria, Denmark, the Netherlands and Sweden. Most bilateral donors have reduced their aid or redirected it to civil society programmes since 1996, and state that they will requires a more supportive environment before full-scale aid programmes resume. A total of 24.97 million euros was disbursed in bilateral aid from EU member states from 1996-99.

The member states tend to work closely with the EU and other international financial organisations such as the World Bank and IMF, promoting similar objectives, also now focusing on poverty reduction as the primary aim of their programmes. The major part of member state contributions to aid is now effected through their share in programmes of the EU, the World Bank and the EBRD. The UK's Department for International Development (DFID) emphasise the work they do with the multilateral agencies to promote sound economic policies, and to support countries' efforts to play a wider part in the international community, including membership of the WTO. As with a number of other donors, DFID also works with multilateral donors to ensure the quality of aid programmes and to look for new ways to help the fight against poverty, provide opportunities for poorer people, and promote civil society.

Aid from major donors and international financial organisations

This is covered in an appendix at the end of this article.

Analysis of aid to Belarus

Results of donor policy

Aid agencies and international financial institutions (IFIs) have, quite rightly, come in for criticism as to the value they have given, and especially the value of their advice. But ten years after the collapse of communism, most of the former centrally planned countries are very different places. Most, when not blighted by conflict, have become very much part of the international community.

The direct impact of foreign aid in recipient countries is a contentious and inconclusive issue, and is not discussed at length here. But the externalities, the spin-off effects of foreign aid, can be crucial to the process of reform. The sheer presence of foreign faces on the streets, and the diversity of culture and experience that they bring, has helped in the onerous task of transition in former centrally-planned countries. Foreign aid has played its part in this. In addition, aid has brought skills, expertise and resources that countries need, and that neither local governments nor foreign investors could bring themselves.

All international financial organisations and donor agencies, including the EU, employ local staff who manage, sometimes entirely, the local office and provide considerable expertise themselves. Local staff members often benefit from training, seminars and study tours abroad that lead to further international contacts. When these local staff move to other jobs they take the skills and practices they have learned with them. The more foreign aid projects in the field, the greater the spin-off effects. Projects involving academic study (e.g. the EU's Tempus programme) can create lasting academic links. Exchange programmes for students provide a relatively cost-effective way of fostering international contacts. Belarus, like other former Soviet states, has a highly educated workforce, and it is easy to see how productive these links can be.

Put simply, well-targeted foreign aid programmes do not simply target senior policy-makers. They work at a level below this, effectively helping create a critical mass of well-trained middle-level staff with local contacts and international links, who can and do provide the diversity in approach that a country such as Belarus needs.

Belarus needs assistance more than most, and on grounds of need the foreign aid community should be there in force. But it is not. The international community has ceased to be proactive in the provision of aid to Belarus. Donors have been slow to implement the programmes that are available, and projects that were providing significant benefit while specifically not supporting any political regime (like Belarus Economic Trends) have been allowed to lapse. The EU is left with an increasingly impoverished and potentially unstable country on its doorstep. By withdrawing foreign aid programmes they can only exacerbate this position.

Foreign aid is needed most when political dialogue is at a low ebb and policy is 'bad'. Projects that have an impact at the local level, that build capacity and that foster international links, are then even more important. These will pay off at that point in the future when dialogue is stronger and when policies finally become acceptable. On these grounds, there is a case for implementing more, rather than fewer, foreign aid projects in Belarus.

Conclusion: a strategy for the 'worst case' is required

The 'Belarus dilemma', whether or not to be proactive in giving aid when political relations are so poor, is not easily solved. It is right to encourage co-operation between donors and governments of recipient countries in the provision of foreign aid, particularly technical assistance. It is understandable to restrict aid when the level of co-operation and political dialogue are low. But when this strategy is not working, as is so obviously the case with Belarus, a new strategy is required.

Even when political relations are poor, the EU, like other donors, can still provide valuable technical assistance in building capacity within the ministries, national banks and other key institutions. That capacity will still be there for the long term, and at some point political relations will improve. Programmes are already in place to do this. It just needs donors to be proactive in targeting areas for assistance, rather than simply allowing political relationships to dominate policy and thus allowing potentially valuable aid programmes to stop. Continuing and developing aid projects under the present regime is fine, as long as the direct beneficiary (the Ministry, the bank, the institution) is still committed and the results are still being achieved.

The EU should adopt a positive and proactive aid policy towards Belarus. But this will require a change in the criteria for aid provision that avoids the need to rely solely on progress in political reform. Such criteria might include:

- Poverty reduction: this can be addressed at the local level, and a strategy could be developed to find ways to implement poverty reduction projects that do not support a political regime; micro-credit schemes may provide a way forward here.
- Trade promotion: foreign aid can quite legitimately be used to help develop trade, which will benefit both donor country and recipient; cross-border projects focusing on customs arrangement, and SME development projects might become a priority.
- Capacity building: aid could be targeted on non-politically-sensitive capacity-building projects (Belarus Economic Trends is the best example) to build competence and international links for when political relations improve. This would focus on the middle level professionals and administrators who implement policy. The long-term benefits could be enormous.

The case for a strategy of assistance for this, a 'worst case' scenario, is strong. At present the only strategy is quietly to withdraw. A positive strategy of offering assistance in areas that help build capacity and can be implemented at the local level can provide major benefits to a recipient country even when political relations are at their worst. When that country is right on the EU's doorstep, the need to develop a strategy for the worst case is even greater.

Appendix

Summary of aid from IFIs and other major donors

EBRD

The EBRD has an existing portfolio of projects in Belarus, but is currently restricting lending to the private sector, particularly SMEs. Loans to date have totalled 112.4 million euros. It too has adopted a set of economic and political benchmarks that Belarus would have to achieve for the Bank to resume its full set of investment activities. The EBRD sees the issue of EU enlargement as paramount, and accepts that as Belarus is shortly to be an neighbour the Bank should retain a presence, although activities will be severely restricted until the country makes progress on democracy, the rule of law, human rights and economic reform.

United Nations

The work of the United Nations (UN) and its agencies is aimed at promoting dialogue between Belarus and other countries, so that Belarus can share and learn from the experiences of other countries.

The United Nations office opened in Belarus in 1992 as a partnership between the United Nations Development Programme and the United Nations Department of Public Information. Since then a number of UN institutions have established a presence in Belarus. These include the World Bank, IMF, IFC, and UN agencies including the World Health Organisation (WHO), UN High Commissioner for Refugees (UNHCR), United Nations Children's Fund (Unicef), Joint United Nations Programme on HIV/AIDS, United Nations Population Fund and International Labour Organisation (ILO).

The UN has provided Belarus with assistance in a wide range of humanitarian and development fields including reform of social support systems, development of small and medium sized enterprises and access to information technology and communications. Programmes to alleviate environmental health problems, such as the aftermath of Chernobyl, have also been prominent in the UN programme in Belarus. Further projects to help with the growing problem of refugees and migrants have been introduced.

More recently programmes to support the development of democracy and an open society have played a fundamental role in the programmes provided. Raising the awareness of UN principles and the international conventions and agreements to which Belarus is a party has now become a major focus of UN programmes in Belarus.

Much foreign assistance targeted at pressing current issues such as drug addition and the spread of AIDS has been provided through the UN. For humanitarian assistance, the

UN manages emergency assistance and humanitarian responses to wars, natural disasters, etc.

The UN has run projects in education and training to assist in providing opportunities for the young and for people in rural areas now that the state support systems under central planning have largely collapsed.

World Bank

The World Bank undertakes three types of operation: lending, analysis and technical assistance. It aims to assist the client country in achieving the goals it has set in terms of economic development, and in particular poverty reduction.

The World Bank's programme in Belarus has so far focused on long-term economic development, emphasising health, education, social protection (safety-nets) and protection of the environment. During 1992-94 the Bank's activities included lending to support institutional development, forestry development and the environment. However, the continuation of price controls and slow progress in transition to a market economy, especially in the key sectors of agriculture, enterprise restructuring, and trade and exchange rate liberalisation, has led to a slowdown in the Bank's financial assistance to Belarus.

The Bank has remained active in analysis of the Belarusian economy, in public education programmes and in promoting debate on the economy's future with a range of stakeholders such as NGOs, government agencies and research institutions. In this way the Bank has focused attention on the major problems affecting the country and its future development even though the assistance programme has been restricted.

In September 2000 the Belarusian authorities decided to unify the exchange rates. This was seen as a significant step towards market reform, and resulted in a new level of co-operation between the World Bank and the Belarusian government. A $22.6 million social infrastructure project was initiated. This focuses on improving the lives of some of the more vulnerable sectors of the population by financing the rehabilitation of over 450 buildings across the country. This includes such fundamentals as better lighting, hot water and heating for schools, hospitals, orphanages and community homes for the elderly and disabled. According to initial feedback published by the World Bank, the pilot project in Minsk resulted in a fall in absenteeism in schools due to minor sickness, and fewer cases of children with eye problems thanks to the installation of flicker-free lights.

The World Bank now consults widely on the compilation of its assistance strategy for Belarus, including with government officials, women's groups, NGOs, trades unions, academics, journalists, government officials, politicians and other civil society representatives, business associations and university students.

Proposed areas for future intervention by the World Bank include health issues such as HIV/AIDS, environmental policy, especially alleviation of the effects of Chernobyl, social protection, private sector development, and various infrastructure projects.

The World Bank stresses that, whilst ensuring that all voices are heard in the development of foreign aid projects, especially from the poorer and more needy income groups, successful implementation of aid projects requires commitment from the government. The World Bank thus sees an important role in working in partnership with the authorities.

International Finance Corporation

The IFC is part of the World Bank group. One of its main priorities is to develop co-operation with the small and medium sized enterprise sector. Growth in SMEs is an area where significant improvements in employment and economic growth can be fostered.

The Small Business Development Project operates a network of offices throughout Belarus to provide links with local business communities. This permits an exchange of information with the IFC Co-ordination Centre about local developments, the business environment, and areas where assistance from the IFC could provide benefit.

The project aims to improve the quality, outreach and sustainability of SME support institutions, expand and improve access for SMEs to legal information, and assist in improving the legislative environment for SMEs by making comments and recommendations on legislative and other impediments to the SME sector. The project also increases public awareness of economic issues through information campaigns in the local and national media. Partner organisations include business associations and support centres, business incubators to support businesses at the very early stages of growth, trade unions, unions of entrepreneurs, NGOs, international organisations and donors. The project also provides a nation-wide training programme for SMEs, including individual entrepreneurs and start-up businesses.

The IFC works closely with partner organisations in monitoring the legal and business environment and in the provision of support services, so assisting the SME sector which is so critical to the growth of new business and employment in the post-planning era.

International Monetary Fund

The IMF, an international organisation with 182 member countries, was created to promote economic stability, particularly exchange rate stability, and international monetary co-operation. Economic stability creates a platform for sustained economic growth and increased employment. The IMF has focused much recent activity on helping countries to overcome short-term balance of payments problems.

The IMF has been present in Belarus since 1992, using IMF funds on three occasions to provide credit and loans to assist the government's reform programme. Loans outstanding at the end of 1998 amounted to SDR 184.4 million, which is not high by international standards. More recently, in 1999-2000, the IMF decided not to provide loans to Belarus in spite of the widespread exchange rate depreciation. Belarus has received no credits from the IMF since 1995 due to the lack of progress in reform.

Although not technically a donor, the IMF has provided Belarus with technical assistance in public expenditure management, tax and customs, bank supervision, monetary policy and central bank organisation, and in statistical analysis of balance of payments and government finance. It has provided training for a number of government officials in macro-economic policy management.

US Agency for International Development (USAID)

Although not a multi-lateral agency, USAID has been a significant donor. As with other donors, USAID has strategically targeted its aid on the consolidation of democracy, emphasising that a democratic, market-oriented and independent Belarus could significantly increase stability in the East European region. This is important to the US, even though it has little direct strategic interest in the region. In particular, as with other donors, US government policy is to focus on civil society development projects.

USAID projects include support for the independent media and NGOs, law programmes, and small-scale privatisation. Under a USAID project to increase productivity in farming, farmers from the USA have worked with local farmers in Belarus over a period of months to help maximise agricultural productivity.

From Aid To Foster Care: A Case Study

Margaret Bamford

The children of Belarus are victims. They are victims of poverty, ill health and a political regime that has discouraged economic investment and development. The nuclear disaster at Chernobyl has compounded the problem. Whatever the reasons, the birth rate continues to decline. Life expectancy remains lower than twenty years ago. The divorce rate at 75% of all marriages is the highest in Europe. The population is falling and is now under 10 million. The health of many children remains a matter of concern and the numbers of children being admitted to orphanages doubled between 1990 and 1999. There are now nearly 30,000 children being brought up in orphanages out of a total child population of 2.5 million. This is a country still struggling to maintain essential health and welfare services.

Individuals and organisations in the West are providing help. Therapeutic holiday schemes for children in Italy, Germany, the Netherlands and Britain have raised awareness of the acute needs of children being brought up in orphanages. Each of these countries has provided, either through state aid, individual or voluntary effort, considerable amounts of support. Material conditions in some orphanages are improving as lavatories and washing facilities are improved, structural repairs tackled, rooms painted, gardens and play areas developed, and van loads of toys delivered.

It is easy to understand why nations want to provide such help. My immediate reaction on visiting in January 1998 was the same. I was accompanying my husband on a business trip with camera and notebook, keen to take photographs of a strange and cold country. I was totally unprepared. I found the photographs hard to take. I was an experienced social worker and had worked with many children with disabilities throughout my professional life. But I had never seen anything like the situation I was invited to record. I took refuge behind the camera and took careful notes for the articles I knew I would have to write on my return home to raise funds for drugs, medical equipment and other essential items of humanitarian aid. On returning to the UK my approach was tentative, but the response was overwhelming and enough money was soon raised to purchase a substantial consignment of aid. I borrowed two vans from the County Council and three colleagues helped me drive overland to Minsk. The sense of achievement was wonderful and the recipients were so grateful. But then I began to think. Magnificent as had been the response to the appeal for help, aid could only be a short-term solution; it would soon be used and gone. Would it not be better to leave driving vans across Europe to those far more able than I to maintain the necessary regular flow of humanitarian aid and put my thirty-five years in social work to better use? I thought of the orphanages…

With limited family support services and without willing relatives, parents can feel there is no alternative to institutional care. Parents of disabled Belorusian babies often select the orphanage option not only because of the stigma that still attaches to disability but also because of the deteriorating economic situation. Adults need to work to survive; they cannot afford for one parent to stay at home. Medicines are also expensive. In the orphanages all healthcare is provided free of charge. Many disabled children, even very mildly disabled children, are admitted at five days old and remain in an orphanage or institution for the rest of their lives.

The idea of a pilot fostering project for disabled children was not greeted in Belarus with overwhelming enthusiasm! First it was difficult to explain. There was no word in Russian for foster care. Even the most child-centred heads of orphanages could only foresee 'problems'. 'Who could possibly want to look after a disabled child, far less someone else's disabled child?' 'Even if they did, how would they be paid?' 'How would the children be educated?' 'What would happen when they were no longer children?' These were perfectly legitimate questions best dealt with directly. So a delegation of senior Government officials from Belarus was invited to West Sussex. They visited a range of childcare facilities particularly for children with disabilities and talked to foster carers. They also noted carefully the laws and regulations to protect the children. They were clearly impressed.

But changing traditions is not easy. Respect and courtesy were essential as negotiations proceeded. Gradually, however, support evolved and a three-year partnership was agreed. The British Government (Department for International Development), Unicef, the Government of Belarus, the Belarusian Association for Handicapped Children and West Sussex County Council agreed to collaborate to establish a three-year pilot fostering project.

Training in a different culture and in a different language was not easy. Staff in orphanages knew the height, weight, health and standard of academic attainment of their children, but not about their relationships with Mum, Dad, grandparents or brothers and sisters. Theories of attachment and emotional development were new. Two young men who had been brought up in an orphanage had a powerful impact when, in their own language, they described how it felt 'not belonging'.

After nearly two years, the first children have left orphanages to live with substitute families. It is very early days. None of the children has been in placement for longer than eighteen months. There have been no disruptions. Support is provided regularly at the local pedagogical centre where representatives of all disciplines are on hand to provide specialist advice and there is regular contact between foster carers locally for mutual support and friendship. Three children who had been diagnosed as oligophrenic (small brained) have begun to blossom and the prognosis for their normal development is good.

All the foster families struggle financially. One Mum baked cakes to sell at the market, another knitted prolifically, another created traditional straw artefacts for the tourist industry, and a foster Dad baked bread for the farm collective with which he worked. All the rural families cultivated their land and grew their own vegetables. Most reared their own chickens, geese, pigs and had a cow or two. Their hard work and determination to provide for their expanding families was an object lesson in resourcefulness and self-sufficiency. They were determined to make it work with minimal resources and none of the benefits of the domestic support taken for granted by the most impoverished of Western families. Washing was undertaken by hand, vegetables were salted or pickled for the winter and meat and fish smoked to preserve them for as long as possible.

No organisation is in a position to commit scarce resources readily to working in other countries. All have to make careful political and professional judgements about the value of involvement. West Sussex County Council has agreed to continue supporting the initiative on the basis that experience elsewhere confirms that temporary release of staff for limited periods can have considerable benefits. The opportunity of working in less developed countries can be professionally and personally rewarding. New skills learned, new knowledge acquired and a renewed focus and enthusiasm for the job are all assets for the Department and staff involved.

The EU and Belarus: Where Next?

Ann Lewis

This book sets out to present the reader with a diverse range of views on Belarus and its relations with the EU. It would be invidious to attempt to summarise those views. But it may be worth picking out some of the main threads and pointing up some of the policy proposals that are scattered throughout the book.

More than a decade after independence, Belarus retains many of the features of the Soviet republic it was before independence, with the president enjoying the powers hitherto the prerogative of the Communist Party. Its state-controlled economy has latterly preserved a certain economic stability and helped prevent obvious extremes of poverty and wealth. The country has largely avoided the corrupt oligarchs and mafia-style capitalism suffered by some of its Slav neighbours as a result of botched privatisation, though at the cost of stultifying central control. It has some of the trappings of a democratic state, but little of the reality, notwithstanding some modification in President Lukashenko's rhetoric since his re-election in 2001. It remains cut off from the European democratic mainstream.

One point on which all contributors seem to be agreed is that, at time of writing (summer 2002), President Lukshenko is well entrenched in power, enjoys the support (from enthusiastic to grudging) of the majority of the population, and is much more popular than any other politician, however flawed the process by which he was re-elected in 2001. Among the reasons for this are:

- Belarusians are passively content with their lot; they are not prosperous, but they feel secure with their steady pay and soviet-style welfare and support system;
- They were scarred by the economic turmoil of the early years of independence, and are now resistant to radical change;
- This is reinforced by the deep conservatism of all but the very young;
- Belarusians are mostly content with the policy of close relations with Russia, to which there is no tradition of hostility;
- Conversely, there is no strong movement in favour of closer links with the West, except perhaps among the young; and few are sufficienly well-informed to question the President's characterisation of the West as inherently unfriendly, if not hostile, to Belarus;
- Lukashenko and his associates control all the levers of administrative power and most of the media;
- There has been no charismatic personality or coherent opposition force to present an attractive alternative.

If there is to be change in Belarus sooner rather than later (when a younger generation that does not share these attitudes comes to political maturity), it will probably result from a combination of an erosion of economic stability, the emergence of a critical mass of opinion in favour of reform, and the appearance of a credible alterative leadership.

Among the factors important to Lukashenko's hold on power, economic stability is perhaps the most crucial. So, is the economic situation sustainable?

The consensus among the economists writing in this book is that it is not, at least in the long term. Some of the foundations on which the former relative prosperity was built no longer look so durable. Assets are being exhausted, industries are out-moded by Western standards, the system deters rational decision-making, innovation is discouraged rather than encouraged, and there is nothing to attract Western investment.

But the biggest question-mark hangs over Russia's willingness to continue indefinitely to subsidise Belarus in the way that has kept it afloat up to now. President Putin is clearly not interested in the Union with Belarus, and has emphasised the need to rationalise economic aspects of the relationship to make Belarus less dependent on its big neighbour. While Putin probably has no particular wish to get rid of his most loyal ally, there may be a limit to his willingness to prop him up. Belarus's significance to Russia, such as it was, is declining as Russia develops a new relationship with the West after September 11. And Lukashenko's belief that Russia gets its *quid quo pro* through access to military bases and facilities may also be undermined by Russia's rapprochement with Nato.

A declining level of Russian subsidy, the unification of Belarus's exchange rate, and the harmonisation of various economic instruments are adding to the pressures on the Belarusian economy which are contributing to falling living standards. If Lukashenko is forced as a consequence to reduce the social security net and cannot protect his people from hardship, that will undermine the main pillar of his support.

But if Lukashenko continues to lose support, where will an alternative leadership come from? This was the fundamental problem in the latest parliamentary and presidential elections. Civil society is alive and flourishing in Belarus. But although the opposition forces and parties were eventually able to agree on a single candidate for the presidency (a big step forward in itself), they were widely perceived as disorganised, unwilling to work together and without coherent strategy or tactics. Given the track record of previous opponents of the President, it is not surprising that few have the stomach for the fight. But until a leader or leaders emerge with political courage, commitment and organisational skills, it will be hard to turn even a wave of popular enthusiasm for change into a coherent political force. The system is heavily stacked against any challenge to the incumbent, especially in view of Lukashenko's strangle-hold over the media.

In these circumstances, what should the EU and its member-states do? How much does the EU care what goes on in Belarus?

So far Belarus has been a low priority for the West in general and the EU in particular. Though eccentric, it is small, stable, of little economic or strategic interest, and safely within the Russian orbit. It has done nothing to make the EU disposed to help it, and much that flouts the most basic principles of Western democracy. The EU has no particular interest in bringing Belarus into membership of the EU, and none at all in detaching it from Russia.

But Belarus is coming nearer to the EU – or rather, the EU is coming nearer to Belarus. With EU enlargement Belarus will have three EU members on its borders and form a substantial part of the last frontier for people and goods moving, legally or illegally, to Western Europe from Russia and points east. Inevitably it will move up the EU agenda, because of its potential to be either a threat or a useful partner in regional arrangements across the board. The new EU members, especially Poland and Lithuania, will have a particularly strong interest in maintaining something of their existing close relationship with Belarus (though not at the expense of their relations with the EU).

Above all the EU must, as a matter of principle, have an interest in seeing democracy, human rights and the rule of law established in Belarus as in the rest of Europe.

EU policy towards Belarus has gone through three main stages. In the early post-independence years, the EU paid little attention to Belarus but did offer modest support and aid in the interest of furthering political and economic reform. This achieved little in the chaotic conditions of the time. Following Lukashenko's unconstitutional extension of his powers in 1996, a severe clamp-down was imposed amounting to a virtual breaking off of relations. This failed to produce any improvement in the political scene in Belarus. In recent years policy has eased up very slightly in the hope that dialogue would help promote some liberalisation. While this has helped the development of civil society it has not led to wider political change. With the mid-2002 impasse over the OSCE office in Minsk, relations seem to have reached stalemate.

The current step-by-step approach, whereby the EU offers Belarus benefits in terms of trade, economic relations, aid, etc as it reaches various 'benchmarks' of economic and political reform, is consistent with the policy of conditionality applied to other Central and East European countries. It appears to enjoy almost universal support among EU governments. Some critics claim it is a crude instrument which fails to take account of the specific conditions in individual countries.

Has this policy worked in Belarus? It has encouraged the development of civil society through support for independent organisations (though Vitali

Silitski argues that Western aid in the political sphere has hindered rather than helped the formation of a coherent opposition in the country). Beyond that it is hard to say that EU policy has done much to further the cause of democracy in Belarus. Lukashenko has not moved an inch in response to pressure from the West, refusing to act under duress (as he might put it), but also no doubt aware that any liberalisation might threaten his own position. Furthermore he has presented the EU's attitude as demonstrating hostility to Belarus, and used this to shore up his domestic position. To that extent the EU's policy may have been counterproductive. But Belarus is clearly feeling isolated, and keeps probing for possible chinks in the position of the EU and other Western institutions.

The key problem with the benchmarking approach is that it assumes the target country is the demandeur, that the EU has something to offer that the country's leadership wants sufficiently for it to be willing to make concessions. In the case of Belarus, this is not so – or at least not yet. Whatever the population might want (and there is so far no discernible ground-swell in favour of close relations with the EU), Lukashenko has shown little interest in any deal involving political concessions; rather the reverse. This could change if he came to see Western help as the only way of shoring up his embattled country. But in those circumstances, unless there were root-and-branch reform of a kind hard to associate with Lukashenko, the West might be wary of doing anything that would help prolong his tenure.

However, EU policy is not entirely static. In view of impending enlargement, discussions are taking place in 2002 on a 'new neighbours' initiative intended to give fresh impetus to relations with Belarus, Ukraine and Moldova. The thinking behind this is that the EU should adopt a more strategic approach to three countries which will sooner or later be on its borders, and which are all engaged in a process of transition which it is in the West's interest to see completed successfully in order to avoid regional instability. The aim would be to send a positive political signal by offering the three countries a new kind of relationship with the EU, perhaps involving more extensive trade liberalisation and co-operation than set out in the Partnership and Co-operation Agreements. This would essentially be an extension of current policy, with an improvement in the carrots on offer but still incorporating the principles of differentiation and conditionality, with each country moving at its own pace depending on progress on internal political and economic reform.

Meanwhile, some analysts are beginning to consider whether an alternative approach might be more successful. Three main lines of thinking are set out in this book. (Apologies to the contributors concerned whose carefully laid out arguments are only sketched below.)

The first and least dramatic is a policy of increased engagement. Advocates of this approach (including both Belarusian and Western commentators) argue that the EU should not give up on the whole of Belarus because its government is autocratic. While it should not deal with Lukashenko and his immediate entourage until they mend their ways, it should do much more to engage with the rest of society. This means not only non-state organisations but also parliamentarians, professionals, business people and the middle ranks of the bureaucracy, who are likely to be important in running the country for the foreseeable future and from whose ranks any credible alternative to Lukashenko is most likely to come. Any interaction with Westerners, it is argued, is likely to broaden minds and introduce new thinking, thus helping to create the critical mass which will be essential for any fundamental change.

To be effective a policy of greater engagement would require a substantial increase in EU and bilateral contacts and aid. Kenneth Charman's article outlines a possible new strategy on aid. A more radical version of the policy of engagement would include opportunities for Belarusians to work temporarily in the EU, see a different way of life for themselves, and perhaps accumulate a little capital.

Against this, sceptics would argue that, apart from the NGOs with which the West already maintains contacts, there are no forces in Belarus worth cultivating because all are subject to Lukashenko's will and any attempt to broaden contacts will be taken by the President as acknowledgement of his regime.

The second proposal (elaborated here by Heinz Timmermann) is that, as Russia seeks to develop its relations with the EU, the latter should use the dialogue to encourage Russia to put pressure on Belarus to follow its own path of liberalisation, since the Russia-Belarus Union will otherwise complicate efforts to integrate Russia into European structures because of the incompatibility of the two countries' economic and political systems.

The EU has for some time been raising the Belarus question in discussions with Russia. This approach could prove more fruitful as Russia seeks further integration with the EU and Western organisations, though the Russians are likely to be motivated more by domestic and bilateral concerns in any dealings with Belarus. And relations with Belarus are unlikely to be high on what will be an increasingly crowded EU/Russia agenda.

The third and most radical suggestion (put forward here by Catherine Guicherd) is that policy towards Belarus should be subsumed in a broader policy encompassing Russia, Ukraine, Moldova and Belarus, dubbed by its advocates the 'Eastern Dimension'. The argument is that since these countries are so closely linked, and the issues of most interest to the EU at least in the case of the last three are all ones of regional scope (migration, crime, environment, etc), it makes sense to deal with them on a broader basis.

The advantage claimed for such an approach is that it would avoid the EU's having to differentiate between the various countries on grounds of their domestic policy when it has similar interests with all of them. But the main argument against is essentially the same: that it would leave no scope for conditionality, for the EU to treat countries more favourably as they make progress towards democracy and thus use the prospect of better relations to promote change. For this reason many in the EU are likely to be wary of such an approach. A further difficulty is that it is hard to see either Russia or the EU wanting their relations even in specialised areas subsumed into a wider grouping. And Ukraine at least has made it clear that it wishes to be dealt with on an individual basis and not as part of a wider group. But this could alter as interests and priorities change.

This kind of regional approach does however already exist in the form of the EU's various regional aid programmes, which attempt to deal with specific regional issues on a broad basis. There would no doubt be scope for expanding this sort of co-operation without necessarily establishing a political umbrella for the process.

If, as many authors argue, the current system in Belarus in unsustainable in the long term (though no-one hazards a guess as to how long that term might be), the EU can sit on the sidelines and wait until the country is forced to reform and liberalise. In the meantime this could involve considerable hardship and possible instability in Belarus, and consequent migratory pressures towards Western Europe. A policy of greater engagement by the EU and others, by whatever means, might help to bring forward that change and make the transition less painful. But so far EU member-states show few signs of wanting to stray from the principle of conditionality in the uncertain hope of inducing change.

In the end it is for Belarus to determine its own future. But it seems unlikely that the country can remain indefinitely outside the main current of democratic development in Europe.

Abbrevations

AMG	Advisory and Monitoring Group
AVN	Russian military news agency
BDG	Belorusskaya Delovaya Gazeta (Belarusian Business Newspaper)
BET	Belarus Economic Trends
BIS	Bank for International settlements
BNR	Belarusian National People's Republic
BPF	Belarusian Popular Front
BSA	Belarusian Students Association
BSDP	Belarusian Social Democratic Party
BSSR	Belorussian (or Belarusian) Soviet Socialist Republic
BSF	Belarusian Soros Foundation
BSTRC	Belarusian State Television and Radio Company
CCDF	Coordinating Council of Democratic Forces
CEC	Central Electoral Commission
CEE	Central and Eastern Europe
CFE	Conventional Forces in Europe
CIA	Central Intelligence Agency
CIS	Commonwealth of Independent States
CoE	Council of Europe
CSB	Central and South-eastern Europe and the Baltic States
DFID	Department for International Development (of the UK)
EBRD	European Bank for Reconstruction and Development
ECHO	European Office for Emergency Humanitarian Assistance
EIB	European Investment Bank
EIDHR	European Initiative for Democracy and Human Rights
ERI	European Research Institute
EU	European Union
FSU	Former Soviet Union
GDP	Gross Domestic Product
GNP	Gross National Product

ICBM	Intercontinental Ballistic Missile
ICCPR	International Covenant on Civil and Political Rights
IFC	International Finance Corporation
IFI	International Financial Institution
IISEPS	Independent Institute for Socio-economic and Political Studies
ILEOM	(OSCE) Limited Election Observation Mission
ILO	International Labour Organisation
IMF	International Monetary Fund
INOGATE	Inter-state Oil and Gas to Europe
INTAS	International Association for the Promotion of Co-operation with Scientists from the NIS of the former Soviet Union
IPU	Inter-Parliamentary Union
ISP	Internet Service Provider
JHA	Justice and Home Affairs
KGB	Committee for State Security
MD	Military District
MFA	Ministry for Foreign Affairs
MID	Ministry of Internal Affairs
MOD	Ministry of Defence
NAFTA	North American Free Trade Area
Nato	North Atlantic Treaty Organisation
NIS	Newly-independent States (of the former Soviet Union)
NISEPI	Independent Institute for Socio-economic and Political Studies
NGO	Non-governmental organisation
NKVD	State Committee for Internal Affairs
NRTC	National Radio and Television Centre
ODIHR	Office for Democratic Institutions and Human Rights
OECD	Organisation for Economic Co-operation and Development
ORT	Russian Public Television
OSCE	Organisation for Security and Co-operation in Europe
OSI	Open Society Institute
PCA	Partnership and Co-operation Agreement
PCB	Party of Communists of Belarus
PVO	Anti-Aircraft Defence
RFE	Radio Free Europe
RL	Radio Liberty

RSFSR	Russian Soviet Federal Socialist Republic
SDR	Special Drawing Rights
SME	Small and Medium Enterprise
Tacis	Technical Assistance to the NIS and Mongolia (originally Technical Assistance for the CIS)
Tempus	Trans-European Mobility Scheme for University Students
TEPSA	Trans European Policy Studies Association
UCP	United Civil Party
UN	United Nations
UNDP	United Nations Development Programme
UNHCR	United Nations High Commission for Refugees
Unicef	United Nations Children's Fund
USAID	United States Agency for International Development
VAT	Value Added Tax
WSCC	West Sussex County Council
WHO	World Health Organisation
WTO	World Trade Organisation

Notes on contributors

Dr Anders Åslund

Senior associate, Carnegie Endowment for International Peace, Washington. Specialises in and has written extensively on post-communist economoic transformations, especially in Russia and Ukraine. Has served as a senior economic adviser to the governments of Russia, Ukraine and Kyrgyzstan. Has also been a Professor at the Stockholm School of Economics and a Swedish diplomat.

Margaret Bamford

Recently retired as Assistant Director of Social Services for West Sussex Council having spent 35 years in social work, including 10 years in Northern Ireland. Has specialised in health-related social work with children and adults. Has published, taught and acted as external examiner to a number of social work courses.

Dr Kenneth Charman

Economist and consultant with extensive experience of Eastern Europe and the former Soviet Union. Lived and worked in Kazakhstan 1993-96, and in Belarus 1998-2000 as managing editor of 'Belarus Economic Trends'. Has written articles on the Belarusian economy. Since 2000 has managed policy advice projects in Eastern Europe and Central Asia for the European Commission.

Steven Eke

Journalist and news analyst, BBC World Service. Has travelled extensively in the former Soviet Union on projects aimed at promoting democratisation and the development of civil society. Spent more than 2 years in Belarus over several visits during the decade from 1990 and closely followed the situation in the Belarusian media.

Dr Larisa V Filinskaya

Senior Lecturer, Department of Sociology, Belarusian State University. PhD from Kharkov University, Ukraine. Special interest in the sociology of politics and social gerontology.

Dr Nadezhda Golubkova

Leading analyst, Centre for Sociological and Political Studies, Belarusian State University. PhD from Belarusian State University. Special interest in sociology of youth, ethnic sociology, sociology of labour and sociology of deviation.

Dr Catherine Guicherd

Independent European security analyst. Her article is part of a larger study on EU policy towards Ukraine, Belarus and Moldova written in residence at the Stiftung Wissenschaft und Politik (Berlin). She was previously Deputy to the Secretary-General of the Nato Parliamentary Assembly.

Grzegorz Gromadzki

Independent analyst who co-operates with the Stefan Batory Foundation in Warsaw. He works on relations between enlarging EU and CIS countries and also on Nato enlargement.

Malcolm Hawkes

Russian researcher, International Secretariat, Amnesty International, London. Author of several reports on Belarus published by Human Rights Watch and Article 19. As Belarus researcher for Human Rights Watch based in Moscow 1997-2000, he travelled frequently to and within Belarus writing on violations of freedom of expression in that country.

Mikhail Khvostov

Deputy Prime Minister and Minister for Foreign Affairs of the Republic of Belarus since November 2000. Member of diplomatic service of Belarus from 1982, served in New York and Washington. Deputy Minister for Foreign Affairs 1994-97, Ambassador to Canada 1997-2000.

Kimmo Kiljunen

Vice-Chairman of the OSCE Parliamentary Assembly, Chairman of its Moldova and Member of its Belarus Working Group. Member of Parliament in Finland since 1995. Director of the Institute of Development Studies at Helsinki University 1986-95. Has worked with various international organisations and written over a dozen books on development, international and political affairs.

Dr Elena Korosteleva

British Academy Post-doctoral Research Fellow, University of Glasgow, and Research Network Coordinator for an INTAS project (99-00245) on 'The Comparative Analysis of Charismatic Political Leadership in Russia, Belarus and Ukraine'. Her research interests include democratisation and the quality of new East European systems, and charismatic political leadership across Europe.

Ann Lewis

Free-lance consultant. Former member of British Diplomatic Service, where she spent most of her career dealing with Central and Eastern Europe, including postings in Moscow and East Berlin.

Dr Steven Main

Senior Lecturer at the Conflict Studies Research Centre, a Ministry of Defence research unit based at the Royal Military Academy Sandhurst. His main research areas are Russian-Belarusian relations; Russia's role in the Baltic Sea region; Russian military reform; and Moscow's relationship with the Russian regions.

Ambassador Sergei N Martynov

Head of Belarus Missions to the EU and Nato and Ambassador to Belgium. Previously First Deputy Foreign Minister, Ambassador to the USA, and Deputy Permanent Representative to the UN. Much of career was devoted to multilateral disarmament. Served as Chairman of the UN Disarmament Commission in New York and President of the Conference on Disarmament in Geneva.

Professor David Marples

Professor of Russian and East European History, University of Alberta. His most recent books include 'Belarus: a Denationalised Nation' (Harwood Academic Publishers, 1999) and 'Motherland: Russia in the 20th Century' (Longman, 2002). He is also Vice-President of the Association for the Study of Nationalities.

Anastasia Nesvetailova

PhD candidate, Department of International Politics, University of Wales, Aberystwyth. Graduated in economics from Belarusian State University. Awarded Chevening Scholarship to study in UK. From September 2002, Lecturer in Economic Geography, University of Liverpool.

Dr Lidia G Novikova

Deputy Director, Centre for Sociological and Political Studies, Belarusian State University. PhD from Belarusian State University. Special interest in sociology of religion and youth.

Jaroslav Romanchuk

President of Mises Scientific Research Centre, Minsk, since 2000, and economic analyst at 'Strategy' Analytical Centre since 1997. Previously businessman, then economic analyst for various think-tanks, newspapers, and the Commission for Economic Policy and Reforms of the Belarusian Parliament. Deputy Chairman of United Civil Party since April 2000.

Dr Clelia Rontoyanni

Research Fellow, Russia and Eurasia Programme, Royal Institute of International Affairs (Chatham House). Her current research, which is supported by the Social and Economic Research Council, concerns Russian, Belarusian and Ukrainian positions on Nato and the European Security and Defence Policy. Previously she worked at Glasgow University on Russia's relations with Belarus and Ukraine (also funded by the ESRC).

Professor David Rotman

Director, Centre for Sociological and Political Research, Belarusian State University. Doctor of Sociology. Special interest in the methodology of sociological research.

Dr Astrid Sahm

Assistant Professor, Department of Social Science, Mannehim University. Her PhD thesis was on Environmental and Energy Policy in Ukraine and Belarus, published under the title 'Transformaton in the Shadow of Chernobyl'. Her current research focuses on problems of integration policy and regional co-operation in Belarus, Poland and Ukraine.

Dr Vitali Silitski

Associate Professor, European Humanities University, Minsk. PhD in political sciences from Rutgers University, USA. Does research on politics of economic reform in Central and Eastern Europe and on democratisation and authoritarianism in the post-Communist world. Worked as an analyst for Goncharik's presidential campaign. 2001-2002 Visiting Fellow, Central European University, Budapest.

Dr Elizabeth Teague

Russian affairs analyst, Ministry of Defence, London. Previously research analyst at the Foreign and Commonwealth Office, analyst of Soviet politics for Radio Free Europe/Radio Liberty, adviser to the OSCE High Commissioner on National Minorities, and analyst of Russian politics for the Jamestown Foundation.

Dr Heinz Timmermann

Head of Research Unit, Russian Federation and Newly Independent States, German Institute for International and Security Affairs (Stiftung Wissenschaft und Politik), Berlin, since 2001. From 1969 member of the Bundesinstitut fur ostwissenschaftliche und internationale Studien in Cologne, latterly as Head of the Research Unit, Russia and East-West Relations.

Rob van de Water

Has worked since 1977 for the Socialist Group in the European Parliament and is currently a senior political adviser specialising in relations with Eastern Europe. Together with Jan Marinus Wiersma he published in 2001 a book on the Echelon system.

Dr Hans-Georg Wieck

Head of the OSCE Advisory and Monitoring Group in Belarus 1997-2001. Member of German Foreign Service 1954-93, including Ambassador in Tehran, Moscow and New Delhi, Permanent Representative to Nato Brussels, and President of German Foreign Intelligence Agency. After retirement, Adviser to President Shevardnadze of Georgia.

Jan Marinus Wiersma

Historian and former International Secretary and Vice-President of the Dutch Labour Party. Member of the European Parliament since 1994, he became an expert on relations with Eastern Europe. Since 1999 he has been President of the European Parliament Delegation for relations with Belarus, Ukraine and Moldova.

Dr Leonid Zlotnikov

Consultant, International Finance Corporation, Minsk. Previously economic specialist at various research centres, manager-in-chief of a firm of consultants, Assistant Professor at European Humanities University, Minsk. One of founders of United Civil Party and member of its Political Council up to June 2000. Chairman of Alternativa-XXI, an NGO engaged in research and education.